Sustainability Management in Heritage and Tourism

Takamitsu Jimura

Sustainability Management in Heritage and Tourism

The Concept and Practice of Mottainai in Japan

Takamitsu Jimura
Faculty of Humanities
Musashi University
Tokyo, Japan

ISBN 978-3-031-40268-5   ISBN 978-3-031-40269-2 (eBook)
https://doi.org/10.1007/978-3-031-40269-2

© The Editor(s) (if applicable) and The Author(s) 2023
This work is subject to copyright. All rights are solely and exclusively licensed by the Publisher, whether the whole or part of the material is concerned, specifically the rights of translation, reprinting, reuse of illustrations, recitation, broadcasting, reproduction on microfilms or in any other physical way, and transmission or information storage and retrieval, electronic adaptation, computer software, or by similar or dissimilar methodology now known or hereafter developed.
The use of general descriptive names, registered names, trademarks, service marks, etc. in this publication does not imply, even in the absence of a specific statement, that such names are exempt from the relevant protective laws and regulations and therefore free for general use.
The publisher, the authors, and the editors are safe to assume that the advice and information in this book are believed to be true and accurate at the date of publication. Neither the publisher nor the authors or the editors give a warranty, expressed or implied, with respect to the material contained herein or for any errors or omissions that may have been made. The publisher remains neutral with regard to jurisdictional claims in published maps and institutional affiliations.

This Palgrave Macmillan imprint is published by the registered company Springer Nature Switzerland AG.
The registered company address is: Gewerbestrasse 11, 6330 Cham, Switzerland

Paper in this product is recyclable.

Preface

My first encounter of the concept of 'sustainability' or 'sustainable development' was the time when I was collecting information on tourism programmes, including modules on heritage, at master's level offered by universities in the UK. At that time, I already developed a certain level of interest in the notion and I enrolled on the master's programme called MSc in Tourism, Conservation and Sustainable Development offered by the University of Greenwich in 2002. It was more than 20 years ago.

Since that time, I have published papers on tourism and heritage, especially cultural heritage tourism and tourism at World Heritage sites. I have also published papers on tourism or destination marketing, making the most of the knowledge I acquired through my work experience in Japan and at business schools of different British universities. In these publications, I often referred to sustainability or sustainable development as it was one of the key themes closely linked to tourism, heritage or marketing. Therefore, I gradually came to think that I should write a new monograph, focusing on sustainability of heritage and tourism industries. I am grateful to Palgrave Macmillan and anonymous reviewers who gave me kind and constructive feedback on my book proposal. Consequently, the title, aim and scope of the book were finalised.

This book is aimed primarily at academics, researchers, students and practitioners whose main interests are sustainability studies, tourism, heritage studies and/or Japanese studies. Nonetheless, the book will appeal to more diverse types of readers such as people who are interested in learning about examples of sustainability management from real world.

Tokyo, Japan Takamitsu Jimura

Acknowledgements

First of all, I am really grateful to Palgrave Macmillan and Ms Jessica Harrison who worked as an editor for the publisher for giving me an opportunity to write a monograph on sustainability management in Japan's heritage and tourism industries, and Springer Nature and its Project Coordinator (Books), Ms Asma Azeezullah (Ms.), for her patience and continuous support, especially when I decided to move back to Japan from the UK.

I am also very thankful to a number of people working in heritage or tourism sector in Japan who served me when I used their services as a visitor, passenger, guest or customer and who gave me a range of useful information on their businesses based on their knowledge and experience. My gratitude also goes to people and organisations who supported my writing journey in various ways such as allowing me to ask various questions or to take photographs of their shops or products.

I would like to deeply thank my mother, brothers and mother-in-law for their support. Finally, I would like to express my profound thanks to my wife, Akemi Jimura. I could not have completed this book project without her understanding, patience and encouragement.

Contents

Part I Introduction   1

1 Introduction – Sustainability and Japan's Heritage and Tourism   3

Part II Sustainability of Heritage   33

2 Sustainability of Japan's Tangible Cultural Heritage   35

3 Sustainability of Japan's Intangible Cultural Heritage   69

4 Sustainability of Japan's Natural Heritage   99

Part III Sustainability of Tourism   129

5 Sustainability of Japan's Transport Sector   131

6 Sustainability of Japan's Accommodation Sector   171

7 Sustainability of Food and Beverage Sector in Japan   207

8 Sustainability of Visitor Attractions and Events Sector in Japan   239

9 Sustainability of Tourism Intermediaries in Japan   273

Part IV   Conclusions   297

10 Conclusions – Reflections and Futures   299

Abbreviations and Acronyms

Abbreviations

ACA	the Agency for Cultural Affairs
ANA	All Nippon Airways
ANTA	All Nippon Travel Agents Association
ATAG	the Air Transport Action Group
CO_2	carbon dioxide
CSR	corporate social responsibility
DBC	the Doggy Bag Committee
DMO	destination marketing organisation
ESG	environmental, social, and governance
EST	Environmentally Sustainable Transport
EU	the European Union
GBM	the Green Belt Movement
GDP	gross domestic product
GGN	the Global Geoparks Network
GRI	the Global Reporting Initiative
HHCG	Hotel Hokke Club Group
IATA	the International Air Transport Association
ICH	Intangible Cultural Heritage (UNESCO's listing system)
ICOM	International Council of Museums
IT	information technology
JAL	Japan Airlines
JATA	the Japan Association of Travel Agents

JES	the Japan Ecotourism Society
JGC	the Japan Geopark Committee
JGLA	Japan Glamping Association
JGN	the Japanese Geoparks Network
JH	Japan Heritage
JNG	Japanese National Geopark
JNR	Japan National Railways
JPC	Japan Productivity Center
JPY	Japanese Yen
JR	Japan Railway or Japan Railways
JTA	the Japan Tourism Agency
JYHG	Japan Youth Hostels Guide
LCC	low-cost carrier
LPG	liquefied petroleum gas
MAFF	the Ministry of Agriculture, Forestry and Fisheries
MCO	the Mottainai Campaign Office
MDGs	the Millennium Development Goals
MEOC	Marimo Exhibition and Observation Centre
MEXT	the Ministry of Education, Culture, Sports, Science and Technology
MHLW	the Ministry of Health, Labour and Welfare
MLIT:	the Ministry of Land, Infrastructure, Transport and Tourism
MOE	the Ministry of the Environment
MOFA	the Ministry of Foreign Affairs
NDC	Nationally Determined Contribution
NEAS	the National Environment Agency of Singapore
NGO	non-governmental organisation
NMWA	the National Museum of Western Art
NPF	Natural Parks Foundation
NPO	non-profit organisation
NPS	the National Park Service (USA)
OECD	the Organisation for Economic Co-operation and Development
OTA	Osaka Taxi Association
OUP	Osaka Urban Prefecture
PRO	the Public Relations Office, the Government of Japan
RV	recreational vehicle
SAF	sustainable aviation fuel

SBJ	Statistics Bureau of Japan
SDGs	Sustainable Development Goals
SL	steam locomotive
SME	small and medium-sized enterprise
SWT	Special Wards of Tokyo
TBL	the triple bottom line
TDR	Tokyo Disney Resort
TMP	Tokyo Metropolitan Prefecture
UGG	UNESCO Global Geopark
UN	the United Nations
UNESCO	the United Nations Educational, Scientific and Cultural Organization
UNFCCC	the United Nations Framework Convention on Climate Change
UNWTO	the World Tourism Organization
USJ	Universal Studios Japan
VFR	visiting friends and relatives
WH	World Heritage
WHS	World Heritage site
WWII	World War II

Acronyms

AFEJ	Armed Forces of the Empire of Japan
AR	augmented reality
CABV	Cenotaph for the Atomic Bomb Victims
CHA	cultural heritage attractions
DCRAA	Development of Comprehensive Resort Areas Act
DMO	destination marketing or management organisation
ERIH	European Route of Industrial Heritage
eWOM	e-word-of-mouth
FA	the Forestry Agency
FAC	Foundation for Ainu Culture
FGH	Former Glover House
FRF	Fuji Rock Festival
FSES	Former Shiroyama Elementary School
FSS	First Service School
GDP	gross domestic product
GFO	Grand Front Osaka

Abbreviations and Acronyms

GTA	Greater Tokyo Area
HNPMH	Hiroshima National Peace Memorial Hall for the Atomic Bomb Victims
HPM	Hiroshima Peace Memorial
HPMC	Hiroshima Peace Memorial Ceremony
HPMM	Hiroshima Peace Memorial Museum
HPMP	Hiroshima Peace Memorial Park
HTB	Huis Ten Bosch
ICH	Intangible Cultural Heritage (the name of the scheme adopted by UNESCO)
ICOMOS	International Council of Monuments and Sites
IJA	Imperial Japanese Army
IJN	Imperial Japanese Navy
IJNA	Imperial Japanese Naval Academy
IR	integrated resort
ISPA	International Spa Association
JH	Japan Heritage
JMSDF	Japan Maritime Self-Defence Force
JNTO	Japan National Tourism Organization
JR	Japan Railway
JTDA	Japan Thoron Development Association
KCTA	Kyoto City Tourism Association
KNA	Kure Naval Arsenal
KNHM	Kure Naval History Museum
KUP	Kyoto Urban Prefecture
METI	Ministry of Economy, Trade and Industry
MEXT	Ministry of Education, Culture, Sports, Science and Technology
MICE	meetings, incentives, conferences (conventions) and exhibitions (events)
MMAF	Ministry of Agriculture, Forestry and Fisheries
MoW	Memory of the World
NABM	Nagasaki Atomic Bomb Museum
NABVMPPC	Nagasaki Atomic Bomb Victims Memorial Peace Prayer Ceremony
NAM	National Ainu Museum
NAMP	National Ainu Museum and Park
NAP	National Ainu Park

Abbreviations and Acronyms

NHV	Nagasaki Holland Village
NME	National Museum of Ethnology
NNPMH	Nagasaki National Peace Memorial Hall for the Atomic Bomb Victims
NPP	Nagasaki Peace Park
OAMP	Office of Ainu Measures Promotion
OCCI	Okayama Chamber of Commerce and Industry
OCSC	Osaka Cotton Spinning Company
OCVB	Okinawa Convention and Visitors Bureau
OHCHR	Office of the United Nations High Commissioner for Human Rights
OPGM	Okunoshima Poison Gas Museum
OUP	Osaka Urban Prefecture
OUV	Outstanding Universal Value
PE	Parque Espana
PIIF	public interest incorporated foundation
SS	Summer Sonic
SSF	Sapporo Snow Festival
SWT	Spatial Wards of Tokyo
TDL	Tokyo Disneyland
TDR	Tokyo Disney Resort
TDS	Tokyo DisneySea
TKSP	Toei Kyoto Studio Park
TMP	Tokyo Metropolitan Prefecture
TSM	Tomioka Silk Mill
UGC	user-generated content
URA	Urban Renaissance Agency
USAF	United States Armed Forces
USJ	Universal Studios Japan
WH	World Heritage
WHC	World Heritage Centre
WHS	World Heritage site
WOM	word-of-mouth
WWII	World War II

List of Figures

Fig. 1.1	3Rs (Reduce, reuse and recycle) + Another R	11
Fig. 2.1	Himeji Castle after its extensive repair work between 2009 and 2015	42
Fig. 2.2	World's largest gilt bronze statue of Vairocana at Todai-ji Temple	44
Fig. 2.3	Canal in Omi-Hachiman	48
Fig. 2.4	Taketomi Island, Taketomi Town (Okinawa Prefecture)	52
Fig. 2.5	Nirayama Reverberatory Furnaces	61
Fig. 3.1	Minamiza theatre	76
Fig. 3.2	Cormorant fishing (*ukai*) on the Nagaragawa River	81
Fig. 3.3	City centre of Onomichi	88
Fig. 4.1	Japanese giant salamander at the World Fresh Water Aquarium	115
Fig. 5.1	Tokyo Metro: Vision for sustainability management	144
Fig. 5.2	Tokyo Metro: five main themes for sustainability management and SDGs	145
Fig. 5.3	Passenger boats connecting Tsuchido and Mukaishima in Onomichi City	161
Fig. 6.1	Door signs for room cleaning options at Hotel Hokke Club Kyoto	183
Fig. 6.2	A notice board in a bathroom of hotel room at Intergate Hotel Osaka	184
Fig. 6.3	Saigetsuro wing of Kanaguya *ryokan*	188

List of Figures

Fig. 6.4	An example of *michi no eki*: Happiness Fukue in Hagi City, Yamaguchi Prefecture	194
Fig. 7.1	A popular seafood bowl at Nishiyo restaurant	216
Fig. 8.1	Yomeimon Gate of Nikko Toshogu Shrine	242
Fig. 8.2	Main Hall (Hondo) of Kawasaki Daishi Temple	243
Fig. 8.3	Konpon Chudo of Enryaku-ji Temple	247
Fig. 8.4	Rikugien (a Japanese garden)	248
Fig. 8.5	Universal Studios Japan	255
Fig. 8.6	*Uchiwa* (Japanese paper fan) featuring Hirosaki Neputa Matsuri	263
Fig. 9.1	Tour operators and travel agents in the tourism distribution system	274
Fig. 10.1	SL Taiju departing from Kinugawa-Onsen station	304
Fig. 10.2	Plastic or paper shopping bag sold at a shop of Kasho Sanzen	315
Fig. 10.3	Akashi City's logo for being selected as a SDGs Future City	316
Fig. 10.4	Slogan including SDGs at a nursery in TMP	316

List of Tables

Table 1.1	Sustainable Development Goals	9
Table 4.1	Japan's natural parks	102
Table 7.1	Eateries and food/drink takeaways and deliveries in Japan	210
Table 7.2	Japan's top 10 fast food businesses by sales between April 2020 and March 2021	214
Table 8.1	Olympics and Paralympics and World Expos held in Japan	259

Part I

Introduction

1

Introduction – Sustainability and Japan's Heritage and Tourism

1   Aim and Scope of the Book

This opening chapter serves as an introductory chapter for the whole of this monograph, discussing key points and main themes that are essential for the book. In this chapter, this section demonstrates the aim and scope of the book. The monograph examines what 'sustainability' means and 'how sustainability management' is conducted in two closely interrelated industries, heritage and tourism sectors. This chapter answers these enquiries in a broad context across the world, but subsequent chapters (Chaps. 2, 3, 4, 5, 6, 7, 8, and 9) focus on the investigation of those in Japan from the perspective of concept and practice of '*mottainai*' in the country.

It is generally agreed that sustainability is a vital notion for all lives and natural environments on the earth and needs to be maintained and managed properly to enable all of them to continue to exist and survive. In relation to this, it should be noted that human beings are part of the ecosystem on the earth and their lives and activities can affect other lives and natural environment on the earth in various ways, causing negative or positive impacts on them, and vice versa. In our current society, human beings engage in and are involved in a wide variety of activities, including those associated with primary, secondary and tertiary industry; energy production and consumption; cultural and natural heritage; and leisure, recreation, entertainment and tourism. Of these, this monograph sheds light on heritage and tourism, focusing on sustainability and sustainability management in these two fields. As signified above, there are close relationships between 'heritage' and 'tourism' and they are investigated by heritage/tourism researchers (e.g. Timothy & Boyd, 2003; Jimura, 2019; Timothy, 2020). Given this background, it can be stated that there is a certain need to investigate sustainability and sustainable management specifically in heritage and tourism sectors.

Another key aspect of this book is exploring the concept and practice of sustainability and sustainability management in heritage and tourism industries in Japan, referring to a notion called '*mottainai*' in Japanese. In the author's view, there is no single English word that has exactly the same meaning as *mottainai*. It is also not easy or straightforward to explain its meaning and nuance in English, although a literal translation of *mottainai* can be, for instance, 'what a waste!'. The author is a Japanese individual and spent his life for 30 years in Japan before he moved to the UK in 2002. In the author's opinion, *mottainai* denotes an ethical and recommended attitude towards the use of a variety of resources that are needed to sustain human life. When the author was a child, his family members, especially his grandmother, often used the word, '*mottainai*', when she thought any of my actions or behaviour were 'wasting' something to blame and correct such attitudes. At that time, the author felt somewhat annoyed every time his grandmother said *mottainai* to him, although he realised later the reasons why she had said this word to him repeatedly and the significance of what this word denotes. In light of such author's own experience, *mottainai* should be comprehended not only as an idea that promotes an environmentally friendly way of life of human beings by eliminating or minimising wasting something but also as a moral and righteous path of humanity in the traditional value system of Japanese society, and has been serving Japanese people as a discipline and important life lesson.

Bearing these fundamental points in mind, the next section discusses basic ideas of 'sustainability', 'sustainability management' and '*mottainai*' with their relevant notions.

1 Introduction – Sustainability and Japan's Heritage and Tourism 5

2 Sustainability, Sustainability Management and *Mottainai*

2.1 Sustainability and Sustainable Development

According to Cambridge Dictionary (2020), the word 'sustainability' means 'the quality of being able to continue over a period of time' generally and 'the quality of causing little or no damage to the environment and therefore able to continue for a long time' in the context of the natural environment. This book considers both of them, but it is fair to state that of various aspects that the concept of sustainability may contain, historically its environmental aspect has been understood and examined as a primary dimension of 'sustainability' in the real world as well as academia, including heritage and tourism domains. As for the notion of sustainability, categorising it into weak and strong sustainability is paramount to understand the core of sustainability (Fennell & Cooper, 2020). Weak and strong sustainability is examined by both in academia (e.g. Pearce, 1993; Turner et al., 1994; Hunter, 1997) and in the real world (e.g. The Organisation for Economic Co-operation and Development (hereafter OECD), 2005a, b). Although the understandings of weak and strong sustainability somewhat differ by author/organisation, key differences between these two are whether and to what extent natural resources (capitals) are valued in its own right and regardless of their usefulness for human life and activities, and can be substituted for man-made resources (capitals). It is also fair to say that weak sustainability corresponds to techno-centrism, whilst strong sustainability corresponds to eco-centrism (Acott et al., 1998).

When the concept of sustainability is discussed, the notion of 'sustainable development' is also often discussed in a variety of study fields, including heritage and tourism (Jimura, 2019). To comprehend the idea of sustainable development and its background, it would be beneficial to review the birth of and advancement of relevant notions. Regarding theories of 'development', in a broad sense, their origin can be confirmed in the nineteenth century in the history of industrialisation, imperialism and colonisation (Jimura, 2019). Since then, theories of development have evolved, generating various new perspectives on development. In this process, a core of theories of development has been changing, originally economy-centred views followed by society-centred and culture-centred ones, and then environment-centred and community-centred ones.

In the context of the development of the notion of sustainable development, the rise of environmentalism should also be considered. Environmentalism can be understood as a philosophy, ideology and movement, and Paehlke (1996) states that environmentalism is the first ideology that is deeply rooted in the natural sciences. The Industrial Revolution occurred first in the UK between the mid- eighteenth century and the early nineteenth century, and then spread to other European countries and the USA during the nineteenth century. Technological changes in manufacturing led to economic and social changes in society and people's lives. At that time, economic and social developments were main interests of entrepreneurs, workers and the general public, and there were no or little concerns about the impacts of industrial activities made by human beings on the natural environment. As time went by, however, more and more individuals started raising concerns about issues in their surrounding natural environments and then such independent responses developed into collective concerns shared at local, regional and even national levels. This series of movements can be seen as the beginning and development of environmentalism.

Environmentalism also promoted the emergence of conservationism. According to Fennell (1999), conservationism has three main areas of activity: The maintenance of harmony between humans and nature, the efficient use of natural resources, and not saving natural resources 'for' use but saving those resources 'from' use. Probably, the establishment and adoption of an idea of national parks is one of the best examples of practice and implementation of environmentalism and conservationism. The world's first national park, the Yellowstone National Park (USA), was founded in 1872. Today, national parks are found in many countries in different regions of the world, including Japan.

Conservation movements have further developed after the end of the Second World War and Stabler (1996) and Fennell and Cooper (2020) argue that those in the 1950s and 1960s were a forerunner to and basis of the concept and practice that are recognised as 'sustainable development' today. There are somewhat different definitions of sustainable development. However, it is fair to state that the definition of sustainable development that was suggested by the Brundtland Commission in 1987 is the most widely accepted and used definition – 'development which meets the needs of current generations without compromising the ability of future generations to meet their own needs' (World Commission on Environment and Development, 1987). Key principles of sustainable development can be comprehended as realisation of the triple bottom line (hereafter TBL) (economic, socio-cultural and environmental) of sustainability as goals of the development process (Jimura, 2019). TBL also signifies the 3P elements of sustainability, which refers to 'people', 'planet' and 'profit', and sustainable development should serve the protection and maximisation of the benefits of the 3Ps.

2.2 Sustainable Development Goals (SDGs) and Sustainability Management

Between 1987 and 2000, the magnitude of sustainable development had been increasingly recognised by a number of stakeholders, including international organisations such as the United Nations (hereafter UN). In this process, several meetings were held, projects were launched and documents were created, including:

* 1987 – Brundtland Report (Our Common Future)
* 1992 – The Rio Earth Summit ('Agenda 21')
* 1998 and
  1999 – The Seventh Session of the UN Commission on Sustainable Development (also called CSD-7)

However, the idea and principles of sustainable development were still an 'armchair theory' and just looked good on paper. Therefore, more concrete themes and goals that sustainable development should focus on and achieve within a certain period of time needed to be developed. To this end, Millennium Development Goals (hereafter MDGs) with eight goals and 18 targets for 2015 were set up as a result of the UN's Millennium Summit in 2000, and the eight goals were:

1. To eradicate extreme poverty and hunger.
2. To achieve universal primary education.
3. To promote gender equality and empower women.
4. To reduce child mortality.
5. To improve maternal health.
6. To combat HIV/AIDS, malaria, and other diseases.
7. To ensure environmental sustainability.
8. To develop a global partnership for development.

Overall, a certain degree of improvement had been made in all of these eight goals by 2015. In the author's view, however, further improvement should still be made for all the goals, particularly 1 and 7 above.

In 2016, MDGs were succeeded by UN Sustainable Development Goals (hereafter SDGs) with 17 goals, including 169 targets and a set of 330 indicators (Fennell & Cooper, 2020; UN, n.d.) (see Table 1.1). These goals should be attained by 2030.

Needless to say, SDGs are vital for all stakeholders, including heritage and tourism sectors and people, organisations and businesses involved in the sectors, at local, regional, national and international levels. In light of the aim and scope of this book, of these, organisations and businesses in heritage and tourism industries in Japan are particularly relevant stakeholders. They are expected to 'manage' sustainability of their activities and businesses day to day and over a long period of time in order to take their responsibility accordingly as members of society and as part of the ecosystem on the earth. Hence, 'sustainability management' is crucial for them to understand the meaning of sustainability and sustainable development of their organisations and companies, and to implement their activities and businesses, embedding sustainability in them. Sustainability management is defined as 'the formulation, implementation, and evaluation of both environmental and socioeconomic sustainability-related decisions and actions' (Starik & Kanashiro, 2013, 12). This definition can be applied to all organisations and businesses in heritage and tourism sectors and is also adopted in this book. However, many of key

1 Introduction – Sustainability and Japan's Heritage and Tourism

Table 1.1 Sustainable Development Goals

Number	Goal	Explanation
1	No poverty	End poverty in all its forms everywhere
2	Zero hunger	End hunger, achieve food security and improved nutrition and promote sustainable agriculture
3	Good health and well-being	Ensure healthy lives and promote well-being for all at all ages
4	Quality education	Ensure inclusive and equitable quality education and promote lifelong learning opportunities for all
5	Gender equality	Achieve gender equality and empower all women and girls
6	Clean water and sanitation	Ensure availability and sustainable management of water and sanitation for all
7	Affordable and clean energy	Ensure access to affordable, reliable, sustainable and modern energy for all
8	Decent work and economic growth	Promote sustained, inclusive and sustainable economic growth, full and productive employment and decent work for all
9	Industry, innovation and infrastructure	Build resilient infrastructure, promote inclusive and sustainable industrialization and foster innovation
10	Reduced inequalities	Reduce inequality within and among countries
11	Sustainable cities and communities	Make cities and human settlements inclusive, safe, resilient and sustainable
12	Responsible consumption and production	Ensure sustainable consumption and production patterns
13	Climate action	Take urgent action to combat climate change and its impacts
14	Life below water	Conserve and sustainably use the oceans, seas and marine resources for sustainable development
15	Life on land	Protect, restore and promote sustainable use of terrestrial ecosystems, sustainably manage forests, combat desertification, and halt and reverse land degradation and halt biodiversity loss
16	Peace, justice and strong institutions	Promote peaceful and inclusive societies for sustainable development, provide access to justice for all and build effective, accountable and inclusive institutions at all levels
17	Partnerships for the goals	Strengthen the means of implementation and revitalize the global partnership for sustainable development

Source: Fennell and Cooper (2020) and UN (n.d.)

stakeholders in heritage and tourism industries, especially those in tourism sector, are not charities, non-profit organisations (hereafter NPOs) or non-governmental organisations (hereafter NGOs) but commercial companies that are profit-driven. Considering this, sustainability management also needs to be defined in the context of their businesses as 'corporate sustainability management'. Corporate sustainability management is defined as 'profit-driven corporate response to environmental and social issues that are caused through the organization's primary and secondary activities' (Salzmann et al., 2005, 13). In light of the significance of each of TBL, however, the author believes that not only 'environmental and social issues' but also 'economic issues' should be included in a comprehensive definition of corporate sustainability management, and this monograph follows it.

2.3 Mottainai

As explained in Sect. 1, the Japanese word *mottainai* signifies a virtuous and admirable approach towards the usage of diverse resources that are necessary to maintain human life. It must also be remembered that *mottainai* should be understood as a form of discipline that people are expected to follow in the traditional value system of Japanese society as well as a conception that promotes eco-friendly ways of life of humankind. Although *mottainai* is a concept and practice that was born in Japan, it has spread all over the world in the twenty-first century. In this process, a role played by Professor Wangari Maathai (1940–2011) was immense. She was a Kenyan environmental activist and the first African woman to win the Nobel Prize (Nobel Peace Prize) in 2004. She launched the Green Belt Movement (hereafter GBM), an environmental NGO, in 1977, and GBM has planted over 51 million trees in Kenya (GBM, 2021a). In February 2005, Professor Maathai was invited to Japan by the Mainichi Newspapers Co., Ltd. to attend an event associated with the Kyoto Protocol (The Mottainai Campaign Office (hereafter MCO), n.d.). During an interview by the Mainichi Newspapers, she encountered the word *mottainai* (MCO, n.d.). According to MCO (n.d.), she was deeply impressed by the spirit and principle of *mottainai* and suggested to spread it across the world as a slogan for environmental conservation. In

1 Introduction – Sustainability and Japan's Heritage and Tourism

fact, she talked about the concept of *mottainai* at several different international events, including the 49th Session of the Commission on the Status of Women that was held in New York in March 2005 (MCO, n.d.).

Following Professor Maathai's visit to Japan, the Mainichi Newspapers launched the Mottainai Campaign in 2005 to foster environmentalism and conservationism amongst people all over the world and to reduce the amount of waste generated through human activities (The Public Relations Office, the Government of Japan (hereafter PRO), 2018). For this campaign, the Mainichi Newspapers worked together with Itochu Corporation, one of the largest Japanese general trading companies (PRO, 2018). In the meantime, Professor Maathai set up the Mottainai Campaign in Kenya to avoid waste plastic from littering the natural environment (GBM, 2021b). Nowadays, 'reduce', 'reuse' and 'recycle' are recognised widely across the world as the three essential elements (3Rs) for the concept and practice of sustainability and its management, and this view is also shared by MCO based in Japan and GBM in Kenya. In addition to reduce, reuse and recycle, both MCO and GBM recognise that 'respect' is also a necessary element for the understanding and practice of sustainability and its management and regard 'respect' as the fourth 'r' element (in total 4Rs) (PRO, 2018; GBM, 2021b) (see Fig. 1.1). Here, 'respect' means that people should respect all resources around them, make the most of these resources and use the resources with a sense of gratitude (GBM, 2021b). The importance of 'respect' is also acknowledged by the Japanese Government as evidenced by, for instance, a web resource that the government prepared for the 34th G8 summit held in Toyako Town in Hokkaido in 2008 (The Ministry of Foreign Affairs (hereafter MOFA), n.d.).

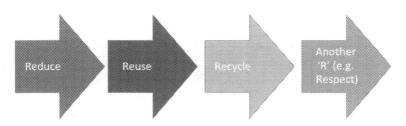

Fig. 1.1 3Rs (Reduce, reuse and recycle) + Another R. (Source: Author)

3 Overview of Heritage and Tourism Industries – World and Japan

3.1 Heritage Sector

Generally, the realm of heritage sector tends to cover only 'cultural' and 'built' (man-made) heritage. According to the University of Birmingham (n.d.), '[t]he heritage sector covers museums, buildings, archaeology, archives and conservation'. For example, however, World Heritage sites (hereafter WHSs) and other international schemes for the conservation of various types of heritage that are adopted by the United Nations Educational, Scientific and Cultural Organization (hereafter UNESCO) view that the notion of heritage contain natural heritage as well as tangible and intangible cultural heritage (Jimura, 2019). This book follows the wider concept of heritage suggested by Jimura (2019) to examine sustainability and its management in the heritage sector in a comprehensive manner. As this monograph comprehends the heritage sector as a broad industry, the book should also look at diverse kinds of key stakeholders in the heritage sector. Regarding the tangible and intangible cultural heritage sector, for instance, Inspiring Interns (2018) states that museums, historic buildings, archives, archaeology, education, events, and conservation are covered under the umbrella of heritage sector. As the book also covers natural heritage, more different types of components such as national parks should also be included in the heritage sector. In this monograph, consequently, all people (e.g. workers and visitors) and organisations (e.g. businesses, NGOs and NPOs) that play an important role in the aforementioned diverse components should be regarded as main stakeholders in the heritage sector. In addition, Deacon et al. (2003) suggest an intriguing categorisation of the heritage sector, 'the formal heritage sector' and 'the informal heritage sector', referring to a case of South Africa, based on whether or not heritage resources are formally registered with the South African Heritage Resources Agency. This is another important approach to the classification of heritage and heritage sector, and this monograph examines both sorts of the heritage and heritage sector.

Like many other countries, the heritage sector of Japan is multifaceted and extensive, including both public and private bodies. Concerning the cultural heritage and its sector, the Agency for Cultural Affairs (hereafter ACA) can be seen as the primary public stakeholder at national level. ACA is in charge of conservation, utilisation and promotion of Japan's tangible and intangible cultural heritage and holds jurisdiction over a range of laws and regulations on cultural heritage (e.g. Act on Protection of Cultural Properties (*Bunkazai Hogo-ho*)). Regarding the natural heritage and its sector, the Ministry of the Environment (hereafter MOE) is regarded to be the principal stakeholder at national level. MOE is responsible for conservation of Japan's natural environment and resources, including fauna and flora, and holds jurisdiction over a variety of laws and regulations on natural heritage (e.g. Act on Nature Conservation (*Shizenkankyo Hozen-ho*) and Act on Natural Parks (*Shizenkoen-ho*)). Japan's municipalities, including prefectures and cities, may also establish their own ordinances (*jorei*) for the conservation of their cultural and natural heritage. Other key stakeholders in Japan's heritage sector include museums (tangible cultural heritage), traditional festivals (*matsuri*) (intangible cultural heritage) and national parks (natural heritage), and their representative examples are the National Art Centre, Aomori Nebuta Matsuri, and Setonaikai National Park respectively.

3.2   Tourism Sector

The tourism sector consists of many different stakeholders on the host (supply) and guest (demand) sides of tourism and intermediaries. Jimura (2019) enumerates such key stakeholders as follows:

Host (supply) side of tourism:

- Transport sector
- Accommodation sector
- Food and drink (catering) sector
- Visitor attraction and events sector
- Tour operators based in a tourist destination

- Retail sector
- Public sector (National, regional or local government)
- Destination marketing organisations
- Local communities

Guest (demand) side of tourism:

- Tourists (overnight visitors) and same-day visitors
- International and domestic visitors

Intermediaries:

- Tour operators
- Travel agents

In relation to this, the emergence and advancement of online travel agents (e.g. Expedia), hotel booking sites (e.g. Booking.com) and travel review sites (e.g. Tripadvisor) should also be noted as they can also be understood as main stakeholders in the tourism sector worldwide (Jimura, 2011; Jimura & Lee, 2020). Furthermore, it should also be remembered that tourism is an integrated or synthesised system (Swarbrooke, 1999; Page & Connell, 2020). This signifies that many components included in the tourism sector are linked and influence each other (Swarbrooke, 1999). Considering the scope of this book, sustainability and its management in Japan's transport, accommodation, foods and drinks (catering), visitor attractions and events sectors, and intermediaries are examined in the book.

As for Japan's tourism and tourism sector, the Japan Tourism Agency (hereafter JTA) is the key public stakeholder at national level. JTA was established in 2008 as an affiliated agency of the Ministry of Land, Infrastructure, Transport and Tourism, aiming to foster tourism as Japan's main industry and to establish Japan as a major tourist destination country (JTA, n.d.). JTA holds jurisdiction over laws and regulations on tourism (e.g. Basic Act on Promoting Tourism-oriented Nation (*Kanko-rikkoku Suishin Kihon-ho*)). In Japan's transport sector, airlines (e.g. Japan Airlines) and train companies (e.g. Central Japan Railway Company) are representative elements that support Japan's domestic tourism. Japan has diverse types of accommodation, but they can be categorised into Western-style and Japanese-style inns (Jimura, 2011). The former includes the hotels that are unique to Japan (e.g. *business hotel* in Japanese English) as well as international hotel chains (e.g. Hilton), whilst the latter can be sub-divided into *ryokan* and *minshuku* (Jimura, 2019). Such coexistence can also be confirmed in the food and drink sector in Japan as evidenced, for example, by the presence of McDonald's and Kentucky Fried Chicken and restaurant chains originated in Japan (e.g. Tenya) and independent restaurants. In the visitor attraction sector, museums (e.g. Tokyo National Museum), religious sites (e.g. Kiyomizu-dera Temple), gardens (Kenroku-en Garden) and castles (e.g. Hikone Castle) can be regarded as popular types of attractions (Jimura, 2019) and some of them are also main elements in Japan's tangible cultural heritage sector. In the event sector, Japan is full of traditional and contemporary festivals and events, and the traditional festivals in Japan are called *matsuri* (Jimura, 2019). As stated in Sect. 3.1, *matsuri* is a significant component in the intangible heritage sector in Japan. Similar to the situation of many other countries, the vast majority of tour operators and travel agents are small or medium-sized enterprises, although Japan has some big tour operators and travel agents such as the JTB Group, Japan's largest tour operator.

3.3 Interrelationships Between Heritage and Tourism

It is clear that there has been a significant relationship between heritage and tourism in academia and the real world (e.g. Jimura, 2019, 2022; Timothy, 2020; Wise & Jimura, 2020). In this long-standing and mutual relation, heritage and tourism have been affecting each other in every region of the world and Japan is not an exception.

A numerous types of cultural heritage and natural heritage have been utilised by the host (supply) side of tourism as tourism resources, has attracted, and has been visited or appreciated by the guest (demand) side of tourism (Jimura, 2019, 2022). Needless to say, however, natural heritage on the earth exists regardless tourism, even human beings. It also needs to be noted that most of cultural heritage in the world and Japan were not initially created and developed by mankind for tourism purposes. Probably, the only type of cultural heritage that was built initially and chiefly for tourism purposes would be amusement or theme parks (Jimura, 2022), although some people may not see them as 'cultural heritage'. In other words, in principle, tourism is not the original and main purpose of cultural and natural heritage. Nevertheless, both cultural and natural heritage is widely recognised as an essential and main element of certain types of tourism as proven by the existence of various niche and special interest tourism today (e.g. cultural heritage tourism, literary tourism, religious tourism, ecotourism, wildlife tourism, and adventure tourism).

As discussed above, heritage has been exploited for tourism and has influenced tourism as an attraction factor and/or tourism resource that tourist destinations have. On the other hand, tourism has also affected cultural and natural heritage in diverse ways. This is also comprehended as the impacts of tourism on heritage or changes in heritage, and they can be positive or negative for heritage. In terms of TBL, for example, tourism can bring economic benefits to cultural and natural heritage and its stakeholders who own, conserve and/or manage the heritage (Jimura, 2019, 2022). Such financial resources can be reinvested or spent for heritage conservation. It is also widely agreed that tourism can revitalise or damage cultural heritage. Revitalisation can occur, for example, when local people re-discover the value of their cultural heritage such as local crafts when they are appreciated by tourists. On the other hand, damage can be done, for instance, when excessive commodification of local culture occurs and its authenticity is damaged. For some kinds of natural heritage such as national parks in the USA, it is usual for the parks to be visited and enjoyed by visitors, including local people. However, an excessive number of visitors or their irresponsible behaviour may cause negative, sometimes even irreversible, damage on flora and fauna of the natural parks.

4 Theory and Practice of Sustainability in Heritage and Tourism Industries – World

4.1 Business Ethics

The term 'ethics' is used in various contexts and many different study fields, including business studies. According to Abdullah and Valentine (2009, 93), for example, 'Ethics is defined as the study of morality and the application of reason which sheds light on rules and principle, which is called ethical theories that ascertains the right and wrong for a situation'. 'Morally right and wrong' included in their definition is also a core of many definitions suggested by other researchers. In addition to 'right and wrong', Fischer (2004) and Manzini (2006) state that ethics is also a matter of what is 'good and bad'. In relation to the scope of this book, a special focus must be given to 'business ethics' because many stakeholders in the heritage and tourism sectors, especially the latter, engage in a specific type of business. Heller and Heller (2011, 30) note that business ethics is not independent from ethics as a whole but part of it and define business ethics as 'the study of how individuals, at all levels of an organization, try to make decisions and live their lives according to a standard of or right or wrong behavior' in their paper on business ethics education. Morally right, good or acceptable 'behaviour' of individuals, organisations and companies is also an essence of the definition of business ethics suggested by Cacioppe et al. (2008).

Huimin and Ryan (2011) suggest that ethical business practice would not be formed without three factors, namely, compliance with a legal framework, an identification of that which is thought to be right, and an ability to implement what are considered to be ethical standards of behaviour. Of these, the first factor is seen as the most basic and minimum requirement to be seen as ethical business practice (Huimin & Ryan, 2011) and it is commonly used in the vast majority of countries. The second factor works as a basis of ethical codes of conduct (Huimin & Ryan, 2011) that is a collection of instructions for decision-making in an ethical manner that are usually created at organisation level (Levy &

Ramim, 2009) but can also be developed at individual level. In the tourism sector, for example, Tourism Australia, a governmental destination marketing organisation for the country, established their code of conduct and makes it available at their website (www.tourism.australia.com › dam › assets › document). Lastly, the third factor can provoke the establishment and implementation of policies of corporate social responsibility (hereafter CSR) (Huimin & Ryan, 2011).

4.2 Corporate Social Responsibility (CSR)

Except some types of stakeholders in the heritage and tourism sectors such as governmental bodies, NPOs and charitable organisations, most of the stakeholders in these sectors, especially those in the tourism sector, are private businesses that are usually profit-driven (e.g. railways and coach companies, hotels and bed and breakfasts, and restaurants and bars). Nowadays, however, it is obvious that not only non-profit-driven organisations but also profit-driven ones are expected to take their responsibilities accordingly as members of society. Although the origins of the concept that is perceived as CSR today have a long and extending history, it is fair to say that this notion was born in the twentieth century, particularly after the 1950s (Carroll, 2008) and originated in the USA (Gjølberg, 2010). CSR of many enterprises has been increasingly integrated with their strategic management and corporate governance during the 2000s (Carroll, 2008) and this trend seems to have been continuing or even more prominent nowadays across the world, especially in developed countries.

In the aforementioned current context, CSR denotes actions and policies employed by organisations that consider their stakeholders' expectations and the sustainability of their performance in terms of TBL (Aguinis, 2011; Wells et al., 2016). This indicates that the magnitude of TBL can be confirmed in the context of CSR as well as in the context of sustainability and sustainability management (see Sects. 2.1 and 2.2 respectively). As stated earlier, nowadays the expectation of society is a main driving force for CSR. This can also be understood as a collective need or even pressure from the general public. Other driving forces behind CSR are enhanced reputation, cost savings and management support (Wells et al., 2016). Thus, many organisations are or at least seem to be keen to practice CSR, but generally it is a demanding task mainly due to financial, socio-cultural, technological or legal factors that may exist within and outside the organisations (Wells et al., 2016). In the tourism sector, for instance, McDonald's UK (n.d.) states that it uses low energy LED light bulbs, energy saving equipment and waterless urinals, and recycles used cooking oil into biodiesel to fuel more than half of its delivery trucks, and these are examples of its CSR activities. Compared with the tourism sector, it is more difficult to find examples of CSR activities in the heritage sector. One of rather limited examples of those in the heritage sector is volunteer programmes that are run by large urban museums in Australia. These programmes involve participation and engagement of their urban communities (Edwards, 2007), although museums are also a key element of the tourism sector.

4.3 Institutional Framework for Sustainability

Theory and practice of sustainability and sustainability management have been embodied through the development of significant notions such as business ethics and CSR and their implementation in the real world. Such activities for sustainability are often planned and conducted at organisational level, intending to achieve each organisation's sustainability goal through its sustainability management. However, the meanings and objectives of these activities should also be considered at a wider scale such as sectoral, national and even international level to make these actions more meaningful in a broader context and to realise more sustainable society in the future by working collectively rather than independently. To this end, various institutional frameworks have been established at diverse levels.

Concerning institutional frameworks associated with sustainability at international level, the Rio Earth Summit held in 1992 was a milestone, and its resulting document was Agenda 21 (see Sect. 2.2). At the Rio Earth Summit, the United Nations Framework Convention on Climate Change (hereafter UNFCCC) was also signed. UNFCCC is an international environmental treaty that aims to tackle climate change, which became effective in 1994. Indeed, UNFCCC was an innovative and beneficial treaty for sustainability of our society and natural environment of the earth; however, it was like a broad picture or vision for the future rather than a specific action plan. UNFCCC also lacks enough clarity in its measurable targets and deadlines to achieve the targets. To improve such drawbacks, the Kyoto Protocol to UNFCCC was adopted in 1997 and became effective in 2005. Simply speaking, the protocol aimed to reduce the amount of greenhouse gas emissions from human activities. Reduction targets to be achieved by 2020 differed by country, considering various factors. The Paris Agreement that was adopted in 2015 and became effective in 2016 can be understood as a successor to the Kyoto Protocol. This agreement regulates various measures against climate change. Each country that signed the agreement has a duty to develop, submit and maintain its Nationally Determined Contribution (hereafter NDC) and is obliged to take domestic actions to make its NDC. However, there is no penalty even if countries fail to make its NDC.

Such institutional frameworks for sustainability have been established at regional intergovernmental level, for example, Europe and the European Union (hereafter EU). EU has a very large number of environmental laws (e.g. Council Directive 1999/31/EC of 26 April 1999 on the landfill of waste). These laws are interrelated with other international environmental legislation. As EU member states are 'governed' by EU, EU's environmental laws influence those of the member states. Furthermore, each country in the world has its own environmental laws and regulations. To cite a case, UK's main laws related to sustainability include Environmental Protection Act 1990, Environment Act 1995 and Climate Change Act 2008. Regulations for Greenhouse Gas Emissions from Aircraft are American regulations associated with its transport sector. China made a major revision of its Environmental Protection Law in 2015, and the revised law has stricter punishments on polluters (Mondaq, 2020).

1 Introduction – Sustainability and Japan's Heritage and Tourism

4.4 Reduce, Reuse and Recycle (3Rs)

As discussed in Sect. 2.3, nowadays 'reduce', 'reuse' and 'recycle' (3Rs) are widely acknowledged as the three main pillars for the idea and implementation of sustainability. In fact, these 3Rs are utilised to raise people's awareness of sustainability and to encourage its practice by diverse stakeholders at different levels, including:

- International organisations (e.g. UN, UNESCO, the United Nations Environment Programme, and the World Tourism Organization),
- Regional intergovernmental organisations (e.g. EU and the Association of Southeast Asian Nations),
- National governments (e.g. Canada, South Africa, and the United Arab Emirates),
- Associations in a certain sector (e.g. ABTA – The Travel Association, UK), and
- Individual companies/organisations (e.g. Finnair, Eurostar, Starbucks, Disneyland Resort, TUI Group, and the National Trust for Places of Historic Interest or Natural Beauty).

When the 3Rs are used together in the context of sustainability or sustainability management, there would be some differences in what 3Rs signify amongst organisations/businesses. Overall, however, the essence of the 3Rs appears to be similar regardless of stakeholders of sustainability. For instance, the National Environment Agency of Singapore (hereafter NEAS) (2020) explains each of the 3Rs in their document called '3R Guidebook for Hotels' as follows:

- Reduce – to avoid waste at source so as to minimise the quantity of waste that needs to be treated or disposed of,
- Reuse – to use an object or material again, either for its original or similar purpose, without significantly altering the physical form of the object or material, and
- Recycle – the process of transforming waste materials into reusable form which may or may not be similar to the original product (NEAS, 2020).

In the real world, each of the 3Rs has been considered and practiced by various stakeholders in the heritage and tourism sector. To cite some relevant cases, Subway UK conducts strict operational procedures that are followed by its franchisees in order to 'reduce' the amount of food waste to an average of less than 1% per store (Subway UK, 2020). Many hotels, particularly those who are part of international hotel chains (e.g. ibis hotels in the Accor Group), give their guests who stay with them for two nights or longer an option to 'reuse' towels. In the heritage sector, it is a common practice, especially in European countries, to 'reuse' their historic buildings, changing their purposes and usage to meet current demands (e.g. from warehouses to retail spaces) (Jimura, 2019). McDonald's UK 'recycles' the cardboard boxes used in more than 89% of their restaurants, and more than 85% of their packaging is made from renewable resources (McDonald's UK, n.d.).

In some industries, 3Rs of sustainability can be extended further. As shown in Sect. 2.3, 'respect' is added to the 3Rs and in total the 4Rs are regarded as essential elements of *mottainai* from the viewpoints of MCO and GBM. Alternatively, 'recover' can also be the 4th R of sustainability (e.g. Yang et al., 2017), and this seems to be prominent in waste management in the manufacturing and construction sectors. 'Recover' in this context means to convert produced waste into new resources or energy. Toyota Europe (n.d.) states that it can 'recover' even the finest waste residues and make the most of them as an alternative fuel source for car industry.

5 Theory and Practice of Sustainability in Heritage and Tourism Industries – Japan

5.1 Business Ethics

'*Dotoku*' and '*rinri*' are the Japanese words that denote 'ethics'. These two terms have similar meanings and some native speakers of Japanese may use them interchangeably. In author's view, however, there would be slight differences in the meanings between the two words. '*Dotoku*' would be associated with ethics of Japanese society as a whole, whilst *rinri* would be related to ethics of certain groups, industry or occupations.

Generally and traditionally, collectivism has been very prominent in societies in East Asian countries, including Japan, and has had strong influence on people in these countries, affecting their ways of thinking and behaviours (Jimura, 2019, 2022). In relation to collectivism in these nations, Confucianism and Confucian ethics are crucial, because they have been deeply rooted in their societies and working as a foundation of collectivism in their society (Jimura, 2019, 2022). For this reason, it could be stated that the vast majority of Japanese individuals have been constantly exposed to implicit pressure from Japanese society, because the society as a whole expects them to respect '*dotoku*' and follow tacit rules that are believed to be vital to maintain the 'harmony' of Japanese society.

It is also fair to say that the existence of collectivism is confirmed in most industries, sectors, companies, organisations and groups in Japan except those which were originally established in foreign countries, especially in the West. *Rinri* would be a more appropriate Japanese word than *dotoku* when ethics is discussed in the context of a specific sector or group of stakeholders. In Japanese, the word *kigyo* denotes companies, enterprises, firms or businesses. Thus, '*kigyo rinri*' would be the most appropriate phrase that has a meaning equivalent to 'business ethics'. In light of the aforementioned nature of Japanese society and ever-increasing importance of business ethics across the world, following and respecting business ethics in the heritage and tourism sectors in Japan is vital for any organisations involved in these sectors.

Like other countries, business ethics in Japan is embodied in several ways by various organisations/businesses in the heritage and tourism sectors. For example, Japan's hoteliers (e.g. APA Group) has established a personal information protection policy for their guests and Shinto shrines (e.g. Dewa Sanzan Jinja) has developed a privacy policy for their admirers, and these policies are accessible at their official websites. Japan's restaurants (e.g. Royal Host, a domestic restaurant chain) make the information about allergens and ingredients of their dishes available on site as well as at their official websites.

5.2 Corporate Social Responsibility (CSR)

As a whole, the rise and development of CSR to date in Japan is similar to those in the USA and other developed countries (see Sect. 4.2). This implies that CSR is not a recent concept in Japan as well and its history can be traced back to 1956 when CSR was discussed at the meeting of Japan Association of Corporate Executives (Kawamura, n.d.). Like the USA, however, CSR had also not been a well-acknowledged notion that is widely understood and practiced by Japanese enterprises until 2003. In general, the year 2003 is regarded as the first year of CSR practice in Japan, because many large Japanese companies have started publishing their annual CSR report and setting up their CSR departments or sections since that time (Kawamura, n.d.). Nowadays, CSR is a familiar idea amongst the general public as well as company workers, and many Japanese individuals could understand what CSR means without its Japanese translation. However, the idea of CSR is also recognised well as '*kigyo no shakaiteki sekinin*', the Japanese translation of CSR.

Organisations or businesses in Japan's heritage and tourism sectors have been planning and conducting a variety of CSR activities, including those for supporting and (re)vitalising cultural heritage, conserving natural heritage, saving natural resources, protecting human rights, and encouraging women's social advancement. In their CSR activities, collaborations beyond the boundary between the heritage sector and the tourism sector can be confirmed. All Nippon Airways (hereafter ANA) have been supporting a conservation project for 'Angkor', a cultural WHS, in cooperation with Sophia University and MOFA (Jimura, 2019) by providing free air tickets between Japan and Cambodia for those involved in clean-up activities on site and conducting awareness-raising activities through their in-flight magazines. This is a good example of CSR activities jointly implemented by organisations/enterprises in the tourism (ANA), heritage and education (Sophia University) and public (MOFA) sectors. Another CSR activity in a collaborative manner can also be found at 'Sacred Sites and Pilgrimage Routes in the Kii Mountain Range', a cultural WHS in Japan. The '*michi-bushin*' programme was established and managed by key stakeholders in the heritage and public sectors such as Wakayama World Heritage Centre, Wakayama Prefecture and Tanabe City. The programme aims to restore and maintain footpaths that connect shrines and temples within the WHS, and any businesses, organisations or individuals can participate in the programme as volunteers (Jimura, 2016). Some businesses in the tourism sector such as Nankai Electric Railway and Suntory (foods and drinks) took part in the *michi-bushin* programme as part of their CSR activities (Jimura, 2019).

5.3   Institutional Framework for Sustainability

As discussed in Sect. 4.2, a range of institutional frameworks for sustainability have been developed at international, regional intergovernmental and national levels. In Japan, there are also various laws and regulations that are associated with sustainability. The examples of institutional frameworks that are directly associated with the heritage or tourism sector are introduced in Sects. 3.1 and 3.2, and they are also linked with sustainability to some extent. Needless to say, however, Japan also has a wide variety of laws and regulations directly related to sustainability and they are applied to organisations and businesses across different sectors.

Concerning climate change, Act on Promotion of Global Warming Countermeasures (*Chikyu Ondanka Taisaku Suishin-ho*) was enacted in 1998. This act obliges organisations/businesses that emit a large amount of greenhouse gas to report the amount of their greenhouse gas emission to MOE annually. Within the heritage and tourism sectors, this act would be most relevant to transport businesses and is actually applied to Japan Airlines, for instance. On the other hand, Act on Prevention of Water Pollution (*Suishitsu Odaku Boshi-ho*) would be associated more with hotel and food and drink businesses. MOE and this act require the businesses to monitor the quality of their drain water at least annually. MOE promotes sustainability not only through these institutional frameworks but also its award scheme named '*Kankyo Sustainable Kigyo*', meaning 'environmentally sustainable companies'.

The Ministry of Economy, Trade and Industry has jurisdiction over laws and regulations on energy use. Act on Rationale Use of Energy (*Shoene-ho*) regulates energy use by factories and transport enterprises, and encourages rationalisation of their energy use. In the tourism sector, for example, this act is applied to major railway companies with 300 or more coaches (e.g. West Japan Railway Company). In relation to accommodation and catering businesses, Act on Food Sanitation (*Shokuhin Eisei-ho*) is a very important law and has a long history since 1947. The Ministry of Health, Labour and Welfare (hereafter MHLW) and the Consumer Affairs Agency exercise jurisdiction over this act. The law defines food additives that are allowed to be used by food/drink businesses to make or process products and requires them to place a food sanitation supervisor (*shokuhin eisei sekinin-sha*) at each of their business venue and factory. MHLW is also in charge of a basic law directly linked with accommodation businesses, Act on Accommodation Businesses (*Ryokan gyo-ho*). This law specifies several types of accommodation in Japan and requirements that must be met by individuals or organisations that plan to launch their accommodation business. Like many other nations, the emergence and development of online holiday rental businesses (e.g. Airbnb) are confirmed in Japan in recent years. Considering this social background, some districts were exempted from the application of the act and new regulations were established at prefectural and local levels (e.g. Osaka Urban Prefecture and Ota Ward in Tokyo Metropolitan Prefecture).

5.4 Reduce, Reuse and Recycle (3Rs)

As shown in Sect. 2.3, the idea of 'reduce', 'reuse' and 'recycle' (3Rs) is strongly interrelated with the concept of *mottainai*. Compared with *mottainai*, 3Rs are a newer notion for the general public in Japan. In the 1990s, however, 3Rs were already examined by Japanese researchers in some different study fields such as environmental studies (e.g. Suzuki et al., 1995) and waste management (e.g. Yasui, 1999). As of 2006, moreover, e's Inc. (2006) asserts that even primary school students may know what 3Rs mean. Hence, nowadays 3Rs as well as *mottainai* can be acknowledged as familiar concepts for Japanese people.

1 Introduction – Sustainability and Japan's Heritage and Tourism

To raise awareness of 3Rs and promote 3Rs activities, several associations consisting of members from different sectors have been formed in Japan. The Council for Promotion of 3Rs is a good example of such organisations, and its members include diverse industry groups, public interest incorporated foundations, general incorporated foundations and consumer groups. Advancing 3Rs in Japan also seems to be a top priority for MOE. To this end, MOE produces leaflets and books for awareness-raising, introduces good practices of 3Rs activities, conducts campaigns with various 3Rs-related events across Japan, and sets October as a month for promoting 3Rs.

Many practices of 3Rs that are implemented outside Japan (see Sect. 4.4) or something similar to them can also be found in Japan's heritage and tourism sectors. For example, Yoshinoya is a Japanese fast-food chain whose main product is Japanese beef bowl (*gyudon*). The company reviewed the volume of boiled rice in *gyudon* and began to serve more different sizes of *gyudon* to 'reduce' the amount of wasted rice. Traditionally, it has not been a common practice in Japan to bring leftovers at a restaurant back to home. In relation to this situation, the Doggy Bag Committee (hereafter DBC) was established in 2009 to encourage the use of doggy bags amongst consumers in Japan, aiming to 'reduce' the amount of leftovers (DBC, n.d.). By doing so, people can also 'reuse' the leftovers as meals they enjoy at home. Encouraging their guests to 'reuse' towels is also a common activity adopted by many hotels in Japan, for instance, the Hankyu Hanshin Daiichi Hotel Group. In Japan, a separate collection of household rubbish has been advanced highly by local governments, but the levels of separation differ by local council. For instance, Kusatsu City (2019) asks its residents to separate their household rubbish into ten main categories to 'recycle' the rubbish as much as possible, particularly plastic bottles, glass bottles, cans, and papers. Such an approach is also employed in the tourism sector. East Japan Railway Company have installed three types of rubbish bins, one for cans and glass bottles, one for newspapers and magazines, and the other for all other types of rubbish in stations. This categorisation can enhance the level of 'recycling' of paper, steel and aluminium.

6 Structure of the Book

This final section of this chapter elucidates the structure of this monograph. This book comprises four parts and has 10 chapters. Part I is formed by this chapter only and works as an introduction to the whole of the book. It also provides readers with this book's key concepts (sustainability, sustainability management and *mottainai*), main focuses (heritage and tourism sectors and interrelationships between them) and essential themes (business ethics, cooperate social responsibility, institutional frameworks for sustainability, and 3Rs). Part II sheds light on sustainability of heritage in Japan and consists of three chapters (Chaps. 2, 3, and 4) that examine tangible cultural heritage, intangible cultural heritage, and natural heritage respectively. Then, Part III explores sustainability of tourism in Japan in five chapters (Chaps. 5, 6, 7, 8, and 9) which focus on transportation, accommodation, food and beverage, visitor attractions and events, and tourism intermediaries, respectively. Part IV is the final part of this monograph and has Chap. 10 that functions as a concluding chapter of this book.

References

Abdullah, H., & Valentine, B. (2009). Fundamental and ethics theories of corporate governance. *Middle Eastern Finance and Economics, 4*(4), 88–96.

Acott, T. G., La Trobe, H. L., & Howard, S. H. (1998). An evaluation of deep ecotourism and shallow ecotourism. *Journal of Sustainable Tourism, 6*(3), 238–253.

Aguinis, H. (2011). Organizational responsibility: Doing good and doing well. In S. Zedeck (Ed.), *APA handbook of industrial and organizational psychology* (Vol. 3, pp. 855–879). American Psychological Association.

Cacioppe, R., Forster, N., & Fox, M. (2008). A survey of managers' perceptions of corporate ethics and social responsibility and actions that may affect companies' success. *Journal of Business Ethics, 82*(3), 681–700.

Cambridge Dictionary. (2020). *Sustainability*. Available at: https://dictionary.cambridge.org/dictionary/english/sustainability. Accessed 31 Dec 2020.

1 Introduction – Sustainability and Japan's Heritage and Tourism

Carroll, A. B. (2008). A history of corporate social responsibility: Concepts and practices. In A. Crane, A. McWilliams, D. Matten, J. Moon, & D. S. Siegel (Eds.), *The Oxford handbook of corporate social responsibility* (pp. 19–46). Oxford University Press on Demand.

DBC. (n.d.). *Home.* Available at: https://www.doggybag-japan.com/home-en. Accessed 22 Jan 2021.

Deacon, H., Mngqolo, S., & Prosalendis, S. (2003). Protecting our cultural capital – A research plan for the heritage sector: Session IX: Wrapping up. *South African Museums Association Bulletin, 29*(1), 34–39.

Edwards, D. (2007). Corporate social responsibility of large urban museums: The contribution of volunteer programs. *Tourism Review International, 11*(2), 167–174.

e's Inc. (2006). *Reduce, reuse, recycle* [in Japanese]. Available at: https://www.es-inc.jp/library/writing/2006/libwri_id002995.html. Accessed 22 Jan 2021.

Fennell, D. A. (1999). *Ecotourism: An introduction.* Routledge.

Fennell, D. A., & Cooper, C. (2020). *Sustainable tourism: Principles, contexts and practices.* Channel View Publications.

Fischer, J. (2004). Social responsibility and ethics: Clarifying the concepts. *Journal of Business Ethics, 52*(4), 381–390.

GBM. (2021a). *Who we are.* Available at: http://www.greenbeltmovement.org/. Accessed 2 Jan 2021.

GBM. (2021b). *Mottainai Campaign.* Available at: http://www.greenbeltmovement.org/what-we-do/advocacy/mottainai-campaign. Accessed 2 Jan 2021.

Gjølberg, M. (2010). Varieties of corporate social responsibility (CSR): CSR meets the "Nordic Model". *Regulation & Governance, 4*(2), 203–229.

Heller, N. A., & Heller, V. L. (2011). Business ethics education: Are business schools teaching to the AACSB ethics education task force recommendations? *International Journal of Business and Social Science, 2*(20), 30–38.

Huimin, G., & Ryan, C. (2011). Ethics and corporate social responsibility – An analysis of the views of Chinese hotel managers. *International Journal of Hospitality Management, 30*(4), 875–885.

Hunter, C. (1997). Sustainable tourism as an adaptive paradigm. *Annals of Tourism Research, 24*(4), 850–867.

Inspiring Interns. (2018). *What is the heritage sector?* Available at: https://www.inspiringinterns.com/blog/2018/05/what-is-the-heritage-sector/. Accessed 7 Jan 2021.

Jimura, T. (2011). The websites of Japanese ryokan and eWOM: Their impacts on guests' expectation and experience. *International Journal of Asian Tourism Management, 2*(2), 120–133.

Jimura, T. (2016). World heritage site management: a case study of sacred sites and pilgrimage routes in the Kii mountain range, Japan. *Journal of Heritage Tourism, 11*(4), 382–394.

Jimura, T. (2019). *World heritage sites: Tourism, local communities and conservation activities.* CABI.

Jimura, T. (2022). *Cultural and heritage tourism in Japan.* Routledge.

Jimura, T., & Lee, T. (2020). The impact of photographs on the online marketing for tourism: The case of Japanese-style inns. *Journal of Vacation Marketing, 26*(3), 354–364.

JTA. (n.d.). *About the JTA.* Available at: https://www.mlit.go.jp/kankocho/en/about/index.html. Accessed 10 Jan 2021.

Kawamura, M. (n.d.). *Nihon ni okeru CSR no keifu to genjo* (The history and current situation of CSR in Japan) [in Japanese]. Available at: https://www.nli-research.co.jp/files/topics/38077_ext_18_0.pdf. Accessed 20 Jan 2021.

Kusatsu City. (2019). *Kusatsu-shi no gomi no dashikata* (Classifying different types of waste) [in Japanese]. Available at: https://www.city.kusatsu.shiga.jp/kurashi/gomirecycle/gominodashikata/dashikata.html. Accessed 22 Jan 2021.

Levy, Y., & Ramim, M. (2009). Initial development of a learners' ratified acceptance of multibiometrics intentions model (RAMIM). *Interdisciplinary Journal of E-Learning and Learning Objects, 5*(1), 379–397.

Manzini, E. (2006) Design, ethics and sustainability. *Guidelines for a Transition Phase. University of Art and Design Helsinki (June)*, 9–15.

McDonald's UK. (n.d.). *What is McDonald's corporate social responsibility (CSR) policy?* Available at: https://www.mcdonalds.com/gb/en-gb/help/faq/19263-what-is-mcdonalds-corporate-social-responsibility-csr-policy.html. Accessed 14 Jan 2021.

MCO. (n.d.). *Who we are.* Available at: https://web.archive.org/web/20090126004726/http://mottainai.info/english/who.html. Accessed 2 Jan 2021.

MOFA. (n.d.). *Team Toyako – The Mottainai Campaign.* Available at: https://www.mofa.go.jp/policy/economy/summit/2008/kids/eco/index_02.html. Accessed 2 Jan 2021.

Mondaq. (2020) *China: China's evolving environmental protection laws.* Available at: https://www.mondaq.com/china/clean-air-pollution/955486/china39s-evolving-environmental-protection-laws. Accessed 16 Jan 2021.

NEAS. (2020). *3R guidebook for hotels*. Available at: https://www.nea.gov.sg/docs/default-source/resource/3r-guidebook-for-hotels.pdf. Accessed 17 Jan 2021.
OECD. (2005a). *Weak sustainability*. Available from http://stats.oecd.org/glossary/detail.asp?ID=6611. Accessed 31 Dec 2020.
OECD. (2005b). *Strong sustainability*. Available from http://stats.oecd.org/glossary/detail.asp?ID=6577. Accessed 31 Dec 2020.
Paehlke, R. C. (1996). Environmentalism and the future of progressive politics. In M. A. Cahn & R. O'Brien (Eds.), *Thinking about the environment* (pp. 256–260). M. E. Sharpe.
Page, S. J., & Connell, J. (2020). *Tourism: A modern synthesis* (5th ed.). Routledge.
Pearce, D. (1993). *Blueprint 3: Measuring sustainable development*. Earthscan.
PRO. (2018). *MOTTAINAI: Reduce, reuse, recycle – And respect*. Available at: https://www.gov-online.go.jp/pdf/hlj/20180701/28-29.pdf. Accessed 2 Jan 2021.
Salzmann, O., Steger, U., & Ionescu-Somers, A. (2005). *Quantifying economic effects of corporate sustainability initiatives – Activities and drivers*. IMD 2005-28, November 2005, p. 3.
Stabler, M. (1996). Managing the leisure natural resource base: utter confusion or evolving consensus. In *4th World Leisure and Recreation Association Congress, Cardiff* (pp. 4–6).
Starik, M., & Kanashiro, P. (2013). Toward a theory of sustainability management; uncovering and integrating the nearly obvious. *Organization and Environment, 26*(1), 7–30.
Subway UK. (2020). *Our CSR initiatives*. Available at: https://www.subway.com/en-gb/aboutus/socialresponsibility/nutritionalleadership#:~:text=Reducing%20waste%20and%20sustainability&text=We%20aim%20to%20reduce%20food,the%20day%2C%20only%20as%20required. Accessed 17 Jan 2021.
Suzuki, T., Ohnishi, M., Takeshima, M., & Minami, K. (1995). Projects for the lifestyle of "OHMI" having on little effects on the environment [in Japanese]. *Kankyo-system Kenkyu, 23*, 643–648.
Swarbrooke, J. (1999). *Sustainable tourism management*. CABI.
Timothy, D. (2020). *Cultural heritage and tourism: An introduction* (2nd ed.). Channel View Publications.
Timothy, D., & Boyd, S. (2003). *Heritage tourism*. Prentice-Hall.

Toyota Europe. (n.d.). *Better earth*. Available at: https://www.toyota-europe.com/world-of-toyota/feel/environment/better-earth/better-earth. Accessed 17 Jan 2021.

Turner, R. K., Pearce, D., & Bateman, I. (1994). *Environmental economics: An elementary introduction*. Harvester Wheatsheaf.

UN. (n.d.). *The 17 goals*. Available at: https://sdgs.un.org/goals. Accessed 1 Jan 2021.

University of Birmingham. (n.d.). *Heritage sector*. Available at: https://intranet.birmingham.ac.uk/as/employability/careers/resources/cal/heritage.aspx. Accessed 7 Jan 2021.

Wells, V. K., Smith, D. G., Taheri, B., Manika, D., & McCowlen, C. (2016). An exploration of CSR development in heritage tourism. *Annals of Tourism Research, 58*, 1–17.

Wise, N., & Jimura, T. (Eds.). (2020). *Tourism, cultural heritage and urban regeneration – Changing spaces in historical places*. Springer.

World Commission on Environment and Development. (1987). *Report of the world commission on environment and development: Our common future*. UN Documents: Gathering a Body of Global Agreements.

Yang, H., Xia, J., Thompson, J. R., & Flower, R. J. (2017). Urban construction and demolition waste and landfill failure in Shenzhen, China. *Waste Management, 63*, 393–396.

Yasui, M. (1999). *Wagakuni no haikibutsu shori no genjo to kadai* (Current situation and issues in Japan's waste management) [in Japanese]. Available at: https://core.ac.uk/download/pdf/236663841.pdf. Accessed 22 Jan 2021.

Part II

Sustainability of Heritage

2

Sustainability of Japan's Tangible Cultural Heritage

1 Introduction

At international level, for example, the United Nations Educational, Scientific and Cultural Organization (hereafter UNESCO) (n.d.) states that the term tangible cultural heritage encompasses three main categories as follows:

- Movable cultural heritage (paintings, sculptures, coins, manuscripts)
- Immovable cultural heritage (monuments, archaeological sites, and so on)
- Underwater cultural heritage (shipwrecks, underwater ruins and cities)

According to UNESCO (n.d.), natural sites with cultural aspects such as cultural landscapes are natural heritage. On the other hand, UNESCO regards cultural landscapes as cultural or mixed heritage in the context of World Heritage (hereafter WH) (Leask, 2006; Jimura, 2019). WH is a UNESCO's international initiative for the conservation of cultural and natural heritage all over the world. The essence of WH is the WH Convention, an international agreement adopted by the General Conference of UNESCO in 1972. Historically, tangible cultural heritage and properties have often been damaged/destroyed and/or forced to be sold/robbed during armed conflicts such as World War II. To protect tangible cultural heritage and properties in such a challenging situation, UNESCO signed the Hague Convention for the Protection of Cultural Property in the Event of Armed Conflict in 1954.

Generally, the terms *isan* (heritage) and *zai* (properties) are used interchangeably in the heritage sector of Japan. The Agency of Cultural Affairs (hereafter ACA) is an extra-ministerial bureau affiliated with the Ministry of Education, Culture, Sports, Science and Technology; and, a government body that is in charge of promotion and conservation of Japan's cultural heritage. A typology of tangible cultural heritage employed by ACA is somewhat different from UNESCO's. According to ACA (n.d.-a), main categories of Japan's tangible cultural heritage are:

- Tangible Cultural Properties – structures and buildings (*Yukei Bunkazai – Kenzobutsu*)
- Tangible Cultural Properties – fine arts and crafts (*Yukei Bunkazai – Bijutsukogeihin*)
- Cultural Landscapes (*Bunkateki Keikan*)
- Preservation Districts for Groups of Historic Buildings (*Dentoteki Kenzobutsugun Hozonchiku*)
- Buried Cultural Properties (*Maizo Bunkazai*)
- Folk Cultural Properties (*Minzoku Bunkazai*)
- Monuments (*Kinenbutsu*)

Of these seven main categories, *Minzoku Bunkazai* include both tangible and intangible cultural properties that Japanese people developed and have passed down to their current generations (ACA, n.d.-b), whilst *Kinenbutsu* encompass even broader sorts of properties that have a high historic/scientific, artistic/aesthetic and scientific values to Japan (ACA, n.d.-c). Comparing the typologies employed by UNESCO (international) and ACA (Japan), ACA does not acknowledge underwater cultural heritage and properties as a main category of Japan's tangible cultural heritage. It should also be noted that Japan has not ratified the Convention on the Protection of the Underwater Cultural Heritage, a key international treaty for conservation of underwater cultural heritage, as of writing. Nevertheless, the Japanese Government still appreciates the importance of its underwater cultural heritage and started working on its conservation (Nakada, 2019; Jimura, 2022) (see Sect. 6 for details). In relation to Japan's tangible cultural heritage, Jimura (2022) also looks at subsequent eight kinds of heritage as its representative examples and examines their importance in their own right and as tourism resources:

- Religious sites, buildings and collections
- Japanese-style inns
- Cultures of indigenous peoples
- Industrial heritage sites and properties
- War heritage
- Urban heritage (Coexistence of historic and contemporary cultural heritage)
- Spaces and places for consumption (e.g. shopping centres)
- Theme parks

The aforementioned ACA's seven main categories of Japan's tangible cultural heritage are employed as key themes of subsequent sections and discussed in terms of their sustainability, applying the concept of *mottainai* and referring to its practice. All eight types of tangible cultural heritage discussed by Jimura (2022) also fit the scope of this chapter. Of these, however, 'Japanese-style inns' are discussed in 'Chapter 6 Sustainability of Japan's Accommodation Sector' in 'Part 3 Sustainability of Tourism', because they are one of the most important players in Japan's accommodation sector. Moreover, contemporary tangible cultural heritage such as multifunctional buildings, shopping centres and theme parks are explored across the chapters in Part 3 as generally their presence as heritage is less established than historic tangible cultural heritage amongst people of Japan, although they have been playing essential roles in Japan's tourism industry today.

2 Tangible Cultural Properties – Structures and Buildings (*Yukei Bunkazai – Kenzobutsu*)

As shown in Sect. 3.1 of Chap. 1 and Sect. 1 of this chapter, ACA is the leading governmental stakeholder at national level that is responsible for conservation, utilisation and promotion of Japan's tangible and intangible cultural heritage. ACA is in charge of laws and regulations associated with cultural heritage and the most important law concerning Japan's cultural heritage is Act on Protection of Cultural Properties (*Bunkazai Hogo-ho*). Concerning Tangible Cultural Properties – structures and buildings (*Yukei Bunkazai – Kenzobutsu*), furthermore, following Japanese laws are also relevant and important:

- Building Standards Act (*Kenchiku Kijun-ho*)
- City Planning Act (*Toshi Keikaku-ho*)
- Landscape Act (*Keikan-ho*)

According to ACA (n.d.-d), the Japanese Government has been conserving Japan's tangible cultural heritage (structures and buildings) through two listing and one register systems as follows:

- National Treasures (*Kokuho*)
- Important Cultural Properties (*Juyo Bunkazai*)
- Registered Tangible Cultural Properties (*Toroku Yukei Bunkazai*)

Both National Treasures (*Kokuho*) and Important Cultural Properties (*Juyo Bunkazai*) are listing schemes adopted by the Japanese Government for the conservation of Japan's tangible cultural heritage. In principle, only historic structures and buildings are eligible to be listed as National Treasures or Important Cultural Properties, and the history of these two listing systems with the current style can be traced back to 1950. Important Cultural Properties are significant historic tangible cultural heritage of Japan. Of these, particularly invaluable one is listed as National Treasures. Thus, National Treasures is superior to Important Cultural

Properties and seen as the most prestigious category of Japan's tangible cultural heritage. On the other hand, Registered Tangible Cultural Properties (*Toroku Yukei Bunkazai*) is a register system for the conservation of modern cultural heritage (structures and buildings) based on the submissions of reports developed by local governments and owners of properties to the Japanese Government via prefectures (ACA, n.d.-d). This register system was newly added when Act on Protection of Cultural Properties was revised in 1996 to conserve a variety of modern tangible cultural properties that face a risk of extinction in a quickly changing Japanese society (ACA, n.d.-d). According to ACA (n.d.-e), Japan has 228 structures/buildings (291 wings) as National Treasures, 2523 structures/buildings (5241 wings) as Important Cultural Properties (these numbers include National Treasures) and 12,681 structures/buildings as Registered Tangible Cultural Properties as of February 2021.

The vast majority of structures/buildings designated as National Treasures (*Kokuho*) are historic Japanese-style structures/buildings, and a few exceptions are Western-style ones such as Oura Church in Nagasaki Prefecture and State Guest House Akasaka Palace in Tokyo Metropolitan Prefecture (hereafter TMP). The latter is also the first building that was built during the Meiji period (1868–1912) to be listed as National Treasure. Some tangible cultural properties encompass both structures/buildings listed as National Treasures and those designated as Important Cultural Properties (*Juyo Bunkazai*) (e.g. Enryaku-ji Temple in Shiga Prefecture). Modern, neither historic nor contemporary, tangible cultural structures/buildings that are 50 years old or older are qualified to be registered as Registered Tangible Cultural Properties (*Toroku Yukei Bunkazai*) (ACA, 2020). For instance, Tokyo Tower was registered as Registered Tangible Cultural Properties in 2013, although it looks a present-day structure at a glance. In fact, however, the tower was built in 1958 and has been seen as one of iconic landmarks of post-war Tokyo and Japan.

Next, sustainability management of Japan's tangible cultural heritage (structures/buildings) is discussed in terms of the triple bottom line (hereafter TBL) of sustainability, applying the concept of *mottainai* and referring to its practice. First, economic sustainability is explored. Protection through the aforementioned listing/register systems indicates that structures/buildings on any of such schemes may obtain grants and/

or subsidies for their conservation activities from various agencies, including national or local government and public interest incorporated foundations. Such financial supports are crucial as generally it is highly challenging to conserve these structures or buildings continuously due to the facts that most of them are made of wood (flammable and easy to decay) and constantly face external threats of natural disasters because Japan are frequently hit by earthquakes and typhoons (Jimura, 2019, 2022). Many of Japan's tangible cultural heritage (structures/buildings), including religious buildings and historic houses, also try to be economically sustainable in their own right. To this end, they are open to the general public as visitor attractions, often charging admission fees. For instance, Former Shizutani School (Okayama Prefecture) comprises of several buildings including a lecture hall that is listed as National Treasure (*Kokuho*) and charges 400 Japanese Yen as its admission fee for adults.

Being open to the general public as people's place to visit also has an implication for socio-cultural sustainability of Japan's tangible cultural heritage (structures/buildings). That is because, these structures and buildings could retain their socio-cultural sustainability by providing visitors with enjoyment and educational opportunities. Playing such roles in their local community and even in wider communities also signifies that these structures and buildings are expected to take their social responsibility accordingly when they are used widely by diverse people with different purposes. Furthermore, the concept of *mottainai* is not respected and practiced, if such tangible heritage with valuable cultural meanings is not utilised by people of Japan in a current context and/or does not play any important role in Japanese society today. This also implies that even culturally significant structures/buildings can be forgotten and abandoned by people as time goes by, and would not be passed on to future generations.

Identifying and realising a best balance between conservation and visits (tourism) has always been a key task for tangible cultural heritage (structures/buildings) that are open to the general public as visitor attractions (Jimura, 2019, 2022). This point is also closely associated with environmental sustainability of tangible cultural heritage (structures/buildings). If structures or buildings utilised as visitor attractions cannot deal with their visitors in an appropriate manner in terms of visitor number, flow and behaviour; the structures or buildings would have negative environmental impacts on their properties such as wear and tear, vandalism and rubbish (Jimura, 2007, 2011). Furthermore, issues such as an excessive number of visitors, irresponsible visitor behaviour and increased amount of rubbish will also negatively affect the surrounding natural environment of the structures or buildings. Environmental sustainability of these structures or buildings can also be retained or enhanced through their conservation activities. For instance, the practice of reduce, reuse and recycle (3Rs), especially the first two, can be observed at many Tangible Cultural Properties – structures and buildings (*Yukei Bunkazai – Kenzobutsu*).

To cite a case, the main buildings of Ise Jingu (Ise Grand Shrine) in Mie Prefecture have been rebuilt in the same form every 20 years for over 1300 years (Jimura, 2019). This ritual is called '*shikinen sengu*' and the most recent one was held in 2013. The wood used for the current main buildings but still in a good condition is reused in the construction and repair of many other shrines across Japan (Adams, 1998). In the case of the latest *shikinen sengu*, the wood was reused for the reconstruction and/or repair of many Shinto shrines that had been hit severely by the 2011 Tohoku Earthquake and Tsunami. This practice can also reduce the amount of abandoned wood generated from *shikinen sengu*. The example of reduce and reuse confirmed in *shikinen sengu* of Ise Jingu can also be regarded as the application of *mottainai* concept to tangible cultural heritage (structures/buildings) and practice of *mottainai* spirit. Another example of the practice of reduce and reuse is found at Himeji Castle (Hyogo Prefecture) (see Fig. 2.1). The castle has five buildings (eight wings) listed as National Treasures (*Kokuho*) and more than 70 structures and buildings designated as Important Cultural Properties (*Juyo Bunkazai*). It should also be noted that Himeji Castle is one of the first two properties in Japan that were inscribed as World Heritage sites (hereafter WHSs) in 1993 together with Buddhist Monuments in the Horyu-ji Area (Nara Prefecture). During the castle's latest extensive repair project between 2009 and 2015, repair work for roofs of the castle's *daitenshu* (large castle tower) was conducted between 2009 and 2012. Of around 80,000 roofing tiles, about 64,000 (approximately 80%) were reused after their good condition had been confirmed (Koyo Seiga, n.d.).

Fig. 2.1 Himeji Castle after its extensive repair work between 2009 and 2015. (Source: Author)

3 Tangible Cultural Properties – Fine Arts and Crafts (*Yukei Bunkazai – Bijutsukogeihin*)

Tangible Cultural Properties – fine arts and crafts (*Yukei Bunkazai – Bijutsukogeihin*) is the second main category of Japan's tangible cultural heritage (ACA, n.d.-a). According to ACA (n.d.-f), Tangible Cultural Properties – fine arts and crafts consists of subsequent seven sub-categories:

- Paintings (*Kaiga*),
- Sculptures (*Chokoku*)
- Crafts (*Kogeihin*)
- Calligraphic works and Classical books (*Shoseki* and *Tenseki*)

2 Sustainability of Japan's Tangible Cultural Heritage

- Ancient documents (*Komonjo*)
- Archaeological artifacts (*Kokoshiryo*)
- Historic resources (*Rekishishiryo*)

Like Tangible Cultural Properties – structures and buildings (*Yukei Bunkazai – Kenzobutsu*), Tangible Cultural Properties – fine arts and crafts (*Yukei Bunkazai – Bijutsukogeihin*) are also designated by ACA and Act on Protection of Cultural Properties (*Bunkazai Hogo-ho*) is the most significant law for the conservation of cultural heritage belonging to this category. The two listing systems (National Treasures and Important Cultural Properties) and one register system (Registered Tangible Cultural Properties) employed for the preservation of Tangible Cultural Properties – structures and buildings are also adopted for the conservation of Tangible Cultural Properties – fine arts and crafts. According to ACA (n.d.-e), Japan has 897 fine arts and crafts as National Treasures, 10,808 fine arts and crafts as Important Cultural Properties (this number includes National Treasures) and 17 structures/buildings as Registered Tangible Cultural Properties as of February 2021. Of 897 properties listed as National Treasures, 254 are Crafts (*Kogeihin*) and 228 are Calligraphic works and Classical books (*Shoseki* and *Tenseki*), and of 10,808 properties listed as Important Cultural Properties, 2723 are Sculptures (*Chokoku*) and 2471 are Crafts (*Kogeihin*). Figure 2.2 shows the world's largest gilt bronze statue of Vairocana at Todai-ji Temple (Nara Prefecture) that is Sculpture listed as National Treasure. Todai-ji-Temple is also one of the components of a cultural WHS called Historic Monuments of Ancient Nara that was inscribed in 1998. Concerning tourism, Todai-ji Temple is a well-established visitor attraction amongst people of Japan and the statue of Vairocana is a cultural icon that represents not only Todai-ji Temple but also Nara City or Nara Prefecture as a whole.

Next, sustainability management of Japan's tangible cultural heritage (fine arts and crafts) is explored from a standpoint of TBL of sustainability, applying the concept of *mottainai* and referring to its practice. In relation to economic sustainability, basically financial costs that are required to repair the fine arts and crafts listed as National Treasures (*Kokuho*) or Important Cultural Properties (*Juyo Bunkazai*) are likely to

Fig. 2.2 World's largest gilt bronze statue of Vairocana at Todai-ji Temple. (Source: Author)

be smaller than those needed for the restoration of the structures and buildings listed as National Treasures or Important Cultural Properties. However, ACA can still support the repair of the fine arts and crafts financially by designating their restoration works as government subsidised projects based on Act on Protection of Cultural Properties (*Bunkazai Hogo-ho*) (ACA, 2018). Like WH status given by UNESCO can be seen as an important marker for authenticity by heritage tourists and work as an established brand in tourism and destination marketing (Jimura, 2011, 2016, 2019), the status as National Treasures or Important Cultural Properties may also attract Japanese (and possibly international) tourists who are interested in Japan's cultural heritage. This can lead to generation of or an increase in their income from tourism.

Some National Treasures (*Kokuho*) and Important Cultural Properties (*Juyo Bunkazai*) are always available for visitors to appreciate if they visit

2 Sustainability of Japan's Tangible Cultural Heritage 45

the sites owning these properties, often paying admission fees. On the other hand, other National Treasures and Important Cultural Properties are not usually open to visitors and can be available for the general public only through special exhibitions usually for a limited time with additional entrance fees. To cite a case, Kinpusen-ji Temple (Nara Prefecture) arranges a special exhibition of statues of three Buddhist saints listed as Important Cultural Properties, charging extra admission fees, between 27 March and 5 May 2021 (Kinpusen-ji Temple, n.d.). One of the purposes of this special exhibition is to raise money needed for an extensive restoration project of its Nio-mon gate listed as National Treasure (Inori no Kairo, n.d.). Special exhibitions whose main displays are National Treasures and/or Important Cultural Properties can also be held outside the premises of their owners, typically at museums or galleries, charging entrance fees, and they can attract a large number of visitors. For instance, Tokyo National Museum (hereafter TNM) hosted a special exhibition of 14 statues of Buddhist saints of Kofuku-ji Temple (Nara Prefecture) between 31 March and 7 June 2009 to commemorate the 1300th anniversary of the temple (TNM, n.d.). Of these statues, Asura statue is particularly famous and popular amongst Japanese people. Consequently, nearly one million visitors enjoyed this special exhibition (Tomura & Onzo, 2011).

As confirmed above, economic sustainability of Tangible Cultural Properties – fine arts and crafts (*Yukei Bunkazai – Bijutsukogeihin*) listed as National Treasures (*Kokuho*) or Important Cultural Properties (*Juyo Bunkazai*) can be maintained through grants/subsidies from public bodies, especially ACA, and serving as tourism resources. As also discussed earlier, some fine arts and crafts listed as National Treasures or Important Cultural Properties are not always accessible for people as visitor attractions. In other words, owners of such invaluable properties may 'reduce' opportunities for displaying with certain intentions. For example, some owners may have too many National Treasures and/or Important Cultural Properties to display all at the same time due to a lack of appropriate spaces and/or human resources. More importantly, the conditions (e.g. lighting and luminosity) ideal for exhibiting precious fine arts and crafts for visitors are often not sustainable for their conservation. Put differently, socio-cultural sustainability of this type of tangible cultural heritage may not be upheld if it is always accessible for visitors, prioritising its exploitation as visitor attractions.

Nevertheless, making important fine arts and crafts presented to as many people as possible is meaningful in terms of their socio-cultural sustainability as well as their economic sustainability. That is because; much more people could have opportunities to see and experience such fine arts and crafts if they are open to the general public and can be appreciated as visitor attractions. This could also enhance wider people's awareness of Japan's cultural heritage, which can lead to a higher level of socio-cultural sustainability of these properties. In tourism settings, owners of fine arts and crafts are on the host side of tourism, and should be able to develop and polish their knowledge on measures to achieve a good balance between heritage conservation and use of heritage as tourism resources from their daily experience. These owners may also exchange and share their knowledge and experience each other. Stated differently, the notion of *mottainai* is not appreciated and practiced in terms of economic and socio-cultural sustainability, if treasured fine arts and crafts are just conserved without generating any financial benefits or they are exploited excessively without considering their conservation.

4 Cultural Landscapes (*Bunkateki Keikan*)

The concept and practice of 'cultural landscapes' in heritage conservation is not unique to Japan but can be observed internationally (e.g. WHSs designated by UNESCO) and other countries (e.g. the Cultural Landscape Foundation in the USA) (Jimura, 2019). How cultural landscapes are defined is somewhat different by organisation or country. Nevertheless, there is a key point in common: Cultural landscapes testify the history of outstanding interactions between human beings and the natural environment, particularly humankind's involvement in and impacts of their life and activities on the natural environment surrounding them (Jimura, 2019). In Japan, *Bunkateki Keikan* is one of the categories of tangible cultural heritage suggested by ACA and corresponds to the notion of the aforesaid cultural landscapes. In fact, English translation of *Bunkateki Keikan* advocated by ACA is 'Cultural Landscapes'

(ACA, n.d.-g). According to Act on Protection of Cultural Properties (*Bunkazai Hogo-ho*), 'Cultural Landscapes are formed by the climate of a given region and people's lives or work there, and are indispensable for understanding the livelihood and work of the Japanese people' (ACA, n.d.-g). Considering this definition of cultural landscapes in the Japanese context (i.e. *Bunkateki Keikan*), the aforementioned key point in the notion of cultural landscapes can also be applied to *Bunkateki Keikan* (Cultural Landscapes).

As signified above, Act on Protection of Cultural Properties (*Bunkazai Hogo-ho*) is an essential act for comprehension and preservation of Cultural Landscapes (*Bunkateki Keikan*). In light of main traits of Cultural Landscapes, however, it is fair to say that Landscape Act (*Keikan-ho*) is the Japanese law that is the most important for and relevant to Cultural Landscapes. This act was promulgated in 2004 and the Ministry of Land, Infrastructure, Transport and Tourism holds jurisdiction over it. The law aims to promote formation of beautiful and united landscapes of cities, towns and villages in Japan. Other important laws to control changes in landscapes and conserve their beauty and unity include City Planning Act (*Toshi Keikaku-ho*), Act on Natural Parks (*Shizenkoen-ho*) and Act on Urban Green Space Conservation (*Toshi Ryokuchi-ho*).

Of diverse Cultural Landscapes (*Bunkateki Keikan*) existing across Japan, particularly significant ones are registered by ACA as Important Cultural Landscapes (*Juyo Bunkateki Keikan*) based on applications from local governments (prefectures, cities, towns or villages) (ACA, n.d.-g). This register system was introduced in 2004 as an amendment of Act on Protection of Cultural Properties (*Bunkazai Hogo-ho*). In principle, any alterations to the current state of Important Cultural Landscapes or actions that may affect their conservation require a prior notification to the Commissioner for ACA under Act on Protection of Cultural Properties (ACA, n.d.-g). In return, the Japanese Government can financially support a variety of projects for Important Cultural Landscapes, including research, conservation and awareness-raising activities (ACA n.d.-g). As of February 2021, there are 65 Important Cultural Landscapes throughout Japan from north (Hokkaido Prefecture) to south (Okinawa Prefecture), although 55 out of 65 are located in the west half of Japan. For example, Wetland in Omi-Hachiman is Important Cultural

Landscape situated in Shiga Prefecture and around 354 hectares in area. Its natural environment comprising of a satellite lake of Lake Biwa and common reed beds. These main features of the local natural environment are deeply associated with traditional activities of local residents residing around there such as common reed industries (cultivation and processing) and water transportation by canal that runs through the local area (see Fig. 2.3).

Most of Important Cultural Landscapes (*Juyo Bunkateki Keikan*), including the above-stated Wetland in Omi-Hachiman, involve diverse matters associated with TBL of sustainability. As shown above, ACA can financially assist research, conservation and learning activities for Important Cultural Landscapes. In addition, local governments may have subsidies mainly for repair and maintenance of Important Cultural Landscape(s) located in their administrative districts. For instance, Takashima City (Shiga Prefecture) has two Important Cultural

Fig. 2.3 Canal in Omi-Hachiman. (Source: Author)

2 Sustainability of Japan's Tangible Cultural Heritage

Landscapes, namely 'Waterfront of Kaizu, Nishihama, and Chinai' and 'Waterfront of Harie and Shimofuri'. The local government can monetarily support 50% (up to five million Japanese Yen) of repair costs for the appearance of elements of its Important Cultural Landscapes (Takashima City, 2017). Chizu Town in Tottori Prefecture has Important Cultural Landscape listed as Forestry landscape of Chizu. In the case of Chizu, the town can financially assist 70% (up to eight million Japanese Yen) of restoration costs for the appearance of elements of its Important Cultural Landscape (Chizu Town, 2019). Such monetary assistances from national and/local government are crucial for economic sustainability of Important Cultural Landscapes.

As the cases of Wetland in Omi-Hachiman and Forestry landscape of Chizu imply, a local industry developed in each Important Cultural Landscape, cultivation and processing of common reads and forestry respectively, is also a key for economic sustainability of Important Cultural Landscapes (Nanri et al., 2009). Key characteristics of Important Cultural Landscapes can also function as main visitor attractions of local areas and play an important role as tourism resources, attracting visitors and contributing to the areas' economic sustainability. In the case of the aforementioned Wetland Omi-Hachiman, such attraction factors include canals, canal tours with traditional boats, and beautiful canal-side and wetland sceneries. In the east half of Japan, cultural landscapes of the Tsuchibuchi Yamaguchi hamlet in Tono City (Iwate Prefecture) that is part of Important Cultural Landscape called 'Tono Arakawakogen Farm, Tsuchibuchi Yamaguchi Community' is the setting of the book titled The Legends of Tono. This book was written by Kunio Yanagita, the pioneer of Japanese folklore studies, and published in Japanese in 1910. Since that time, The Legends of Tono has still been read widely by Japanese people and has also been translated to different languages. For these reasons, it could be stated that main features of Important Cultural Landscape of Tono City have been contributing to city's development as a destination of cultural, heritage and/or literary tourism.

Needless to say, tangible cultural heritage registered as Important Cultural Landscapes (*Juyo Bunkateki Keikan*) should be explored in terms of their socio-cultural and environmental sustainability as well. First, it is obvious that cultural landscapes registered as Important Cultural

Landscapes are expected to maintain their environmental sustainability, because the natural environment that has been interacting with local communities nearby is a vital element of all Important Cultural Landscapes without exceptions. It can also be confirmed at many areas with Important Cultural Landscape(s) that socio-cultural sustainability of Important Cultural Landscapes and their relationships with local communities and wider audience have been maintained or even enhanced through varied activities planned and conducted on site. Such activities include volunteering for repair work, work experience programmes with local farmers and fishermen, nature observations, and experiencing rural life (ACA, 2019).

5   Preservation Districts for Groups of Traditional Buildings (*Dentoteki Kenzobutsugun Hozonchiku*)

Like 'cultural landscapes', the concept and practice of 'groups of buildings' in heritage conservation can be found not only in Japan but also at international stage. To cite a case, 'groups of buildings' are one of the types of cultural WHSs (Jimura, 2019). In the context of WHSs, groups of buildings mean 'groups of separate or connected buildings which, because of their architecture, their homogeneity or their place in the landscape, are of outstanding universal value from the point of view of history, art or science' (Jimura, 2019, 137). In Japan, groups of buildings are protected mainly through register systems called Preservation Districts for Groups of Traditional Buildings (*Dentoteki Kenzobutsugun Hozonchiku*) and its higher and upgraded version named Important Preservation Districts for Groups of Traditional Buildings (*Juyo Dentoteki Kenzobutsugun Hozonchiku*).

Overall pictures of and relations between Preservation Districts for Groups of Traditional Buildings (*Dentoteki Kenzobutsugun Hozonchiku*) and Important Preservation Districts for Groups of Traditional Buildings (*Juyo Dentoteki Kenzobutsugun Hozonchiku*) are similar to the outlines of and relationships between Cultural Landscapes (*Bunkateki Keikan*) and

Important Cultural Landscapes (*Juyo Bunkateki Keikan*). Preservation Districts for Groups of Traditional Buildings and Important Preservation Districts for Groups of Traditional Buildings were introduced in 1975 as a revision of Act on Protection of Cultural Properties (*Bunkazai Hogo-ho*), intending to improve the level of conservation of diverse kinds of historic quarters across Japan. City Planning Act (*Toshi Keikaku-ho*) is also an important law associated with these conservation systems. Local governments (cities, towns and villages) can designate traditional districts in their administrative areas as Preservation Districts for Groups of Traditional Buildings and develop conservation plans based on municipal ordinances in order to carry out conservation activities accordingly (ACA, n.d.-h).

Of a number of Preservation Districts for Groups of Traditional Buildings (*Dentoteki Kenzobutsugun Hozonchiku*), especially valuable ones for Japan are registered by ACA as Important Preservation Districts for Groups of Traditional Buildings (*Juyo Dentoteki Kenzobutsugun Hozonchiku*) based on applications from municipalities (ACA, n.d.-h). ACA and prefectural Boards of Education provide cities, towns and villages with guidance and advice to preserve and utilise Important Preservation Districts for Groups of Traditional Buildings (ACA, n.d.-h). These public organisations also financially aid restoration, landscaping, and installation of disaster prevention facilities and tourist signs (ACA, n.d.-h).

As of March 2021, 123 districts situated in 101 municipalities in 43 prefectures are designated as Important Preservation Districts for Groups of Traditional Buildings (*Juyo Dentoteki Kenzobutsugun Hozonchiku*) and the listed quarters are approximately 3788 hectares in area (ACA, n.d.-i). There are diverse sorts of Important Preservation Districts for Groups of Traditional Buildings, including:

* Agricultural hamlets (*noson-shuraku*)
* Agricultural hamlets in islands (*shima no noson-shuraku*)
* Brewery quarters (*jozo-machi*)
* Castle quarters (*jyoka-machi*)
* Merchant quarters (*shoka-machi*)
* Mountainous hamlets (*sanson-shuraku*)

- Port quarters (*minato-machi*)
- Post quarters (*shukuba-machi*)
- Quarters surrounding shrines or temples (*monzen-machi*)
- Restaurant quarters (*chaya-machi*)
- Samurai quarters (*buke-machi*)
- Shrine-family quarters (*shake-machi*)
- Temple-centred quarters (*jinai-machi*)
- Temple-cluster quarters (*tera-machi*)
- Traditional country quarters (*zaigo-machi*)

For instance, Taketomi Island, Taketomi Town (Okinawa Prefecture) is Important Preservation District for Groups of Traditional Buildings inscribed as agricultural hamlets in islands (*shima no noson-shuraku*) (see Fig. 2.4). This district comprises three hamlets that are located in the centre of Taketomi Island (Taketomi Town, 2020). It has traditional agricultural village scenery consisting of historic single-story Okinawan-style houses surrounded by stone walls brightened with flowering plants (Jimura, 2022). Such Okinawan-style houses should also be recognised as tangible cultural properties that reflect heritage of indigenous people of Okinawa Prefecture, Uchinanchu people (Jimura, 2022).

Fig. 2.4 Taketomi Island, Taketomi Town (Okinawa Prefecture). (Source: Author)

2 Sustainability of Japan's Tangible Cultural Heritage 53

Like other categories of tangible cultural heritage suggested by ACA, economic sustainability of Important Preservation Districts for Groups of Traditional Buildings (*Juyo Dentoteki Kenzobutsugun Hozonchiku*) can be supported by subsidies from national and local governments. Currently, many Important Preservation Districts for Groups of Traditional Buildings are established tourist destinations (e.g. Ouchi-juku in Fukushima Prefecture and Kawagoe in Saitama Prefecture). This signifies that tourism can makes an important contribution to economic sustainability of preservation districts through tourist spending. It should also be noted that cultural significance of the districts can be also appreciated by people external to the districts typically tourists. A good level of public awareness of these districts can also invite a high level of their socio-cultural sustainability in the society of Japan. To keep conserving whilst utilising historic buildings in the districts is also effective to secure environmental sustainability as these practices can decrease the amount of building materials, particularly timber, required to construct new buildings and the volume of waste materials, especially scrap wood.

In Important Preservation Districts for Groups of Traditional Buildings (*Juyo Dentoteki Kenzobutsugun Hozonchiku*), presence of community groups for conservation is commonly confirmed. In many cases, such community groups were created before the listing as Important Preservation Districts for Groups of Traditional Buildings. For instance, Ogimachi district in Shirakawa Village (Gifu Prefecture) was registered as Important Preservation District for Groups of Traditional Buildings in 1976. Prior to this, a community group named the Society for Conservation of Natural Environment of Ogimachi, Shirakawa-go was established in 1971 (Jimura, 2007, 2011) and the group is still actively working on a range of conservation activities at local level. This suggests that the meaning of socio-cultural and environmental sustainability of traditional district has been appreciated by local communities for a long time, reaching milestones successfully such as the designation as Important Preservation Districts for Groups of Traditional Buildings in 1976 and inscription as part of cultural WHS called Historic Villages of Shirakawa-go and Gokayama in 1995.

TBL of sustainability in the context of Important Preservation Districts for Groups of Traditional Buildings (*Juyo Dentoteki Kenzobutsugun*

Hozonchiku) can be discussed, also referring to the concept and practice of *mottainai*. Sanmachi, Takayama City (Gifu Prefecture) is a merchant quarter and its traditional buildings have 100–150 years history. These houses have very solid structures and were built with domestic timber of excellent quality (Takayama City, 2015). Nowadays, it would be impossible to newly build such buildings due to limited availability of traditional building materials and huge financial costs. Thus, Takayama City and local residents feel that these houses should not be scrapped and replaced with new ones built from scratch, following the spirit of *mottainai* (Takayama City, 2015). As can be confirmed from the discussions above, the scheme of Important Preservation Districts for Groups of Traditional Buildings has many advantages for owners of traditional buildings and local people (Yeay, 2018). Nevertheless, it should be remembered that many Important Preservation Districts for Groups of Traditional Buildings have been facing various challenges, including a shortage of next generations who take over their historic houses, an increase in the number of unoccupied houses and residents who move to other places, and a decrease in the number of local households and local population (Yeay, 2018). These issues are challenges for the vast majority of remote and/or rural areas of Japan, and many Important Preservation Districts for Groups of Traditional Buildings are situated in such regions.

6 Buried Cultural Properties (*Maizo Bunkazai*)

According to ACA (n.d.-j), Buried Cultural Properties (*Maizo Bunkazai*) are 'cultural properties that lie underground (known as archaeological sites)'. Precisely speaking, however, it would be more appropriate to understand Buried Cultural Properties as a sub-category of archaeological sites as archaeological sites often include a wider types of cultural properties in the international context. In Japan, there are around 460,000 sites where any cultural properties would exist underground and approximately 9000 archaeological excavation works are conducted in Japan annually for investigation purposes (ACA, n.d.-j).

2 Sustainability of Japan's Tangible Cultural Heritage

Following Act on Protection of Cultural Properties (*Bunkazai Hogo-ho*), a notification must be submitted to the education boards of prefectures/designated cities before a construction work is conducted at any sites where cultural properties would exist underground and when such properties are found (ACA, n.d.-j). An individual or organisation who uncovers cultural properties need to submit them to the chief of the governing police office except the case that their owners are known (ACA, n.d.-j). The education board is responsible to decide how they deal with reported properties. In principle, it is expected that sites will be preserved as they have been, although it is not always possible. In such a case, developers are asked to conduct excavation works and investigation of properties, covering costs required for these works (ACA, n.d.-j). However, if excavation works are conducted for non-profit purposes (e.g. construction of private houses), costs for investigations can be financially supported by subsidies from the national government (ACA, n.d.-j). Such monetary backings can improve the level of economic sustainability of cultural properties lying underground. Otherwise, developers may not report the discovery of cultural properties to the education board even if they find such properties underground.

In fact, construction or development works at spots where cultural properties may lie underground are often disturbed or delayed because of the finding of cultural properties. This is common at sites located in municipalities with a long history. To cite a case, Kyoto City is an ancient capital of Japan between the beginning of the Heian period and the beginning of the Meiji period (794–1869). Many important cultural properties made during the Heian period and even much older the Yayoi period (the tenth to the sixth centuries BC) were discovered during the construction works of Karasuma Subway Line and Tozai Subway Line (Ito, 1995; Araki, 2011). The finding of these properties delayed the completion of the construction works, especially those for Tozai Subway Line, and made the extension of these subway lines challenging. This factor may hinder the development of Kyoto City as an urban space and the convenience for local inhabitants, commuters to the city and tourists. Simultaneously, however, it is also true that such careful policies and practices have been playing a key role in the discovery and conservation of cultural properties laying underground. In this sense, these cautious approaches have been making a good contribution to socio-cultural and environmental sustainability of underground cultural properties and their surrounding environments.

After discovered cultural properties are handed in to the governing police office, the education board carefully examines whether the properties have a value as Buried Cultural Properties (*Maizo Bunkazai*) (ACA, n.d.-j). Amongst cultural properties appreciated as Buried Cultural Properties, the properties whose owners cannot be identified belong to prefectures (ACA, n.d.-j). Buried Cultural Properties are cultural heritage that needs to be conserved for future generations and be accessible for as many people as possible (ACA, n.d.-j). To this end, TBL of sustainability is imperative and should be respected. Items valued as Buried Cultural Properties are usually exhibited at private or public museums. In the case of the former, museums may charge visitors for some admission fee and this income can improve economic sustainability of Buried Cultural Properties and the museums as a whole (e.g. Kobe City Museum). In the case of the latter, whilst, Buried Cultural Properties are typically housed by local folk museums and available for visitors often without charging entrance fees (e.g. Chofu City Folk Museum in TMP and Chiba City Folk Museum). Recognition as Japan's cultural heritage (Buried Cultural Properties) and serving as exhibitions at museums are useful to maintain or enhance their socio-cultural sustainability. Moreover, some excavation sites could allow the general public to observe their excavation works, ensuring the safety of workers and visitors and conservation of their surrounding natural environments (e.g. the ruins of Inohana-jo Castle in Chiba Prefecture). All of these works are essential to conserve and utilise cultural properties lying underground in a sustainable manner. Indeed, a series of the above-mentioned works and procedures can be time-consuming and require financial resources. Nevertheless, the concept of *mottainai* cannot be reflected in its practice, if underground cultural properties are never discovered, and conserved and displayed for current and future generations.

Last but not least, it is worth noting that the Japanese Government also acknowledges the magnitude of conservation of underwater ruins. Although conservation frameworks for this type of cultural properties have not been matured enough compared to those for Buried Cultural

Properties (*Maizo Bunkazai*), some advancements can still be confirmed. For instance, ACA developed guidelines for conservation of underwater ruins in 2017 (ACA, 2017) to promote the movements and activities for the conservation of this kind of properties.

7 Folk Cultural Properties (*Minzoku Bunkazai*)

As shown in Sect. 6, Buried Cultural Properties (*Maizo Bunkazai*) are often exhibited at museums, particularly at local folk museums. Needless to say, such local folk museums are places where tangible Folk Cultural Properties (*Minzoku Bunkazai*) are housed, conserved and displayed. The concept of Folk Cultural Properties adopted by ACA contains cultural properties that have emerged from ordinary people's everyday life and consist of tangible and intangible properties (ACA, n.d.-k). Following the scope of this chapter, however, this section sheds light on Tangible Folk Cultural Properties (*Yukei Minzoku Bunkazai*). Each municipality of Japan can register their Tangible Folk Cultural Properties, and ACA inscribes particularly important ones as Important Tangible Folk Cultural Properties (*Juyo Yukei Minzoku Bunkazai*). Conservation or restoration of these properties can be financially supported by ACA (ACA, n.d.-k); therefore, this policy is helpful to retain economic sustainability of Tangible Folk Cultural Properties designated by a municipality or ACA. According to ACA (n.d.-k), Important Tangible Folk Cultural Properties are associated with any of following ten dimensions of human life. The number in brackets indicates the number of Tangible Folk Cultural Properties belonging to each category as of March 2021 (ACA, n.d.-l):

* Food, clothing and shelter (29)
* Production and livelihood (97)
* Traffic, transport and communication (19)
* Trade (1)
* Social life (1)

- Faith (40)
- Folklore knowledge (7)
- Folk performing arts, entertainment and game (23)
- Life event (3)
- Annual event (3)

In the category of 'production and livelihood', for instance, traditional finishing tools used in certain geographical areas are designated as Important Tangible Folk Cultural Properties. These areas include, for example, Rumoi (Hokkaido Prefecture) and Boso Peninsula (Chiba Prefecture).

As stated above, Tangible Folk Cultural Properties (*Yukei Minzoku Bunkazai*) can be appreciated by wide audience mainly by being exhibited at local folk museums, and this policy and practice can contribute to the enhancement of socio-cultural sustainability of Tangible Folk Cultural Properties. The wide audience in this context encompass local residents as well as tourists. In relation to local people, Tangible Folk Cultural Properties play a key role in education in Japan's elementary and junior high schools. Social Studies is one of main subjects at Japan's elementary and junior high schools, and Regional Studies is an essential component of Social Studies. Students are expected to familiarise themselves with history, traditions, geographies and main characteristics of their community through Regional Studies, and it is sure that Tangible Folk Cultural Properties in their community are appropriate and effective educational materials (Kikuchi, 1981; Tamura, 2017). As such educational activities could raise local children's awareness and understanding of their local Tangible Folk Cultural Properties, socio-cultural sustainability of local Tangible Folk Cultural Properties could also be strengthened. Put differently, making the most of local Tangible Folk Cultural Properties for educational purposes can be comprehended as an 'ethical' 'reuse' of Tangible Folklore Cultural Properties. To practice the idea of *mottainai*, children should be given plenty of opportunities to study the past, customs, geographies and key features of their hometown and local Tangible Folk Cultural Properties should be utilised fully for such learning opportunities.

8 Monuments (*Kinenbutsu*)

Monuments (*Kinenbutsu*) are the final type of tangible cultural assets discussed in this chapter and their value as heritage are acknowledged by the Japanese Government under Act on Protection of Cultural Properties (*Bunkazai Hogo-ho*). According to the definition of ACA (n.d.-c), the notion of Monuments contains a wide variety sorts of natural properties as well as tangible cultural properties, and can be divided into following three groups:

* Historic Sites (*Shiseki*) – Shell mounds, ancient mounded tombs, ruins of castle quarters, castles or forts, former private residences, and other sites of a high historic or scientific value to Japan
* Places of Scenic Beauty (*Meisho*) – Gardens, bridges, gorges, seashores, mountains, and other places of scenic beauty of a high artistic or aesthetic value to Japan
* Natural Monuments (*Tennen Kinenbutsu*) – Animals, plants, minerals, and geological features of a high scientific value to Japan.

Of these three groups, properties in the Historic Sites category and some properties in the Places of Scenic Beauty category (i.e. gardens and bridges) can be seen as tangible cultural heritage that is the scope of this chapter.

Either the Japanese Government or municipalities can designate Monuments. Similar to many other kinds of tangible cultural heritage examined in this chapter, the Japanese Government gives an exceptional status of Special Historic Sites (*Tokubetsu Shiseki*), Special Places of Scenic Beauty (*Tokubetsu Meisho*), and Special Natural Monuments (*Tokubetsu Tennen Kinenbutsu*) to those are of especially high value for Japan (ACA, n.d.-c). To cite a case, the precinct of Chuson-ji Temple (Iwate Prefecture) is designated as Special Historic Site in 1979. Chuson-ji Temple also has valuable Tangible Cultural Properties (*Yukei Bunkazai*), including buildings and sculptures, listed as National Treasures (*Kokuho*) or Important Cultural Properties (*Juyo Bunkazai*). This means that the temple's tangible cultural heritage is conserved through a combination of multiple conservation frameworks. Here, it should also be noted that conservation practice based on country's own conservation scheme(s) is a requisite to be listed as a WHS by UNESCO. In fact, Chuson-ji Temple is a component of a cultural WHS, Hiraizumi – Temples, Gardens and Archaeological Sites Representing the Buddhist Pure Land, which was inscribed in 2011. On the other hand, Japanese gardens are representative examples of Special Places of Scenic Beauty. Many of them are temple gardens (e.g. Motsu-ji Temple in Iwate Prefecture), whilst others are not. For instance, Rikugi-en (TMP), Kenroku-en (Ishikawa Prefecture) and Ritsurin Koen (Kagawa Prefecture) are generally understood as *daimyo teien* that were originally created by the feudal lords during the Edo period (1603–1868).

Moreover, some types of tangible cultural heritage examined by Jimura (2022) are also conserved through the Monuments (*Kinenbutsu*) system. As for Japan's industrial heritage, Nirayama Reverberatory Furnaces (Shizuoka Prefecture) was inscribed as Historic Sites (*Shiseki*) in 1922 (see Fig. 2.5). The structures were also designated as Heritage of Industrial Modernisation (*Kindaika Sangyo Isan*) by the Ministry of Economy, Trade and Industry in 2007. As confirmed in the case of Chuson-ji Temple above, conservation through domestic frameworks could lead to the designation of a cultural WHS named Sites of Japan's Meiji Industrial Revolution: Iron and Steel, Shipbuilding and Coal Mining in 2009, and Nirayama Reverberatory Furnaces is a property included in this WHS. On the other hand, Genbaku Dome (Hiroshima Prefecture) is one of the most recognised and iconic war heritage of Japan. The building called Genbaku Dome today is the ruin of the Hiroshima Prefectural Industrial Promotion Hall. The hall was severely damaged by the atomic bombing of Hiroshima on 6 August 1945. Genbaku Dome was designated as Historic Site in 1995 and then a cultural WHS in 1996. Different from the case of Nirayama Reverberatory Furnaces, Genbaku Dome was listed as a WHS soon after its inscription as Historic Site. This facts may imply that Genbaku Dome was not conserved by a domestic conservation system when the Japanese Government started working on the listing of Genbaku Dome as a WHS.

Like other kinds of tangible cultural heritage recognised by ACA, in principle Monuments (*Kinenbutsu*) are expected to be conserved now and for the future as they have been. The national government can

Fig. 2.5 Nirayama Reverberatory Furnaces. (Source: Author)

financially aid municipalities to enable them to conserve and utilise their Monuments, typically their Historic Sites (*Shiseki*), in a suitable and active manner. Like the cases of other sorts of tangible cultural heritage, such assistance can back the enhancement of economic sustainability of Monuments. Certain types of Historic Sites (*Shiseki*) (ruins of castle quarters, castles or forts, and former private residences) or Places of Scenic Beauty (*Meisho*) (Japanese gardens) have been serving as popular tourism resources and attracting a number of people as visitor attractions. Of these, former private residences and Japanese gardens usually charge visitors for entrance fees. The income raised as admission fees could also make these Monuments economically sustainable. It is also true that such active presence of Monuments in a local community and wider society can ensure their socio-cultural sustainability. From the perspective of *mottainai*, Monuments should also be not only conserved well but also utilised fully, strengthening their socio-cultural sustainability.

9 Conclusion

A wide variety of tangible cultural properties is valued as tangible cultural heritage and conserved through international and domestic systems. Regarding the international schemes, for instance, UNESCO's WHS listing scheme is a representative one, and WH Convention functions as a core of the scheme. In relation to the domestic schemes, overall Japan's conservation systems for tangible cultural heritage are led and managed by the Japanese Government, more precisely speaking ACA. Act on Protection of Cultural Properties (*Bunkazai Hogo-ho*) legally governs the conservation and utilisation of diverse important cultural properties that can be valued as cultural heritage of Japan. Concerning the categories of cultural properties, this chapter follows those used by ACA and examines seven different kinds of tangible cultural properties, using real examples from various regions of Japan and linking them back to the concept and practice of sustainability and *mottainai*.

It is confirmed that TBL (economic, socio-cultural and environmental) of sustainability of tangible cultural heritage is a vital issue in the conservation and utilisation of diverse types of tangible cultural properties explored in this chapter. Of the three areas of sustainability, socio-cultural sustainability would be particularly paramount for tangible cultural heritage. That is because; such tangible cultural heritage mirrors traditional society and culture of Japan, especially those of peculiar regions, in a visible and touchable manner. In other words, these elements reflect uniqueness of the society and culture of Japan and specific regions that are closely associated with people's identity as a Japanese person and an inhabitants of specific geographical areas. Therefore, tangible cultural heritage can and are expected to play a central role in educational and leisure activities not only for local people, including children,

2 Sustainability of Japan's Tangible Cultural Heritage

but also for visitors. Here, connections with visitors signify relationships between tangible cultural heritage and tourism.

As discussed earlier in this chapter, tangible cultural heritage such as Important Tangible Cultural Properties (*Juyo Yukei Bunkazai*) and Important Preservation Districts for Groups of Traditional Buildings (*Juyo Dentoteki Kenzobutsugun Hozonchiku*) is acknowledged well as tourism resources by both host and guest sides of tourism. In fact, there are countless examples showing popularity of tangible cultural heritage as visitor attractions. For instance, Senso-ji Temple (TMP) has National Treasures (*Kokuho*) and Important Cultural Properties (*Juyo Bunkazai*), and its garden is designated as Places of Scenic Beauty (*Meisho*). The temple attracts more than 10 million visitors annually before the COVID-19 pandemic. Although the temple does not charge visitors for entrance fees, it charges those who want to obtain *goshuin* for 500 Japanese Yen as of writing. *Goshuin* are stamps people who visit Shinto shrines/Japanese Buddhist temples can get and regarded as evidences of their visits (Jimura, 2022). In addition to subsidies from the national or local government for the conservation and utilisation of tangible cultural heritage, the income raised from tourism can also enhance economic sustainability of Japan's tangible cultural heritage.

To maintain or enhance TBL of sustainability of Japan's tangible cultural heritage, it is also essential that the concept of *mottainai* is respected and practiced in everyday management of tangible cultural heritage. This indicates that the heritage should be not only conserved but also utilised in a sustainable way. To this end, tangible cultural heritage should establish and uphold its position in local communities and wider Japanese society, and develop and keep good relationships with a variety of its stakeholders. As confirmed in this chapter, these stakeholders include the national and relevant local governments, owners of properties, local communities and visitors. All of them are expected to observe ethics of heritage conservation and utilisation and take their responsibility for their actions for sustainability management in the tangible cultural heritage sector. This would be particularly important for tangible cultural heritage as it physically deteriorates over time and can be materially damaged by accidents, natural disasters or irresponsible behaviours of people.

References

ACA. (2017). *Suichu-isan-hogo no arikata ni tsuite* (Guidelines for conservation of underwater ruins) [in Japanese]. Available at: https://www.bunka.go.jp/seisaku/bunkazai/shokai/pdf/r1392246_01.pdf. Accessed 10 Mar 2021.

ACA. (2018). *Kokuho Juyo Bunkazai Bijutsukogeihin no shuri* (Repair of national treasures, important cultural properties and fine arts and crafts) [in Japanese]. Available at: https://www.bunka.go.jp/tokei_hakusho_shuppan/shuppanbutsu/bunkazai_pamphlet/pdf/92723301_01.pdf. Accessed 24 Feb 2021.

ACA. (2019). *Bunkateki Keikan no hogo no shikumi* (Mechanisms for conservation of cultural landscapes) [in Japanese]. Available at: https://www.bunka.go.jp/tokei_hakusho_shuppan/shuppanbutsu/bunkazai_pamphlet/pdf/r1393016_02.pdf. Accessed 27 Feb 2021.

ACA. (2020). *Toroku Yukei Bunkazai Kenzobutsu seido no goannai* (Introduction to the registered tangible cultural properties system) [in Japanese]. Available at: https://www.bunka.go.jp/tokei_hakusho_shuppan/shuppanbutsu/bunkazai_pamphlet/pdf/pamphlet_ja_06_ver02.pdf. Accessed 19 Feb 2021.

ACA. (n.d.-a). *Introduction to cultural properties*. Available at: https://www.bunka.go.jp/english/policy/cultural_properties/introduction/. Accessed 17 Feb 2021.

ACA. (n.d.-b). *Folk cultural properties*. Available at: https://www.bunka.go.jp/english/policy/cultural_properties/introduction/folk/. Accessed 17 Feb 2021.

ACA. (n.d.-c). *Monuments*. Available at: https://www.bunka.go.jp/english/policy/cultural_properties/introduction/monuments/. Accessed 17 Feb 2021.

ACA. (n.d.-d). *Tangible cultural properties (structures)*. Available at: https://www.bunka.go.jp/english/policy/cultural_properties/introduction/buildings/. Accessed 19 Feb 2021.

ACA. (n.d.-e). *Bunkazai-shitei-to no kensu* (Number of Designated Cultural Properties) [in Japanese]. Available at: https://www.bunka.go.jp/seisaku/bunkazai/shokai/shitei.html. Accessed 19 Feb 2021.

ACA. (n.d.-f). *Tangible cultural properties (fine arts and crafts)*. Available at: https://www.bunka.go.jp/english/policy/cultural_properties/introduction/crafts/. Accessed 22 Feb 2021.

ACA. (n.d.-g). *Cultural landscapes*. Available at: https://www.bunka.go.jp/english/policy/cultural_properties/introduction/landscape/. Accessed 26 Feb 2021.

2 Sustainability of Japan's Tangible Cultural Heritage

ACA. (n.d.-h). *Preservation districts for groups of traditional buildings*. Available at: https://www.bunka.go.jp/english/policy/cultural_properties/introduction/historic_buildings/. Accessed 2 Mar 2021.

ACA. (n.d.-i). *Juyo Dentoteki Kenzobutsugun Hozonchiku ichiran* (List of important preservation districts for groups of traditional buildings) [in Japanese]. Available at: https://www.bunka.go.jp/seisaku/bunkazai/shokai/hozonchiku/judenken_ichiran.html. Accessed 2 Mar 2021.

ACA. (n.d.-j). *Buried cultural properties*. Available at: https://www.bunka.go.jp/english/policy/cultural_properties/introduction/buried_properties/. Accessed 10 Mar 2021.

ACA. (n.d.-k). *Folk cultural properties*. Available at: https://www.bunka.go.jp/english/policy/cultural_properties/introduction/folk/. Accessed 15 Mar 2021.

ACA. (n.d.-l). *Juyo Yukei Minzoku Bunkazai* (Important tangible folk cultural properties) [in Japanese]. Available at: https://kunishitei.bunka.go.jp/bsys/categorylist?register_id=301. Accessed 15 Mar 2021.

Adams, C. (1998). Japan's Ise Shrine and its thirteen-hundred-year-old reconstruction tradition. *Journal of Architectural Education, 52*(1), 49–60.

Araki, T. (2011). Shinsen-en to goryoe: kin'en no henshitsu to sono keiki (Shinsen-en Temple and goryoe: The transition of kin'en and its trigger) [in Japanese]. *Senshu-daigaku Jinbunkagaku-kenkyusho geppo, 25*, 1–10.

Chizu Town. (2019). *Chizu-cho Juyo Bunkateki Keikan seibijigyo hojokin kofu yoko* (Guideline on applications for subsidies for Juyo Bunkateki Keikan in Chizu Town) [in Japanese]. Available at: https://public.joureikun.jp/chizu_town/reiki/act/frame/frame110001517.htm. Accessed 27 Feb 2021.

Inori no Kairo. (n.d.). *Kinpusen-ji* (Kinpusen-ji Temple) [in Japanese]. Available at: http://inori.nara-kankou.or.jp/inori/hihou/kimpusenji/event/arfeyxb1hr/. Accessed 24 Feb 2021.

Ito, A. (1995). Kyoto-bonchi no Yayoijidai-iseki (Buried cultural properties created in the Yayoi period in the Kyoto Basin) [in Japanese]. *Annual Report of the Center for Archaeological Operations*, 137–183.

Jimura, T. (2007). *The impact of World Heritage site designation on local communities – A comparative study of Ogimachi (Japan) and Saltaire (UK)*. Doctoral Thesis, Nottingham Trent University.

Jimura, T. (2011). The impact of world heritage site designation on local communities – A case study of Ogimachi, Shirakawa-mura, Japan. *Tourism Management, 32*(2), 288–296.

Jimura, T. (2016). World heritage site management: A case study of sacred sites and pilgrimage routes in the Kii mountain range, Japan. *Journal of Heritage Tourism, 11*(4), 382–394.

Jimura, T. (2019). *World Heritage sites: Tourism, local communities and conservation activities.* CABI.

Jimura, T. (2022). *Cultural and heritage tourism in Japan.* Routledge.

Kikuchi, I. (1981). On folklore cultural properties for a teaching material in the social study – Taking farm houses with the Yamato Ridge of a roof as an example [in Japanese]. *Kobunkazai Kyoiku Kenkyu Hokoku, 10*, 23–32.

Kinpusen-ji Temple. (n.d.). *Hibutsu honzon tokubetsu gokaicho* (Special exhibition of sculptures of Buddhist saints) [in Japanese]. Available at: https://www.kinpusen.or.jp/niomon/index.html. Accessed 24 Feb 2021.

Koyo Seiga. (n.d.). *Sekai-isan Himeji-jo no yane to mukiau* (Repair of roofs of Himeji Castle, a cultural World Heritage site) [in Japanese]. Available at: https://koyoseiga.co.jp/case/himeji/. Accessed 21 Feb 2021.

Leask, A. (2006). World Heritage site designation. In A. Leask & A. Fyall (Eds.), *Managing World Heritage sites* (pp. 5–19). Butterworth-Heinemann.

Nakada, T. (2019). *Suichu-bunkaisan hogo-jyoyaku to maizo-bunkazai hogo-gyosei* (Convention on the protection of the underwater cultural heritage and buried cultural property protection administration in Japan) [in Japanese]. Available at: https://www.spf.org/opri/newsletter/453_3.html?latest=1. Accessed 16 Jan 2021.

Nanri, M., Yokohari, M., & Ochiai, M. (2009). Transformation processes and conservation strategies of reed beds in the "Suigo" landscape in Omihachiman, Japan [in Japanese]. *Journal of the Japanese Institute of Landscape Architecture, 72*(5), 731–734.

Takashima City. (2017). *Takashima-shi Juyo Bunkateki Keikan seibijigyo hojokin kofu yoko* (Guideline on applications for subsidies for Juyo Bunkateki Keikan in Takashima City) [in Japanese]. Available at: http://www.city.takashima.lg.jp/reiki/reiki_honbun/r152RG00002052.html. Accessed 27 Feb 2021.

Takayama City. (2015). *Sanmachi* [in Japanese]. Available at: https://www.city.takayama.lg.jp/kurashi/1000021/1000119/1000847/1001005/1001006.html. Accessed 5 Mar 2021.

Taketomi Town. (2020). *Teketomi-jima, Taketomi-cho (Okinawa-ken)* (Taketomi Island, Taketomi Town (Okinawa Prefecture)) [in Japanese]. Available at: https://www.bunka.go.jp/seisaku/bunkazai/shokai/hozonchiku/pdf/r1392257_117.pdf. Accessed 2 Mar 2021.

Tamura, H. (2017). Shogakko shakaika ni okeru chiikisozai no kyozaika ni tsuite (Using regional materials as learning materials for Social Studies in elementary schools) [in Japanese]. *Saitama-daigaku Kyoiku-gakubu kiyo, 66*(2), 549–557.

TNM. (n.d.). *The national treasure ASHURA and masterpieces from Kohfukuji.* Available at: https://www.tnm.jp/modules/r_free_page/index.php?id=652. Accessed 24 Feb 2021.

Tomura, T., & Onzo, N. (2011). Kokuho Asura-ten ni miru marketing no shinchoryu (A new marketing trend confirmed in the special exhibition of asura) [in Japanese]. *Japan Marketing Journal, 30*(3), 107–119.

UNESCO. (n.d.). *What is meant by "cultural heritage"?* Available at: http://www.unesco.org/new/en/culture/themes/illicit-trafficking-of-cultural-property/unesco-database-of-national-cultural-heritage-laws/frequently-asked-questions/definition-of-the-cultural-heritage/. Accessed 17 Feb 2021.

Yeay. (2018). *Shitteokitai Dentoteki Kenzobutsugun Hozonchiku no kenchiku rule* (Construction regulations for Preservation Districts for Groups of Historic Buildings you should know) [in Japanese]. Available at: https://sell.yeay.jp/reading/knowledge/10113/#:~:text=%E4%BC%9D%E7%B5%B1%E7%9A%84%E5%BB%BA%E9%80%A0%E7%89%A9%E7%BE%A4%E4%BF%9D%E5%AD%98%E5%9C%B0%E5%8C%BA%E3%81%AE%E5%95%8F%E9%A1%8C,%E3%81%AB%E7%9B%B4%E9%9D%A2%E3%81%97%E3%81%A6%E3%81%84%E3%81%BE%E3%81%99%E3%80%82. Accessed 5 Mar 2021.

3

Sustainability of Japan's Intangible Cultural Heritage

1 Introduction

Similar to the case of tangible cultural heritage explored in Chap. 2, intangible cultural heritage across the globe has been preserved through international initiatives and domestic schemes unique to each nation. At international stage, for instance, Intangible Cultural Heritage (hereafter ICH) is a universal conservation scheme adopted by the United Nations Educational, Scientific and Cultural Organization (hereafter UNESCO), and can be regarded as UNESCO's three major initiatives for conservation of cultural heritage in the world together with World Heritage (hereafter WH) and Memory of the World (Jimura, 2019). According to UNESCO (n.d.-a), representative types of ICH are:

- Oral traditions
- Performing arts
- Social practices
- Rituals
- Festive events
- Knowledge and practices concerning nature and the universe
- Knowledge and skills to produce traditional crafts

ICH Convention adopted in 2003 serves as a foundation of the conservation practice through UNESCO's ICH scheme.

As of March 2021, Japan has 22 elements that are on its list of ICH (UNESCO, n.d.-b). Kabuki theatre, Ningyo Johruri Bunraku puppet theatre, and Nohgaku theatre are the first three elements of Japan that were added on the lists in 2008, whilst the most recent addition is Traditional Skills, Techniques and Knowledge for the Conservation and Transmission of Wooden Architecture in Japan, which was designated in 2020 (UNESCO, n.d.-b). All of the three elements listed in 2008 are recognised as 'performing arts', and Ningyo Johruri Bunraku Puppet Theatre and Nogaku Theatre are also acknowledged as 'oral traditions and expressions' and 'traditional craftsmanship'. On the other hand, Traditional Skills, Techniques and Knowledge for the Conservation and Transmission of Wooden Architecture in Japan is comprehended as 'knowledge and practices concerning nature and the universe' and 'traditional craftsmanship'. It is noteworthy that Sustainable Development Goals (hereafter SDGs) connected with each element of ICH are indicated clearly at the UNESCO's web page for each ICH element. According to UNESCO (n.d.-c), the aforementioned Traditional Skills, Techniques and Knowledge for the Conservation and Transmission of Wooden Architecture in Japan is connected with subsequent five SDGs:

- SDG 4: Quality education
- SDG 8: Decent work and economic growth
- SDG 9: Industry, innovation and infrastructure
- SDG 12: Responsible consumption and production
- SDG 15: Life on land

Amongst these, this ICH element is strongly connected with SDGs 8 and 12 (UNESCO, n.d.-c). Furthermore, the connections between world's ICH elements and SDGs are visually presented at the tab named Sustainable Development that is part of the web page called 'Dive into intangible cultural heritage!' (UNESCO, n.d.-d).

As a difference in years between adoptions of WH Convention in 1972 and ICH Convention in 2003 may imply, generally movements for conservation of intangible cultural heritage at universal level seems to

3 Sustainability of Japan's Intangible Cultural Heritage

have emerged and become apparent later than those for conservation of tangible cultural heritage. In relation to Japan, however, listing and conservation of Japan's intangible cultural heritage, particularly important ones to the country, were already addressed in Articles 71–77 of Act on Protection of Cultural Properties (*Bunkazai Hogo-ho*) when the law was enacted in 1950. Since that time, Act on Protection of Cultural Properties has been functioning as a key act for conservation of Japan's intangible and tangible cultural properties, going through seven-time amendments to date (The Agency of Cultural Affairs (hereafter ACA), 2021). ACA is a government organisation responsible for promotion and conservation of Japan's cultural heritage. ACA specifies main categories of Japan's cultural properties that should be appreciated as heritage (ACA, n.d.-a). Of these, Intangible Cultural Properties (*Mukei Bunkazai*) is the name of the main category specifically for Japan's intangible cultural heritage (see Sect. 2 for details). On the other hand, the group called Folk Cultural Properties (*Minzoku Bunkazai*) comprises both tangible and intangible folk cultural heritage, and this chapter sheds light on the latter (see Sect. 3 for details). Moreover, there is another group for Japan's intangible cultural heritage that is named Conservation Techniques (*Hozongijutsu*) (see Sect. 4 for details).

ACA and its parent government department, the Ministry of Education, Culture, Sports, Science and Technology (hereafter MEXT), also launched a programme called Japan Heritage (*Nihon Isan*) in 2015 (see Sect. 5 for details). Unlike the aforementioned three conservation schemes for Japan's intangible cultural heritage and those for tangible cultural heritage (see Chap. 1), Japan Heritage focuses much more on utilisation of cultural heritage than its conservation. The programme aims to build regions of Japan as established brands, enable local inhabitants to rediscover their identity, and ultimately revitalise diverse regions of Japan (ACA, n.d.-b). To this end, Japan Heritage packages certain regions' diverse tangible and intangible heritage under certain themes, conserve and utilise collections of such heritage in a comprehensive and holistic manner, generate appealing regional narratives, and attract the attention of domestic and international audience (ACA, n.d.-b). Concerning Japan's intangible cultural heritage, Jimura (2022) also examines following seven types as its representative examples and discusses their importance in their own right and as tourism resources:

- Religions
- *Matsuri* (traditional festivals)
- Foods and drinks
- *Onsen* (hot springs)
- Cultures of indigenous peoples
- War heritage
- Popular culture

Amongst these, *matsuri*, cultures of indigenous peoples, and foods and drinks are associated with a Japan's elements listed as ICH by UNESCO. Intangible cultural heritage related to *matsuri* and cultures of indigenous peoples is examined in Sect. 3 as Intangible Folk Cultural Properties (*Mukei Minzoku Bunkazai*). On the other hand, intangible cultural heritage associated with foods and drinks is discussed in Sect. 6 as other type of intangible cultural heritage that is not covered in Act on Protection of Cultural Properties (*Bunkazai Hogo-ho*) whose implementation is managed by MEXT and ACA.

2 Intangible Cultural Properties (*Mukei Bunkazai*)

ACA's category of Intangible Cultural Properties (*Mukei Bunkazai*) denotes a variety of Japan's intangible cultural assets (performing arts and craft techniques) with high historic or artistic value for the nation (ACA, n.d.-c). Amongst Intangible Cultural Properties, a minister of MEXT lists particularly valuable ones as Important Intangible Cultural Properties (*Juyo Mukei Bunkazai*) (ACA, n.d.-c). To conserve intangible cultural heritage in a sustainable manner, both the Japanese Government and UNESCO designate intangible cultural properties through their own conservation systems, Important Intangible Cultural Properties and ICH respectively, have conservation frameworks such as a relevant law or

3 Sustainability of Japan's Intangible Cultural Heritage

treaty, and guide and support conservation activities, following the frameworks. Some Important Intangible Cultural Properties are also conserved through the ICH scheme. For instance, *kabuki* was designated as Important Intangible Cultural Property in 1965 and was also added to the lists of ICH elements as Kabuki theatre in 2008. Kabuki theatre is also associated with SDGs 4 (Quality Education), 8 (Decent Work and Economic Growth) and 16 (Peace, Justice and Strong Institutions) (UNESCO, n.d.-d) (see Table 1.1 in Chap. 1).

Here, it should be noted that the Japanese Government and Act on Protection of Cultural Properties (*Bunkazai Hogo-ho*) place great importance on people who can represent, embody and practice Important Intangible Cultural Properties (*Juyo Mukei Bunkazai*) as well as Important Intangible Cultural Properties themselves. It is an intriguing and noteworthy practice and unique to Japan's approach towards the conservation of intangible cultural heritage. Such people are regarded as the holder(s) of a certain Important Intangible Cultural Property who have acquired advanced mastery of knowledge and technique required for the specific Important Intangible Cultural Property (ACA, n.d.-c). This would testify the magnitude of human factors in the practice and conservation of intangible cultural heritage and its succession to future generations. Holder(s) of Important Intangible Cultural Properties can be recognised in one of following three forms:

* Individual recognition – recognition as each individual
* Collective recognition – recognition as two or more individuals
* Group recognition – recognition as an association or organisation

Although it is not an official title specified in Act on Protection of Cultural Properties (*Bunkazai Hogo-ho*), the holders of Important Intangible Cultural Properties (*Juyo Mukei Bunkazai*) who are recognised through individual recognition are usually called Living National Treasures (*Ningen Kokuho*). Individual recognition is used in the recognitions of both performing arts and craft techniques as Important Intangible Cultural Properties. To cite a case, *rakugo* is a story-based verbal entertainment at Japan's *yose* theatres. *Rakugo* consist of *koten rakugo* and *shinsaku* (*sosaku*) *rakugo*. In general, the former means *rakugo* developed during the Edo, Meiji or Taisho period, whilst the latter denotes the newer ones created during the Showa period (1926–1989) and thereafter. Of these, *koten rakugo* is Important Intangible Cultural Property and three masters of *koten rakugo* have been acknowledged as Living National Treasures through individual recognition. Overall, examples of collective recognition can be confirmed more in performing arts than craft techniques, whilst those of group recognition can be found more in craft techniques than performing arts. For instance, Ogie-bushi is one of traditional *shamisen* vocal genres and was awarded a status as Important Intangible Cultural Property in 1993 through collective recognition. On the other hand, Yuki-tsumugi is high-class silk fabrics originated in today's Ibaraki Prefecture and Tochigi Prefecture and has around 400-year history. Yuki-tsumugi was listed as Important Intangible Cultural Property in 1956 via group recognition and as an ICH element in 2010. The Japanese Government financially supports the conservation of Important Intangible Cultural Properties by subsequent measures:

* To provide special grants (two million Japanese Yen annually) to Living National Treasures
* To subsidise training programmes for successors or public performances that are planned and implemented by the above-mentioned recognised group holders, local governments or other relevant entities
* To arrange and carry out training workshops and other activities to train successors of traditional performing arts at the National Theatre of Japan in Tokyo Metropolitan Prefecture (hereafter TMP).

As discussed so far, Important Intangible Cultural Properties (*Juyo Mukei Bunkazai*) are highly significant intangible assets. Nevertheless, it should be remembered that there are other valuable intangible cultural properties that need to be documented and publicised for current and future generations. That is because; these properties are essential to comprehend historical transitions of performing arts and craft techniques (ACA, n.d.-c). These intangible cultural properties are understood by the Japanese Government as such, and the national government itself may make their record or subsidise local governments to enable them to work on such a task, following Article 77 of Act on Protection of Cultural

Properties (*Bunkazai Hogo-ho*). In recent years, especially since early 2020, the Japanese Government acknowledges that there is a need to develop a new register system for the conservation of much wider Intangible Cultural Properties (*Mukei Bunkazai*), considering the negative impacts of COVID-19 on this type of heritage (ACA, 2021). This new register system can be named, for instance, Registered Intangible Cultural Properties (*Toroku Mukei Bunkazai*). The new register scheme will also need to be embedded in Act on Protection of Cultural Properties and utilised fully by national and local governments when it is established to realise proper conservation of an extensive range of Japan's intangible cultural properties (ACA, 2021).

Like the cases of Japan's tangible cultural heritage (see Chap. 2), it is confirmed from the arguments above that financial supports from the Japanese Government can enhance economic sustainability of diverse kinds of Intangible Cultural Properties (*Mukei Bunkazai*), especially Important Intangible Cultural Properties (*Juyo Mukei Bunkazai*). In relation to economic sustainability of Important Intangible Cultural Properties, it is also important to understand that both performing arts and craft techniques have been maintaining or improving their economic sustainability through their interactions with the general public. In other words, people who spend their money to enjoy the above-stated performing arts or purchase the products generated through the aforementioned craft techniques monetarily assist these intangible cultural properties.

Kabuki, *ningyo johruri*, *bunraku*, and *nohgaku* are representative examples of performing arts that are listed as Important Intangible Cultural Properties (*Juyo Mukei Bunkazai*), well known to Japanese people, and regularly performed in front of audience. In this book, the term *bunraku* is understood as *ningyo johruri* originated and based in Osaka and generally the word *nohgaku* encompasses both *noh* and *kyogen*. The income raised as ticket fees is a vital financial resource that can maintain or enhance economic sustainability of these performing arts. In addition, souvenir shops and restaurants on theatres can also contribute to their economic sustainability. It is also true that socio-cultural sustainability of these performing arts can be maintained or improved by being appreciated and enjoyed by their keen fans and wider audience, including young people, students, children, and even foreign people living in Japan and international tourists. That is because; such practice can raise people's awareness of Japan's traditional performing arts, which is vital for their long-term sustainability.

Of the aforementioned performing arts, it is fair to say that currently *kabuki* is most approachable and popular performing arts amongst Japanese people. *Kabuki* has various programmes and they are performed at many theatres in Japan, but Kabukiza and Shinbashi Enbujo in TMP, Minamiza in Kyoto Prefecture (see Fig. 3.1), and Osaka Shochikuza are four main theatres of *kabuki*. The locations of these main theatres imply that *kabuki* can be enjoyed in two main urban regions situated in the eastern and western parts of Japan. Touring *kabuki* and local theatres play a key role in making *kabuki* accessible for wider audience. Moreover, overseas performances were also held in France, Russia and Poland between 2017 and 2018 (Shochiku, n.d.-a). The information about the overseas performance was found at the official English website of *kabuki*

Fig. 3.1 Minamiza theatre. (Source: Author)

3 Sustainability of Japan's Intangible Cultural Heritage

(https://www.kabukiweb.net/) that is owned and managed by a private company, Shochiku. All of these practices and activities are beneficial for economic and socio-cultural sustainability of *kabuki*.

As implied above, the production and performance of *kabuki* has been dominated by a private company, Shochiku, since 1895 when the company was established. According to Shochiku (n.d.-b), the relations between Shochiku and *kabuki* started in 1890 when two founders of the company watched a *kabuki* performance in a theatre in Kyoto City. Since that time, *kabuki* has always been one of the main pillars of Shochiku's entertainment businesses, and Shochiku has also been developing *kabuki* as an entertainment and fostering *kabuki* culture (Shochiku, n.d.-b). Hence, it is clear that Shochiku has been playing an essential role in the modern history of *kabuki* and its economic and socio-cultural sustainability. In the author's view, *kabuki* would not be able to enjoy its success today without the presence of Shochiku. What the company has been doing can also be understood as representation of *mottainai* spirit as *kabuki* might have disappeared or declined if Shochiku has not been involved in *kabuki*. Nevertheless, there has also been an opinion amongst Japanese people that the production and performance of *kabuki* should not be dominated by a private company, because *kabuki* is intangible cultural heritage of Japan. Stated differently, part of Japanese people would see what Shochiku has been doing is legal but not ethical. This means that Shochiku's *kabuki* businesses can be challenged in terms of its business ethics and corporate social responsibility. Moreover, Shochiku registered the word *kabuki* and many relevant words as trademarks to prevent unauthorised use, although the scope of this effect is somewhat limited because of objections from other parties. This action taken by Shochiku may be a right one in terms of its businesses, but this must have provoked another controversy and may have damaged the company's image.

Craft techniques listed as Important Intangible Cultural Properties (*Juyo Mukei Bunkazai*) comprise a wide range of skills for porcelain/pottery, papermaking, staining, lacquerware, doll making, metalworking, and wood/bamboo-working. These traditional crafts themselves are Japan's tangible cultural heritage, but they embody Japan's craft techniques, intangible cultural heritage. Some of these traditional crafts, particularly invaluable ones, are usually understood as artworks that are not expected to be sold to consumers as products. These artworks may not be able to generate income through a financial transaction, but can still contribute to economic and socio-cultural sustainability of traditional crafts. That is because; for example, such artworks can serve as museum exhibitions, attracting visitors with admission fees and being appreciated by the general public. On the other hand, the majority of these traditional crafts are made as products to be sold to consumers. The income raised through retail activities can support economic sustainability of traditional crafts and the craft techniques that are required to produce these crafts. Price ranges differ by type of traditional crafts and prices differ even within the same type of traditional crafts. According to the official website of Kakiemon porcelains with the *nigoshide* body, for instance, the prices of products range between 27,500 and 66,000 Japanese Yen as of March 2021 (Kakiemon, n.d.).

In relation to socio-cultural sustainability, it is clear that many traditional crafts and craft techniques of Japan have been suffering from a lack of successors (Kuroda, 2000). As the case of *honminoshi* papermaking indicates, even craft techniques listed as Important Intangible Cultural Properties (*Juyo Mukei Bunkazai*) are not exceptions (Chunichi Shimbun, 2020). Fortunately, however, a young person started learning *honminoshi* papermaking since 2020 under the supervision of Tadashi Sawamura, Living National Treasure (*Ningen Kokuho*) (Chunichi Simbun, 2020).

3 Folk Cultural Properties (*Minzoku Bunkazai*)

As Sect. 7 in Chap. 2 shows, ACA's notion of Folk Cultural Properties (*Minzoku Bunkazai*) means cultural properties that have emerged from ordinary people's daily lives and comprises tangible and intangible properties (ACA, n.d.-d). In light of the scope of this chapter, this section highlights Intangible Folk Cultural Properties (*Mukei Minzoku Bunkazai*). The conservation framework for Intangible Folk Cultural Properties is similar to those for Tangible Folk Cultural Properties (*Yukei Minzoku*

3 Sustainability of Japan's Intangible Cultural Heritage

Bunkazai) (see Sect. 7 in Chap. 2) and the aforementioned Intangible Cultural Properties (*Mukei Bunkazai*) (see Sect. 2). Each municipality of Japan can register their Intangible Folk Cultural Properties. Amongst these, ACA designates especially important ones as Important Intangible Folk Cultural Properties (*Juyo Mukei Minzoku Bunkazai*) and can support their conservation and practice in various ways, including financial assistance. This is beneficial for economic sustainability of Important Intangible Folk Cultural Properties.

Japan has 318 properties listed as Important Intangible Folk Cultural Properties (*Juyo Mukei Minzoku Bunkazai*) and each of the 47 prefecture of Japan has at least one Important Intangible Folk Cultural Property as of writing (ACA, n.d.-e). According to ACA (n.d.-e), Important Intangible Folk Cultural Properties consist of subsequent three main groups and several sub-groups in each main group:

* Manner and custom (production and livelihood, life and ritual, entertainment and sport, social life (folklore knowledge), annual event, festival (faith), and other)
* Folk performing art (*kagura* (dance and music at Shinto shrine), *dengaku* (dance and music for agricultural festival), *furyu* (elegant and tasteful dance and music), storytelling and performing art for celebration, *ennen* and *okonai* (dance and music at Japanese Buddhist temple), performing art of foreign origin, and other)
* Folk technique (production and livelihood; food, clothing and shelter; and, other)

Of these, 'folk technique' was added as a new group of Important Intangible Folk Cultural Properties as part of the amendment of Act on Protection of Cultural Properties (*Bunkazai Hogo-ho*) in 2004.

As Jimura (2022) point out referring to *matsuri* and cultures of indigenous peoples, some Important Intangible Folk Cultural Properties (*Juyo Mukei Minzoku Bunkazai*) are appreciated and used as tourism resources as well as Japan's intangible cultural heritage. For instance, Aomori Nebuta Matsuri (Aomori Prefecture) is a very popular *matsuri* amongst tourists and inscribed as a manner and custom (festival (faith)), whilst Ainu *Koshiki-buyo* (traditional Ainu dance) (Hokkaido Prefecture) can be enjoyed by tourists at a local theatre and is listed as a folk performing art (other). Dual meaning and role of intangible folk cultural properties as heritage and tourism resources can also be confirmed in the other main group of Important Intangible Folk Cultural Properties, folk technique. For example, cormorant fishing (*ukai*) on the Nagaragawa River (Gifu Prefecture) is Important Intangible Folk Cultural Properties listed in 2015 as a folk technique (production and livelihood). Traditionally, cormorant fishermen of this area have trained cormorants to catch *ayu* fish (sweetfish). *Ukai* is held after dark under a bonfire at the bow, using a traditional wooden boat during May and November. This type of boat is eco-friendly and beneficial for environmental sustainability of *ukai* implementation as it has no engine. A cormorant fisherman handles several cormorants using ropes. The bonfire makes *ayu* surprised and cormorants catch *ayu*. Currently, *ukai* is a popular visitor attraction during summer. Once, the author enjoyed watching *ukai* performed in Oze quarter in Seki City, sharing a traditional wooden boat with other visitors (see Fig. 3.2). Thus, it is fair to say that *ukai* has been highly commoditised and commercialised as a tourism resource, opening it to the general public with admission fees (3400 Japanese Yen for an adult in the case of Oze). In fact, serving as a visitor attraction can bring income to fishermen that is significant to sustain their livelihoods, and can also increase employment opportunities for local residents (Nakahara & Kitano, 2008). This aspect is crucial for economic sustainability of *ukai*. Today, *ukai* is seen as an embodiment of a traditional folk technique rather than a mere fishing method because the technique has been inherited from generations to generations by specific local families (Deguchi & Deguchi, 2016). Hence, it is essential for socio-cultural sustainability of *ukai* to be practiced and performed regularly and continuously even for tourism purposes. *Ayu* caught through *ukai* are not wasted. In fact, they are often cooked and served at local Japanese restaurants as a local speciality. This practice can be regarded and appreciated as a representation of *mottainai* spirit and practice of 'reuse' of a natural resource (see Sects. 2.3 and 5.4 in Chap. 1 respectively).

It should be noted that cormorant fishing (*ukai*) on the Nagaragawa River is also a component of An Ancient Castle Town with the Spirit of Nobunaga's Hospitality (Gifu Prefecture), one of the 'stories' designated

Fig. 3.2 Cormorant fishing (*ukai*) on the Nagaragawa River. (Source: Author)

as Japan Heritage (*Nihon Isan*) (see Sect. 5 for detail). This is a representative example of dual listing for conservation of cultural heritage adopted by the Japanese Government, although the emphasis of the Japan Heritage scheme is utilisation of cultural heritage, including tourism, rather than its conservation (see Sect. 1). According to Deguchi and Deguchi (2016), local communities of Nagara in Gifu City and Oze in Seki City where *ukai* has been practiced, have developed an action plan and have implemented various activities with the national and local governments, aiming to make *ukai* to be inscribed as a UNESCO's ICH element. If realised, cormorant fishing (*ukai*) on the Nagaragawa River will be protected by both domestic and international conservation schemes. In fact, the protection of Japan's intangible folk cultural heritage through domestic and international initiatives has already been realised as, for instance, the case of Paantou of the Miyako Island demonstrates. Paantou of the Miyako Island was designated as Important Intangible Folk Cultural Property

(*Juyo Mukei Minzoku Bunkazai*) in 1993 and inscribed as an ICH element as part of Raiho-shin, ritual visits of deities in masks and costumes in 2018. This ICH element is strongly connected with SDG 4 (Quality Education) and also associated with SDG 16 (Peace, Justice and Strong Institutions).

As demonstrated in Sect. 2, the Japanese Government is very keen and concerned about the conservation of intangible cultural heritage that are not listed as Important Intangible Cultural Properties (*Juyo Mukei Bunkazai*). The national government is also eager and concerned about the conservation of intangible folk cultural heritage that is not protected through Important Intangible Folk Cultural Properties (*Juyo Mukei Minzoku Bunkazai*). With regard to the conservation of such properties, the Japanese Government video-records their practices (e.g. Umazekku Horse Seasonal Festival in Sanuki (Kagawa Prefecture)) or develop a survey report on their current statuses (e.g. Kashima miroku (Ibaraki Prefecture)) (ACA, n.d.-d).

4 Conservation Techniques (*Hozongijutsu*)

Conservation techniques have been well recognised and examined as a critical element of conservation of a range of cultural heritage, especially tangible one (e.g. Rogerio-Candelera et al., 2013). Generally, however, such techniques themselves are not always appreciated as objects of conservation, and valued and conserved as intangible cultural heritage through a public conservation scheme. In Japan, the importance of Conservation Techniques (*Hozongijutsu*) has been officially acknowledged in Act on Protection of Cultural Properties (*Bunkazai Hogo-ho*) since its amendment in 1975 (Articles 147–152). The Japanese Government selects and designates traditional techniques and skills that are vital for conservation of Japan's tangible and intangible cultural heritage as Selected Conservation Techniques (*Sentei Hozongijutsu*) (ACA, n.d.-a). This listing system also formally recognises groups and individuals who have Selected Conservation Techniques (ACA, n.d.-a). In addition, the national government develops and maintains its own record of Selected Conservation Techniques and organises training opportunities for successors of various Selected Conservation Techniques. Furthermore, the government also financially back training programmes conducted by groups and individuals with Selected Conservation Techniques (ACA, n.d.-a). Such monetary assistance is beneficial for their economic sustainability.

As of writing, 81 conservation techniques are inscribed as Selected Conservation Techniques (*Sentei Hozongijutsu*): 46 techniques are for conservation of tangible cultural heritage, 30 for conservation of intangible cultural heritage, and five for conservation of both (ACA, n.d.-f). Amongst these 81 Selected Conservation Techniques, 17 are included in UNESCO's ICH element named Traditional skills, techniques and knowledge for the conservation and transmission of wooden architecture in Japan. Of these 17 techniques, 15 are for tangible cultural heritage (e.g. woodworking), one for intangible cultural heritage (production and purification of *urushi* lacquer) and one for tangible and intangible cultural heritage (making of *enzuke* gold leaf) (ACA, n.d.-g). This dual listing signifies that the 17 conservation techniques are valued by and protected through both domestic and universal initiatives for conservation of intangible cultural heritage. It is worth noting that the ICH element, Traditional skills, techniques and knowledge for the conservation and transmission of wooden architecture in Japan, is potentially related to three cultural World Heritage sites in Japan all of which comprise historic monuments such as Shinto shrines and/or Japanese Buddhist temples (UNESCO, n.d.-c). That is because; maintenance and repair of such historic wooden buildings require special skills and knowledge represented by diverse types of elaborate wood joinery that does not use nails or metal fittings. This practice enables large wooden structures such as Shinto shrines and Japanese Buddhist temples to survive for a long period. Carpenters with such special know-how and techniques are called and respected as *miyadaiku*, and their knowledge and skills have been passed down from generation to generation for more than a thousand years. Socio-cultural sustainability of such exceptional techniques can be achieved and maintained through their continuous succession to date and in the future. Nevertheless, currently their socio-cultural sustainability has been facing a risk mainly due to a lack of successors of such special techniques (Hashitsume, 2020). To tackle this problem, for instance, the aforementioned supports from the Japanese Government would be crucial.

It is sure that a recent extensive repair project of Himeji Castle demonstrates the magnitude of conservation techniques for preservation of Japan's tangible cultural heritage (see Sect. 2 in Chap. 2). In principle, such conservation works attempt to reuse original or existing materials of Japan's historic wooden buildings as much as possible to preserve object authenticity of such structures and reduce the amount of waste materials. Such a policy and practice can contribute to environmental sustainability of Japan's historic timber structures and forests where trees are cut down to produce timber. This approach can also be understood as an ethical approach adopted by organisations and enterprises engaging in repair projects for Japan's historic wooden structures, particularly large ones. Thus, it is fair to say that these stakeholders are expected to take their social responsibility accordingly and embody the spirit of *mottainai* through their works. Tangible cultural heritage such as Japanese-style castles, Shinto shrines and Japanese Buddhist temples often serve as popular visitor attractions. Therefore, the level of techniques required for conservation of this type of cultural heritage can also influence visitor perception of and experience with such cultural heritage.

On the other hand, the significance of techniques for conservation of Japan's intangible cultural heritage can be more overlooked or disregarded by visitors than the importance of techniques for conservation of Japan's tangible cultural heritage. That is mainly because; intangible cultural heritage supported by specific conservation techniques is often associated with particular plays/events such as Japan's traditional performing arts (e.g. *kabuki*) or music (e.g. *kagura*), which may not be performed when visitors want to appreciate or enjoy. Currently, serving only their primary purposes in original settings might not be enough for some Selected Conservation Techniques (*Sentei Hozongijutsu*) for Japan's intangible cultural heritage to be maintained and inherited to next generations. To cite a case, *Awa ai* (Awa natural indigo) is a traditional dye that has been produced in Awa domain (today's Tokushima Prefecture) since the early Edo period (1603–1868). Although the production of *Awa ai* has experienced a certain level of decline in its history, it has been surviving until today. *Awa ai* would not be able to survive and maintain a certain amount of its production if it has been used only to create *Awa ai* products (Kawahito, 2010). *Awa ai* has been able to survive to date as it has also been utilised in tourism and education settings and purposes (Kawahito, 2010). *Awa ai* must be involved in even a wider variety of activities and supported by diverse types of assistances to continue to be sustainable in terms of each pillar of triple bottom line (hereafter TBL) and to be passed down to future generations (Kawahito, 2010).

5   Japan Heritage (*Nihon Isan*)

As outlined in Sect. 1, ACA and MEXT have been managing the Japan Heritage (*Nihon Isan*) scheme since 2015. According to ACA (n.d.-b), the scheme has following three primary objectives:

- To recognise the narratives that bind Japan's regional cultural properties
- To maintain and use these regional cultural properties in a cohesive manner
- To strategically and effectively promote the narratives pertaining to cultural properties within Japan and abroad

As implied from these objectives, Japan Heritage intends to create 'stories' based on tangible and intangible cultural heritage of specific regions, focuses more on its utilisation in an integrated manner rather than its conservation, and tries to promote certain localities as appealing destinations for domestic and international tourists. Considering this, Japan Heritage can be regarded as an initiative that epitomises the use of heritage as tourism resources, which is a significant theme in Part 2 (Chaps. 2, 3, and 4) of this monograph. In light of the magnitude of 'stories' in the concept of Japan Heritage, the Japan Heritage system is discussed in this chapter as such stories can be understood as intangible cultural heritage.

As confirmed from Chaps. 1, 2, and 3, Japan has various public listing and register systems for conservation of its tangible and intangible cultural heritage. A core of these schemes is financial supports from the governments, especially the national government, for heritage conservation. Indeed, this has been assisting and enhancing economic sustainability of cultural heritage that is listed or registered by these public schemes. Relying on monetary assistances from public sector did not have major issues when financial conditions of the national, regional and local governments were healthy and stable like Japan in the 1980s. Since the burst of Japanese economic bubble in 1991, however, the Japanese economy has been stagnant for three decades. Thus, Japan's tangible and intangible cultural heritage has been expected to be sustainable, particularly financially sustainable, in its own right as much as possible. Suga and Ogawa (2018) suggest that such a shift in approaches towards cultural heritage consists of three stages namely 'preservation and conservation-focused', 'maintenance and open-to-public-focused' and 'utilisation-focused', and state that the vast majority of Japan's cultural heritage is in the third phase (utilisation-focused). This important change in the Japanese Government's policy can be confirmed in, for instance, the document named 'Plan for utilisation of cultural resources to establish Japan as a tourism-oriented country' (*Kanko-rikkoku no jitsugen no tameno bunkashigen no katsuyohosaku*) (published by MEXT in 2010 (Nakagawa, 2010). Established in 2015, Japan Heritage (*Nihon Isan*) is expected to play a paramount role in the utilisation-focused stage.

In light of the aforementioned main objectives of Japan Heritage, furthermore, it is obvious that listing as Japan Heritage is expected to make a great contribution to tourism development at designated regions, disseminating stories unique to each region and attracting a larger number of domestic and international tourists. Moreover, Japan Heritage should have been able to maximise its contribution to inbound tourism by working together with Tokyo 2020 Olympic and Paralympic Games (Jimura, 2020). Thus, actions to achieve the three primary objectives of Japan Heritage and tourism development at regions having Japan Heritage should work in a collaborative way, and ultimately the listing system of Japan Heritage aims to revitalise local communities of the regions with Japan Heritage (ACA, n.d.-h). Revitalisation of local communities, especially those in remote and/or rural regions, is essential for their long-term sustainability of Japanese society. To this end, diverse assets of the regions, including cultural and natural heritage, tourism developed in a sustainable manner and/or WH status, have been utilised in Japan (Jimura,

3 Sustainability of Japan's Intangible Cultural Heritage 87

2011, 2019, 2022). In addition to these, the Japan Heritage scheme may also be effective to support revitalisation of many local communities in Japan.

In 2020, 21 stories were newly inscribed as Japan Heritage (*Nihon Isan*) and the total number of stories listed as Japan Heritage reached 104. As the Japanese Government aimed to designate 100 stories as Japan Heritage by 2020, new listings have been suspended for a while. Although each story highlights a specific region, such a region can be a city/prefecture or extend over two or more prefectures. For instance, 19 tangible and intangible cultural properties of Onomichi City (Hiroshima Prefecture) are listed as Japan Heritage named Onomichi – A Historic Port City Prefect for Wandering. Onomichi is surrounded by hills on three side and its south side faces the Seto Inland Sea. Onomichi has flourished as a hub of maritime transportation since the twelfth century and has enjoyed its prosperity. Successful merchants played a key role in city's development, especially the construction of countless Japanese Buddhist temples. The cityscape is also characterised by a number of narrow streets and stone paths, particularly in the city centre (see Fig. 3.3). The city has a relatively small land area, but is filled with a variety of tangible and intangible attraction factors. Therefore, Onomichi City can be described as a city like a miniature landscape garden (Japan Heritage, n.d.). Although Onomichi was already a popular tourist destination even before its inscription as Japan Heritage in 2015, the designation has been further disseminating the city's attractiveness both domestically and internationally (Nishii, 2016). Undoubtedly, Onomichi City is an established tourist destination, but the city has been suffering from depopulation and ageing society like many local municipalities in Japan. In the city centre, many houses are built on a steep slope and along a narrow street. Many local residents, especially elderly ones, once lived in such houses have moved to a different city and the number of abandoned or vacant houses has increased. This worrying situation needs to be improved to maintain economic, socio-cultural and environmental sustainability of the city. To tackle this problem, Onomichi City has been teaming up with a non-governmental organisation called Onomichi Vacant House Renovation Project. They work as intermediaries between owners of vacant houses and people who want to live in the houses to maximise the

Fig. 3.3 City centre of Onomichi. (Source: Author)

level of usage of these houses. Their work represents a spirit of *mottainai* and is crucial for the sustainable future of the city.

As stated earlier, a locale where a 'story' of Japan Heritage (*Nihon Isan*) exists can extend over two or more prefectures. For example, the story of The Cities of Iga and Koka – Exploring the Birthplace of the Real Ninja includes Iga City (Mie Prefecture) and Koka City (Shiga Prefecture). As Ito (2018) asserts, *ninja* is very popular amongst people in the West. Given a wide variety of international tourists enjoying *ninja*-related attractions in Japan, a high level of popularity of *ninja* can also be confirmed amongst people in the East (e.g. Hong Kong). Various *ninja* amine or manga (e.g. Ninja Hattori-kun and Naruto) have been contributing to today's popularity of *ninja* across many regions of the world (Ito, 2018). It is generally believed that there were many different *ninja* schools in Japan between the fourteenth and seventeenth centuries. Normally, however, Iga and Koka are recognised widely as two major *ninja* schools. Iga *ninja* based in and around today's Iga City (Mie Prefecture), whilst Koka *ninja* resided in today's Koka City (Shiga Prefecture). Interestingly, Iga City and Koka City are next to each other, although it is generally believed that Iga and Koka worked for different lords during the Sengoku period (the medieval era of the Warring States). A prominent heritage common to Iga City and Koka City is *ninja*; hence, it is natural that these two cities are included in one Japan Heritage (*Nihon Isan*) and their story is created with a central focus on *ninja*. On the other hand, the story of Henro – A Spiritual Journey through Shikoku includes all of four prefectures in the Shikoku Island (Tokushima, Kagawa, Ehime and Kochi). The Japanese word *henro* means pilgrimages and this story is comprehended as the Shikoku Pilgrimage visiting 88 temples that are associated with Kukai, the originator of Shingonshu sect of Japanese Buddhism. In the cases of these two stories extending over two or more cities or prefectures, one city or prefecture may not have cultural properties that are enough to create a unique and attractive story in its own right. However, these cities or prefectures can still develop such a story together by creating a synergy under the Japan Heritage scheme.

6 Other Type of Intangible Cultural Heritage

This section examines Japan's foods and drinks as a representative example of Japan's intangible cultural heritage whose conservation is not covered in Act on Protection of Cultural Properties (*Bunkazai Hogo-ho*). The application of Act on Protection of Cultural Properties is managed by MEXT and ACA, whilst main laws related to foods, drinks and agricultural products are supervised by the Ministry of Health, Labour and Welfare, the Consumer Affairs Agency, and the Ministry of Agriculture,

Forestry and Fisheries (hereafter MAFF). Overall, 'conservation' of Japan's foods and drinks does not seem to be a key interest of the Japanese Government compared with that of various types of intangible cultural heritage discussed in Sects. 2, 3, and 4. Instead, the national government appears to be eager to promote and export Japan's foods and drinks (e.g. *wagyu* beef and *sake*) overseas in recent years. Nevertheless, the value of Japan's traditional food culture as intangible cultural heritage and the magnitude of its conservation are acknowledged at international level as evidenced by the listing of Washoku, traditional dietary cultures of the Japanese, notably for the celebration of New Year as an ICH element in 2013 (Jimura, 2022). This designation is a considerable factor that can encourage socio-cultural sustainability of *washoku* in the long run, helping the succession of this heritage to future generations of Japan. As can be seen in Sect. 5, the mission of the Japan Heritage (*Nihon Isan*) scheme contains attracting domestic and international tourists to places having Japan Heritage. Following two stories of Japan Heritage feature a food and food culture distinctive in a peculiar region:

- Transporting Food and Culture along the 'Mackerel Road' (Fukui Prefecture) – *saba* (mackerel)
- From Cedar to Citrus (Kochi Prefecture) – *yuzu* (yuzu citron)

Japan's foods and drinks, especially traditional ones such as *washoku*, are intangible cultural heritage of Japan, and intangible cultural heritage often works in tourism settings and serve as tourism resources. In fact, Henderson (2009) asserts that foods and drinks are important visitor attractions available in many different forms, and can affect or be central to visitor experience. More specifically, foods and drinks are important to realise tourism in a sustainable manner for subsequent reasons:

- Tourist consumption of local foods has been increasing and it can generate a multiplier effect that will benefit the local economy,
- Increasing concerns on the environmental impacts of transporting foods across the world have led researchers to argue that purchasing and using locally produced foods is an essential practice for the tourism industry to reduce its carbon footprint, and

3 Sustainability of Japan's Intangible Cultural Heritage

* Promoting high-quality cuisine or distinctive local foods is one of the ways for a tourist destination to compete with other tourist destinations and continue to attract a certain number of visitors (Sims, 2009).

In relation to this, MAFF and many regions of Japan have been working together to establish foods and drinks unique or distinctive to particular regions as a well-recognised local brands in Japanese and international markets. MAFF also financially supports a wide range of activities for this purpose (MAFF, 2008).

According to Japan Agricultural Development and Extension Association (2007), preceding successful examples of local food and drink brands include:

* Furano Wine (Furano City, Hokkaido Prefecture)
* Yubari Melon (Yubari City, Hokkiado Prefecture)
* Utsunomiya Gyoza (dumpling) (Utsunomiya City, Tochigi Prefecture)
* Shimonita Negi (spring onion) (Tomioka City, Gunma Prefecture)
* Matsusaka Gyu (*wagyu* beef) (Mie Prefecture)
* Uji Wazuka Cha (green tea leaf) (Wazuka Town, Kyoto Prefecture)
* Miwa Somen (*somen* noodle) (Nara Prefecture)
* Kuma Shochu (distilled beverage) (Kumamoto Prefecture)
* Seki Saba and Seki Aji (fish) (Oita City, Oita Prefecture)
* Okinawa Kokuto (muscovado) (Okinawa Prefecture)

The above-listed foods or drinks have a potential to contribute not only to economic, socio-cultural and environmental sustainability of these foods and drinks but also to tourism development and sustainable development of places with such established brands. To this end, a fair amount of financial benefits need to be received by relevant local workers, historical connections between a region and a food/drink peculiar to the region must be recognised widely by local residents, especially young people, and natural environment essential for the making of certain foods or drinks needs to be maintained for the sustainable future of a region and foods or drinks unique to the region.

7 Conclusion

Like diverse kinds of Japan's tangible cultural properties, various types of Japan's intangible cultural properties are also appreciated as intangible cultural heritage and protected by international and Japanese initiatives. As for international schemes, UNESCO's lists of ICH elements can be seen as the most founded one. As WH Convention functions for World Heritage sites, the Convention for the Safeguarding of the ICH works for ICH elements as the principle of this universal listing system developed for conservation of intangible cultural heritage across the globe. Concerning Japanese systems, Act on Protection of Cultural Properties (*Bunkazai Hogo-ho*) is the main law that regulates the protection and use of both tangible and intangible cultural properties whose value is acknowledged as cultural heritage of Japan. ACA officially suggests three main groups of intangible cultural properties, namely Intangible Cultural Properties (*Mukei Bunkazai*), Intangible Folk Cultural Properties (*Mukei Minzoku Bunkazai*) and Conservation Techniques (*Hozongijutsu*). Amongst these, the Japanese Government designates particularly valuable ones as Important Intangible Cultural Properties (*Juyo Mukei Bunkazai*), Important Intangible Folk Cultural Properties (*Juyo Mukei Minzoku Bunkazai*) and Selected Conservation Techniques (*Sentei Hozongijutsu*). Part of intangible cultural heritage belonging to any of these three categories are also listed as components of UNESCO's ICH elements. Such dual listing by domestic and international conservation schemes may be able to enhance the level of conservation and people's awareness of Japan's intangible cultural heritage, and lead to enhancement of its sustainability, especially its socio-cultural sustainability, in the long run.

As of writing, Japan has 22 elements that included in its list of ICH elements. Relations between each ICH element and any of 17 SDGs are found at the tab called Sustainable Development that is part of the web page named 'Dive into intangible cultural heritage!' owned by UNESCO, and some relations are strong ones. Ten SDGs have associations with any of Japan's 22 ICH elements. Amongst these ten SDGs, five SDGs have

3 Sustainability of Japan's Intangible Cultural Heritage

strong relationships with any of Japan's 22 ICH elements. These associations are confirmed as follows:

* SDG 2: Zero Hunger
  Connected to six ICH elements (strongly connected to three out of the six)
* SDG 4: Quality Education
  Connected to 13 ICH elements (strongly connected to one of the 13)
* SDG 5: Gender Equality
  Connected to five ICH elements
* SDG 8: Decent Work and Economic Growth
  Connected to nine ICH elements (strongly connected to four out of the nine)
* SDG 9: Industry, Innovation and Infrastructure
  Connected to one ICH element
* SDG 11: Sustainable Cities and Communities
  Connected to four ICH elements
* SDG 12: Responsible Consumption and Production
  Connected to six ICH elements (strongly connected to two out of the six)
* SDG 14: Life below Water
  Connected to one ICH element
* SDG 15: Life on Land
  Connected to five ICH elements
* SDG 16: Peace, Justice and Strong Institutions
  Connected to 16 ICH elements (strongly connected to two out of the 16)

From this list, it is fair to say that Japan's ICH elements are associated with sustainability of all of TBL, especially sustainability of food availability, education, work condition, economic development, consumption and production practice, world's peace and justice.

Once, Japan's approaches towards cultural heritage focused on its preservation and conservation. As the Japan's economy has been declining, its emphasis has shifted to its maintenance and making it open to public. Today, Japan's cultural heritage is expected to focus on its utilisation mainly to be sustainable in its own right, particularly financially sustainable. That is mainly because; the national, regional and local governments have been suffering a lack of budgets for cultural heritage in recent years, although financial assistances have been a primary way to maintain or enhance economic sustainability of a range of cultural heritage of Japan, including intangible one. Such monetary supports also help relevant stakeholders to practice their intangible cultural heritage and conduct a range of training sessions and workshops chiefly for successors of intangible cultural heritage. In relation to making the most of cultural heritage for its own sustainability in the future, the Japan Heritage (*Nihon Isan*) scheme is noteworthy. Different from the framework managed by MEXT and ACA, this initiative highlights utilisation rather than conservation of Japan's heritage. Concerning utilisation, using local cultural heritage as a tourism resource has been increasing important. With regard to this, the Japan Heritage scheme can play a paramount role. The system packages a wide variety of tangible (e.g. former residences) and intangible (e.g. foods) cultural heritage unique or prominent in a certain locale to create an attractive 'story' and lure domestic and international tourists. If a relevant region(s) makes the most of its Japan Heritage status in a sustainable manner, balancing conservation and utilisation, and local communities and visitors, it is safe to say that the region embodies the spirit of *mottainai* through the Japan Heritage system.

References

ACA. (2021) *Mukei no bunkazai no toroku-seido no sosetsu ni mukete* (Towards the creation of a register system for intangible cultural properties) [in Japanese]. Available at: https://www.bunka.go.jp/seisaku/bunkazai/shokai/pdf/92816101_01.pdf. Accessed 26 Mar 2021.

ACA. (n.d.-a). *Introduction to cultural properties*. Available at: https://www.bunka.go.jp/english/policy/cultural_properties/introduction/. Accessed 26 Mar 2021.

ACA. (n.d.-b). *Outline of Japan heritage*. Available at: https://japan-heritage.bunka.go.jp/en/about/index.html. Accessed 26 Mar 2021.

ACA. (n.d.-c). *Intangible cultural properties*. Available at: https://www.bunka.go.jp/english/policy/cultural_properties/introduction/intangible/. Accessed 28 Mar 2021.

ACA. (n.d.-d). *Folk cultural properties*. Available at: https://www.bunka.go.jp/english/policy/cultural_properties/introduction/folk/. Accessed 12 Apr 2021.

ACA. (n.d.-e). *Kuni-shitei Bunkazai-to Database: Juyo Mukei Minzoku Bunkazai* (Cultural properties database: Important intangible folk cultural properties) [in Japanese]. Available at: https://kunishitei.bunka.go.jp/bsys/categorylist?register_id=302. Accessed 12 Apr 2021.

ACA. (n.d.-f). *Kuni-shitei Bunkazai-to Database: Sentei Hozongijutsu* (Cultural Properties Database: Selected Conservation Techniques) [in Japanese]. Available at: https://kunishitei.bunka.go.jp/bsys/searchlist. Accessed 22 Apr 2021.

ACA. (n.d.-g). *Bunkaisan online: Mukei Bunkaisan* (Cultural heritage online: Intangible cultural heritage) [in Japanese]. Available at: https://bunka.nii.ac.jp/special_content/ilink4. Accessed 22 Apr 2021.

ACA. (n.d.-h). *Japan heritage*. Available at: https://www.bunka.go.jp/english/policy/cultural_properties/japan_heritage/. Accessed 29 Apr 2021.

Chunichi Shimbun. (2020). *Minowashi-shokunin e shugyo tsumu* (A young person started learning the making of honminoshi paper) [in Japanese]. Available at: https://www.chunichi.co.jp/article/3455. Accessed 30 Mar 2021.

Deguchi, A., & Deguchi, M. (2016). Wasen wo ikashita kasenkankoshuun (River tourism and transport utilising Japanese-style boats) [in Japanese]. *Konan daigaku kiyo bunkaku-hen, 166*, 193–212.

Hashitsume, K. (2020). Lucidation of motor skills focusing on the line of sight of the beginning to cut in wood cutting skills [in Japanese]. *Takenaka daikudogu-kan kenkyu kiyo, 31*, 39–52.

Henderson, J. C. (2009). Food tourism reviewed. *British Food Journal, 111*(4), 317–326.

Ito, G. (2018). Particularities of boys' manga in the early twenty-first century: How naruto differs from dragon ball. *Mechademia, 11*(1), 113–123.

Japan Agricultural Development and Extension Association. (2007). *Chiiki brand no senko jirei ichiran* (List of preceding successful examples of local brands) [in Japanese]. Available at: https://www.jadea.org/houkokusho/chizai/other/4b723fe2028.pdf. Accessed 2 May 2021.

Japan Heritage. (n.d.). *Onomichi – A historic port city prefect for wandering*. Available at: https://www.japan.travel/japan-heritage/popular/5bca15cb-078a-4992-a6de-81631516a607. Accessed 30 Apr 2021.

Jimura, T. (2011). The impact of world heritage site designation on local communities – A case study of Ogimachi, Shirakawa-mura, Japan. *Tourism Management, 32*(2), 288–296.

Jimura, T. (2019). *World heritage sites: Tourism, local communities and conservation activities*. CABI.

Jimura, T. (2020). Changing faces of Tokyo: Regeneration, tourism and Tokyo 2020. In N. Wise & T. Jimura (Eds.), *Tourism, cultural heritage and urban regeneration – Changing spaces in historical places* (pp. 141–155). Springer.

Jimura, T. (2022). *Cultural and heritage tourism in Japan*. Routledge.

Kakiemon. (n.d.). *Seihin ichiran* (A list of products) [in Japanese]. Available at: https://kakiemon.co.jp/product/. Accessed 30 Mar 2021.

Kawahito, M. (2010). Collaboration and future of Awa natural indigo [in Japanese]. *Sen'i Gakkaishi, 66*(11), 386–391.

Kuroda, K. (2000). Traditional arts of today and the future [in Japanese]. *Hyomengijutsu, 51*(10), 960–964.

MAFF. (2008). *Norinsuisanbutsu shokuhin no chiiki brand-ka no suishin ni mukete* (Encouraging to establish agricultural, forest and fishery products and foods as local brands) [in Japanese]. Available at: https://www.maff.go.jp/j/kanbo/tizai/brand/b_e-meeting/pdf/data1.pdf. Accessed 2 May 2021.

Nakagawa, M. (2010). *Kanko-rikkoku no jitsugen no tameno bunkashigen no katsuyohosaku* (Plan for utilisation of cultural resources to establish Japan as a tourism-oriented country) [in Japanese]. Available at: https://www.mlit.go.jp/common/000116084.pdf. Accessed 29 Apr 2021.

Nakahara, N., & Kitano, S. (2008). Dento-gyoho ga soshutsusuru gaibukeizaikoka to sono hyoka (External economic impacts of traditional fishing methods and evaluation of the impacts) [in Japanese]. *Chiiki gyogyo kenkyu, 49*(1), 63–81.

Nishii, T. (2016). Nihon Isan to Onomichi Shimin Isan: Onomichi-shi no rekishi machizukuri (Japan heritage and Onomichi Citizen heritage: Redevelopment of Onomichi City, utilising its history) [in Japanese]. In S. Ikenoue, T. Hanaoka, Y. Ishiguro, & S. Ishimori (Eds.), *What is Onomichi type destination management? Strategy of tourism for social innovation using heritage diversity* (pp. 23–28). Hokkaido University.

Rogerio-Candelera, M. A., Lazzari, M., & Cano, E. (Eds.). (2013). *Science and technology for the conservation of cultural heritage*. CRC Press.

Shochiku. (n.d.-a). *Kabuki: Overseas performance*. Available at: https://www.kabukiweb.net/news/overseas/. Accessed 29 Mar 2021.

Shochiku. (n.d.-b). *Shochiku to kabuki* (Shochiku and kabuki) [in Japanese]. Available at: https://www.shochiku.co.jp/play/kabuki/about/. Accessed 29 Mar 2021.

Sims, R. (2009). Food, place and authenticity: Local food and the sustainable tourism experience. *Journal of Sustainable Tourism, 17*(3), 321–336.

Suga, T., & Ogawa, M. (2018). Public administration of cultural properties and Japan heritage: A case study on Sakura City in the frontier of regional revitalization. *Chiba daigaku jinbunkokyo-gaku kenkyuronshu, 36,* 198–209.

UNESCO. (n.d.-a). *What is intangible cultural heritage?* Available at: https://ich.unesco.org/en/what-is-intangible-heritage-00003. Accessed 25 Mar 2021).

UNESCO. (n.d.-b). *Japan – Elements on the lists of intangible cultural heritage.* Available at: https://ich.unesco.org/en/state/japan-JP?info=elements-on-the-lists. Accessed 25 Mar 2021.

UNESCO. (n.d.-c). *Traditional skills, techniques and knowledge for the conservation and transmission of wooden architecture in Japan.* Available at: https://ich.unesco.org/en/RL/traditional-skills-techniques-and-knowledge-for-the-conservation-and-transmission-of-wooden-architecture-in-japan-01618. Accessed 25 Mar 2021.

UNESCO. (n.d.-d). *Dive into intangible cultural heritage! – Sustainable Development.* Available at: https://ich.unesco.org/en/dive&display=sdg#tabs. Accessed 25 Mar 2021.

4

Sustainability of Japan's Natural Heritage

1 Introduction

As noted in Sect. 3.1 of Chap. 1, in many cases, the concept of 'heritage' includes only 'cultural' and 'built' (man-made) heritage; however, 'natural' heritage is also contained in the notion of heritage in certain contexts as confirmed in the World Heritage scheme employed by the United Nations Educational, Scientific and Cultural Organization (hereafter UNESCO). Jimura (2019) also states that the idea of heritage should include natural heritage as well as cultural one. In order to explore sustainability and its management in the heritage sector in an exhaustive manner, this book follows this understanding and this chapter serves to discuss sustainability of Japan's natural heritage. As also demonstrated in Sect. 3.1 of Chap. 1, the Ministry of the Environment (hereafter MOE) is the main public stakeholder regarding Japan's natural landscapes, environment and resources. MOE is in charge of the conservation and management of natural heritage of Japan, applying various relevant legislations. Such laws include Act on Nature Conservation (*Shizenkankyo Hozen-ho*) and Act on Natural Parks (*Shizenkoen-ho*). In addition, Act on Landscapes (*Keikan-ho*) is also related to Japan's natural heritage, especially its landscapes, and jointly governed by MOE, Ministry of Agriculture, Forestry and Fisheries (hereafter MAFF) and Ministry of Land, Infrastructure, Transport and Tourism (hereafter MLIT). Concerning Japan's natural heritage and its utilisation for tourism purposes, Act on Ecotourism Promotion (*Ecotourism Suishin-ho*) is a key law that was enacted in 2007 and put in force in 2008, and is under the jurisdiction of MOE, MAFF, MLIT and Ministry of Education, Culture, Sports, Science and Technology (see Sect. 5 for details). Japan's municipalities at different levels may also constitute ordinances (*jorei*) to protect their natural heritage, considering the characteristics of their natural landscapes, environment and resources. For instance, Hirose River is a symbolic river of Sendai City (Miyagi Prefecture) and runs through its city centre. The city established Ordinance on Water Quality of Hirose River in 1974 to preserve clear stream and natural environment of the river.

The aforementioned Act on Natural Parks (*Shizenkoen-ho*) aims to enhance the conservation and utilisation of Japan's natural parks. Japan has three different kinds of natural parks, namely National Parks, Quasi-National Parks and Prefectural Natural Parks (see Sect. 2 for details). Like tangible and intangible cultural heritage of Japan (see Chaps. 2 and 3 respectively), several National Parks or properties situated in National Parks are conserved through international schemes as well as Japanese ones. To cite a case, three National Parks (Shiretoko, Ogasawara and Yakushima) are listed as natural World Heritage sites (hereafter WHSs). Moreover, four National Parks (Nikko, Fuji-Hakone-Izu, Yoshino-Kumano and Setonaikai) encompass properties designated as cultural WHSs namely Shrines and Temples of Nikko; Fujisan, sacred place and source of artistic inspiration; Sacred Sites and Pilgrimage Routes in the Kii Mountain Range; and, Itsukushima Shinto Shrine respectively (MOE, n.d.-a). Furthermore, the centre of Kushiro Wetland (7863 ha) of Kushiroshitsugen National Park (Hokkaido Prefecture) has been preserved by Ramsar Convention since 1980 (Kushiro International Wetland Centre, n.d.). This is another example of dual protection through domestic and international conservation initiatives.

Furthermore, domestic law and systems developed primarily for the conservation of Japan's cultural heritage also work for the protection of Japan's natural heritage. As Sect. 8 of Chap. 2 shows, Monuments

4 Sustainability of Japan's Natural Heritage

(*Kinenbutsu*) is one of the main categories of heritage that is conserved through the application of Act on Protection of Cultural Properties (*Bunkazai Hogo-ho*). Monuments comprise subsequent three sub categories:

* Historic Sites (*Shiseki*) – Shell mounds, ancient mounded tombs, ruins of castle quarters, castles or forts, former private residences, and other sites of a high historic or scientific value to Japan.
* Places of Scenic Beauty (*Meisho*) – Gardens, bridges, embankments, gorges, seashores, mountains, and other places of scenic beauty of a high artistic or aesthetic value to Japan.
* Natural Monuments (*Tennen Kinenbutsu*) – Animals, plants, minerals, and geological features of a high scientific value to Japan.

As confirmed above, the two sub categories, Places of Scenic Beauty and Natural Monuments, include properties that are usually comprehended and treated as natural heritage rather than cultural heritage (e.g. mountains and animals). Concerning all of the three sub categories, the properties with particularly high value for Japan are awarded an outstanding status of Special Historic Sites (*Tokubetsu Shiseki*), Special Places of Scenic Beauty (*Tokubetsu Meisho*), or Special Natural Monuments (*Tokubetsu Tennen Kinenbutsu*) by the Japanese Government. In light of these, this chapter centres around the natural landscapes and environment listed as Special Places of Scenic Beauty, and flora and fauna designated as Special Natural Monuments (see Sect. 3 for details) in terms of their sustainability and practice of *mottainai* spirit.

In addition to the aforementioned various public bodies, regulations and schemes, the conservation and sustainability of Japan's natural heritage are also supported by initiative led by non-governmental organisations (hereafter NGOs). To cite a case, the Japan Geopark Committee (hereafter JGC) designates Japan's geoparks, support their listing as the United Nations Educational, Scientific and Cultural Organization (hereafter UNESCO) Global Geoparks, and evaluate and give advice about activities conducted there (JGC, 2017) (see Sect. 4 for details).

2 National Parks, Quasi-National Parks and Prefectural Natural Parks

2.1 Overview

This section discusses Japan's natural parks, namely National Parks, Quasi-National Parks and Prefectural Natural Parks in view of their sustainability and *mottainai*. As the starting point of this section, similarities and differences between these three sorts of Japan's natural parks are summarised in Table 4.1. As of June 2021, there are 34 National Parks, 56 Quasi-National Parks and 311 Prefectural Natural Parks across all eight geographical regions of Japan (MOE n.d.-a; Natural Parks Foundation (hereafter NPF), n.d.). The areas designated as natural parks account for more than 14% of the national territory, and this proportion is higher than many other countries (MOE, n.d.-b). In addition, over 1.3 million hectares of sea area are included as part of National Parks or Quasi-National Parks, and this accounts for around 4% of Japan's territorial sea (MOE, n.d.-b). Since established, Japan's three different kinds of natural parks have been playing a central role in the conservation of Japan's natural landscapes and environment (NPF, n.d.). As shown in Sect. 2.1 of Chap. 1, the world's first national park, the Yellowstone National Park (USA), was founded in 1872. On the other hand, the history of Japan's National Parks commenced in the twentieth century when Act on National Parks (*Kokuritsukoen-ho*) was enacted in 1931. Following this, three areas were listed as Japan's first National Parks in 1934. After amended several times, the act was replaced with Act on Natural Parks

Table 4.1 Japan's natural parks

Type	Main relevant law/regulation	Listing body	Management body
National Parks	Act on Natural Parks (*Shizenkoen-ho*)	Japanese Government	Japanese Government
Quasi-National Parks	Act on Natural Parks (*Shizenkoen-ho*)	Japanese Government	Prefecture
Prefectural Natural Parks	Prefectural ordinances	Prefecture	Prefecture

Source: Author

(*Shizenkoen-ho*) in 1957. Act on Natural Parks covers a newly introduced concept and category of Quasi-National Parks as well as those of National Parks. Japan's National Park system aims to enhance conservation and utilisation of Japan's exceptional natural beauty and landscapes, and ultimately intends to contribute to health, recreation and edification of Japanese citizens (MOE, n.d.-b).

2.2   Main Features of National Parks in Japan

Japan's National Parks have two main features (MOE, n.d.-b). First, National Parks in Japan encompass a wide variety of places and properties with diverse purposes, including where people live, work and visit (e.g. farmlands and religious sites), applying a certain level of restrictions on the usage of and activities on lands and properties situated in National Parks (MOE, n.d.-b). This approach towards the designation of National Parks is also confirmed in other countries typically the UK and South Korea (MOE, n.d.-b). On the other hand, in principle, National Parks in nations such as the USA, Canada and Australia are established by purchasing the grounds to be listed as National Parks, and such areas are used for the purpose of National Parks only (MOE, n.d.-b). This difference affects the numbers of inhabitants residing in National Parks. The numbers of people living in National Parks are around 0.65 million in Japan and around 0.29 million in the UK (MOE, n.d.-b). On the other hand, only about 20,000 people reside in National Parks in the USA (MOE, n.d.-b). This is noteworthy as the population of the USA (approx. 332 million) is much larger than those of Japan (approx. 125 million) or the UK (approx. 68 million). Another big difference is that compared with the approach taken by Japan, the UK and South Korea, the approach adopted by the USA, Canada and Australia would be more advantageous for the conservation and management of National Parks as a whole, although the latter would be more costly than the former. That is chiefly because; the national governments (e.g. National Park Service (hereafter

(NPS) (USA)) own most of the lands and properties comprising National Parks, and this fact would be beneficial for overall control of National Parks and application of stricter/new restrictions on the utilisation of and activities on lands and properties in National Parks.

The second main feature of Japan's National Parks is that precisely speaking, its National Park scheme intends to conserve Japan's natural landscapes rather than its natural environment or biodiversity (MOE, n.d.-b). In other words, Act on Nature Conservation (*Shizenkankyo Hozen-ho*) is more relevant to the preservation of Japan's natural environment or biodiversity than Act on Natural Parks (*Shizenkoen-ho*). Nevertheless, Act on Natural Parks and three types of natural parks still contribute to the conservation of Japan's natural environment and biodiversity, because generally people view and appreciate natural landscapes not just as sceneries but as a broader notion that embraces both natural environment and biodiversity (MOE, n.d.-b).

2.3 Sustainability Management of National Parks in Japan

The triple bottom line (hereafter TBL) of sustainability is an essential notion for diverse types of protected areas, including national parks, across the world. For instance, financial resources needed for maintenance of National Parks in Japan are the matter connected with economic sustainability, a pillar of TBL of sustainability (De Vos et al., 2016). Considering the aims and tasks of Japan's National Parks, it is clear that the parks are directly associated with environmental sustainability, another aspect of TBL of sustainability (Rodríguez-Rodríguez & Martínez-Vega, 2017). In light of the aims and characteristics of National Parks of Japan, moreover, they are also closely related to socio-cultural sustainability, the other pillar of TBL of sustainability' (Cottrell et al., 2013).

With regard to economic sustainability of Japan's National Parks, MOE has a considerable amount of budget for National Parks every financial year (April to March in Japan). The budget consists of funds for public projects and those for non-public projects. The amount of the budget for public works has been much larger than that for non-public works, although overall the former has been decreasing and the latter has been increasing in recent years (MOE, n.d.-c). MOE's budget for Japan's National Parks can also be classified into five groups by purpose as follows:

- Developing conservation and management plans of National Parks
- Implementing popularisation and enlightenment activities about National Parks
- Promoting appropriate use of National Parks amongst visitors and users
- Conducting activities to protect domestic species and eliminate alien species in National Parks, and restoring natural environment of the parks
- Carrying out conservation and management activities of National Parks with local communities and volunteering workers (MOE, n.d.-c).

In addition, every year MOE makes calls for applications for subsidies open to municipalities of Japan regarding their plans to improve facilities and services at National Parks. For example, municipalities' plans to enhance digitalisation of exhibitions at relevant National Parks are eligible to be subsidised in the financial year of 2021 (April 2021 to March 2022).

Concerning socio-cultural sustainability of Japan's National Parks, visitor numbers is an important information that signifies relationships between National Parks and Japanese people. Generally and historically, National Parks of Japan do not seem to have been fully utilised by its people as places to enjoy leisure and recreational activities. In fact, the numbers of visitors to National Parks in Japan are (much) lower than those to national parks in other countries (e.g. Canada). Furthermore, the number of visitors to Japan's National Parks has been decreasing in recent years due to changes in social trends and people's needs (MOE, n.d.-d). A decline in visitor numbers may be understood as a positive change if only preservation of natural landscapes, environment and biodiversity should be considered. As discussed in Sect. 2.1, however, Japan's National Parks intend to enhance not only the conservation of such natural resources but also their utilisation for Japanese people's well-being, recreation and edification. Given this, a decrease in visitor numbers is not a welcome situation for Japan's National Parks. This may also trigger a decline of tourism industry in nearby local communities and/or local economy as a whole, and make upkeep and management of National Parks challenging (MOE, n.d.-d). This circumstance also indicates that the strength of interrelations between National Parks and Japanese people, including local residents and visitors, might have also been weakened. This is worrying as it implies that socio-cultural sustainability of Japan's National Parks has also been weakening. In relation to socio-cultural sustainability of national parks, accessibility and universal design standards have been established as concepts commonly significant for national parks in many countries. To cite a case, NPS, a public managing agency for national parks in the USA, has a web page specifically for accessibility and universal design standards (NPS, 2021). Following such a world trend, since 2013, Japan's National Parks have also started working to enhance the level of accessibility of visitors with diverse needs by improving their services and facilities, considering universal design standards. For example, Japan's National Parks rent supporting equipment for disabled visitors and some of them also broadened wooden paths on the ground or water of the parks (MOE, n.d.-d).

In order to strengthen environmental sustainability, Japan's National Parks have been developing and implementing a range of ideas, often supported by local communities and volunteering workers. In fact, there are a lot of examples regarding controlling and restricting activities that can threaten or damage National Parks (MOE, n.d.-d). In principle, building of new structures and expansion of existing structures are highly regulated in National Parks in Japan. Moreover, logging, collection of soils and stones, picking of plants and capture of animals are also controlled tightly. More specific strategies targeting conservation and/or regeneration of certain features of National Parks are also confirmed. To cite a case, MOE supports setting up devices on the sea bed of Iriomote-Ishigaki National Park (Okinawa Prefecture) in order to help implantation of corals (MOE, n.d.-d). Measures for environmental sustainability are also adopted regarding visitor's activities and moves within National Parks. For instance, usage of snowmobiles and off-road vehicles are restricted at highly protected areas in National Parks. Furthermore, exploring National Parks by private car is also prohibited in certain areas of National Parks during particular periods since 1974 to protect flora and fauna vulnerable to air pollution (MOE, n.d.-d).

2.4 *Mottainai* Spirit and National Parks in Japan

Currently, activities that are understood as embodiment of the *mottainai* spirit are found in a number of natural areas not only in Japan but also across the globe. This trend seems to have become prominent in foreign countries during the past 15–20 years since Professor Wangari Maathai, a Kenyan environmentalist and Nobel peace prize winner, encountered and was impressed by the notion and spirit of *mottainai* when she visited Japan in 2004 (see Sect. 2.3 of Chap. 1). A wide range of activities that mirror the spirit of *mottainai* can be found in Japan's National Parks and other natural areas. These activities are generally planned as conservation, awareness-raising and/or enlightenment activities, and tend to be implemented and supported by various public (e.g. local governments at different levels), private (e.g. businesses) and/or non-profit organisations (hereafter NPOs). It should also be noted that in reality different types of organisations work together to organise and implement a variety of *mottainai* activities across Japan. For example, Fukushima Prefecture has been engaging in diverse enlightenment activities in the prefecture, teaming up with environmental NPOs, building 'Mottainai Network Fukushima' and advocating '*mottainai*' as the network's slogan in order to develop and expand environmental practices in natural areas in the prefecture (MOE, n.d.-e). Moreover, natural areas such as local natural parks are also utilised by teachers and instructors as learning resources for environmental education for students in primary, junior high and high schools in Japan. For instance, disposable wooden chopsticks made from timber from forest thinning can be used as a learning material and can be looked at in terms of the spirit of *mottainai*. Teachers and/or instructors may ask students whether students know how disposal wooden chopsticks are usually made and to what extent students think the spirit of *mottainai* is embedded and embodied in the production of disposable wooden chopsticks from timber from forest thinning to produce.

2.5 Tourism and National Parks in Japan

As mentioned in Sect. 2.3, the number of visitors to Japan's National Parks has been declining in recent years because of changes in social trends and people's demands (MOE, n.d.-d). Historically, the number of visitors to Japan's natural parks, namely National Parks, Quasi-National Parks and Prefectural Natural Parks had remained at the same level between 1975 and 1983 (MOE, n.d.-f). The number started increasing gradually since 1984 and reached its peak, over 1 billion, in 1991 (MOE, n.d.-f). However, the number has stated decreasing since 1992 and this trend has continued at least until 2018 (MOE, n.d.-f). In fact, the number of visitors to Japan's natural parks in 2018 was around 0.91 billion decreased by 0.4% from 2017 (MOE, n.d.-f). As for reasons and backgrounds of the increase between 1984 and 1991 and the decrease since 1992, Numata's (2019) consideration is insightful. Numata (2019) suggests that the disposable money of Japanese people for leisure, including the costs to visit natural parks, had increased between 1984 and 1991 as Japan had experienced economic bubble during this period, but they have become less affluent after Japan's economic bubble burst in 1992. The author also regards it as a main reason of a decline in the number of visitors to natural parks in Japan. The other key reason indicated by Numata (2019) is that Japanese people, especially those living in urban or suburban areas, have had less leisure time and cannot afford to enjoy nature visiting natural parks. Instead, handier ways to feel nature such as home gardening have become popular amongst city dwellers (Numata, 2019). In fact, several friends of the author residing in Japan's urban areas started enjoying home gardening recently, growing vegetables and/or herbs at back garden or even at balcony of apartment houses.

Nevertheless, it could be stated that Japan's natural parks, particularly National Parks, are still primary destinations for Japanese citizens to enjoy and appreciate a variety of natural heritage of Japan. In 2018, in fact, the numbers of visitors to 34 National Parks, 56 Quasi-National Parks and 311 Prefectural Natural Parks were around 0.37 billion, 0.29 billion and 0.25 billion respectively (MOE, n.d.-f). In 2018, the top three National Parks in terms of visitor numbers were Fuji-Hakone-Izu,

Setonaikai, and Joshin'etsukogen, and their visitor numbers were about 136 million, 43 million and 22 million respectively (MOE, n.d.-f). As MOE (n.d.-f) suggests, a key reason for their high popularity seems to be their locations and accessibility from extensive urban areas. Fuji-Hakone-Izu extends over four prefectures (Shizuoka, Yamanashi, Tokyo and Kanagawa) and encompasses Mount Fuji and two areas famous for hot springs (Hakone and Izu). Overall, these areas are easy to access by coach and/or train as well as by car from Tokyo Metropolitan Prefecture and its surrounding prefectures in the Kanto region. On the other hand, Setonaikai is the National Park surrounding the Seto Inland Sea and extends over 11 prefectures in the western part of Japan (Kansai, Chugoku, Shikoku and Kyushu regions). Many of popular tourist destinations within the National Park can be accessed by public transport, for instance Tomonoura (Hiroshima Prefecture) by train and bus, Shimonoseki (Yamaguchi Prefecture) by train and the Shodo Island by ferry.

Visitors to Japan's natural parks can enjoy a variety of outdoor activities, including hiking, trekking, climbing, kayaking and birdwatching. Diverse facilities and services are available to support and control visitor activities. These facilities include visitor centres, parking spaces, camp sites, toilets, signposts, interpretation panels, mountain trails and boardwalks. As suggested in Sect. 2.3, universal design standards have been increasingly considered in recent years when these facilities (e.g. toilets and boardwalks) are built or renovated. On the other hand, nature guides are a typical example of services available for visitors in National Parks. According to several market reports, the needs for outdoor goods and activities have been increasing amongst people in Japan during the COVID-19 pandemic. In fact, however, the number of visitors to National Parks have dropped tremendously because of COVID-19 as many facilities and services available there have been suspended. This caused a huge decrease in the amount of income raised through tourism (e.g. parking fees) and many National Parks have been struggling with a lack of budget for cleaning up activities and maintenance of footpaths and boardwalks (Mainichi Shimbun 2020). To improve this situation, MOE has been making the most of the campaign called *Kokuritsu Koen Mankitsu Project* (Fully Enjoying National Parks Project). The project commenced in 2016, involving eight National Parks, and aims to establish Japan's National Parks as world-class destinations that can lure visitors from all over the world (Travel Voice, 2021). As part of this project, for instance, MOE (n.d.-g) tries to promote National Parks as places for 'workation' during and post the COVID-19 pandemic.

3 Monuments (*Kinenbutsu*)

As stated in Sect. 1, Monuments (*Kinenbutsu*) is one of the main categories of Japan's cultural heritage that is conserved through the use of Act on Protection of Cultural Properties (*Bunkazai Hogo-ho*). Amongst three sub categories comprising Monuments, two, namely Places of Scenic Beauty (*Meisho*) and Natural Monuments (*Tennen Kinenbutsu*) contain the elements that are seen as natural heritage. Thus, these two are set as main focuses of this section.

3.1 Places of Scenic Beauty (*Meisho*)

Places of Scenic Beauty (*Meisho*) include Japan's gardens, bridges, embankments, gorges, seashores, mountains, and other places of scenic beauty of a high artistic or aesthetic value. In other words, Places of Scenic Beauty consist of nature-oriented ones (e.g. gorges, seashores and mountains) and culture-oriented ones (e.g. gardens, bridges and embankments). The Agency of Cultural Affairs (hereafter ACA) (2013) states that culture-oriented ones have been developed based on nature-oriented ones. For instance, gardens can be understood as 'recreation' and 'miniaturisation' of nature, more specifically beautiful landscapes or sceneries, in an artificial way; whilst, bridges and embankments are man-made structures, and are designed and built to fit and work well with their surrounding natural environment. In summary, ACA (2013) views that many elements that are recognised as Places of Scenic Beauty have been formed through a solid integration of nature and culture. In this sense, Places of Scenic Beauty have many common points with Cultural Landscapes (*Bunkateki Keikan*), one of main groups of Japan's cultural heritage (see Sect. 4 of Chap. 2 for details). However, it should be noted that Places of Scenic Beauty highlight their ornamental value, whilst Cultural Landscapes focuses on their value as evidence of interactions between human activities and nature (ACA, 2013).

Places of Scenic Beauty (*Meisho*) are designated by the Japanese Government or prefectures. Of Monuments listed by the central government, particularly significant ones are given the status of Special Places of Scenic Beauty (*Tokubetsu Meisho*). According to ACA (n.d.), there are 387 Places of Scenic Beauty and 36 Special Places of Scenic Beauty at the time of writing. Moreover, Japan has more than 1000 Places of Scenic Beauty listed by prefectures (ACA, 2013). The number of designated properties has been growing gradually and steadily, and this trend appears to indicate that a wider variety of culture-oriented and nature-oriented properties have been protected through the listing as Places of Scenic Beauty. Nevertheless, ACA has been concerned with conservation and sustainability of the places and properties that own a high value to Japan/ prefectures but are yet to be protected through the Places of Scenic Beauty scheme (ACA, 2013). ACA (2013) regards urbanisation and development of the areas as main reasons of threats they have been facing. Between 2011 and 2013, ACA conducted a survey with Japan's municipalities regarding the places and properties listed as Places of Scenic Beauty and those not listed but with high value (ACA, 2013). The major outcome of this nation-wide survey is an extensive list of Places of Scenic Beauty and their equivalents that was created based on the information submitted by municipalities (ACA, 2013). This list helps the Japanese Government to grasp the latest and exhaustive information about these places and properties and to shape future direction for their conservation and sustainability management.

Indeed, Places of Scenic Beauty and their equivalents should be maintained well and passed on to future generations through proper conservation activities and sustainability management. However, it should also be remembered that not only cultural environment but also natural environment have kept and will keep changing as far as humankind continue to interact with them and people's activities keep occurring in these environments (Jimura, 2019; Wise & Jimura, 2020), and Places of Scenic Beauty are not exceptions. In relation to this point, a representative example of people's activities at Places of Scenic Beauty is tourism. It is clear that Places of Scenic Beauty, especially Special Places of Scenic Beauty, have an ability to lure a number of visitors like the case of Japan's natural parks indicates (see Sect. 2.5 of this chapter). With regard to the notion of *mottainai*, Places of Scenic Beauty do not practice the spirit of *mottainai* sufficiently, if they are not well visited or appreciated by day trippers or tourists. That is because; the utilisation of Places of Scenic Beauty in a sustainable manner can make contribution to economic sustainability (e.g. income raised through tourism) and socio-cultural sustainability (e.g. solid and meaningful presence in local and wider communities) of themselves and their surrounding areas without compromising their environmental sustainability. To cite a case, Itsukushima (Hiroshima Prefecture) is widely acknowledged as one of the top three must-see landscapes of Japan, and is listed as both Special Places of Scenic Beauty (*Tokubetsu Meisho*) and Special Historic Sites (*Tokubetsu Shiseki*). To cope with increasing environmental pressures caused by a rise of visitor numbers coming to the Itsukushima Island by ferry, the mayor of Hatsukaichi City, where Itsukushima belongs to, decided to introduce visitor tax of 100 Japanese Yen per person per visit (CNN Travel, 2019). The city intends to spend financial resources gained through its visitor tax for various environmental/tourism-related purposes, including installation of rubbish collection points for visitors, refurbishment of public toilets, and spatial separation of visitor and residential zones, in order to be a more sustainable tourist destination (Hatsukaichi City, 2020).

3.2 Natural Monuments (*Tennen Kinenbutsu*)

Like Places of Scenic Beauty (*Meisho*), Natural Monuments (*Tennen Kinenbutsu*) can also be designated by prefectures as well as the Japanese Government, and particularly significant ones are awarded the position of Special Natural Monuments (*Tokubetsu Tennen Kinenbutsu*). At the time of writing, Japan has 958 Natural Monuments listed by the central government and 75 Special Natural Monuments (ACA, n.d.). Natural Monuments include animals, plants, minerals and geological characteristics of a great scientific value for Japan. In relation to National Monuments and nature-oriented Places of Scenic Beauty, there has been a debate on the appropriateness, effectiveness and limitations in conserving such natural heritage through the application of Act on Protection of Cultural Properties (*Bunkazai Hogo-ho*), the law created primarily for the conservation of cultural heritage and under jurisdiction of ACA (Neki, 1995). However, Neki (1995) also mentions that Act on Protection of Cultural Properties can work with relevant laws that are under jurisdiction of MOE such as Act on Nature Conservation (*Shizenkankyo Hozen-ho*) and Act on Natural Parks (*Shizenkoen-ho*) in a complementary way to safeguard National Monuments and nature-oriented Places of Scenic Beauty. Moreover, Act on Conservation of Endangered Species of Wild Fauna and Flora (*Shu no Hozon-ho*) was established in 1992. This law is conjointly administered by MOE, MAFF and Ministry of Economy, Trade and Industry and can also be effective for the conservation of National Monuments and nature-oriented Places of Scenic Beauty.

Compared with other types of Japan's natural heritage and its conservation categories and systems, the most distinctive feature of Natural Monuments (*Tennen Kinenbutsu*) and Special Natural Monuments (*Tokubetsu Tennen Kinenbutsu*) is the inclusion of specific animal and plant species. Environmental sustainability of these animal and plant species has been maintained across Japan through not only the application of Act on Protection of Cultural Properties (*Bunkazai Hogo-ho*) but also various measures planned and conducted by relevant municipalities and associations (e.g. prefectural ordinances). Besides, it is also true that these animal and plant species, particularly those listed as Natural Monuments, have also been utilised for educational and tourism purposes, and such usage has been contributing to their economic and socio-cultural sustainability. Regarding specific animal species designated as Natural Monuments, fireflies of Misato and their birthplace (Tokushima Prefecture) has been used for both educational and tourism purposes. Yoshinogawa City where the Misato area is situated in has a public museum called Misato Fireflies Museum. The museum provides local pupils as well as visitors with displays and interpretation about five different types of fireflies that can be observed there. Furthermore, Misato Fireflies Festival is held between the end of May and the mid- June annually, although the festival was cancelled in 2020 and 2021 due to the COVID-19 pandemic (Awanavi, 2021). The festival can also be seen as evidence that can prove the utilisation of the fireflies as an attraction factor for visitors as well as local residents. On the other hand, weeping cherry trees of Kakunodate (Akita Prefecture) is a good example of the use of peculiar plant species listed as Natural Monuments for tourism. These weeping cherry trees are a symbol of Semboku City in spring and appreciated by local inhabitants and visitors. In 2021, Kakunodate Cherry Blossom Festival was held between the mid- April and early May, although various measures were adopted (e.g. enforcement of face coverings) and limitations were imposed (cancellation of lighting-up of cherry blossoms at night) because of the COVID-19 pandemic to ensure the health and safety of people (Tazawako-Kakunodate, 2021).

As a whole, the level of utilisation of animal and plant species that are inscribed as Special Natural Monuments (*Tokubetsu Tennen Kinenbutsu*) for educational and tourism purposes seem to be rather limited compared to those designated as Natural Monuments (*Tennen Kinenbutsu*). That is because; there is a strong need to maintain and enhance their environmental sustainability owing to their scarcity and invaluableness. Nevertheless, examples of utilisations of plant and animal species listed as Special Natural Monuments for educational and tourism purposes can still be found in Japan. For instance, algae balls (*marimo*) of Lake Akan (Hokkaido Prefecture) are a plant species designated as Special Natural Monuments. Aegagropila linnaei grown in Lake Akan has a spherical shape and furry appearance, and is very famous amongst Japanese people as one of Hokkaido's icons. Thus, it is natural that the algae balls of Lake Akan are also recognised as a key attraction factor of Lake Akan. In fact, small algae balls are bottled and sold at souvenir shops by Lake Akan. Indeed, manufacturers of the bottlings or souvenir shops do not do anything illegal as the algae used for the bottlings are collected at different lakes and shaped as algae balls manually. However, some visitors may think that they are purchasing authentic algae balls of Lake Akan due to such a misleading situation. Visitors need to do spend more time and money to see and experience authentic algae balls of Lake Akan. A typical way to do so is to visit the Chului Island in the lake by sightseeing boat and call in Marimo Exhibition and Observation Centre (hereafter

MEOC) (MEOC, n.d.). On the other hand, Japanese giant salamanders are an animal species listed as Special Natural Monuments. Like other animal species designated as Special Natural Monuments (e.g. Japanese crested ibises), the vast majority of Japanese people do not have opportunities to see Japanese giant salamanders in their daily lives. However, the people still have chances to see and appreciate this animal in tourism and/or educational settings. For example, the author visited the World Fresh Water Aquarium (Gifu Prefecture) in 2020 and saw and learned about Japanese giant salamander (see Fig. 4.1). In summary, making Natural Monuments and Special Natural Monuments available and accessible for educational and/or tourism purposes through the aforementioned various ways whilst conserving them can also be understood as the reflection of *mottainai* spirit.

Fig. 4.1 Japanese giant salamander at the World Fresh Water Aquarium. (Source: Author)

4 Geoparks in Japan

It could be stated that nowadays 'geopark' is a well-established and familiar concept in academia and real world, and can also be seen as a global notion (McKeever & Zouros, 2005). Although many different definitions of geoparks are suggested, these definitions do not differ much and the mission common to these definitions is the protection of geological heritage. It is also confirmed from several definitions that generally geoparks focus not only on their conservation in a sustainable manner but also on their utilisation and contribution to economic and socio-cultural development and sustainability of the areas in and around geoparks (McKeever & Zouros, 2005). In the author's view, generally, these features of geoparks are similar to national parks, although Guo and Chung (2016) deem that geoparks tend to focus more on their usage than their conservation compared with national parks. The term 'geopark' has more than 30-year history. 'Protection of geosites', 'fostering geotourism' and 'promotion of local economic development' were set as the main aims of Gerolstein District Geopark (Germany) when it was established in 1989 (Henriques & Brilha, 2017). Geotourism can be defined as 'tourism which focuses on an area's geology and landscape as the basis of fostering sustainable tourism development' (Dowling, 2013, 59). Today, the aforementioned three are widely accepted by geoparks across the world, including those in Japan, as major three pillars of the mission of geoparks. Currently, a number of nations in different regions of the world, including Japan, have geoparks in their territories, designating the areas with significant geological features through their own geopark schemes.

UNESCO is a key international organisation when the development of geopark initiative at global level and international network of geoparks are examined. The history of UNESCO's engagement with geoparks commenced in 2001 (Global Geoparks Network (hereafter GGN), 2018). Three years later, in 2004, representatives of eight Chinese and 17 European geoparks met at UNESCO headquarters in Paris to launch GGN (Jimura, 2019). This network enables geoparks in different countries to exchange their knowledge and experiences and foster mutual cooperations (UNESCO, 2017a). It is innovative and noteworthy because both Western and Eastern knowledge and experiences were incorporated in the initial stage of GGN (Jimura, 2019). In 2015, 195 Member States of UNESCO ratified the creation of a new label, the UNESCO Global Geoparks (hereafter UGGs), at its 38th General Conference (GGN, 2018). UNESCO (2017a) defines UGGs as 'single, unified geographical areas where sites and landscapes of international geological significance are managed with a holistic concept of protection, education and sustainable development'. UGGs have four fundamental features, namely, 'geological heritage of international value', 'management', 'visibility', and 'networking', and they are requirements for geoparks around the world to be inscribed as UGGs (UNESCO, 2017b). The ratification of establishment of UGGs means that the national governments of the aforementioned Member States officially acknowledge that it is significant for them to manage their geological sites and landscapes with exceptional value in a holistic manner (UNESCO, 2017a). UNESCO intends to enhance the levels of conservation and usage of geological heritage across the globe through UGGs. To this end, UNESCO works closely with GGN to provide Member States with necessary supports that are essential for geoparks in their domains to obtain UGG status.

As signified above and also stated in Sect. 1, Japan has its own conservation and listing system for its geological heritage named 'the Japanese National Geoparks' (hereafter JNGs) and domestic network called 'the Japanese Geoparks Network' (hereafter JGN). In addition, JGC was established in 2008 and is officially certified by the Japanese National Commission for UNESCO as the Japanese National Committee that governs JNGs' application procedures to be listed as UGGs (JGC, 2020). JGC is also in charge of designation of geoparks in Japan as JNGs and having JNG status is essential for Japan's geoparks to apply for the listing as UGGs (JGC 2020). JGC also makes sure that geoparks in Japan follow the Operational Guidelines for UGGs set by UNESCO (JGC, 2020). On the other hand, JGN is a non-profit organisation established in 2010 and serves as a networking platform for geoparks across Japan (JGN, 2021). As of April 2021, JGN comprises of members (nine UGGs and 34 JNGs) and associate members (13 geoparks in Japan aiming to be recognised as JNGs and then UGGs) (JGN, 2021), and supports JNGs and geoparks in Japan in various ways. As implied above, the main aim of

JGN is to function as a focal point for its members and associate member to share and exchange their knowledge and experiences, and in fact JGN has been achieving its key aim (Watanabe, 2011).

In 2010, JNG held its first annual conference at Itoigawa (Niigata Prefecture). The conference had presentations on research outcomes about and reports on activities at various geoparks in Japan. Itoigawa is one of the first three JNGs that were listed as UGGs in 2009. As indicated by the programme of this conference, an increasing number of key stakeholders such as local people, local governments and researchers have become interested in geoparks in Japan (Watanabe, 2011). This trend is crucial for socio-cultural and environmental sustainability of Japan's geoparks. Along with activities for conservation and education, tourism is also key activities for Japan's geoparks. In fact, the quality of tourism facilities and services are one of the assessment criteria in the evaluation of geoparks that apply for JNG or UGG status (Watanabe, 2011). Nonetheless, geoparks in Japan were not established well as tourist destinations at least as of 2010, as confirmed by the findings from visitor surveys conducted by Fukami and Arima (2011) at four different geoparks in the Kyushu region of Japan. With regard to this, tourism, especially geotourism, at geoparks in Japan should be developed further, considering their economic, socio-cultural and environmental sustainability.

Indeed, 'fostering geotourism' is one of the aforementioned three main objectives of geoparks together with 'protection of geosites' and 'promotion of local economic development'. These three key targets are interrelated each other and associated with economic, socio-cultural and environmental sustainability of geoparks and its surrounding communities. More specifically, well-conserved geosites in geoparks or geoparks as a whole can attract people who enjoy geotourism activities there, and this can bring economic benefits to local communities, businesses and governments if all are implemented in a sustainable manner. Concerning UGGs, moreover, their essential characteristics include 'geological heritage of international value', 'management', 'visibility', and 'networking'. Of these four, 'visibility' is closely connected with geotourism. That is because; UGGs needs to have good level of visibility to stimulate geotourism in the areas where UGGs sit and this indicates that local residents and visitors can easily find the information on UGGs they are

4   Sustainability of Japan's Natural Heritage

interested in or want to visit (UNESCO, 2017b). To this end, all UGGs are expected to provide visitors as well as local inhabitants with useful information in a clear manner via various types of media, including dedicated websites, informative leaflets and detailed maps (UNESCO 2017b). For example, all of nine UGGs situated in Japan have their own dedicated websites with a variety of information as of June 2021, and this should be effective to increase the level of visibility of UGGs in Japan amongst prospective visitors.

Furthermore, the spirit of *mottainai* is well reflected in the three main aims of geoparks and four key features of UGGs as they intend not only to conserve their outstanding geological heritage but also to fully utilise them for educational and tourism purposes. In relation to tourism, visitors' active engagements with geological heritage are encouraged through diverse measures. To cite a case, Sakurajima-Kinkowan, a JNG in Kagoshima Prefecture, puts a slogan '*Nagameru dakedewa mottainai*' ('Let's fully enjoy the JNG by experiencing a range of activities') on its website. In other words, this JNG encourages their visitors not only to appreciate unique geological characteristics but also to explore the park and its surrounding areas and/or join taster sessions and guided tours (Sakurajima-Kinkowan Geopark, 2021). It should also be noted that UGGs are expected to contribute to UN Sustainable Development Goals (hereafter SDGs) as an initiative run by UNESCO, a specialised agency of UN. For instance, the above-mentioned Itoigawa Geopark has been making contribution to six SDGs through diverse activities as follows:

- SDG 4 (Quality Education) and SDG 13 (Climate Action): Disaster prevention and education (e.g. Implementation of education for disaster prevention at Mount Niigata-Yakeyama),
- SDG 8 (Decent Work and Economic Growth) and SDG 11 (Sustainable Cities and Communities): Promotion of regional development (e.g. Training of local guides and arrangement of guided tours), and
- SDG 14 (Life below Water) and SDG 15 (Life on Land): Preservation and conservation (e.g. Capture of black basses (alien species) at Taumigaike Pond to protect local dragonflies) (Itoigawa Geopark, n.d.).

5   Act on Ecotourism Promotion (*Ecotourism Suishin-ho*)

As demonstrated in Sect. 4, the focus of geoparks and geotourism is the conservation and utilisation of geo heritage, an abiotic factor; whilst, the core of national parks and tourism there is the preservation and use of flora and fauna, a biotic factor (see Sect. 2). The other main type of natural heritage in Japan examined in this chapter is Monuments (*Kinenbutsu*) (see Sect. 3) and this group includes cultural, natural and geo heritage of Japan. As stated in Sect. 1, Act on Ecotourism Promotion (*Ecotourism Suishin-ho*) was established in 2007 and enforced in 2008. The act is unique, because, to date, it is the only Japanese national law that was developed for a specific kind of tourism, ecotourism. As can be confirmed through the targets of Act on Protection of Cultural Properties (*Bunkazai Hogo-ho*), some sorts of Japan's natural heritage are conserved through the legal framework created primarily for the conservation of Japan's cultural heritage. Like the aforementioned category of Monuments shows, moreover, cultural and natural heritage can be included in the same group for conservation. Such an integrated approach can also be confirmed in a key notion in Act on Ecotourism Promotion, which is called 'Specific Natural Tourism Resources' (*Tokutei Shizen Kanko Shigen*). According to Article 2 of the act, Specific Natural Tourism Resources comprise two sorts of tourism resources as follows:

1. 'Tourism resources relevant to habitats of flora and fauna or other natural environments', and
2. 'Tourism resources relevant to manners and customs closely associated with natural environments and those deeply connected with traditional livelihood cultures'.

It is clear that the above-mentioned integrated approach to the conservation and usage of cultural and natural heritage is confirmed in the second type of Specific Natural Tourism Resources.

The other key characteristic of the act is the formation of 'Ecotourism Promotion Council'. According to Article 5 of Act on Ecotourism

Promotion (*Ecotourism Suishin-ho*), municipalities of Japan (i.e. cities, towns and villages) can organise their Ecotourism Promotion Councils, involving key stakeholders of ecotourism at local level such as local councils, specific businesses, local residents, NPOs, experts in Specific Natural Tourism Resources of local areas or in tourism, and land owners. The council intends to create grand designs of ecotourism promotion for local areas and coordinate clerical works required for the promotion. Furthermore, the municipalities can apply for Japanese Government's designation of their grand designs of ecotourism promotion for local areas (Article 6). The Japanese Government can approve the grand designs submitted by municipalities if (1) they follow the principles of Act on Ecotourism Promotion, and (2) the measures included in the grand designs are appropriate and effective to conserve natural and cultural resources to be listed by municipalities as Special Natural Tourism Resources. Municipalities can select their Special Natural Tourism Resources once the national government endorses municipalities' grand designs (Article 8).

For selection and approval of Special Natural Tourism Resources, municipalities need to study on natural and cultural resources of their areas, and work collaboratively with key stakeholders such as land owners of habitats of flora and fauna to be listed as Special Natural Tourism Resources. This series of processes can improve the level of socio-cultural and environmental sustainability of natural and cultural resources to be designated as Special Natural Tourism Resources, if it goes well in a harmonious manner. However, it should also be remembered that aspirations and views of members of the aforementioned Ecotourism Promotion Council at a local area are not always unified. Such examples can be found in the Yakushima Island (Kagoshima Prefecture). Yakushima was listed as a WHS in 1993 as one of Japan's two first natural WHSs (World Heritage Centre, n.d.). In Japan, Yakushima is also seen as a forerunner of ecotourism practice and implementation. It is generally agreed that ecotourism in Yakushima started in the mid-1990s (Matsumoto et al., 2004). In 2011, an ordinance plan was submitted to the local council. The ordinance aimed to list three spots in the island as Special Natural Tourism Resources and to restrict the usage of these three spots (The Forestry Agency (hereafter FA), n.d.). However, the plan was rejected by the local council mainly because part of local businesses was not happy with the restriction on usage of the three spots (FA, n.d.). In such a circumstance, Act on Ecotourism Promotion (*Ecotourism Suishin-ho*) cannot work effectively for the establishment and advancement of ecotourism in local areas, and socio-cultural or environmental sustainability of natural and cultural resources acknowledged as Special Natural Tourism Resources cannot be enhanced. In this situation, ecotourism in local areas would also not be promoted and developed enough and this signifies that economic sustainability of local natural and cultural resources cannot be strengthened. That is because; in this situation, these resources would not be fully experienced by ecotourists and a good amount of financial benefits for local communities would not be generated through ecotourism activities.

On the other hand, the case of the sea area of the Kerama Island (Okinawa Prefecture) demonstrates that a consensus on Special Natural Tourism Resources was formed amongst local governments, other local government agencies and local diving associations after five-year discussions and negotiations (Ryukyu Shimpo, 2014). The consensus was about the limit on divers' numbers entering the sea area to be listed as Special Natural Tourism Resources, but still guaranteed divers' access to the sea area (Ryukyu Shimpo, 2014). Forming a consensus amongst stakeholders with different aspirations and priorities is often a very challenging task, but this can lead to an ideal balance between activities and practices for economic, socio-cultural and environmental sustainability.

In light of the aim and scope of this book, here it should also be noted that basically it is fair to say that the belief of ecotourism matches well the principle of *mottainai*. In fact, for instance, Matsubara (2013) conducted questionnaire surveys with the first-year university students in Kyoto City and their parents to examine their awareness and practice of *mottainai*. Her research reveals that ecotourism is identified as one of the topics the students learned when they studied on environmental issues and *mottainai* (Matsubara, 2013).

6   Conclusion

Japan's natural heritage includes biotic (e.g. flora and fauna) and abiotic (e.g. geo sites) factors, and has been conserved and utilised through various domestic frameworks and initiatives. Of these, Japan's natural park scheme aims to preserve and use both biotic and abiotic factors. The main feature of the natural park system of Japan is the protection and usage of places with scenic beauty, and the most important law for Japan's natural parks is Act on Natural Parks (*Shizenkoen-ho*). Japan's natural parks have three major categories, namely National Parks, Quasi-National Parks and Prefectural Natural Parks. Generally speaking, National Parks are seen as the most prestigious type of Japan's natural parks in terms of their scenic beauty, and are inscribed and managed directly by the Japanese Government. In addition to Act on National Parks, other Japanese laws such as Act on Nature Conservation (*Shizenkankyo Hozen-ho*) and Act on Landscapes (*Keikan-ho*) are also associated with the protection of natural parks in Japan.

In principle, Monuments (*Kinenbutsu*) are one of the main categories of Japan's cultural heritage and are regulated by a national law for conservation of cultural heritage (i.e. Act on Protection of Cultural Properties (*Bunkazai Hogo-ho*)). Nevertheless, this category contains sub categories that comprise natural heritage. One sub category, Places of Scenic Beauty (*Meisho*), embraces seashores and mountains of a high artistic or aesthetic significance; whilst, the other sub category, Natural Monuments (*Tennen Kinenbutsu*) contain biotic (animals and plants) and abiotic (minerals and geological characteristics) elements of an outstanding scientific worth. Thus, it is fair to say that the Monuments category can be adopted for the conservation of a wide variety of cultural and natural heritage of Japan, although there would be a certain level of limitation in applying a cultural focused law (i.e. Act on Protection of Cultural Properties) to the conservation of natural heritage. With regard to this, as mentioned in Sect. 3.2, other domestic laws such as Act on Conservation of Endangered Species of Wild Fauna and Flora (*Shu no Hozon-ho*) can help the protection of precious animals and plants. Other national laws such as Act on Protection and Control of Wild Birds and Mammals and Hunting

Management (*Choju Hogo Kanri-ho*) and Basic Act on Biodiversity (*Seibutsu Tayosei Kihon-ho*) can also assist the preservation of diverse flora and fauna of Japan. Regarding the conservation and utilisation of abiotic factors, 'geoparks' are also a significant concept and initiative that are adopted at domestic and international levels. These two levels are closely associated each other as demonstrated by the interrelationship between JNGs (domestic level) and UGGs (international level) (see Sect. 4).

Concerning all of the three conservation systems for Japan's natural heritage, their good conservation and proper utilisation supported by a best balance between these two can lead to environmental and socio-cultural sustainability of Japan's natural heritage and communities in and around such natural heritage. Especially, meaningful use of the natural heritage in a local context, including education, would be essential to establish or enhance the existence of natural heritage in and around local communities and amongst wider audience. This is vital for socio-cultural sustainability of natural heritage of Japan and communities in and around the natural heritage. In fact, utilisation of natural heritage for people's health and leisure is also part of mission of Japan's natural parks and geoparks. 'Utilisation' in the context above includes the use of natural heritage for tourism purposes. All of the three kinds of Japan's natural heritage have been used as resources for nature-based tourism such as ecotourism and geotourism or destinations of these sorts of tourism. If ecotourism or geotourism is planned and implemented in a well-balanced manner and key stakeholders take their responsibility accordingly, these tourism activities can contribute not only to environmental and socio-cultural sustainability of the natural heritage and local communities in and around the natural heritage but also to their economic sustainability. Making the most of natural heritage whilst conserving it in a good condition also reflects the spirit of *mottainai*. Due to the COVID-19 pandemic, the number of visitors to Japan's National Parks in 2020 decreased a lot compared to 2019. The number of tourists who stayed overnight in a National Park in 2020 was also 43.9% less than 2019 (MOE, 2021). As of July 2021, however, the popularity of nature-based leisure activities, including ecotourism and geotourism, seem to have started increasing again as many people think open-air activities such as nature-based tourism are relatively safe leisure activities under the COVID-19 situation.

References

ACA. (2013). *Meisho ni kansuru sogochosa hokokusho* (Report on the results of survey on places of scenic beauty) [in Japanese]. Available at: https://www.bunka.go.jp/tokei_hakusho_shuppan/tokeichosa/pdf/meishou_chousa.pdf. Accessed 16 June 2021.

ACA. (n.d.). *Kuni-shitei Bunkazai-to Database: Shiseki, Meisho, Tennen Kinenbutsu* (Cultural properties database: Historic sites, places of scenic beauty and natural monuments [in Japanese]. Available at: https://kunishitei.bunka.go.jp/bsys/categorylist?register_id=401. Accessed 16 June 2021.

Awanavi. (2021). *Misato Hotaru Matsuri* (Misato Fireflies Festivals) [in Japanese]. Available at: https://www.awanavi.jp/spot/21863.html. Accessed 18 June 2021.

CNN Travel. (2019). *Miyajima, Japan to impose a tourist tax*. Available at: https://edition.cnn.com/travel/article/miyajima-japan-tourist-tax-intl-hnk/index.html. Accessed 16 June 2021.

Cottrell, S. P., Vaske, J. J., & Roemer, J. M. (2013). Resident satisfaction with sustainable tourism: The case of Frankenwald Nature Park, Germany. *Tourism Management Perspectives, 8*, 42–48.

De Vos, A., Cumming, G. S., Moore, C. A., Maciejewski, K., & Duckworth, G. (2016). The relevance of spatial variation in ecotourism attributes for the economic sustainability of protected areas. *Ecosphere, 7*(2), e01207.

Dowling, R. K. (2013). Global geotourism – An emerging form of sustainable tourism. *Czech Journal of Tourism, 2*(2), 59–79.

FA. (n.d.). *Yakushima Sekaiisan-chiiki kagaku-iinkai no koremade no keii* (Background of the scientific committee for Yakushima World Heritage area) [in Japanese]. Available at: https://www.env.go.jp/park/yakushima/ywhcc/wh/kagaku/10/141026-1-2.pdf. Accessed 14 July 2021.

Fukami, S., & Arima, T. (2011). *Geopark ni taisuru kanko-kyaku no image* (Visitors' perception of geoparks) [in Japanese]. https://doi.org/10.14866/ajg.2011s.0.75.0

GGN. (2018). *Request for proposals: Communication & marketing strategy for UNESCO Global Geoparks*. Available at: http://globalgeoparksnetwork.org/wp-content/uploads/2018/02/RFP-Marketing-Strategy-Final-14-02-2018.pdf. Accessed 30 June 2021.

Guo, W., & Chung, S. (2016). Remaking tourism carrying capacity frameworks for Geoparks. In *4th International conference on advances in social science, humanities, and management (ASSHM 2016)*, pp. 197–205.

Hatsukaichi City. (2020). *Kazei kyakutai ni tsuite* (About taxable) [in Japanese]. Available at: https://www.city.hatsukaichi.hiroshima.jp/uploaded/attachment/35898.pdf. Accessed 16 June 2021.

Henriques, M. H., & Brilha, J. B. (2017). UNESCO Global Geoparks: A strategy towards global understanding and sustainability. *Episodes, 40*(4), 349–355.

Itoigawa Geopark. (n.d.). *Geoparks and education for sustainable development/Sustainable Development Goals* [in Japanese]. Available at: https://geo-itoigawa.com/what/gp_esd.html. Accessed 30 June 2021.

JGC. (2017). *Nihon Geopark Iinkai kaisoku (Constitution of JGC)* [in Japanese]. Available at: https://jgc.geopark.jp/files/jgc_kaisoku_20171222.pdf. Accessed 16 June 2021.

JGC. (2020). *Japan Geopark Committee (JGC)*. Available at: https://jgc.geopark.jp/en/. Accessed 30 June 2021.

JGN. (2021). *Japanese Geoparks network*. Available at: https://geopark.jp/en/. Accessed 30 June 2021.

Jimura, T. (2019). *World heritage sites: Tourism, local communities and conservation activities*. CABI.

Kushiro International Wetland Centre. (n.d.). *Our wetlands: Ramsar sites in Kushiro area*. Available at: https://www.kiwc.net/english/wetlands/index.html#c01. Accessed 1 June 2021.

Mainichi Shimbun. (2020). *Corona-ka Kokuritsu Koen nimo – Shunyu kyuwarigen hozen ni eikyo* (The impact of COVID-19 on Japan's National Parks – The revenue decreased by 90% and it negatively affects conservation of the parks) [in Japanese]. Available at: https://mainichi.jp/articles/20200627/dde/001/040/035000c. Accessed 8 June 2021.

Matsubara, S. (2013). Consciousness and behavior of teens relating to mottainai in daily life: Influence of customs in daily life and lessons given in school [in Japanese]. *Journal of Human and Living Environment, 20*(2), 155–165.

Matsumoto, F., Tashiro, S., & Ohnishi, A. (2004). The present circumstances and challenges of Ecotour guides in Yakushima [in Japanese]. *The Bulletin of the Faculty of Agriculture, Kagoshima University, 54*, 15–29.

McKeever, P. J., & Zouros, N. (2005). Geoparks: Celebrating Earth heritage, sustaining local communities. *Episodes, 28*(4), 274–278.

MEOC. (n.d.). *The Marimo of Lake Akan*. Available at: https://marimo-web.org/en/index.html. Accessed 19 June 2021.

MOE. (2021). *2020 nen no zenkoku oyobi Kokuritsu Koen to ni okeru riyo doko* (Visitor trend in 2020 – Japan and Japan's National Parks) [in Japanese]. Available at: http://www.env.go.jp/nature/2021/04/14/mat01-02.pdf. Accessed 21 July 2021.

MOE. (n.d.-a). *Overview of national parks.* Available at: https://www.env.go.jp/en/nature/nps/park/parks/index.html. Accessed 1 June 2021.

MOE. (n.d.-b). *Kokuritsu Koen towa* (What national parks are) [in Japanese]. Available at: https://www.env.go.jp/nature/np/pamph5/02.pdf. Accessed 3 June 2021.

MOE. (n.d.-c). *Kokuritsu Koen no kanri-taisei* (Management system for National Parks) [in Japanese]. Available at: https://www.env.go.jp/park/about/index.html. Accessed 6 June 2021.

MOE. (n.d.-d). *Hogo to riyo* (Conservation and utilisation) [in Japanese]. Available at: http://www.env.go.jp/park/about/protect/index.html. Accessed 6 June 2021.

MOE. (n.d.-e). *Kankyo NPO to tono renkei kyodo torikumi jirei* (Examples of collaborative works with environmental NPOs) [in Japanese]. Available at: https://www.env.go.jp/policy/kihon_keikaku/lifestyle/h2007_02/mat5.pdf. Accessed 7 June 2021.

MOE. (n.d.-f). *Shizen Koen to riyoshasu no gaiyo* (Summary of the number of visitors to natural parks in Japan) [in Japanese]. Available at: https://www.env.go.jp/park/doc/data/natural/data/naturalpark_gaiyo.pdf. Accessed 8 June 2021.

MOE. (n.d.-g). *Gaiyo – Kankyo-sho ga suishinsuru Kokuritsu Koen Mankitsu Project no 2021 nen iko no torikumi hoshin-an* (Summary – Plan to implement Fully Enjoying National Parks Project in 2021 and thereafter) [in Japanese]. Tokyo: MOE.

Neki, A. (1995). Can the places of scenic beauty and natural monuments be considered as "Cultural properties"? [in Japanese]. *Nagaoka University of Technology Research Report, 17*, 109–117.

NPF. (n.d.). *Natural parks of Japan.* Available at: http://en.bes.or.jp/invitation/. Accessed 2 June 2021.

NPS. (2021). *Accessibility & universal design standards.* Available at: https://www.nps.gov/dscw/ds-accessibility-universal-design.htm. Accessed 6 June 2021.

Numata, S. (2019). Biodiversity and tourism: the current efforts and issues [in Japanese]. *Japanese Journal of Ecology, 69*, 23–27.

Rodríguez-Rodríguez, D., & Martínez-Vega, J. (2017). Assessing recent environmental sustainability in the Spanish network of National Parks and their statutory peripheral areas. *Applied Geography, 89*, 22–31.

Ryukyu Shimpo. (2014). *Kerama-kaiiki diving kisei – Raigetsu nimo jyorei-an* (Restriction on diving activities in the sea area of the Kerama Islands) [in

Japanese]. Available at: https://ryukyushimpo.jp/news/prentry-224994.html. Accessed 14 July 2021.

Sakurajima-Kinkowan Geopark. (2021). *Home* [in Japanese]. Available at: http://www.sakurajima-kinkowan-geo.jp/. Accessed 30 June 2021.

Tazawako-Kakunodate. (2021). *Kakunodate no Sakura Matsuri* (Kakunodate Cherry Blossom Festival) [in Japanese]. Available at: https://tazawako-kakunodate.com/ja/events/125. Accessed 18 June 2021.

Travel Voice. (2021). *Kankyo-sho ga suishinsuru Kokuritsu Koen Mankitsu Project* (Fully Enjoying National Parks Project promoted by MOE) [in Japanese]. Available at: https://www.travelvoice.jp/20210331-148453. Accessed 8 June 2021.

UNESCO. (2017a). *UNESCO global geoparks*. Available at: http://www.unesco.org/new/en/natural-sciences/environment/earth-sciences/unesco-global-geoparks/. Accessed 29 June 2021.

UNESCO. (2017b). *Fundamental features of a UNESCO global geopark*. Available at: http://www.unesco.org/new/en/natural-sciences/environment/earth-sciences/unesco-global-geoparks/fundamental-features/. Accessed 30 June 2021.

Watanabe, M. (2011). Global geoparks network and geoparks in Japan [in Japanese]. *Chigaku Zasshi, 120*(5), 733–742.

World Heritage Centre. (n.d.). *Yakushima*. Available at: https://whc.unesco.org/en/list/662/. Accessed 14 July 2021.

Wise, N., & Jimura, T. (Eds.). (2020). *Tourism, cultural heritage and urban regeneration – Changing spaces in historical places*. Springer.

Part III

Sustainability of Tourism

5

Sustainability of Japan's Transport Sector

1 Introduction

Tourism can be defined in several ways and different context. 'The World Tourism Organization (hereafter UNWTO) is the United Nations agency responsible for the promotion of responsible, sustainable and universally accessible tourism' (UNWTO, n.d.). To date, the definition of tourism suggested by UNWTO (2001) is one of the most widely accepted ones in academia as well as real world:

> Tourism is defined as the activities of persons travelling to and staying in places outside their usual environment for not more than one consecutive year for leisure, business and other purposes not related to the exercise of an activity remunerated from within the place visited.

UNWTO (n.d.) also defines tourism somewhat differently in their glossary of tourism terms as follows:

> Tourism is a social, cultural and economic phenomenon which entails the movement of people to countries or places outside their usual environment for personal or business/professional purposes. These people are called visi-

tors (which may be either tourists or excursionists; residents or non-residents) and tourism has to do with their activities, some of which involve tourism expenditure.

In academia, 'movement' or 'transport' is also understood as a crucial element of tourism (Smith, 2004). Considering these points, concepts or words such as 'travelling' or 'movement' should be included as an essential component of tourism when tourism is defined. In light of this, the 'transport' sector should also be understood as an integral element of tourism industry (Virkar & Mallya, 2018). Furthermore, transport is also a key part of nations' sustainable economic and social development (Susnienė, 2012). Thus, sustainability management in the transport sector is paramount for sustainability of tourism industry and even for our society as a whole.

The main transport modes widely utilised in tourism industry across the globe are air, land and water transport (Page, 2005; Inkson & Minnaert, 2018; Page & Connell, 2020). All of these three key transport modes are discussed in this chapter, focusing on their sustainability. Regarding each of these three, there are several major means of transport as follows:

- Air (international/domestic and scheduled/charter passenger airline services, light aircrafts (e.g. Cessna Aircraft), and helicopters)
- Land (international, intercity, regional and local trains; subways; trams; bus and coach services; taxi and limousine taxi; private and rental cars; motorbikes, and bicycles)
- Water (international and domestic ferries, and passenger liners)

Needless to say, all of the three main travel modes are operated for tourism purposes in the vast majority of countries across the world, including Japan. On the other hand, some of the transport means are not used at all or not widely utilised in Japan. For instance, charter passenger airline services have been familiar for British holidaymakers but are not common for Japanese ones as international and domestic package holidays organised by Japanese tour operators usually use scheduled flights. Another example is international trains. They are common and established transport in Europe (e.g. Eurostar and Thalys), whilst they cannot be confirmed in Japan mainly due to its geographical feature, an island country relatively far from its neighbouring countries.

Nowadays, sustainability of transport is an international concern as evidenced by the fact that transport is recognised as one of the thematic issues related to the United Nations Sustainable Development Goals (hereafter UN and SDGs respectively) (UN, n.d.). In addition, the Organisation for Economic Co-operation and Development (hereafter OECD) has been working on a project on Environmentally Sustainable Transport (hereafter EST) since 1994 (OECD, n.d.). The project aims to characterise EST and to establish guidelines for the development of policies that can lead to the realisation of EST (OECD, n.d.). Sustainability of transport is also an important agenda at international regional level. To cite a case, sustainability of transport activities is one of the target objectives established by the European Commission in order to improve the environmental quality in the European Union (Vaghi & Percoco, 2011). Thus, it seems to be natural that this theme is also recognised well by Japan's key stakeholders of sustainability management such as Ministry of Land, Infrastructure, Transport and Tourism (hereafter MLIT) as a significant subject for the future of the country and world (MLIT, n.d.). Considering this, this chapter intends to explore sustainability of Japan's transport sector. To achieve this aim, the aforementioned diverse transport modes and means serving for tourism purposes are examined in Sects. 2 (air), 3 and 4 (land), and 5 (water) in detail in terms of sustainability management and *mottainai* spirit both of which are key notions of this book.

2 Flight (International and Domestic)

2.1 Overview and History

There has been a growing concern about the environmental impact of air transport in the media, policymakers and the general public (OECD, 2008; Chiambaretto et al., 2021). Chiambaretto et al. (2021) further state that nowadays aviation has been criticised as a main cause of high carbon emissions and global warming, and this has been leading to the emergence and development of the 'flight shame' movement in European countries. At the same time, however, it should also be noted that air transport and aviation industry, including passenger and freight services, are essential for many people's life and work. They can be blamed in terms of environmental sustainability of the earth and countries, whilst they can also be advantageous for economic and socio-cultural sustainability of the world and society. In fact, for instance, a main industry and major source of income and/or foreign exchange for many small island developing countries is tourism, and tourism cannot be sustainable without air transport (Abeyratne, 1999). Therefore, excessive criticism towards air transport without enough consideration of characteristics of different international regions and/or countries should be avoided.

It could be stated that the history of Japan's air transportation for tourism purposes commenced in the early 1950s, several years after the end of World War II (hereafter WWII). However, ordinary Japanese people had not been able to travel freely for tourism purposes until 1964. The liberalisation of overseas travel in 1964 was triggered by Japan's participation in OECD. In fact, the liberalisation of overseas travel means relaxation of foreign exchange regulations that was advised by OECD when Japan became a member of it (Kurosu, 2014). 1964 was also the year when Tokyo Olympic Games was held. The Games was the first Games hosted by an Asian country and could show Japan's recovery from WWII and ability as a developed country to the international audience (Jimura, 2020). For a long time since 1964, Japan's air transport industry for international and domestic tourism purposes had been dominated by two giants, Japan Airlines (hereafter JAL) (traditionally, international and main domestic routes) and All Nippon Airways (hereafter ANA) (traditionally, domestic routes), and by Japan Air System (local routes) (merged into JAL in 2006), and had been highly regulated by the Japanese Government through *Koku-ho* (Civil Aeronautics Act). Following the deregulation of the Act in 1997, however, two mid-sized airlines, Skymark Airlines and AIRDO, entered the market in 1998. Depending on definitions, but these two airlines can also be seen as Japan's first low-cost careers (hereafter LCCs). Since then, the number of Japan's LCCs has been increasing (e.g. Peach established in 2012); however, most of them have been more or less struggling and supported by JAL or ANA.

It could be stated that overall Japan's air transport sector for tourism purposes had been developing steadily throughout its history until 2019. In principle, this applies to both international and domestic passenger airline services. The Japanese Government launched its Visit JAPAN Campaign in 2003, targeting tourists from overseas countries to increase the number of inbound tourists and to enhance Japan's presence as a tourist destination across the world (Jimura, 2022). Once, Japan had been famous as a main tourist-generating country, whilst it had not been recognised or visited well by foreign tourists. This signifies that Japan's tourism balance of payments had been negative for a long time (Jimura, 2019). Because of Japan's inbound tourism boom in recent years, its tourism balance of payments turned positive in 2014 (Jimura, 2019, 2022) and the country had kept enjoying its inbound tourism boom until 2019 (Japan Tourism Agency (hereafter JTA) 2021). According to JTA (2021), Japan received 31.88 million inbound tourists and sent 20.08 million outbound tourists in 2019, and both are the largest numbers in Japan's tourism history. As everybody can assume, this favourable situation of Japan's air transport sector for tourism purposes, especially international one, was totally changed in 2020 due to the outbreak of COVID-19 all over the world. In 2020, the numbers of inbound and outbound tourists for Japan plummeted to 4.12 million and 3.17 million respectively (JTA, 2021). In addition, domestic flights for tourism purposes were also negatively affected by COVID-19 itself and travel restrictions because of it. Considering the points discussed above, the subsequent section (Sect. 2.2) explores sustainability management of airlines based in Japan.

2.2 Economic Sustainability of Airlines Based in Japan

Amongst the triple bottom line of sustainability, economic sustainability and its management in Japan's airline industry is discussed first. Two main pillars of airline services are those for passengers (people) and freight (cargo). Both are imperative for people's life and work, but the former is much more significant than the latter in the context of tourism and the focus of this section. It is crucial to remember that the products the airline industry offers to consumers (passengers) are not goods but services like many other sectors comprising tourism industry. Basically, the service industry is labour-intensive and the airline industry is not an exception. This means that the delivery of their services relies heavily on human labour and high ratio of personnel cost within a company's expenditure. In fact, the services provided by airlines are supported by employees engaging in diverse jobs such as pilots, flight attendants and mechanics. In principle, the word, 'capital-intensive', is an antonym of 'labour-intensive', and generally, labour-intensive industry is unlikely to be capital-intensive. Nevertheless, the airline industry can be comprehended as not only labour-intensive industry but also capital-intensive industry. That is because, the business of airlines cannot be possible without machines or infrastructure, typically air crafts, which are essential to offer their service to passengers. Purchase and/or maintenance of these assets needs an enormous investment, and this can be a financial burden for the business of airlines.

Throughout the history of Japan's airline services for passengers, the above-mentioned two major companies, JAL and ANA, have been playing a leading role in domestic and international flight services. Supported by the economic recovery and development of Japan after WWII and a steady increase in the number of domestic and international passengers, overall ANA could manage to maintain its economic sustainability until 2019 before the emergence of COVID-19 pandemic. As a whole, JAL had also been developing and expanding their services after WWII, establishing its presence as a major international company based in Japan. Unlike ANA, however, JAL went into bankruptcy in January 2010 and its shares were delisted from Japan's stock exchanges in February 2011. Main reasons of JAL's business failure can be summarised as follows:

- Ownership of excessive numbers of large air crafts
- Unprofitable routes
- Surplus workers
- Financial crisis triggered by the bankruptcy of Lehman Brothers (Ono, 2013; Otsuka & Fujiwara, 2015).

Surprisingly, JAL realised its relisting very quickly in September 2012 under the leadership of Kazuo Inamori, the founder of the Kyocera group.

As everybody knows or can imagine, however, the COVID-19 pandemic has been extensively damaging economic sustainability of the aviation sector all over the world. Economic sustainability of their services for passengers, particularly international flights, has been almost destroyed due to COVID-19. In this very challenging situation, both ANA and JAL have been employing various measures such as sell-out of their aircrafts and secondment of their employees in order to continue to survive as private businesses and to secure a certain level of their economic sustainability. Of these two measures, especially the secondment is noteworthy as the vast majority of organisations or enterprises selected for ANA/JAL's secondment are not related to airline businesses. These organisations or companies cover diverse sorts of workplaces, including local governments, a nationwide high-end supermarket chain, an electric retailer, a telecommunication company and a staffing service company. This is a rather drastic measure but should be helpful for ANA and JAL to keep their experienced employees as well as for the employees to secure their income.

2.3 Socio-cultural Sustainability of Airlines Based in Japan

In the context of business, social sustainability denotes identification and management of positive and negative impacts of businesses on 'people' (UN Global Compact, n.d.). Put differently, social sustainability means that companies conduct their everyday businesses in ways that benefit society and protect people (UN Global Compact, n.d.). Nevertheless, it has been often pointed out that social sustainability is the most neglected pillar of sustainable development compared with economic or environmental sustainability (Trainer, 2005; Boström, 2012). According to Balaman (2019, 86), the areas that social sustainability covers include 'health and social equity, human rights, labor rights, practices and decent working conditions, social responsibility and justice, community development and well-being, product responsibility, community resilience, and cultural competence', all of which would be vital for our society and people's lives. These areas of social sustainability are also relevant to passenger services offered by the airlines based in Japan. For instance, the secondment of ANA and JAL's workers can involve issues in the aforementioned 'labour rights' and/or 'practices and decent working conditions' (see Sect. 2.2). ANA and JAL should look after the mental health of their employees who are currently working outside the companies due to the secondment triggered by the COVID-19 pandemic. That is mainly because, this is the working conditions the employees of ANA or JAL did not expect at all and the jobs they are currently engaging in differ considerably from those they were doing for ANA or JAL prior to the pandemic.

Cases associated with other fields of social sustainability can also be found in airline companies and their businesses. Indeed, the health of employees is a significant aspect of social sustainability for all organisations and enterprises. Due to the natures of their business, however, employees' health is a particularly important dimension of social sustainability for airlines. For instance, pilots or flight attendants are exposed to cosmic ray on duty and may start developing aerotitis because of sudden changes in atmospheric pressure. Both have been recognised as illustrative health concerns for these workers. Such health problems have been gradually mitigated in recent years thanks to various factors, including the advancements in aircraft technology. Thus, it is natural that airlines employ various measures to ensure their employees' health. To cite a case, JAL and their employees and Health Insurance Association work together under 'JAL Wellness Declaration' to maintain the physical and mental health of all employees (JAL, n.d.-a). Needless to say, airlines are also responsible for health and safety of their passengers. For example, the Medical Advisory Group of the International Air Transport Association (hereafter IATA) developed the guidelines that address medical issues in all areas of aviation on their web page (https://www.iata.org/en/programs/safety/health/) (IATA, 2021). For instance, ensuring safety and security of passengers on-board is one of the main tasks for cabin crew.

ANA and JAL are also eager to take their corporate social responsibility (hereafter CSR) as a member of society. ANA runs an education programme for children and future generations called 'ANA Blue Academy'. Furthermore, ANA donates foods and beverages unsold on domestic flights to a charity called Second Harvest Japan and has been supporting the Central Community Chest of Japan for a long time (ANA, n.d.-a). Through these CSR activities, ANA aims to contribute to SDG 8 Decent Work and Economic Growth, SDG 9 Industry, Innovation and Infrastructure, and SDG 11 Sustainable Cities and Communities (ANA, n.d.-a). Of these initiatives, minimising the amount of food and drink waste represents the practice of the 'reduce' element of 'reduce', 'reuse' and 'recycle' (3Rs). This practice also well reflects the *mottainai* spirit originated in Japan and should be valued as embodiment of this spirit. JAL has been supporting many special exhibitions at museums or galleries by transporting invaluable paintings and crafts from foreign countries to Japan. This activity addresses the 'cultural' aspects of socio-cultural sustainability and can contribute to socio-cultural sustainability of the company itself, people and society as a whole. Regarding community resilience as well as CSR, both ANA and JAL have been supporting the recovery of local communities which suffered from natural disasters such as 2011 Tohoku Earthquake and Tsunami by transporting emergency relief goods to disaster-affected areas, making donations to these areas, and promoting the areas as tourist destinations.

2.4 Environmental Sustainability of Airlines Based in Japan

As mentioned in Sect. 2.1, there has been ever-increasing concerns on the environmental impact of air transport, and aviation has been blamed as one of the major causes of climate change. Today, even the movement called 'flight shame' has emerged in Europe. However, it needs to be noted that the voices from the air transport industry should also be heard. For example, the Air Transport Action Group (hereafter ATAG), a non-profit organisation, represents all sectors of the air transport industry (ATAG, 2021a). ATAG (2021b) shows a variety of facts and figures, signifying the importance of their businesses and activities, contributions to society and people, and the significantly lower level of environmental impact of the air transport industry than climate/environmental activists assert:

1. The global aviation industry produces around 2% of all human-induced carbon dioxide (hereafter CO_2) emissions.
2. Aviation is responsible for 12% of CO_2 emissions from all transport sources, compared to 74% from road transport.
3. While air transport carries around 0.5% of the volume of world trade shipments, it is over 35% by value – meaning that goods shipped by air are extremely high value commodities, often times perishable or time-sensitive. Deliveries of fresh produce from Africa to the UK alone supports the livehoods of 1.5 million people, while producing less CO_2 than similar produce grown in the UK, despite the energy used in transport.
4. Jet aircraft in service today are well over 80% more fuel efficient per seat kilometre than the first jets in the 1960s.
5. Alternative fuels, particularly sustainable aviation fuels (hereafter SAFs), have been identified as excellent candidates for helping achieve the industry climate targets. SAF derived sources such as algae, jatropha, or waste by-products have been shown to reduce the carbon footprint of aviation fuel by up to 80% over their full lifecycle.
6. Around 80% of aviation CO_2 emissions are emitted from flights of over 1500 kilometres, for which there is no practical alternative mode of transport.
7. Globally, the average occupancy of aircraft is 82%, greater than other forms of transport.

Nevertheless, it is also true that the air transport industry is expected to make more efforts and decrease their negative environmental impact further.

Regarding the airlines based in Japan, both ANA and JAL are fully aware of the magnitude of SDGs and have been conducting a range of activities to make good contributions to SDGs as members of society (ANA, n.d.-b; JAL, n.d.-b). In many cases, these actions are also comprehended as their CSR activities. The businesses of ANA and JAL are related to all of the 17 SDGs directly or indirectly. Considering the current global concerns and movements, however, SDG 13 Climate Action should be viewed as the goal that is most strongly associated with airline companies all over the world, including ANA and JAL. ANA established three environmental, social, and governance (hereafter ESG) Commitments (ANA, n.d.-b). Of these three ESG Commitments, the one that is most intimately associated with SDG 13 Climate Action is:

* To achieve net-zero emissions from aircraft flight operations by fiscal 2050.

ANA also developed subsequent four different approaches for this commitment:

1. Full utilisation of SAF – To increase usage of SAF produced from sustainable sources such as vegetable oil, sugar, animal fat and waste biomass.
2. Adoption of new technologies – To use aircrafts with improved engines characterised by higher fuel-efficiency and cutting-edge technology.
3. Improvement of flight operations – To 'reduce' fuel consumption by improving aircraft flight operations, regularly cleaning the inside of the engine, and reducing the weight of installed equipment.
4. Use of emission trading system – To use an emission trading scheme for emissions that cannot be reduced through the aforementioned three approaches (ANA, n.d.-b).

All of these four measures employed by ANA to decrease the amount of CO_2 emissions from their flights are commonly adopted by JAL (n.d.-b) and many major airline companies across the world.

3 Rail (Train and Underground)

3.1 Overview and History

Generally, the UK is known as the birthplace of railways and the first railway was opened between Liverpool and Manchester in 1830 (Page, 2015). Between 1835 and 1885, the UK railway network experienced a rapid and extensive growth, increasing the miles of track to 30,000 (Page, 2015). Working together with the Bank Holidays Act 1871, the expansion of railway networks played an important role in the emergence and development of leisure tourism, connecting people's places to live/work and tourist destinations such as seaside resorts, including Blackpool, Brighton and Scarborough. At around the same period, European countries also saw a huge expansion of railway network. Even today, railways can be understood as a primary transport mode for both business and leisure tourism in the UK and other European countries, especially in Western European countries. In the case of the UK, the central government reviewed the national railway network in the late 1960s and consequently a number of railway lines were closed. As of writing, however, the central and relevant local governments are planning to reopen some closed lines (e.g. Northumberland Line between Ashington to Newcastle) as a socially and environmentally sustainable travel mode. They deem that reopening of once-abandoned railway lines can promote an eco-friendly way to travel amongst local residents and tourists, improve rail congestion, and support commuting of people who moved to suburban areas during the COVID-19 pandemic. In fact, railway transport is regarded as a (most) eco-friendly transport mode in academic research (Razumovskaya et al., 2014; Sagar et al., 2016).

The history of railways in Japan commenced in 1872 when the first steam locomotive started running between Shimbashi (Tokyo Metropolitan Prefecture (hereafter TMP)) and Yokohama (Kanagawa Prefecture). Japan's railway network began to expand extensively since the end of the nineteenth and/or the beginning of the twentieth century mainly thanks to the business growth of Japan's government-owned railway enterprise and private railway companies. These advancements contributed to the emergence and/or development of a range of tourist destinations or visitor attractions such as hot-spring resorts and religious sites/buildings (Jimura, 2022). In Japan, moreover, railway stations have often been functioning as nuclei of city/town centres, especially in newly developed cities or towns (Jimura, 2022). In addition, residential areas and a variety of social amenities such as shopping centres and theatres have also been developed along the railway lines (Jimura, 2022). Such development process is prominent in Japan and implies that rail transport is more deeply embedded in everyday life and work of people residing in Japan, especially those in urban areas, compared with air or water transport.

As often described as 'the most environment-friendly way to travel' (Shalom, 2021), Japan's railway companies have also been working on sustainability management of their businesses, contributing to SDGs. Many of them also recognise their activities for SDGs as their key CSR activities. For example, Tokyo's subway lines are managed by two organisations namely Tokyo Toei (public) and Tokyo Metro (private). Tokyo Metro (n.d.) regards following six as the SDGs that are most relevant to their businesses:

- SDG 8 Decent Work and Economic Growth
- SDG 9 Industry, Innovation and Infrastructure
- SDG 11 Sustainable Cities and Communities
- SDG 13 Climate Action
- SDG 16 Peace, Justice and Strong Institutions
- SDG 17 Partnerships for the Goals

According to Tokyo Metro (n.d.), they have also set five main themes in sustainability management in their business activities and have identified SDG(s) that are associated with each theme as follows:

- Theme 1: Realising a Safer and More Resilient Subway (SDGs 11, 13 and 16)
- Theme 2: Contributing to the Active Lives of All People (SDG 11)
- Theme 3: Enhancing the Multifaceted Charms and Value of Tokyo (SDGs 11 and 17)
- Theme 4: Making Thoughtful Choices for a Healthy Planet (SDG 13)
- Theme 5: Cultivating Resources for Our Sustainable Future (SDGs 8, 9 and 16)

Tokyo Metro also makes their passengers aware of their SDG activities through advertisements in their railway carriages (see Figs. 5.1 and 5.2). Subsequent sections shed light on economic, socio-cultural and environmental sustainability of rail transport in Japan.

3.2 Economic Sustainability of Railways in Japan

After World War II, the vast majority of railways in Japan were owned and managed by three different types of organisations until 1987, and they were:

- Nation-owned railway enterprise (i.e. Japan National Railways (hereafter JNR))
- Regional/local government-owned railway enterprises
- Private railway companies

In 1987, JNR was privatised and their railway businesses were taken over by Japan Railways (hereafter JR) Group. JR Group comprises six companies that provide passenger services in different regions of Japan, and one company that offers freight services across Japan as follows:

Fig. 5.1 Tokyo Metro: Vision for sustainability management. (Source: Author)

5 Sustainability of Japan's Transport Sector   145

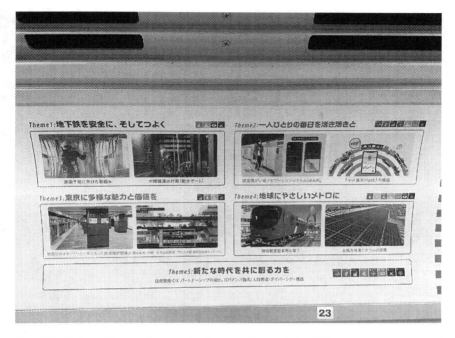

Fig. 5.2 Tokyo Metro: five main themes for sustainability management and SDGs. (Source: Author)

- Passenger: JR Hokkaido, JR East, JR Central, JR West, JR Shikoku and JR Kyushu
- Freight: JR Freight

There are several main reasons why JNR was privatised. Generally, however, subsequent issues are often pointed out as main reasons:

- Huge debts
- Low quality of services
- Issues in National Railway Workers' Union and frequent strikes
- Low morale of employees and in workplace

Amongst these, JNR's huge debts is viewed as the largest reason of the privatisation of JNR. This financial condition signifies that economic sustainability of JNR was lost. The national budgets and tax revenue for other purposes were also spent to improve the financial condition of JNR. This situation was contrary to the spirit of *mottainai* and implies that JNR did not take their CSR accordingly.

After the privatisation of JNR, since 1987 onwards, most of railways in Japan were owned and run by four different kinds of organisations, and they are:

* Regional/local government-owned railway enterprises
* Joint public-private ventures
* JR Group (private companies, but the successor of JNR)
* Private railway companies

Of these four, an increase in the number of joint public-private ventures and the emergence and presence of JR Group can be seen as key differences before and after 1987. In the process of the privatisation, the business of many local train lines with a small number of regular passengers that had often been in debt were taken over by joint public-private ventures or were replaced with local bus services (Furomoto, 2017). Due to the background of their establishment, however, more than half of such joint public-private ventures, particularly those run the services in a local city or rural area has been financially struggling (Toyo Keizai, 2016). Overall, their financial conditions have become even worse recently because of the COVID-19 pandemic. In other words, their businesses have been continuously in debt and the economic sustainability of their business has also not been maintained. Consequently, local train lines managed by some joint public-private ventures were discontinued. For example, Miki Railway that ran the train services between Kakogawa City and Miki City in Hyogo Prefecture stopped running their services in 2008. Nonetheless, several joint public-private ventures have maintained their economic sustainability mainly through expanding their business fields and/or excellent marketing strategies (e.g. Isumi Railway in Chiba Prefecture and Chizu Express in Hyogo, Okayama and Tottori Prefectures).

Although it had already been predicted before JNR was privatised, two out of the six JR companies namely JR Hokkaido and JR Shikoku have been struggling with financial issues. The main problems of these companies are the characteristics of the areas and train lines they are responsible for and the maintenance costs for lines and carriages. Many of these lines connect local towns and/or rural areas with much smaller population than urban zones, and the number of regular passengers tend to be small. Needless to say, however, the companies still need to keep spending a considerable amount of money for the maintenance of lines and carriages. Especially, the economic sustainability of JR Hokkaido has been facing a serious risk. As of writing, none of JR Hokkaido's train lines or line divisions generate profits and a number of the lines have been/will be discontinued in the near future. Given such financial challenges, the Japanese Government announced in December 2020 that they would financially support JR Hokkaido, JR Shikoku and JR Freight for the next ten years (Toyo Keizai, 2021).

3.3 Socio-cultural Sustainability of Railways in Japan

As demonstrated in Sect. 3.1, railways are the most important travel mode for people residing and/or working in Japan's urban areas. Thus, socio-cultural sustainability, especially social sustainability, of railways can influence the everyday life and work of these people extensively. Two incidents that occurred in October 2021 reveals that how fragile railway services are, although the daily life and work of urban dwellers rely heavily on railways services. In the late evening of 7th October, Tokyo was hit by a strong earthquake and thousands of commuters were stranded for several hours (Reuters, 2021). Just three days after, moreover, a fire at an electric power substation caused power outage and this fire accident suspended JR East train services in Tokyo for serval hours, affecting more than 230 k people (Kyodo News, 2021). These troubles happened, although many railway companies in Japan developed and have been updating their own disaster-prevention plans and make them available online to the general public. As the supervising ministry for train companies, MLIT has also been reviewing its disaster-prevention measures regularly. Both plans and measures are essential for socio-cultural sustainability, especially social sustainability, of train companies.

Concerning cultural elements of socio-cultural sustainability of railways and railway companies, it needs to be noted that the vast majority of train companies in Japan have been offering not only railway services but also a wide range of other services. This denotes that their customers are not limited to their passengers. As shown in Sect. 3.1, residential areas and a wide variety of social amenities have been built or developed along railway lines or terminal stations (Jimura, 2022). Of these, the terminal stations and their surrounding areas often consist of extensive complexes and provide consumers with diverse socio-cultural experiences and services (Jimura, 2022). It is believed that this type of business development strategy was first suggested and implemented by Ichizo Kobayashi, the founder of Hankyu Railway, in the early twentieth century (Hankyu Railway, n.d.). Since then, this business approach has also been employed by many other railway companies across Japan, particularly private railway companies covering urban regions. In the case of Hankyu, its flagship department store is situated near its main terminal station (Osaka Umeda), whilst a main musical theatre for its musical theatre troupe (Takarazuka Grand Theatre) is located near its Takarazuka station. Both department store and musical theatre have been key players in sustaining socio-cultural, particularly cultural, sustainability of the company itself and local communities around its railway stations or along its train lines. Offering the above-mentioned cultural opportunities to local communities and beyond is also related to the company's CSR activities. In fact, supporting the promotion of cultural, art and sport activities is one of the main fields of Hankyu's CSR activities (H2O Retailing, n.d.).

A key problem in some railway companies categorised as joint public-private ventures and JR Hokkaido is the discontinuation of train lines whose business is in debt. As signified in Sect. 3.2, such discontinuation can be comprehended as a right and reasonable decision in terms of economic sustainability of these enterprises. Nonetheless, local residents may not be happy with such a decision. Local people may also deem that the enterprises that decided to discontinue their train services and local governments of the affected areas did not fulfil their responsibility in a satisfactory manner. In fact, the discontinuance of local railway lines can influence their neighbouring communities in a negative rather than positive way. Put differently, socio-cultural, especially social, sustainability of such railway companies can be damaged due to the discontinuation of their services. For instance, a joint public-private venture had operated Furusato Ginga Line in Hokkaido Prefecture since 1989 but stopped running their train services in 2006. Although the railway services were replaced with bus services, a few issues affecting local residents/communities arose. To cite a case, many elderly people who went to a hospital by bus felt that the bus services were less convenient than the train services mainly because local buses did not have a toilet (Horihata, 2010). Horihata (2010) also points out that the discontinuation of local train lines led to the disappearance of a focal point where local people once got together for shopping and/or socialising. That is because, as stated above, many cities or towns in Japan have been developed near or around train stations (Jimura, 2022).

3.4 Environmental Sustainability of Railways in Japan

As stated in Sect. 3.1, railway transport is seen as a (most) eco-friendly transport mode in previous academic studies. Generally, this view is also supported widely in the real world regardless of country and is emphasised by key stakeholders such as advocacy groups (e.g. Campaign for Better Transport, UK) and flight-free travel agencies (e.g. Byway, UK) (The Independent, 2021). In Japan, Japan Private Railway Association and each railway company (e.g. JR Central, JR West and JR Kyushu) also highlight the high environmental sustainability of railways. The low level of CO_2 emission and energy consumption are two major reasons why these railway companies assert that railways are the most environmentally friendly travel mode. According to JR West (n.d.), for example, railway services carry 30% of passenger transport in Japan, whilst their energy consumption is only 4% of the total energy amount spent for Japan's passenger transport. MLIT has also been trying to raise people's awareness of eco-friendliness of railway travels through their promotional activities.

Moreover, the railway industry of Japan and its related businesses have been conducting a variety of measures to make their businesses even more environmentally friendly. In the author's view, these activities can be best explained through the concept of 'reduce', 'reuse' and 'recycle' (3Rs) (see Sect. 4.4 in Chap. 1 for details). As for 'reduce' of 3Rs, for instance, many railway companies, especially large ones covering extensive urban areas (e.g. JR East), have been replacing their carriages with more energy-efficient ones to reduce their CO_2 emission and energy consumption. More specifically, a lower level of CO_2 emission and a higher level of energy efficiency can be realised through the introduction of new carriages with lighter weight, lower level of air resistance and LED light bulbs (JR Central, n.d.). To implement such measures, train companies need to work with conglomerates or manufacturers that produce carriages with cutting-edge technology, including Hitachi, Kawasaki Heavy Industries and Nippon Sharyo. Concerning 'reuse' of 3Rs, a number of carriages that have been utilised by large railway companies serving urban areas have been reused in many ways. In general, such large train companies tend to introduce newest carriages to serve their main/busy train lines with a lot of passengers. Following this, the companies may start using the carriages once served for major lines for other train lines they have. If big train companies in urban areas cannot or do not reuse their carriages within their passenger services, they may sell these carriages to local train companies. To cite a case, Tokyu Railway serving TMP and Kanagawa Prefecture sold their old carriages to Nagano Electric Railway (Nagano Prefecture) and Chichibu Railway (Saitama Prefecture) (Diamond Online, 2018a). Thus, the reuse of old carriages by other train companies in Japan can be beneficial for economic sustainability of both large/urban and small/local railway companies in Japan. Last but not least, recycling of old carriages is also a crucial activity for environmental sustainability. According to JEMAI (2020), 57% of train carriages produced in the fiscal year of 2017 were made of aluminium and they were recycled typically as car parts. All of 3Rs activities of train companies reflect the spirit of *mottainai*, minimising the amount of waste produced through their business activities and decreasing the consumption of raw materials.

Some of the activities carried out by railway companies for environmental sustainability can also be viewed as their CSR activities. For example, many railway companies in Japan sold their old train carriages to Jabodetabek Railway that runs passenger services across the metropolitan area of Jakarta, Indonesia (Diamond Online, 2018b). Nonetheless, it should be remembered that this sale did not intend to increase the Japanese companies' profits but was conducted as international co-operation activities (Diamond Online, 2018b). It was possible thanks to rather similar railway technical standards between Japan and Indonesia. Forest-related activities conducted by JR West is other type of activity for environmental sustainability that can also be regarded as a CSR activity. Working collaboratively with Kyoto Model Forest Association and Kyoto Prefecture, JR West set a forest in the prefecture as Forest of Club J-WEST and has been carrying out forest protection activities since 2013 (JR-odekake net, n.d.). Both the forest itself and activities held there are open to the general public, giving diverse people opportunities to think about nature conservation (JR-odekake net, n.d.).

4 Road (Coach/Bus, Taxi/Rent-a-Car and Bicycle)

4.1 Overview and History

Although railway transport is generally seen as the most eco-friendly travel mode except bicycle/walk, travelling by coach or bus is also often viewed as environmentally friendly transport mode. Additionally, travelling by coach or bus is the most popular way to travel in some regions of the world (e.g. South America) for specific factors such as an underdeveloped national railway network. The history of coach travel for tourism purposes can be traced back to the early twentieth century in Western countries such as the UK and the USA, whilst its history in Japan began in 1960s, connecting urban areas and local cities where urban dwellers originally came from. Across the globe, including Japan, coach has been playing in a leading role in package holidays as the primary travel mode amongst different destinations or between airports, attractions and hotels. In recent years, express coach services connecting large cities and local areas have been expanded and used widely by people in Japan, especially amongst youngsters, thanks to the advantages such as their cheaper prices than other travel modes typically train, improved comfortability of seats, and extended time passengers can spend at their destinations (if they travel by night coach). On the other hand, local bus services are also well used by travellers, but they mainly serve local residents and commuters. As argued in Sects. 3.2, 3.3 and 3.4, for example, many local railway services with the limited number of passengers and poor financial condition have been replaced with bus services. Moreover, a countless number of bus routes link local railway stations with residential areas.

Both taxi and rent-a-car are familiar travel modes for people in Japan. Basically, taxi is not used for travelling a long distance, whilst rent-a-car is. Both travel modes can improve flexibility and degree of freedom in people's itinerary and places to visit. Since 2014, Japan had been enjoying an inbound tourism boom until the COVID-19 pandemic came in 2020 (Jimura, 2019, 2022). Both taxi and rent-a-car industries in Japan financially benefited from the boom, although they also had to cope with issues stemming mainly from cultural differences and overseas tourists' lack of knowledge on Japan's traffic rules. Travelling by bicycle can be comprehended as an ultimate travel mode in terms of eco-friendliness. In Japan, bicycle has been much less established as a travel mode compared with in Western European countries such as Denmark, Germany and the Netherlands. Even in Japan, nevertheless, an increasing number of people have been using bicycle as their main travel mode in their daily lives and more and more cities/towns have become bicycle-friendly, for instance, through the installation of bicycle lanes (e.g. Higashimurayama City, TMP). However, it needs to be noted that travelling by bicycle in Japan has several issues, including those in safety. In Japan, the number of bicycle lanes is still small across the country. When bicycle lanes are newly installed, either the edges of roadways or the edges of pavements are converted to bicycle lanes. To cite a case, cyclists can be hit by a car in the case of the former, whilst pedestrians can be hit by bicycle in the case of the latter. Following sections explore economic, socio-cultural and environmental sustainability of various kinds of road transport in Japan.

4.2 Economic Sustainability of Road Transport in Japan

In Japan, coaches have been employed by coach tour/holiday companies (e.g. Hato Bus and Sanq-tripal) as well as by intercity (highway) coach companies (e.g. JR Bus Kanto, Willer Express and Vip Liner). As a whole, economic sustainability of these two types of companies had increased since 2014 or around thanks to the aforementioned inbound tourism boom. This inbound tourism boom had been mainly supported by tourists from Asian countries (Murayama, 2015) such as China, Thailand and Vietnam. Like the vast majority of other transport businesses, however, the economic sustainability of many coach tour/holiday companies and intercity (highway) coach companies has also been deteriorating since March 2020 due to the impact of COVID-19. That is because, these companies have lost most of their international and domestic customers, especially the former, chiefly due to travel restrictions introduced within Japan as well as those between foreign countries and Japan. Needless to say, such restrictions have been initiated to prevent the spread of COVID-19. Consequently, a record number of these companies went into administration in the fiscal year of 2020. As of October 2021, the number of COVID-19 cases has been ridiculously small, and a range of restrictions has been lifted or softened across Japan. Hence, coach tour/holiday companies have just started running tours that visit various suburban or remote locations (Tokyo MX, 2021), enhancing the preventive measures for COVID-19. Reinforcing such measures is also a strategy adopted by intercity (highway) coach companies to reassure their passengers. Overall, however, the economic sustainability of many coach tour/holiday companies and intercity (highway) coach companies and the industries as a whole have already been hugely damaged, and it will take several years to recover from the aftermath of the COVID-19 pandemic.

The aforementioned travel restrictions have also been influencing taxi and rent-a-car industries negatively. Both, particularly taxi, are a familiar travel mode for visitors when they move from an airport or railway station to their final destination such as a visitor attraction, hotel or restaurant. Thus, a large decrease in the number of passengers who travel by air or rail can easily lead to a huge drop in the number of customers who use taxi or rent-a-car (Nomura, 2021). Kanda (2021) also points out that taxi companies in Japan have been more seriously damaged than private railway companies or local bus companies because the businesses of taxi companies rely more heavily on tourism and tourists than those of train or bus companies. Consequently, many taxi companies in many different prefectures (e.g. Aomori, Osaka and Hiroshima) could not maintain their economic sustainability and went into administration or closed their businesses. Although some rent-a-car companies in Japan went bankrupt (e.g. New Step in Okinawa Prefecture in 2020) due to COVID-19, the economic sustainability of rent-a-car industry seems to have been less seriously damaged by the COVID-19 pandemic compared with the taxi industry in Japan. That is probably because, the rent-a-car market in Japan is currently dominated by a relatively small numbers of big enterprises and they are often affiliated companies (e.g. TOYOTA Rent a Car) of Japan-based multinational car manufacturers (e.g. TOYOTA). In recent years, moreover, some companies newly started providing carsharing services (e.g. ORIX Carshare). Their main target should be city dwellers who do not have a car but use it for a few hours occasionally. In comparison to owning or even renting a car, this option is beneficial for users in terms of the fees they need to pay.

In tourism settings, exploring a tourist destination by bicycle is a common tourist activity. Basically and traditionally, a traveller gets to his/her destination by other transport mode such as train, and then rent a bicycle in the destination from a local bicycle shop, tourist information centre or hotel to fully explore the destination and its surrounding areas. Renting a bicycle for several hours or all day is often not so expensive (e.g. around 1000 JPY per day); hence, it can be seen as an economically sustainable travel mode for most Japanese people. In recent years, the popularity of bicycles as a way to commute, travel and/or exercise has been increasing, particularly after the emergence of COVID-19. Many people try to avoid commuting on packed trains for safety reasons, to enjoy visiting places not far from their home, and/or to maintain their physical health during this challenging time. The increased popularity has led to a wider variety of bicycles with a range of prices. Although some types of bicycles (e.g.

electric bicycles) can be rather expensive, there are still many choices for the general public of Japan and the purchase of a bicycle will not be viewed as a financial burden for most households.

4.3 Socio-cultural Sustainability of Road Transport in Japan

Currently, the highway network across Japan extends over 10,000 km and carries around 100 million passengers annually (Ieda & Iwamori, 2019). This signifies that intercity (highway) coach services are one of the essential transport modes for people in Japan, and its significance is particularly high for the areas that cannot be accessed by Shinkansen bullet train (Ieda & Iwamori, 2019) or even by normal train services. Thus, it is fair to say that the highway network and intercity (highway) coach services are crucial to maintain or enhance socio-cultural sustainability of the above-mentioned regions such as rural and/or remote areas. If these regions lose the access to intercity (highway) coach services, they will become isolated areas, and this can negatively affect the quality of life of local inhabitants and socio-cultural sustainability of the areas. This also means that it is challenging for excursionists or tourists, especially the former, to visit tourist destinations located in such regions.

It should also be noted that such isolated areas exist not only in rural/ or remote regions but also in urban regions such as TMP. In the isolated areas in urban regions, for instance, it may take 20 minutes or more by walk from residential districts to the nearest railway station, and there are no or extremely limited number of regular bus services connecting these two places (e.g. some quarters in Setagaya Ward in TMP). In light of such an inconvenient situation and presence of people who have difficulty in mobility/using public transport, many local governments having isolated areas have been introducing community transport services. Community transport services have also been well developed in other nations, especially in the West (e.g. Australia and the UK). Local governments intend that community transport services should serve primarily local residents, although generally same-day visitors or tourists can also use the services. In Japan, small buses are a major travel mode to be adopted for community transport services. Representative routes of community bus services connect key facilities in and around a municipality such as railway station, city hall, hospital, library, museum and/or sports hall. 'Mubus' of Musashino City in TMP is widely accepted as the first community bus service introduced in Japan. The service started in 1995 and is used by around 2.6 million people annually (Musashino City, n.d.). Thus, it is true to say that a wide variety of coach/bus services have been playing essential roles in maintaining socio-cultural sustainability of local communities all over Japan. Furthermore, taxi is another transport mode that can assist people who have mobility issues. As of writing, a number of local governments financially support the use of taxi by elderly and/or disabled residents (e.g. Atsugi City in Kanagawa Prefecture, Onomichi City in Hiroshima Prefecture and Sanuki City in Kagawa Prefecture).

4.4 Environmental Sustainability of Road Transport

Along with railways, coaches and buses are also generally seen as an eco-friendly travel mode across the world. In fact, the eco-friendliness of travelling by coach or bus has been emphasised by service providers in diverse countries, including Japan (e.g. Shinki Bus and Kobe City). Environmental sustainability of their businesses, especially local bus companies' or operators', have been enhanced mainly through the adoption of vehicles with advanced environmentally friendly technologies and/or features. Representative examples of such technologies and/or features and companies or operators adopting them are as follows:

- Hybrid vehicle:

    - Private companies – Meitetsu Bus
    - Public operators –TMP and Kobe City

- Electric vehicle:

    - Private companies – Kanden Tunnel Electric Bus, Keihan Bus, and Nishitetsu Bus
    - Public operators – Iida City (Nagano Prefecture)

5 Sustainability of Japan's Transport Sector

* Natural gas vehicle:

    – Private companies – Yamanashi Kotsu
    – Public operators – Kobe City

* Biofuel vehicle:

    – Private companies – JR Bus Tohoku, Shuhoku Bus, Keikyu Bus, Seibu Bus and JR Shikoku Bus
    – Public operators – Ushiku City (Ibaraki Prefecture) and Higashiomi City (Shiga Prefecture)

* Fuel cell electric vehicle:

    – Private companies – Keio Bus
    – Public operators – TMP and Yokohama City

* Hydrogen fuel cell vehicle:

    – Private companies – Tokyu Bus
    – Public operators – TMP

As of writing, a main obstacle for the providers of coach/bus services to introduce and continue to use the aforementioned eco-friendly vehicles would be high introduction and maintenance costs. This problem is especially serious for small private companies with limited financial resources.

Technologies or features to improve environmental sustainability of travel modes can also be observed in Japan's rent-a-car and taxi industries. Nowadays, some types of eco-friendly vehicles are available for customers to rent at several Japan's rent-a-car companies, including Nippon Rent-a-car, Nissan Rent-a-car and ORIX Rent-a-car. For instance, customers can choose a hybrid vehicle or electric vehicle when they rent a car from these enterprises. Usually, renting an eco-friendly vehicle is more expensive than a petrol vehicle, whilst the former is cheaper than the latter regarding fuel costs. In some cases, therefore, renting an eco-friendly car can be less expensive than a petrol car, particularly when customers drive a long distance. However, exploring non-urban areas by eco-friendly vehicle may face some difficulties, typically a lack of facilities and services (e.g. electric refuelling stations). In relation to rent-a-car, carsharing has been emerging in the Japanese market as another way to rent a vehicle. As discussed in Sect. 4.2, carsharing attracts attentions or interests of drivers who do not own a private vehicle in terms of its economic sustainability. Moreover, environmental sustainability of various carsharing schemes adopted in urban regions of Japan should be noted. The introduction and development of flexible carsharing systems that can satisfy diverse needs of customers may lead to the larger proportion/number of urban households who do not possess a private car.

Liquefied petroleum gas (hereafter LPG) is a common fuel for taxis in Japan. The primary reason why LPG vehicles have been widely adopted as taxis would be LPG's cheaper fuel costs than petrol. On the other hand, LPG cars have not been used commonly as vehicles for private use due to their maintenance costs and the limited number of LPG refuelling stations throughout Japan (Web Cartop, 2019). The good economic sustainability of LPG vehicles is not the only reason why these vehicles share the vast majority of cars used as taxis. In fact, the environmental sustainability of LPG cars is another key reason of their popularity (Osaka Taxi Association (hereafter OTA), n.d.). According to OTA (n.d.), LPG cars have clearer exhaust gas and lower level of vehicle vibration or noise than petrol cars. Compared with other transport modes by road, the eco-friendliness of bicycle is obvious and widely acknowledged by the general public of Japan.

5 Water (Cruise Ship, Ferry, High-Speed Craft and Passenger Boat)

Of a variety of transport modes by water, cruise ships are different from others because their purposes include not only moving people from A to B but also working as visitor attractions during their voyages. The COVID-19 pandemic reveals that the fragility of the economic sustainability of cruise ship companies and their businesses. Due to the highly confined nature of spaces in cruise ships whilst sailing often long itineraries, removing or minimising the risk for COVID-19 infection and spread can be quite challenging and more demanding than other transport modes such as air flights and trains. As a result, a number of cruises have been suspended or cancelled since the pandemic began (e.g. One-week domestic cruise by Asuka II between 29 April and 5 May 2021). In fact, the financial results of Yusen Cruise running Asuka II cruises were greatly in red in the fiscal year of 2020 (Company Activities Total Research Institute, 2021). On the other hand, overall the socio-cultural sustainability of cruises has been enhanced in Japan. This can be justified by the fact that there has been an increase in both the number of Japanese and foreign cruise ships calling at ports in Japan and the number of Japanese people enjoying cruise experiences (Suzuki, 2018). Nevertheless, it has been pointed out that cruises and cruise ships can cause health problems. These problems include the spread of respiratory infections or gastrointestinal illness amongst passengers and crew (Pavli et al., 2016). For example, the former includes the diseases caused by COVID-19 and the latter includes food poisoning. Respiratory infections can also affect the health of local residents residing near the ports cruise ships call at. Thus the socio-cultural sustainability of cruises and cruise ships can be damaged in terms of these possible health issues.

Cruises and cruise ships have been criticised in terms of its environmental sustainability. Diverse major environmental issues can be caused or worsened by cruises and cruise ships. Of these, solid and food wastes, sewage and greywater, and air pollution can be seen as representative examples of environmental issues (Commoy et al., 2005; Murena et al., 2018; Ytreberg et al., 2020). Considering these impacts and following a request from the United Nations Educational, Scientific and Cultural Organization, Italian authorities approved a ban on cruise ships entering the historic centre of Venice (BBC News, 2021). This would be beneficial for socio-cultural and environmental sustainability of this historic city and its beautiful lagoon. Simultaneously, however, economic sustainability of city's economy can be hugely damaged as a result of the ban. In fact, business leaders and local campaigners about negative impacts of the ban on jobs in and around the cruise industry (Euronews, 2021). Although compensation will be available for the people affected by the ban, there is still an important level of concerns as the livelihoods of many local inhabitants rely on the cruise industry (Euronews, 2021). The aforementioned environmental problems can also be confirmed at cruises and cruise ships calling at ports in Japan (Suzuki, 2018; Yuguchi & Sakai, 2018). Unlike Venice, however, a bold decision with a drastic measure that bans or hugely restrict the number of cruise ships calling at Japanese ports has not been made as of writing. Rather, the majority of port cities in Japan seem to have been keen to attract more cruises calling at their ports, expecting their economic contribution to local economy (e.g. Hokkaido Prefecture, Nagoya City, Kobe City and Tokushima Prefecture). Nevertheless, there is a sceptical view towards the economic contribution cruises can really make to local economy and wider society of Japan (Carr & Kiyono, 2019). The level of cruises' economic contribution has been quite limited since March 2020 due to the COVID-19 pandemic. In relation to this, it should also be noted that the majority of cruise passengers in Japan are overseas tourists and most of cruise ships calling at ports in Japan are foreign ships. Hence, the impact of the COVID-19 pandemic on port cities that financially rely on the cruise industry has been immense.

Unlike cruise ships, ferries, high-speed crafts (*kosokutei*) and passenger boats (*watashibune*) do not have the nature as visitor attractions. They are major transport modes by sea and serve same-day visitors/tourists as well as local people. In the case of Japan, the services provided by these three different transport modes by sea can be distinguished mainly by travel distance. Generally, ferries are used for a long-distance travel by sea (e.g. between Otaru City in Hokkaido Prefecture and Maizuru City in Kyoto Prefecture) and usually used by tourists rather than local residents. High-speed crafts are often used for a middle-distance sea travel (e.g. between Kure City in Hiroshima Prefecture and Matsuyama City in Ehime Prefecture) and used commonly by excursionists, tourists and local inhabitants. On the other hand, the vast majority of passengers of passenger boats are local people who take it for commuting to office, school or hospital. This signifies that passenger boasts are usually used for a short-distance travel by sea. Figure 5.3 shows passenger boats connecting Tsuchido in Onomichi City and Mukaishima, a small island belonging to the city. This type of passenger boats can transport bicycles and motorbikes as well as people.

5 Sustainability of Japan's Transport Sector

Fig. 5.3 Passenger boats connecting Tsuchido and Mukaishima in Onomichi City. (Source: Author)

As a whole, transport by sea, including ferries, high-speed crafts and passenger boats, is regarded as a relatively environmentally friendly travel mode. Like the case of vehicles, the environmental sustainability of these three travel ways by sea has also been improved through the advancement in maritime technology. The socio-cultural sustainability of them, especially passenger boats', is particularly important as the service offered with the boats is often essential to sustain local residents' everyday lives. Overall, nevertheless, the economic sustainability of the companies running transport services with ferries, high-speed crafts and/or passenger boats seems to have been weaker in recent years for various reasons. Obviously, the impact of the COVID-19 pandemic has been immense for the enterprises that run transport services by ferry and/or high-speed crafts as tourism activities and commuting have been limited. The companies that manage transport services by passenger boats have been negatively affected by other factors, including the construction of new bridges or removal of toll fees from existing bridges (Terai & Ogihara, 1998).

6   Conclusion

Today, the transport sector and its services are essential for people to sustain their lives and movement, including tourism. In other words, transport modes play a crucial role in maintaining or enhancing the socio-cultural sustainability of people's lives and activities such as commutes and tourism. In light of the definitions of tourism suggested and adopted in the real world and academia, it is confirmed that transport is vital to make tourism happen. The importance of transport in tourism has been getting greater and greater as an increasing number of people have been travel to places outside their usual environments for tourism purposes, including overseas destinations. If Leiper's (1979) tourism system is applied, Japan has a long-standing history as a 'tourist generating region' mainly since the 1980s, whilst its history as a 'tourist destination region' is relatively short after the 2000s. Prior to the COVID-19 pandemic, Japan had been experiencing and enjoying inbound tourism boom. In this impactful phenomenon, the transport sector, particularly airline companies, played a significant role in bringing foreign tourists to Japan. As confirmed across the globe, however, COVID-19 totally changed the situation and a challenging time for the transport sector in Japan still continues as of writing (November 2021).

People travel by air, land or sea. Each of these three has diverse transport modes. As a whole, transport by land, particularly rail, is often evaluated as the most eco-friendly travel mode in terms of its impacts on the natural environment. This also implies that a high level of environmental sustainability of natural environment in surrounding communities can be realised through an appropriate use of the transport by land, especially rail. On the other hand, transport by air is frequently blamed as the least eco-friendly transport mode. This has led to the emergence and spread of anti-flight social movement, flight shame, which is prominent in Europe. Nevertheless, it is crucial that such social movements have not been commonly noticeable across the world, even in other Western countries outside Europe such as the USA. There would be serval reasons why the social movement can be typically found in Europe, particularly rich Scandinavian and Western European nations. For example, the total distances travelled by air across nations within Europe would be larger than those in other regions of the world. That is because, Europe comprises of around 50 countries with a number of holiday and business destinations, although its landmass is less than half of the USA's. This would be one of the main reasons why many low-cost carriers such as easyJet, Ryanair and Norwegian Air Shuttle have been thriving, developing a wide variety of airline routes. The other important geographical feature of Europe is that most nations are next to each other without being divided by sea. This factor should be a key reason why transport by land such as rail or road has also well developed within the European region. Compared with people residing in nations in other regions of the world (e.g. the USA or Japan), those living in European countries have more options or alternatives to air flights (e.g. coaches and trains) when they travel internationally across the borders.

There would also be another reason why the social movement for environment cannot be a truly global phenomenon sympathised by all. Generally, such a movement tends to be led by young, educated people living in rich developed countries such as Scandinavian and Western European who can be seen as 'haves'. Nonetheless, it would be almost impossible for people residing in less developed or developing nations ('have-nots') to see such environmental issues, including the ones caused or worsened by transport, as imminent threats. That is because, less developed or developing nations and their citizens often cannot afford climate change to make a living or increase their living standards. Consequently, less developed or developing countries accelerate environmental problems such as global warming as their economies grow because they cannot afford to use alternative (renewable) energy sources (Davey, 2016). It is also natural for these countries to pursue their economic growth as this is the path every developed country went through. At that time, these developed nations paid no or little attention to global environmental problems. If so, why can today's developed countries force less developed or developing countries to prioritise measures to improve global environmental issues, compromising their economic growth? No developed countries can do so in terms of fairness amongst all the nations in the world.

Transport by sea also includes some different travel modes. Of these, cruise ships and cruises have been accused frequently due to its low level of environmental (and socio-cultural) sustainability and its negative environmental influences on natural environment and people, including water or air pollution, although cruises might be able to contribute to the economic sustainability of the port cities where cruise ships call at. On the other hand, negative environmental impacts of ferries, high-speed crafts and passenger boats would be rather limited, and they, particularly passenger boats, are crucial to maintain the socio-cultural sustainability of local communities.

Owing to external factors beyond the control of the transport sector, typically the COVID-19 pandemic since March 2020, the economic sustainability of most of companies/organisations that provide customers with transport services has been deteriorating and Japanese ones have not been exceptions. Such economic issues have especially been serious for Japanese enterprises whose businesses rely heavily on inbound tourism such as international passenger flights and international cruises. Last but not least, it needs to be remembered that the environmental sustainability of transport services in Japan has been improved and will also be enhanced further mainly through the advancement in transport technology. In addition, it would also be true that the environmental sustainability of transport services can also be strengthened by raising Japanese people's awareness of natural environment. The awareness can be raised, for example, by understanding and even being involved in (1) transport companies' activities for CSR and 3Rs, (2) the concept of SDGs and diverse activities for SDGs (see Figs. 5.1 and 5.2), and/or (3) the notion of *mottainai* and practicing *mottainai* spirit.

References

Abeyratne, R. I. (1999). Management of the environmental impact of tourism and air transport on small Island developing states. *Journal of Air Transport Management, 5*(1), 31–37.

ANA. (n.d.-a). *Social contribution (Japan)*. Available at: https://www.ana.co.jp/group/en/csr/regional_creation/domestic/. Accessed 2 Oct 2021.

ANA. (n.d.-b). *ANA future promise*. Available at: https://www.ana.co.jp/en/jp/topics/ana-future-promise/#contribution-sdgs. Accessed 5 Oct 2021.

ATAG. (2021a). *Who we are*. Available at: https://www.atag.org/about-us/who-we-are.html. Accessed 5 Oct 2021.

ATAG. (2021b). *Facts and figures*. Available at: https://www.atag.org/facts-figures.html. Accessed 5 Oct 2021.

Balaman, S. Y. (2019). *Sustainability issues in biomass-based production chains*. Elsevier.

BBC News. (2021). *Venice bans cruise ships from historic centre*. Available at: https://www.bbc.co.uk/news/world-europe-56592109. Accessed 3 Nov 2021.

Boström, M. (2012). A missing pillar? Challenges in theorizing and practicing social sustainability: Introduction to the special issue. *Sustainability: Science, Practice and Policy, 8*(1), 3–14.

Carr, A., & Kiyono, Y. (2019). *Kanko bokoku ron* (Tourism can ruin Japan) [in Japanese]. Chuokoron-shinsha.

Chiambaretto, P., Mayenc, E., Chappert, H., Engsig, J., Fernandez, A. S., & Le Roy, F. (2021). Where does flygskam come from? The role of citizens' lack of knowledge of the environmental impact of air transport in explaining the development of flight shame. *Journal of Air Transport Management, 93*, 102049.

Commoy, J., Polytika, C. A., Nadel, R., & Bulkley, J. W. (2005). The environmental impact of cruise ships. In R. Walton (Ed.), *Impacts of global climate change* (pp. 1–12). ASCE Press.

Company Activities Total Research Institute. (2021). *Kanpo kessan database – Yusen Cruise* (Japanese government gazette database: Balance sheets of Japanese companies – Yusen Cruise) [in Japanese]. Available at: https://catr.jp/settlements/81368/208236. Accessed 1 Nov 2021.

Davey, T. (2016). *Developing countries can't afford climate change*. Available at: https://futureoflife.org/2016/08/05/developing-countries-cant-afford-climate-change/. Accessed 14 Nov 2021.

Diamond Online. (2018a). *Intai densha wa dokoeiku? – page 3* (Where do old carriages go? – page 3) [in Japanese]. Available at: https://diamond.jp/articles/-/172043?page=3. Accessed 19 Oct 2021.

Diamond Online. (2018b). *Intai densha wa dokoeiku? – page 4* (Where do old carriages go? – page 4) [in Japanese]. Available at: https://diamond.jp/articles/-/172043?page=4. Accessed 19 Oct 2021.

Euronews. (2021). *Economic fears in Venice as cruise ship ban comes into force.* Available at: https://www.euronews.com/2021/08/02/economic-fears-in-venice-as-cruise-ship-ban-comes-into-force. Accessed 3 Nov 2021.

Furomoto, T. (2017). Haishitaisho local-sen no sonzoku-mondai (Issues in survival of local train lines) [in Japanese]. *Kotsu-ken, 34*, 78–92.

H2O Retailing. (n.d.). *Shakaikoken katsudo* (CSR activities) [in Japanese]. Available at: https://www.h2o-retailing.co.jp/ja/csr/society.html. Accessed 17 Oct 2021.

Hankyu Railway. (n.d.). *Ichizo Kobayashi* [in Japanese]. Available at: https://www.hankyu.co.jp/cont/ichizo/column1.html. Accessed 17 Oct 2021.

Horihata, M. (2010). Chiiki-tetsudo haishi ga oyobosu chiiki-shakai eno eikyo (The impact of discontinuance of local train lines on local communities) [in Japanese]. *Obirin ronko: Shizenkagaku sogokagaku kenkyu, 1*, 49–62.

IATA. (2021) *Health & safety for passengers & crew*. Available at: https://www.iata.org/en/programs/safety/health/. Accessed 4 Oct 2021.

Ieda, H., & Iwamori, K. (2019). Allocation and type selection of expressway bus-stops in relation to bus operation strategies in Japan [in Japanese]. *Doboku-keikaku-gaku Kenkyu, 75*(5), I_719–730.

Inkson, C., & Minnaert, L. (2018). *Tourism management: An introduction*. Sage.

JAL. (n.d.-a). *Health and productivity management*. Available at: https://www.jal.com/en/sustainability/human/health-management/. Accessed 2 Oct 2021.

JAL. (n.d.-b). *JAL group actions to achieve SDGs*. Available at: http://www.jal.com/en/sustainability/sdgs/. Accessed 5 Oct 2021.

JEMAI. (2020). *Aluminium seihin no haiki to recycle (tetsudo sharyo)* (Disposal and recycling of aluminium products (train carriages)) [in Japanese]. Available at: http://www.cjc.or.jp/school/a/a-2-3-1.html. Accessed 19 Oct 2021.

Jimura, T. (2019). *World heritage sites: Tourism, local communities and conservation activities*. CABI.

Jimura, T. (2020). Changing faces of Tokyo: Regeneration, tourism and Tokyo 2020. In N. Wise & T. Jimura (Eds.), *Tourism, cultural heritage and urban regeneration – Changing spaces in historical places* (pp. 141–155). Springer.

Jimura, T. (2022). *Cultural and heritage tourism in Japan*. Routledge.

JR Central. (n.d.). *Chikyu ni yasashii norimono tetsudo* (Railway transport is eco-friendly) [in Japanese]. Available at: https://eco.jr-central.co.jp/railway/. Accessed 19 Oct 2021.

JR West. (n.d.). *Chikyu ni yasashii tetsudo* (Railway transport is eco-friendly) [in Japanese]. Available at: https://www.westjr.co.jp/company/action/env/eco/001/. Accessed 19 Oct 2021.

JR-odekake net. (n.d.). *Club J-WEST no mori* (Forest of Club J-WEST) [in Japanese]. Available at: https://www.jr-odekake.net/cjw/about/forest/. Accessed 19 Oct 2021.

JTA. (2021). *Honichi gaikokujin ryokosha su shukkoku nihonjin su* (The numbers of inbound and outbound tourists) [in Japanese]. Available at: https://www.mlit.go.jp/kankocho/siryou/toukei/in_out.html. Accessed 22 Sept 2021.

Kanda, Y. (2021). COVID-19 and public transport: An examination of the coronavirus's impacts and steps toward revival in the post-pandemic world [in Japanese]. *IATSS Review, 46*(1), 40–48.

Toyo Keizai. (2021). *Hokkaido no taboo: JR jogebunriron ga sainen suru riyu* (Taboo of JR Hokkaido: Reasons why their business style may need to be changed) [in Japanese]. Available at: https://toyokeizai.net/articles/-/418110?page=2. Accessed 15 Oct 2021.

Kurosu, H. (2014). *Kaigaitoko Jiyuka 50 shunen ni mukete* (The 50th anniversary of the liberalisation of overseas travel) [in Japanese]. Available at: https://www.tourism.jp/tourism-database/column/2014/02/overseas-travel-liberalization/. Accessed 18 Sept 2021.

Kyodo News. (2021). *Fire-caused power outage hits trains in Tokyo area, 236,000 affected*. Available at: https://english.kyodonews.net/news/2021/10/44b40774fe01-breaking-news-extensive-power-outage-hits-jr-trains-in-tokyo-area.html. Accessed 17 Oct 2021.

Leiper, N. (1979). The framework of tourism: Towards a definition of tourism, tourist, and the tourist industry. *Annals of Tourism Research, 6*(4), 390–407.

MLIT. (n.d.). *Kankyoteki ni Jizokukano na Kotsu* (Environmentally sustainable transport) [in Japanese]. Available at: https://www.mlit.go.jp/sogoseisaku/environment/sosei_environment_fr_000061.html. Accessed 15 Sept 2021.

Murayama, K. (2015). *Honichi-gaikokujin kanko-business nyumon-koza* (Introduction to tourism business targeting inbound tourists to Japan) [in Japanese]. Shoeisha.

Murena, F., Mocerino, L., Quaranta, F., & Toscano, D. (2018). Impact on air quality of cruise ship emissions in Naples, Italy. *Atmospheric Environment, 187*, 70–83.

Musashino City. (n.d.). *Mubus: Aisare Hashiritsuzukete 20nen* (Mubus: 20 years of service) [in Japanese]. Available at: https://musashino-kanko.com/musashi-now/%E8%B5%B0%E3%82%8A%E7%B6%9A%E3%81%91%E3%81%A620%E5%B9%B4/. Accessed 26 Oct 2021.

Nomura, M. (2021). Shingara coronavirus kansensho wo meguru shakaiteki-konran to seisaku (Social chaos caused by the COVID-19 pandemic and policies for recovery) [in Japanese]. *Sanken Ronshu, 48*, 9–16.

OECD. (2008). *The environmental impacts of increased international air transport.* Available at: https://www.oecd.org/greengrowth/greening-transport/41508474.pdf. Accessed 16 Sept 2021.

OECD. (n.d.). *Environmental criteria for sustainable transport.* Available at: https://www.oecd.org/env/greening-transport/environmentalcriteriaforsustainabletransport.htm. Accessed 16 Sept 2021.

Ono, N. (2013). Nihonkoku saijojo no kadai (Tasks for JAL's relisting) [in Japanese]. *Kaetsu University Research Review, 55*(2), 1–13.

OTA. (n.d.). *Taxi wa kankyo ni yasashii* (Taxis are environmentally friendly) [in Japanese]. Available at: https://www.osakataxi.or.jp/eco/. Accessed 30 Oct 2021.

Otsuka, Y., & Fujiwara, T. (2015). Nihonkoku no keieihatan to sohikiteki-yoin (1) (JAL's bankruptcy and its organisational factors) [in Japanese]. *RIPESS Working Paper, 65*, 1–33.

Page, S. (2005). *Transport and tourism: Global perspectives.* Pearson.

Page, S. (2015). *Tourism management* (5th ed.). Routledge.

Page, S. J., & Connell, J. (2020). *Tourism: A modern synthesis* (5th ed.). Routledge.

Pavli, A., Maltezou, H. C., Papadakis, A., Katerelos, P., Saroglou, G., Tsakris, A., & Tsiodras, S. (2016). Respiratory infections and gastrointestinal illness on a cruise ship: A three-year prospective study. *Travel Medicine and Infectious Disease, 14*(4), 389–397.

Razumovskaya, E. M., Lapidus, L. V., Mishakin, T. S., & Popov, M. L. (2014). Features and peculiarities of the Russian passenger rail market development. *Mediterranean Journal of Social Sciences, 5*(18), 165–165.

Reuters. (2021). *Magnitude 6.1 quake jolts Tokyo, causing blackouts but no tsunami warning.* Available at: https://www.reuters.com/world/asia-pacific/earthquake-61-jolts-tokyo-preliminary-magnitude-estimated-61-nhk-2021-10-07/. Accessed 17 Oct 2021.

Sagar, K., Kumar, A., Ankush, G., Harika, T., Saranya, M., & Hemanth, D. (2016). Implementation of IoT based railway calamity avoidance system using cloud computing technology. *Indian Journal of Science and Technology, 9*(17), 1–5.

Shalom, R. (2021). *Why travelling by train is environmentally friendly?* Available at: https://www.saveatrain.com/blog/why-choosing-to-travel-by-train-is-environmentally-friendly/. Accessed 11 Oct 2021.

Smith, S. L. (2004). The measurement of global tourism: Old debates, new consensus, and continuing challenges. In A. A. Lew, C. M. Hall, & A. M. Williams (Eds.), *A companion to tourism* (pp. 25–35). Blackwell Publishing.

Susnienė, D. (2012). Quality approach to the sustainability of public transport. *Transport, 27*(1), 102–110.

Suzuki, K. (2018). Cruise kyakusen kiko-kyaku no kanko-kodo: Hakodate-ken Raiho-kyaku no kekka-hokoku (Activities of cruise passengers: A case of Hakodate) [in Japanese]. *Hokusei Rinshu – Kei, 57*(2), 111–116.

Terai, S., & Ogihara, M. (1998). Study on planning to Islands promotion in case of construct a bridge to connect Honsyu with Shikoku – About the Tourist Industry in Geiyo Islands [in Japanese]. *Toshi-keikaku Ronbunshu, 33*, 127–132.

The Independent. (2021). *What's the most environmentally friendly way to travel?* Available at: https://www.independent.co.uk/climate-change/sustainable-living/sustainable-travel-transport-environmentally-friendly-b1891496.html. Accessed 19 Oct 2021.

Tokyo MX. (2021). *Fukkatsu nerau kanko-gyokai* (Japan's tourism industry aim to revive their businesses) [in Japanese]. Available at: https://news.yahoo.co.jp/articles/23c417b827292f3b0263df2bf12ecc618fc7ce47. Accessed 24 Oct 2021.

Tokyo Metro. (n.d.). *Sustainability juyokadai to themes* (Sustainability materiality and themes). Available at: https://www.tokyometro.jp/corporate/csr/materiality.html. Accessed 11 Oct 2021.

Toyo Keizai. (2016). *Hansu ijo ga akaji: Sanseku tetsudo no kibishii genjo* (More than half of joint public-private ventures for passenger railway lines are in debt) [in Japanese]. Available at: https://toyokeizai.net/articles/-/143321. Accessed 15 Oct 2021.

Trainer, T. (2005). Social responsibility: The most important, and neglected, problem of all? *International Journal of Social Economics, 32*(8), 682–703.

UN. (n.d.). *The 17 goals*. Available at: https://sdgs.un.org/goals. Accessed 15 Sept 2021.

UN Global Compact. (n.d.). *Social sustainability*. Available at: https://www.unglobalcompact.org/what-is-gc/our-work/social. Accessed 2 Oct 2021.

UNWTO. (2001). *Tourism satellite account: Recommended methodological framework*. UNWTO.

UNWTO. (n.d.) *Glossary of tourism terms*. Available at: https://www.unwto.org/glossary-tourism-terms. Accessed 12 Sept 2021.

Vaghi, C., & Percoco, M. (2011). City logistics in Italy: Success factors and environmental performance. In C. Macharis & S. Melo (Eds.), *City distribution and urban freight transport: Multiple perspectives* (pp. 151–175). Edward Elgar.

Virkar, A. R., & Mallya, P. D. (2018). A review of dimensions of tourism transport affecting tourist satisfaction. *Indian Journal of Commerce & Management Studies, 9*(1), 72–80.

Web Cartop. (2019). *Taxi ni saiyosareru LP gas sha ga joyosha ni hiromaranai wake* (The reasons why LPG vehicles are not widely adopted as cars for private use) [in Japanese]. Available at: https://www.webcartop.jp/2019/09/422924/2/. Accessed 30 Oct 2021.

Ytreberg, E., Eriksson, M., Maljutenko, I., Jalkanen, J. P., Johansson, L., Hasellöv, I. M., & Granhag, L. (2020). Environmental impacts of grey water discharge from ships in the Baltic Sea. *Marine Pollution Bulletin, 152*, 110891.

Yuguchi, K., & Sakai, H. (2018). Gaiko cruise kyakusen no kiko no shuchu ga motarasu fu no eikyo ni kansuru kosatsu (Examination of negative impacts caused by concentration of foreign cruise ships at ports in Japan) [in Japanese]. *Kotsugaku kenkyu, 61*, 85–92.

6

Sustainability of Japan's Accommodation Sector

1 Introduction

Chapter 5 indicates that 'movement' or 'transport' is an essential element of tourism according to the definitions of tourism suggested by UNWTO (n.d.) (see Sect. 1 in Chap. 5). In these definitions, staying at 'places outside people's usual environment' can also be regarded as a vital component of tourism. In this context, 'places' is understood as tourist destinations where main activities of same-day visitors and tourists happen with the purposes of leisure, business or visiting friends and relatives (hereafter VFR). Of same-day visitors and tourists, the latter needs a place to stay overnight. The only exception is VFR as their friends or relatives may allow tourists to stay overnight at their home. Thus, accommodation is a crucial part of tourism, especially for tourists. The amounts of spending per visitor at tourist destinations can significantly differ between excursionists and tourists, and this difference often comes from whether or not they spend for accommodation (Jimura, 2022). This implies that a good level of economic sustainability of each accommodation business and the accommodation sector as a whole can also make a good contribution to the economic sustainability of the destination where each accommodation business is situated. Nowadays, the regional and/or local governments of many tourist destinations charge tourist tax. According to Insider (2019), 41 countries charge tourist tax as of 2019. Not in every country, but in many countries (e.g. Italy, Malaysia and the USA), tourist tax is collected by accommodation businesses on behalf of local, regional or national government, and is sometimes called 'hotel tax'. The importance of accommodation sector for the sustainability of local, regional or national economy can also be backed and justified by this fact. In Japan, Tokyo Metropolitan Prefecture (hereafter TMO) is the first regional government that introduced tourist tax in 2002. As of writing, regional and/or local governments in Japan charging tourist tax include Kanazawa City in Ishikawa Prefecture, Kyoto Urban Prefecture and Osaka Urban Prefecture all of which are well-known tourist destinations and urban spaces in Japan. The cases of Fukuoka City and Kitakyushu City, both located in Fukuoka Prefecture, are noteworthy as tourist tax in these two cities is charged by the prefecture as well as the city.

In recent years, particularly under challenging circumstance due to natural disasters (e.g. typhoon and earthquake) or the pandemic (i.e. COVID-19), the accommodation sector in Japan has been playing an important role in supporting the socio-cultural sustainability of people's lives and local communities. Playing such a key role has also been functioning as accommodation companies' corporate social responsibility (hereafter CSR) activities, enhancing or maintaining their socio-cultural sustainability as members of society. To be specific, a number of hotels in different regions of Japan have accepted people who suffered from a natural disaster or pandemic disease voluntarily or responding a request from central, regional or local government. These are really good examples of CSR activities that have been carried out by businesses in the accommodation sector. Moreover, the accommodation sector in Japan has also been eager to maintain or strengthen the level of environmental sustainability of their own businesses and the environments surrounding their businesses. For instance, many hotels in Japan have obtained or have been working to acquire ISO 14001 certification. ISO 14001 specifies the criteria for an environmental management system and outlines a framework that a company/organisation can follow to establish its own effective environmental management system (ISO, n.d.). Compared with the businesses of other sectors forming the tourism industry, those of the accommodation sector involves a wider variety of activities of their customers (guests) such as sleeping, relaxing, bathing, eating, drinking and/or working. Because of such a wide range of their services, furthermore, the customers (guests) of the accommodation businesses are likely to use their services longer (e.g. one night and two days) than those of other sectors in the tourism industry (e.g. one to two hours in a restaurant). Thus, other key notions for this book such as the Sustainable Development Goals (hereafter SDGs), and 'reduce', 'reuse' and 'recycle' (3Rs) are also likely to be embedded in the businesses of the accommodation sector. This also implies that there is a large room to reflect and practice the spirit of *mottainai* in daily businesses of the accommodation sector.

In this introductory section, it should also be emphasised that Japan has diverse sorts of accommodation and there are many possible ways to categorise them into different groups. In light of various elements of accommodation such as natures, prices and origins, this chapter divides Japan's accommodation facilities into subsequent six main groups:

- Western-style hotel (Sect. 2),
- Japanised Western-style hotel (Sect. 3),
- Japanese-style inn (Sect. 4),
- Budget accommodation (Sect. 5),
- Outdoor accommodation (Sect. 6), and
- *Minpaku* (Sect. 7)

Like the previous chapter (Chap. 5) that is about sustainability of Japan's transport sector, this chapter also explores each of the aforementioned major categories of accommodation in terms of economic, sociocultural and environmental sustainability.

2 Western-Style Hotel (Luxury Hotel and Resort Hotel)

Nowadays, Western-style hotels in Japan can be categorised into Western-style hotels with full services (e.g. luxury hotels and resort hotels) and Japanised Western-style hotels with no frills (e.g. *business hotels* in Japanese

English). This section focuses on the former and those with a large hotel capacity and located in urban areas are usually called *city hotels* (Japanese English) in Japan. On the other hand, the subsequent section, Sect. 3, examines the latter.

It is generally agreed that the history of Western-style hotels in Japan commenced in 1860, at the end of the Edo period, when Yokohama Hotel was opened in Yokohama City (Kanagawa Prefecture) (Yokohama Archives of History, 2007; Japan Travel Bureau Foundation (hereafter JTBF) 2019). Yokohama Hotel was founded by C. J. Huffnagel, a former captain of Dutch sailing ship, Nassau (Cwiertka, 2006). The development of this first Western-style hotel in Japan was triggered by the Treaty of Amity and Commerce between Japan and the USA that was signed in 1858 and became effective in 1859. Later, two Western employees of Yokohama Hotel established their own Western-style hotels, namely Royal British Hotel in 1862 and Typhoon Hotel in 1864 (Cwiertka, 2006). Subsequently, more Western-style hotels were built in other Japanese cities that encompassed foreign settlements such as Kobe City (Hyogo Prefecture) and Nagasaki City (Nagasaki Prefecture) (JTBF, 2019). For example, Oriental Hotel was opened in Kobe City in 1870, following the opening of Kobe Port in 1868, and has been loved and protected by their guests, people in the city and the city itself since that time (Oriental Hotel, 2021). Emergence and development of Western-style hotels initially led by foreign investments followed by domestic entrepreneurs include not only the above-mentioned luxury hotels but also resort hotels. The Hakone region consists of some areas famous for hot springs, including Miyanoshita, Gora and Yumoto. In 1878, Fujiya Hotel was founded by Sennosuke Yamaguchi as Japan's first resort hotel (Fujiya Hotel, n.d.). Today, Imperial Hotel Tokyo is seen as one of the three major brands of Japan's Western-style hotels with full services together with Okura Tokyo and Hotel New Otani Tokyo. Imperial Hotel Tokyo was initiated in 1890. Imperial Hotels Group also established a resort hotel in Kamikochi Plateau in Nagano Prefecture in 1933 and a luxury hotel in Osaka City in 1996. Here, it should be noted that in principle the main target guests for Western-style hotels in Japan throughout their history have been overseas tourists visiting Japan for leisure and business purposes and foreign people residing in Japan. This trend had especially been prominent between the late nineteenth century and the 1930s, although an increasing number of ordinary Japanese citizens began to use and enjoying staying at Western-style luxury and resort hotels since the end of World War II, particularly after the 1980s.

As discussed in Part I (Chap. 1) and Part II (Chaps. 2, 3 and 4) of this book, there is a solid relationship between cultural/natural heritage and tourism. To be specific, a range of heritage has been utilised as tourism resources in tourism settings often as visitor attractions (Jimura, 2019, 2022). In tourism settings, nevertheless, visitor attractions are not the only tourism component that can be appreciated as heritage, especially cultural heritage. In fact, accommodation facilities such as Japanese-style inns can also be respected as heritage (Jimura, 2022) (see also Sect. 1 of Chap. 2 and Sect. 4 of this chapter). In addition, the meaning of such cultural heritage can also be recognised by the Japanese Government (the Agency for Cultural Affairs (hereafter ACA)) through its listing systems such as National Treasures, Important Cultural Properties or Registered Tangible Cultural Properties. Concerning Western-style hotels, for instance, main structures of the aforementioned Fujiya Hotel were inscribed as Registered Tangible Cultural Properties by ACA in 1997. Furthermore, Tokyo Station Hotel, part of Tokyo Station Marunouchi Main Building, was opened in 1915 and designated by ACA as Important Cultural Property in 2003. Here, it should also be remembered that the significance of many historic Western-style hotels in Japan, including Fujiya Hotel and Tokyo Station Hotel, have also been acknowledged through another listing system by the Japanese Government (the Ministry of Economy, Trade and Industry), Heritage of Industrial Modernisation. This designation system was launched in 2007, aiming to make the most of listed heritage for revitalisation of associated local communities as well as to appreciate its historic value (Jimura, 2022). In relation to this, it is natural that a number of traditional Western-style hotels in Japan listed as Registered Tangible Cultural Properties have also been inscribed as Heritage of Industrial Modernisation. That is because, the period when these hotels were built and opened matches before and after the Meiji Restoration (1867–1868) when the modernisation of Japan started with the reform of its political and social system, following developed Western countries such as the UK, France, Germany and the USA (Jimura, 2022).

In this process, there was a need to have Western-style hotels in Japan, especially in port cities and resort destinations, to accommodate and welcome foreign nationals visiting or moving to Japan for various purposes. Without the roles these foreign people played and the knowledge and skills acquired from the Western countries, Japan would not be able to realise its modernisation in the late nineteenth century.

In light of the worth of historic Western-style hotels as tangible cultural heritage as well as the role they have been playing in Japanese society, it is fair to say that the socio-cultural sustainability of these hotels has always been significant for Japan and its citizens. Their socio-cultural sustainability has also been maintained by being conserved through different listing schemes adopted by the Japanese Government and being utilised by overseas and Japanese people for more than a century. As stated in Sect. 1, the accommodation sector has also supported local communities as a member of the society and through its CSR activities. Atami City in Shizuoka Prefecture experienced huge landslides and a sediment disaster triggered by heavy rain in July 2021 and many local inhabitants lost their houses or needed to evacuate. Some resort hotels with hot-spring facilities belonging to Itoen Hotels Group accepted victims of the natural disaster (Itoen Hotels, 2021). In this case, some key features of these resort hotels were suitable and beneficial to accommodate the victims. Specifically, these hotels tend to have a large hotel capacity, spacious rooms and big communal bathes usually with hot spring; hence, they were ideal to be temporary places to live for local victims. Some luxury hotels also take a responsibility as a member of society regarding the COVID-19 pandemic. To cite a case, Hotel Nikko Kansai Airport accepted people arriving in Japan via Kansai Airport who needed a hotel quarantine for three or six days upon a request from the Japanese Government. Such activities are primarily associated with the socio-cultural sustainability of Western-style hotels, accommodation sector in Japan and wider society. Simultaneously, however, these activities have also been beneficial to maintain their economic sustainability. In more detail, the Western-style hotels could secure a certain amount of income regularly by accepting disaster victims or people arriving in Japan during the pandemic. This also means that employees of these hotels could secure their jobs in such challenging situations. Overall, Western-style hotels in

Japan are also keen to enhance their environmental sustainability. For instance, Cerulean Tower Tokyu Hotel acquired ISO 14001 in February 2007 and has been trying to establish itself as a hotel that is friendly for human beings as well as natural environment (Cerulean Tower Tokyu Hotel, n.d.).

Overall, Japan's Western-style luxury and resort hotels are fully aware of the magnitude of SDGs and have already been working to make their contributions to them. In fact, all of the aforementioned three top brands of Japan's Western-style luxury hotels show their activities for SDGs on their official websites. Of the 17 SDGs, subsequent seven SDGs are commonly addressed by these hotel brands as the SDGs that they intend to contribute to through their businesses:

- SDG 3 Good Health and Well-being
- SDG 5 Gender Equality
- SDG 8 Decent Work and Economic Growth
- SDG 11 Sustainable Cities and Communities
- SDG 12 Responsible Consumption and Production
- SDG 13 Climate Action
- SDG 17 Partnerships for the Goals

These SDGs are deeply connected with their daily businesses and reflect the importance of 'people' in services, the products they are offering. Amongst these, SDGs 11, 12 and 13 are directly related to 'reduce', 'reuse' and 'recycle' (3Rs). For instance, Imperial Hotels Group has been trying to decrease their energy consumption and CO2 emission by improving both tangible (e.g. improving facilities) and intangible (e.g. raising awareness) approaches (Imperial Hotels Group, 2021). They have also been working to minimise food waste, use of plastic materials, and separate their business rubbish and garbage into different categories strictly following the rule of a municipality each hotel is situated in (Imperial Hotels Group, 2021). Thus, it can be stated that these actions conducted by Imperial Hotels Group mirror the spirit of *mottainai*. Nevertheless, the group is also criticised by some people as Imperial Hotel Tokyo plans to scrap its main and tower buildings built in 1970 and 1983 respectively and construct new main and tower buildings from scratch between 2024 and 2036 (Imperial Hotel Tokyo, 2021). Some people blame this plan because it is not sustainable, especially environmentally, and does not reflect the *mottainai* spirit. In the author's view, the plan is also associated with Japan's long-standing scrap and build culture (LeBlanc, 2017; Jimura, 2019, 2022). Nonetheless, the spirit of place of Imperial Hotel Tokyo will be retained or even enhanced after the construction of new buildings as the plan aims to offer even more excellent services and memorable experience to its guests (Imperial Hotel Tokyo, 2021).

3 Japanised Western-Style Hotel (Business Hotel)

As stated at the beginning of Sect. 2, '*business hotels*' is the other main category of Western-style hotels that exist in Japan. In relation to this, it needs to be remembered that basically *business hotels* should be understood as 'Japanised' Western-style hotels with no frills. At international level, hotels are often categorised mainly by following ways:

- Luxury (30 k JPY or higher per room per night), high-end (30 k JPY or higher per room per night), middle (20 k–30 k JPY per room per night), economy (10 k–20 k per room per night) and budget (10 k or lower per room per night) (Tokyo YMCA, n.d.), or
- Star rating system (e.g. five-star to one-star hotels).

In both categories, factors such as the quality of facilities and services are considered primarily and the categories usually have a positive relationship with prices. It could be stated that Western-style hotels in Japan (luxury hotels, including *city hotels*, and resort hotels) generally have better quality of facilities and services and charge higher prices than Japanised Western-style hotels in Japan (i.e. *business hotels*), although there are some exceptions for the reasons discussed later.

It is generally agreed that the history of *business hotels* commenced in the 1960s. For instance, Hotel Hokke Club Group (hereafter HHCG),

6 Sustainability of Japan's Accommodation Sector

one of the large *business hotel* chains in today's Japan, converted their Japanese-style inns to *business hotels* in the early 1960s and is seen as a pioneer of *business hotels* (HHCG, n.d.). Hiroma (2013) also states that Japan's accommodation sector saw the rise of *business hotels* over the 1960s and early 1970s. However, rooms of *business hotels* at that time were Japanese-style with *tatami* mats, did not have beds and were not en-suite as they were converted from traditional Japanese-style inns (Hiroma, 2013) as the case of HHCG shows. Between the mid-1970s and early 1980s, *business hotels* with Western-style rooms and en-suite facilities appeared and most of their rooms were single rooms (Hiroma, 2013). According to Hiroma (2013), this phenomenon was triggered by the social backgrounds at that time such as World Expo Osaka in 1970 and an increase in the numbers of inbound (international) and Japanese (domestic) tourists. Hiroma (2013) further argues that the development of *business hotels* in Japan's accommodation market is confirmed between the mid and late 1980s as evidenced by the expansion of several *business hotel* chains, including HHCG, Washington Hotels (managed by Fujita Kanko) and Sunroute Hotels (currently managed by Sotesu Hotel Management). In addition to these *business hotel* chains; other *business hotel* brands have also become eminent in the *business hotel* market. They include Dormy Inn (managed by Kyoritsu Maintenance), APA Hotels (managed by APA Group), Hotel Route Inn (managed by Route Inn Japan), Toyoko Inn and Daiwa Roynet Hotels (currently managed by Daiwa House Realty Management).

Although all *business hotels* are not 'budget' hotels, the majority of business hotels fall in this category. It is often said that the aforementioned APA Hotels, Hotel Route Inn and Toyoko Inn are three major brands of *business hotels* (Hotel Jinzai Bank, 2019; Tokyo YMCA, n.d.). One of the main features of *business hotels* is the small size of average rooms, typically between 9 and 15 square meters. This can be perceived as a negative element by guests, however, their positive features such as excellent locations often near railway stations and value for money seem to outweigh the negative feature. Subsequently, the popularity of *business hotels* has been increasing amongst Japanese leisure tourists as well as Japanese business tourists as time goes by. According to Diamond Online (2020), the number of rooms supplied by *business hotels* is larger than the total number of rooms offered by *city hotels*, resort hotels and Japanese-style inns; and the largest proportion of inbound tourists (36.6%) stayed in *business hotels* in 2018. Nonetheless, Diamond Online (2020) argues that the Japan's accommodation market led by *business hotels* may discourage overseas tourists to visit Japan again. That is mainly because, the size of rooms is small and/or this type of hotels lacks a uniqueness and does not reflect Japanese cultures and traditions (Diamond Online, 2020). In this view, staying at *business hotels* may not enable foreign tourists to see and experience Japan's cultural heritage such as Japan's Western-style hotels (see Sect. 2) or Japanese-style inns (see Sect. 4). However, the author disagrees with the view of Diamond Online (2020) and needs to point out that 'inbound tourists' are not homogenous. To be specific, what Diamond Online (2020) claims may apply to Western tourists who come from North America (USA and Canada), Europe (e.g. UK, France and Germany) or Oceania (e.g. Australia). However, it would not apply to Eastern tourists who come from Asia such as Mainland China, Hong Kong, Taiwan, South Korea, Thailand and Vietnam. The author has stayed at a number of *business hotels* in many different cities across Japan since 1994. Through his own observations and experiences, it is sure that *business hotels*, especially those in urban areas, have been very popular amongst Asian guests, especially in the past 10–15 years. On some occasions, more than half of hotel guests seem to be tourists from Asian countries and such hotels often employ Asian people or people who can speak Asian languages as receptionists. According to Japan National Tourism Organisation (2020), in fact, 82.7% of inbound tourists came from Asia (East Asia, Southeast Asia and India) in 2019. For these reasons, the author does not think that the leading position of *business hotels* in Japan's accommodation market and their lack of uniqueness discourage overseas tourists to visit or revisit Japan. In light of these points, it is fair to say that the socio-cultural sustainability of *business hotels* as places to stay for domestic and international tourists has been maintained and has even been enhanced in recent years.

Concerning the socio-cultural sustainability, it should also be noted that *business hotels* have been contributing to Japanese society and citizens through their CSR activities and actions for SDGs. Many *business hotels* also take their responsibilities as members of society by accepting

COVID-19 patients with mild symptoms or people arriving in Japan who need hotel quarantine. For example, APA Hotel & Resort Yokohama Bay, the largest hotel in APA Hotels with 2311 rooms, has been accepting people arriving via Haneda Airport who need hotel quarantine. As mentioned earlier, most *business hotels* are budget hotels, although there are some exceptions. These exceptions are associated with one of current trends in the accommodation sector in Japan, the emergence and expansion of deluxe *business hotels* whose prices tend to be equivalent to those of economy hotels (10 k–20 k per room per night). Well-known examples of deluxe *business hotels* brands are Dormy Inn Premium, Candeo Hotels (managed by Candeo Hospitality Management), Mitsui Garden Hotel Premier (managed by Mitsui Fudosan Hotel Management) and Intergate Hotels (managed by Granvista Hotels & Resorts), although some of them may not see themselves as deluxe *business hotels*. Deluxe *business hotels* are featured by excellent locations, communal bathes sometimes with hot spring, good-quality breakfasts often with local specialities, and/or larger rooms with comfortable beds. The position such deluxe *business hotels* share in Japan's hotel market would be somewhere between *city hotels* and ordinary *business hotels*. Actually, targeting this niche market is a current marketing strategy adopted by Candeo Hotels, enhancing the quality of their services in 3Bs (bath, bed and breakfast) (TBS News, 2021). As of writing, this marketing strategy appears to have contributed to the business success and enhancement of economic sustainability of Candeo Hospitality Management.

Largely, *business hotels* have been conducting diverse sorts of actions in order to strengthen environmental sustainability of their everyday businesses, surrounding natural environment and key stakeholders, including local communities they belong to. Amongst them, particularly large domestic *business hotel* chains have been eager to work on such mission. Particularly, the approaches adopted by Super Hotel is remarkable and unique. First of all, it is clearly stated that Super Hotel supports SDGs on the Japanese homepage of Super Hotel's official website (https://www.superhotel.co.jp/). The number of their *business hotels* that obtained ISO 14001 certification has been increasing every year, and 121 out of 166 hotels have the certification as of December 2021 (Super Hotel, 2021). Access to rooms of Super Hotels is manged by neither traditional key nor card key but is controlled by a unique Personal Identification Number (PIN) that is given to guests when they check in via their self-check in system. This can decrease the amount of plastic rubbish the hotels produce and reduce labour costs. In the COVID-19 pandemic, moreover, this check-in system is beneficial to avoid or minimise contacts between guests and hotel receptionists. Furthermore, hotel receptions do not open 24 hours a day and air conditioning are off in lifts and corridors even in summer. Western-style hotels in Japan such as *city hotels* and resort hotels would not be able to implement such actions because these hotels are expected to always provide their guests with full services. Although these approaches are unique or conspicuous at Super Hotel, following approaches for environmental sustainability have been widely employed by a number of *business hotel* chains.

Nowadays, a vast majority of hotels in Japan, especially *business hotels* (Japanised Western-style hotels), give their guests three or even more options regarding daily cleaning of their hotel rooms. For example, rooms of Hotel Hokke Club Kyoto have three different door signs regarding room cleaning (see Fig. 6.1). If some of their guests who want their rooms cleaned up are happy with ecology cleaning (the tag on the right-hand side in Fig. 6.1), the hotel can reduce the amount of laundry and this leads to 'reduction' of laundry wastewater. This also means that guests who choose ecology cleaning will 'reuse' bed sheets, pillowcases and pyjamas. Another approach is to ask guests to use up a toilet paper before they start using a new one. To cite a case, Intergate Hotel Osaka encourages their guests to do so by putting a small notice board on the wall of a bathroom (see Fig. 6.2). If some guests agree to do so, the hotel could save the amount of toilet papers they need. This can lead to saving timber resources not only in Japan but also in other regions of the world (e.g. Asia, Oceania and South America) (WWF Japan, n.d.). It is also important that in Japan, currently various types of used papers such as copier papers, milk cartons and paper train tickets are 'recycled' as toilet papers. Although part of the reasons why many *business hotels* have been implementing these measures would be to enhance the economic sustainability of their businesses by saving diverse kinds of costs, it is also true that these actions are useful to strengthen the environmental sustainability of their businesses and wider society. Various approaches for environmental

6 Sustainability of Japan's Accommodation Sector

Fig. 6.1 Door signs for room cleaning options at Hotel Hokke Club Kyoto. (Source: Author)

sustainability adopted by *business hotels* may also remind their guests of the importance of *mottainai* spirit. Moreover, the embodiment of 3Rs concept, particularly 'reduce' and 'reuse', can also be confirmed in the aforementioned practices conducted by *business hotels*.

4 Japanese-Style Inn (*Ryokan, Minshuku* and *Shukubo*)

Japanese-style inns differ from Western-style inns in various ways. Amongst these, following points are seen as key features of the former that can differentiate it from the latter:

- Guests need to take off their shoes at the main entrance.
- Guest rooms come with *tatami* mats.

Fig. 6.2 A notice board in a bathroom of hotel room at Intergate Hotel Osaka. (Source: Author)

- Guests sleep on *futon*.
- Traditionally, dinner and breakfast are included in the accommodation fee.
- Dinner and breakfast, particularly the former, use locally sourced ingredients and include local specialities (Jimura, 2022, 101).

There are two main types of Japanese-style inns in Japan, namely *ryokan* and *minshuku* (Jimura, 2011a; Jimura & Lee, 2020; Jimura, 2022). Although the above-mentioned characteristics are common to both *ryokan* and *minshuku*, generally *ryokan* is superior to *minshuku* in many senses. To be specific, *ryokan* and *minshuku* are dissimilar in terms of their locations, management styles, levels and qualities of facilities and services, and accommodation fees (Jimura, 2022). *Ryokan* are often situated in established hot-spring areas (*onsen-chi*), whilst *minshuku* are found in any locations with tourism resources (e.g. hot springs (*onsen*), famous religious sites, splendid mountains or lakes, and popular local specialties) (Jimura, 2022). Usually, *ryokan* have a larger number of guest rooms than *minshuku*. Thus, *ryokan* are more likely to be owned and managed by enterprises than *minshuku* (Jimura, 2011a, 2022). To cite a case, Kagaya situated in Wakura Onsen area in Ishikawa Prefecture has 235 guest rooms and owned and run by Kagaya Group that also manages four other *ryokan* and other service businesses (Kagaya Group, n.d.). On the other hand, *minshuku* usually have a much smaller number of guest rooms (e.g. up to ten) than *ryokan*. Moreover, *minshuku* are usually family-run and owner families often live in the buildings used as *minshuku* (Jimura, 2011a; Jimura & Lee, 2020; Jimura, 2022). In this sense, *minshuku* can be interpreted as a Japanese version of B&Bs. Considering the aforementioned features, it would be natural that *ryokan* tend to have more variety of facilities and services than *minshuku* (Jimura, 2022). In principle, subsequent three are key attraction factors of Japanese-style inns and their quality affects decision-making and expectations of prospective guests:

* Japanese-style guest rooms (*washitsu*),
* Dishes with local specialties, and
* Communal bathes with hot-spring water (Jimura, 2011a).

Usually, Japanese-style guest rooms in *ryokan* are more spacious and sophisticated than those in *minshuku*. Although both *ryokan* and *minshuku* provide guests with dinner and breakfast with local specialties, *ryokan*'s ones, particularly dinner, are customarily served in *kaiseki* style, a traditional Japanese multi-course meal, where dishes are served one by one like a formal French meal. Regarding communal bathes, *minshuku* are inclined to have only one or two communal bathes whose water is not always hot-spring water (Jimura, 2022). In contrast, most of *ryokan* have multiple communal bathes with hot-spring water and luxury rooms at some *ryokan* are even equipped with a small bath with hot-spring water.

Although *ryokan* and *minshuku* are two major kinds of Japanese-style inns, *shukubo* have been recognised increasingly and used widely in recent years by not only domestic but also international tourists. A key difference between *shukubo* and *ryokan* or *minshuku* is that in principle *shukubo* are accommodation facilities for monks and pilgrims (Yasuda, 2021), although they have also been welcoming ordinary people as their guests. Put differently, *shukubo* are temple-run accommodation facilities that provide their guests with accommodation and meals (Beumer, 2016). Hence, it is natural that *shukubo* are in the precinct of/near Japanese Buddhist temples or along main approaches to the temples as the case of *shukubo* of Zenko-ji Temple (Nagano Prefecture) indicates. Staying overnight at *shukubo* should be somewhat different from staying at *ryokan* or *minshuku* since *shukubo* could give their guests opportunities to practice *zazen*, calming their minds, appreciate Japanese gardens, enjoying seasonal beauty, and have *shojin* vegetarian dishes (Redelman, 2012). Therefore, guests of *shukubo* could see, feel, and experience the history and culture of Japan, especially religious ones, through their overnight stays there (Redelman, 2012). After the author lost his father, he took part in two-day trial ascetic training at Eihei-ji Temple (Fukui Prefecture) in winter 2018, staying overnight at *shukubo* situated in its precinct. He could have extraordinary experiences such as *zazen* sessions and a Dharma talk that cannot be experienced through staying at *ryokan* or *minshuku* (Jimura, 2022).

Prior to the COVID-19 pandemic, Japan has been enjoying a rapid and huge increase in the number of inbound tourists for several years, especially since 2014 (Jimura, 2022). During this inbound tourism boom, trends in consumption behaviour of overseas tourists in Japan have also changed as the number of repeat tourists has increased. For example, inbound tourists are inclined to come by famous and established destinations such as Tokyo and Kyoto on their first visits to Japan. On the other hand, many of them start exploring less well-known areas on their repeat visits, prioritising their own interests and preferences. It can also be stated that once inbound tourists, especially those come from Mainland China, spent a lot of their time and money for shopping. Recently, however, they seem to have become more interested in having experiences unique to Japan than just enjoying shopping. For instance, the author's foreign friends are interested in having *ninja* experience in Koka area (Shiga Prefecture) and *geisha* experience in Kyoto. Staying overnight at a Japanese-style inn has also been valued by many inbound tourists as such unique experience in Japan. In fact, the number of foreign guests staying overnight at Japanese-style inns had been increasing until COVID-19 came. This was, for example, evidenced by the fact that nowadays the etiquette that users of communal bathes at Japanese-style inns are expected to observe are available in foreign languages on various websites and on site (Jimura, 2022). In relation to this, *shukubo* have also been getting popular as places to stay overnight amongst inbound tourists as well as Japanese tourists. Actually, guests of *shukubo* could have typical Japanese experiences such as *zazen* and *shojin* vegetable dishes. In other words, accepting non-religious guests at *shukubo* and giving them opportunities to have various experiences unique to Japan can be understood as Japanese Buddhist temples' outreach activities. All of these activities would be beneficial to maintain or enhance the socio-cultural sustainability of Japanese-style inns and could increase the level of people's awareness of these inns. The socio-cultural sustainability has also been retained or strengthened through other approach. Japan has several national listing systems for the recognition and conservation of its intangible and tangible cultural heritage (see Chap. 2). For example, four structures of Mukaitaki *ryokan* (Fukushima Prefecture) were designated as Registered Tangible Cultural Properties in 1996, and the *ryokan* is proud of it (Jimura, 2022). The great hall and Saigetsuro wing of Kanaguya *ryokan* (Nagano Prefecture) were also inscribed as Registered Tangible Cultural Properties in 2003. Figure 6.3 shows the exterior of Saigetsuro wing at night. The *ryokan* arranges a guided tour about its historic building and cultural properties every day. The guided tour is well received by their guests, including the author, and could enhance guests' understanding and awareness of diverse cultural heritage Kanaguya has. Thus, it is fair to say that this guided tour plays a vital role in heightening the socio-cultural sustainability of Kanaguya *ryokan*.

Unlike Western-style hotels (luxury hotels, including *city hotels*, and resort hotels) or Japanised Western-style hotels (*business hotels*), Japanese-style inns are not widely utilised by business tourists. This signifies that their room occupancy rates on weekdays tend to be much lower than weekends except some highly popular *ryokan*. This is one of the reasons why the economic sustainability of Japanese-style inns is difficult to strengthen or even maintain. *Minshuku* and small *ryokan* are often

Fig. 6.3 Saigetsuro wing of Kanaguya *ryokan*. (Source: Author)

family-run and can be understood as small and medium-sized enterprises (SMEs). Low labour productivity is an issue commonly confirmed at Japanese-style inns, especially at such SMEs (Ikado, 2021). This is another problem that may negatively affect the economic sustainability of Japanese-style inns. As discussed in Sect. 2.2 of Chap. 5, in principle the service industry is labour-intensive, and the accommodation sector is its representative example. Amongst several different types of accommodation in Japan, the business of Japanese-style inns is particularly labour-intensive and their labour productivity tends to be low. That is because, their everyday business requires both skilled and manual workers who need to engage in a variety of jobs constantly such as taking care of guests, cooking meals and cleaning up rooms (Ohno, 2019). In Sect. 2.2 of Chap. 5, it is pointed out that the airline industry is not only labour-intensive but also capital-intensive. Japanese-style inns, especially high-end *ryokan*, are also such a business. Stated differently, delivering high-quality services continuously to guests needs specific facilities that require large installation and regular maintenance costs (e.g. hot-spring facilities) as well as a large amount of personnel expenses for their employees who work on diverse duties. Hence, the economic sustainability of Japanese-style inns is difficult to be improved or even retained.

Currently, many Japanese-style inns attempt to make their businesses as eco-friendly as possible and to increase the level of environmental sustainability of their businesses, making contribution to SDGs. Generally, Japanese-style inns can be viewed as a type of business that has a plenty of opportunities to conduct actions for SDGs. That is because, they have often kept running their business for a long time, maintaining their relationships with local communities and surrounding environments, and their businesses include a variety of services such as lodging, food and drink, bathing and retail. Honma (2021) states that Hoshino Resorts is a Japan's advanced accommodation enterprise in relation to SDGs. Some of their brands, especially Kai and Hoshinoya, can be regarded as Japanese-style inns. The company's activities for SDGs include, for instance, generation of electricity through hydro and geothermal energies (Honma, 2021). They are also engaged in 3Rs activities by 'reducing' food waste, 'reusing' containers and tableware, and 'recycling' kitchen waste as compost (Honma, 2021). It is intriguing that Hoshino Resorts believes that their activities for SDGs should not sacrifice their business profit (Honma, 2021). In other words, the economic sustainability of the company's businesses should not be damaged by implementing measures for their contribution to SDGs. If damaged, what Hoshino Resorts are implementing is not appropriate or sensible as a private company whose mission includes the pursuit of business profit. The author echoes this policy and believes that companies' actions for SDGs should not be triggered primarily by the peer pressure from society or global/Western trends but should come originally from their caring attitudes towards environment, society and people.

5 Budget Accommodation (Guest House, Youth Hostel and Capsule Hotel)

Although the majority of *business hotels* (see Sect. 3) and some *minshuku* (see Sect. 4) are seen as Japan's budget accommodation in terms of accommodation fees, Japan has more representative examples of budget accommodation. Today, guest houses, youth hostels and *capsule hotels* are seen as three typical types of budget accommodation. Of these, guest houses and youth hostels are found not only in Japan but also in many other countries. What the category of 'guest houses' include would be somewhat different by nation. Nevertheless, it is safe to say that a guest house usually means a small-sized accommodation facility managed by a family. Unlike *minshuku* or B&Bs, however, meals are not always offered at Japan's guest houses and their owners are unlikely to live in the buildings used as guest houses (Hayashida, 2017). On the other hand, the concept of 'youth hostel' was born in Germany more than 100 years ago (Japan Youth Hostels Guide (hereafter JYHG) n.d.). Nowadays, there are more than 4 k youth hostels across around 80 nations or regions, and there are around 220 youth hostels across Japan (JYHG, n.d.). Main features of youth hostels are a dormitory that accommodates several bunk beds and shared facilities such as a bathroom, lounge and kitchen. Like *business hotels*, in contrast, the concept of '*capsule hotel*' was born and their presence are prominent in Japan. *Capsule hotels* comprise of a large number of tiny bed-sized rooms called capsules and shared facilities such as toilets, communal bathes, saunas and lounges. Nowadays, accommodation facilities whose concepts are similar to *capsule hotels* can be found outside Japan (e.g. Netherlands, Singapore and the UK). They are called capsule hotels or pod hotels. In many cases, however, rooms in these hotels are not actually 'capsules', which means that a room has a sleeping space only. Stated differently, a guest cannot stand up in a capsule (room) at *capsule hotels* in Japan.

Like the above-discussed Western-style hotels, Japanised Western-style hotels and Japanese-style inns, overall, the proportion overseas tourists share within all guests at Japan's guest houses and youth hostels had also been increasing since Japan's inbound tourism boom began. Since the

COVID-19 pandemic emerged, guest houses and youth hostels have been hit especially hard as their main target segments are budget inbound tourists such as young travellers and backpackers whose trips with non-business purposes have been highly limited by the Japanese Government. Compared to guest houses or youth hostels, *capsule hotels* do not seem to have been used widely by inbound tourists. That is probably because, *capsule hotels* are a type of accommodation facilities that cannot be found well in other countries, and the majority of overseas tourists would not be familiar with them. In fact, however, *capsule hotels* have been affected even more badly by the COVID-19 than other kinds of accommodation due to its highly limited private spaces and many chances to see other guests at communal areas (Takizawa, 2021a). However, Takizawa (2021b) also points out that another challenge in the economic sustainability of *capsule hotels* already emerged before the COVID-19 pandemic, around at the end of 2018. As accommodation fees of some *business hotels* started decreasing, *capsule hotels*, particularly advanced ones with more available services, needed to compete them with price (Takizawa, 2021b). In Japan, moreover, most Internet cafes allow their customers to stay over-nights or even for several days; therefore, they became another main competitor for *capsule hotels* (Takizawa, 2021b). For these reasons, it seems to be challenging for *capsule hotels* to maintain their economic sustainability today and in the future.

The aforementioned challenges budget accommodation in Japan, especially *capsule hotels*, has been facing and suffering from signify that not only their economic sustainability but also their socio-cultural sustainability have been deteriorating. That is because, their presence in and value for Japanese people and society have been decreasing due to the current situation of Japan's accommodation market and still-ongoing COVID-19 pandemic, although budget accommodation, particularly *capsule hotels*, mirrors the cultural heritage unique to Japan. Amongst different types of budget accommodation in Japan, *capsule hotels* have been widely used by Japanese people who are not leisure tourists. The situation has been improving in recent years; however, customarily Japan had been infamous for its long working hour culture. Thus, some employees may stay overnight at *capsule hotels* near their offices, saving their time to be spent for commuting. This implies that traditionally *capsule hotels* have shared a certain position in everyday lives of Japanese businesspersons. On the other hand, guest houses have been playing an important role in enhancing the socio-cultural and/or environmental sustainability of local culture and nature surrounding them. For example, many guest houses renovate existing buildings that often reflect cultural and natural characteristics of certain localities (e.g. Japan's traditional folk houses). They also arrange a variety of events and programmes that enables their guests to experience local culture and nature (Matsubara, 2019). Interactions between guests and local residents can be enhanced through various events or programmes such as making local crafts, experiencing farming and participating in outdoor activities (Matsubara, 2019). These practices can raise a wider group of people's awareness of local culture and nature and ensure their socio-cultural and environmental sustainability for future generations.

6 Outdoor Accommodation (Campsite, Glamping Site, Recreational Vehicle and Spending a Night in a Car (*Shachuhaku*))

Camping is an established outdoor activity in Japan and has more than a hundred years of history. This endorses a high level of socio-cultural sustainability of camping as a leisure activity in Japanese society. Japan has 2064 campsites as of 2019 and many of them are located in the countryside where forests, lakes or rivers are nearby (Kubo, 2019). Campsites have been utilised by a range of people, including scouts and school groups as well as adults. Today, the majority of campsites in Japan are *auto campsites* (Japanese English) where people come by car and park the car by a place they put a tent or near an accommodation facility. The number of people enjoying overnight camping at *auto campsites* had increased between 2015 and 2019 (8.6 million in 2019) (Hayashi & Horimatsu, 2021). Of these, 22.6% campers had less than a year experience of camping (Hayashi & Horimatsu, 2021). The popularity of outdoor activities as a whole, including camping, has been increasing since the COVID-19 pandemic began. That is because, people think that they can keep social distancing at campsites where fresh air is also available.

Compared with camping, 'glamping', meaning glamorous camping, is a much more recent phenomenon. Glamping is originated in the UK and has been developed significantly in the last ten years (Adamovich et al., 2021). This concept and practice have spread across the world, including Japan. Its level of recognition and popularity amongst Japan's general public have also increased lately for some reasons, including the aforementioned key reason for the increase in the popularity of campsites. Thus, the socio-cultural sustainability of glamping and glamping sites in Japanese society has also been enhanced in recent years. A main feature of glamping that differentiates itself from camping is that glamping enables campers to be released from labours such as putting a tent or cooking and allows them to focus on enjoying nature (Japan Glamping Association (hereafter JGLA), n.d.). Thanks to such characteristics, glamping is approachable for beginners of camping and can function as an introduction to camping (JGLA, n.d.). In Japan, Ise-Shima Everglades opened in 2004 is seen as a forerunner of Japan's glamping sites, and other well-known glamping sites include Hoshinoya Fuji (Yamanashi Prefecture) and Mahina Glamping Spa Village (Shizuoka Prefecture).

Besides, recreational vehicles (RVs) (*camping cars* in Japanese English) have been increasingly well-liked by people in Japan, especially since the COVID-19 pandemic started because travelling with RVs can minimise interactions with others. More specifically, the number of Japanese customers who purchase or rent a RV has boosted (Hiratsuka, 2021; Mainichi Shimbun, 2021). Consequently, the manufacturers and dealers of RVs have been benefited financially from their popularity. On the other hand, RV rental companies have been financially struggling. That is because, most of their business profits came from inbound tourists whose number has been almost zero since the pandemic began. Inbound tourists to Japan are inclined to rent a RV for a longer period (e.g. six days) than Japanese ones (e.g. two or three days) (Hiratsuka, 2021). Furthermore, the former tends to visit Japan and rent a RV all year round, whilst the demand of the latter is usually highly seasonal (Hiratsuka, 2021). In short, the economic sustainability of RV manufacturers and dealers has been strengthened recently, whilst that of RV rental companies has been weaken.

Lately, an increasing number of people in Japan have been enjoying *shachuhaku* (spending a night in a car) when they travel by car. The most important theme in this sort of travel is whether drivers and their companions are allowed to keep parking their car at a certain parking space and can stay overnight there. For example, it is fine if they stay overnight at a campsite or glamping site. On the other hand, parking their car at a certain parking space and staying overnight there are basically not allowed at motorway service stations or roadside stations (*michi no eki*) (see Fig. 6.4 for an example of *michi no eki*). That is because; these stations aim to enable drivers and their fellow travellers to take a rest or a nap for safety reasons, but do not intend to be used as accommodation facilities such as hotels or campsites. In reality, nevertheless, some motorway

Fig. 6.4 An example of *michi no eki*: Happiness Fukue in Hagi City, Yamaguchi Prefecture. (Source: Author)

service stations and roadside stations connive overnight use of their parking spaces by irresponsible drivers, or part of roadside stations actually allow them to do so. In the author's view, however, much clearer standards should be developed and presented to indicate what drivers and their companions can/cannot do at motorway service stations and roadside stations, and these rules need to be applied to anybody without exceptions to be fair to all. Otherwise, travelling with spending a night in a car will not be socio-culturally sustainable due to a lack of fairness amongst users and/or irresponsible behaviours of some users. In addition, some drivers and their fellow travellers may throw away the garbage generated outside motorway service stations or roadside stations. To tackle this problem, some roadside stations do not install any rubbish bins. Some *shachuhaku* fans are not satisfied with this policy, but the author echoes the roadside stations rather than the fans in terms of the environmental sustainability of these stations and the attitudes the users and fans should have. Here, it needs to be re-emphasised that in principle, service or roadside stations should not be used to stay overnight. The author also feels that this practice is not ideal for the economic sustainability of accommodation sector as the aforementioned drivers and their companions do not make financial contribution to this sector, although accommodation fees often share the largest proportion in tourists' spending.

7   Minpaku

The last category of accommodation discussed in this chapter is *minpaku* properties. It is safe to say that *minpaku* is equivalent to a vacation rental (mainly in the USA) or holiday rental (mainly in the UK) that can be found in many tourist destinations in the world. According to Liang et al. (2021, 2), a vacation rental is 'any portion of a private home, townhouse, apartment, condominium, or other private dwelling in various forms rented to tourists as an alternative to a hotel'. The rise of the sharing economy in recent years has been advantageous for vacation rentals and have become a current trend in the accommodation sector across the globe (Liang et al., 2021). Availability of a range of vacation rentals could give tourists a wider variety of choices in their decision-making process together with other kinds of accommodation such as hotels. The rapid and extensive development of vacation rentals in the last 15–20 years is mainly due to the rise of online marketplaces whose representative examples include HomeAway founded in 2005 and Airbnb established in 2007. These online marketplaces can connect people who want to rent out their properties with those who look for accommodations in specific locations and often want 'stay like locals' (Investopedia, 2021).

Through sharing economy schemes such as *minpaku* in Japan, holiday rental or Airbnb, the owners can make the most of their properties for financial benefits. As this signifies that these properties can generate income for the owners, it could be stated that the economic sustainability of these properties and owners' businesses can be strengthened by being fully utilised through such sharing economy systems. Nevertheless, it should also be noted that making profits by renting out properties using sharing economy scheme is not always easy. In the case of *minpaku*, for instance, the New Act on Private Lodging was enforced in June 2018 to regulate the rapid rise and development of *minpaku* businesses, including the arrival of Airbnb in 2014. According to this Act, the owners cannot run *minpaku* businesses more than 180 days in a fiscal year of Japan. This restriction was introduced mainly to protect conventional accommodation businesses in Japan such as Western-style hotels, Japanised Western-style hotels and Japanese-style inns (see Sects. 2, 3 and 4 for details).

Amongst three main pillars of sustainability, probably the issues associated with socio-cultural sustainability is the most serious and pressing matters for *minpaku* businesses, including Airbnb in Japan. As stated earlier, the New Act on Private Lodging came into force in 2018 and ordinances related to *minpaku* were also established by many regional and local governments in Japan (e.g. Hokkaido Prefecture, Kyoto City, Osaka Urban Prefecture). Several different socio-cultural issues may occur in relation to *minpaku* businesses. According to the City Planning Act, there are three main zone categories by primary purpose of use (residential, commercial or industrial) and 13 sub zone categories in total. Regarding zones where *minpaku* businesses can be run, there are two main options that regional or local authorities can choose (Yokozeki, 2018). The first option is that *minpaku* businesses are allowed in all kinds of zones except the Exclusive Industrial Zones. This option means that owners can manage *minpaku* businesses in the zone categories where hotels or Japanese-style inns cannot run their businesses (Yokozeki, 2018). On the other hand, the second option is that owners can run *minpaku* businesses only in the zones where hotels or Japanese-style inns can operate their businesses (Yokozeki, 2018). Compared with the latter, the former can be regarded as a much more drastic approach in many senses. For instance, the former has a potential to vitalise accommodation business activities in the most areas in a prefecture, city or town, and this can be beneficial for the economic sustainability of these municipalities. Simultaneously, however, the former may instigate socio-cultural issues that can negatively influence the quality of neighbours' lives. Of these issues, noise caused and rubbish dumped by guests of *minpaku* are representative problems (Fukui, 2016; Hirata, 2017). In addition, neighbours are also concerned about extra wear and tear on communal facilities and insecurity triggered by the presence of strangers (i.e. *minpaku* guests). As for the causes of these problems, there is a point to be remembered. *Minpaku* guests use a room and communal facilities only for a short period of time (e.g. one night), whilst neighbours utilise their rooms and communal facilities as their places of residence. Thus, there is usually a certain level of gap in their attitudes and behaviours between the former and the latter.

Nevertheless, it should also be noted that *minpaku* can make a good contribution to the socio-cultural sustainability of local communities, particularly those in suburban or rural localities. Japan as a whole, especially its countryside, has been suffering from depopulation since 2015 and has become an aging society (Jimura, 2011b, 2019, 2022). Consequently, there are a large number of unoccupied or abandoned houses across Japan, particularly in non-urban areas. These unused properties should be utilised fully to activate the existing house market of Japan (Matsunaga, 2019), and *minpaku* is one of effective measures that can make the most of unoccupied or abandoned houses. Subsequently, such approaches and actions can lead to revitalisation of declining local communities. A major concern regarding the environmental sustainability of *minpaku* properties is their hygiene level. As the vast majority of owners of *minpaku* properties are ordinary citizens who are not experts of hygiene matters, the good hygiene level of the properties would not be always guaranteed, although the owners or cleaning staff they employ may clean up rooms for *minpaku* use on a regular basis. In reality, Yamada et al. (2018)'s study reveals that rooms used for *minpaku* tend to have various hygiene issues such as a lack of ventilation, house dust, insects, unknown clothes and/or foods left in a refrigerator. In light of this situation, supervision of relevant local authorities and administrative guidance for proper management should be introduced to increase and maintain a good hygiene level of *minpaku* facilities (Yamada et al., 2018).

8 Conclusion

Like the transport sector (see Chap. 5), the accommodation sector is also a vital element of tourism industry and their businesses include a range of themes associated with the triple bottom line (hereafter TBL) of sustainability. As discussed in this chapter, Japan's accommodation sector comprises of diverse kinds of accommodation facilities and services. Of these, some of accommodation facilities and services are unique or prominent in Japan and they are Japanised Western-style hotels (i.e. *business hotels*) and Japanese-style inns (e.g. *ryokan*, *minshuku* and *shukubo*). In relation to Part II of this book (Sustainability of Heritage), it should also be noted that the value of specific historic Western-style hotels in Japan and some of traditional Japanese-style inns as Japan's cultural heritage have been officially recognised by the Japanese Government. In fact, these structures have been protected through the public listing systems for the conservation of cultural heritage such as Important Cultural Properties. Therefore, TBL of sustainability of the aforementioned properties, particularly their socio-cultural sustainability, is indispensable for themselves, Japan's culture and society, and people in Japan to pass such cultural heritage on to future generations.

Prior to the COVID-19 pandemic, largely, Japan's accommodation sector had been thriving thanks to well-developed domestic tourism consisting of internal tourism and inbound· tourism. Especially, Japan's accommodation sector had enjoyed an increase in the amount of financial benefits thanks to Japan's inbound tourism boom that had become prominent since 2014 until the emergence of COVID-19 in March 2020. Indeed, this phenomenon strengthened the economic sustainability of Japan's accommodation sector as a whole, especially accommodation facilities located in tourist destinations that were well visited by international tourists. As a result, however, the author has to point out that a certain number of accommodation businesses relied too heavily on international tourists, especially those from Asia. Ironically, the COVID-19 pandemic and stricter restrictions on inbound tourists introduced by the Japanese Government revealed the vulnerability of such a business model. Stated differently, a number of accommodation businesses that set international tourists as their main target segment has been struggling and their economic sustainability has also been damaged severely since the spread of the COVID-19 pandemic. Some of such accommodation businesses could not/will not be able to recover from the aftermath of the COVID-19 pandemic even if financial supports are provided by the central, regional and/or local government. In Japan, the national campaign called 'Go To Travel' is adopted by the Japanese Government to help the accommodation sector. The campaign provides a discount on people's travel expenses, spending taxpayers' money, to encourage people's tourism activities and support the businesses of accommodation companies. The Go To Travel campaign is suspended as of January 2022 because of the spread of the Omicron COVID-19 variant across the world and a surge of COVID-19 cases in Japan, although the accommodation sector and people in Japan have been eagerly waiting for the resumption of the campaign.

Concerning the environmental sustainability, the vast majority of accommodation businesses in Japan are aware of the importance of SDGs. Particularly, most Western-style hotels, Japanised Western-style hotels and Japanese-style inns owned and managed by established companies are keen to contribute to SDGs. Their approach to and activities for SDGs are often illustrated on their official websites. In many cases, these enterprises also regard their actions for SDGs as their CSR activities. Nowadays, enterprises', especially large/multinational ones', activities for CSR and SDGs can be viewed as a socially constructed expectation. In light of this, implementing these actions is crucial not only for the environmental sustainability of accommodation businesses and their surrounding environment but also for the socio-cultural sustainability of those.

As represented by a series of activities conducted by Hoshino Resorts, 'reducing' food waste, 'reusing' containers and tableware, and 'recycling' kitchen waste as compost (see Sect. 4), 3Rs concept is often embedded in accommodation businesses' activities for CSR or SDGs and is implemented in many different ways. As indicated by Fukushima City (2017), the foundation of 3Rs is the spirit of *mottainai* in a Japanese context. In Japan's accommodation sector, a solid link between the *mottainai* spirit and 3Rs can be confirmed, for instance, in the initiative the aforementioned Hoshino Resorts launched in 2020. This scheme is called 'Mottainai Project' whose primary aim is to reduce the amount of food waste in the COVID-19 pandemic situation (Hoshino Resorts, 2021). To cite a case, the consumption of milk as part of school lunch or in the restaurant industry began to decrease since the start of the pandemic in 2020 and a large amount of milk could be wasted. Bearing this situation in mind, Hoshino Resorts started making milk jam to reduce the amount of wasted milk (Hoshino Resorts, 2021).

Generally speaking, other kinds of accommodation businesses, especially *minpaku*, do not seem to have been active regarding their activities for TBL of sustainability, SDGs, CSR or 3Rs compared with Western-style hotels, Japanised Western-style hotels and Japanese-style inns. There would be several reasons for this difference and one of the main ones would be people/organisations that own and/or run accommodation businesses. The former is usually owned and/or run by an ordinary person, family or a small company, whilst the latter tends to be owned and/or managed by large or mid-sized enterprises. This signifies that the latter is likely to be more abundant than the former in terms of their financial and human resources that enable the latter to plan and implement activities for SDGs, CSR and/or 3Rs in a comprehensive manner.

References

Adamovich, V., Nadda, V., Kot, M., & ul Haque, A. (2021). Camping vs. glamping tourism: Providers' perspective in the United Kingdom. *Journal of Environmental Management and Tourism, 12*(6), 1431–1441.

Beumer, H. (2016). *Kumano Kodo*. Lulu Press.

Cerulean Tower Tokyu Hotel. (n.d.). *ISO 14001 ninsho ni tsuite* (About acquisition of ISO 14001) [in Japanese]. Available at: https://www.tokyuhotels.co.jp/cerulean-h/corporate/social/osirase_iso/index.html. Accessed 30 Nov 2021.

Cwiertka, K. J. (2006). *Modern Japanese cuisine: Food, power and national identity*. Reaktion Books.

Diamond Online. (2020). *Gaikokujin kankyokyaku wo gakkari saseru Nihon no 'osugiru business hotels'* ('Too many *business hotels*' in Japan make inbound tourists disappointed) [in Japanese]. Available at: https://diamond.jp/articles/-/225366. Accessed 4 Dec 2021.

Fujiya Hotel. (n.d.). *Home* [in Japanese]. Available at: https://www.fujiyahotel.jp/. Accessed 27 Nov 2021.

Fukui, H. (2016). Legal issues and policy on renting private homes and apartments [in Japanese]. *The Japanese Journal of Real Estate Sciences, 30*(2), 37–44.

Fukushima City. (2017). *"3R" is promoted based on the spirit which "is wasteful"*. Available at: https://fukushimacity.j-server.com/LUCFKSC/ns/tl.cgi/https://www.city.fukushima.fukushima.jp/gomi-genryou/kurashi/recycling/genryo/1166.html?SLANG=ja&TLANG=en&XMODE=0&XCHARSET=utf-8&XJSID=0. Accessed 18 Jan 2022.

Hayashi, A., & Horimatsu, M. (2021). How to have fun in the outdoors under the pandemic of the Covid-19 [in Japanese]. *Bulletin of Biwako Seikei Sport College, 18*, 127–134.

Hayashida, S. (2017). *Hostel to guest house no chigai* (Differences between hostels and guest houses) [in Japanese]. Available at: https://tabi-labo.com/285242/yado-definition. 12 Dec 2021.

Hirata, Y. (2017). *Mansion ni okeru minpaku riyo no oyobosu eikyo* (The impacts of *minpaku* use on apartments) [in Japanese]. Japan Society of Home Economics.

HHCG. (n.d.). *President Message* [in Japanese]. Available at: https://www.hokke.co.jp/company.html. Accessed 8 Sep 2023.

Hiratsuka, N. (2021). *Camping car gyokai ga corona tokujyu wo yorokobenai wake 4* (Reasons why the RV industry is not satisfied with a rapid increase in the demand for RVs 4) [in Japanese]. Available at: https://toyokeizai.net/articles/-/464768?page=4. Accessed 17 Dec 2021.

Hiroma, J. (2013). Hotel gyokai no shin-choryu ni kansuru ichikosatsu (Examination of new tends in Japan's accommodation sector) [in Japanese]. *Osaka University of Tourism Kiyo, 13*, 89–96.

Honma, T. (2021). *Hoshino Resorts wa SDGs no sanshin-kigyo datta* (Hoshino Resorts is an advanced company regarding SDGs) [in Japanese]. Available at: https://renergy-online.com/archives/160. Accessed 10 Dec 2021.

Hoshino Resorts. (2021). *Mottainai Project Tsushin Volume 1* (Mottainai Project News Volume 1) [in Japanese]. Available at: https://www.hoshinoresorts.com/information/release/2021/03/139062.html?fbclid=IwAR0u1Yf3s3f0OLXGAawbN3fHreKSRHJVM0Dz9xV_HSGOAgTEDK5ARIc1Be4. Accessed 18 Jan 2022.

Hotel Jinzai Bank. (2019). *Budget Hotel towa (What are budget hotels?)* [in Japanese]. Available at: https://hoteljinzai.com/contents/dictionary/%E3%83%90%E3%82%B8%E3%82%A7%E3%83%83%E3%83%88%E3%83%9B%E3%83%86%E3%83%AB%E3%81%A8%E3%81%AF. Accessed 4 Dec 2021.

Ikado, T. (2021). Efforts of students in *ryokan* management – For improving labor productivity in small-scale lodging industry [in Japanese]. *Chiiki-seisaku Kenkyu, 23*(3), 39–47.

Imperial Hotel Tokyo. (2021). *Oshirase (Notice)* [in Japanese]. Available at: https://www.imperialhotel.co.jp/j/tokyo/news/cat311/20210325_news.html. Accessed 1 Dec 2021.

Imperial Hotels Group. (2021). *Teikoku Hotel no sustainability suishin undo* (Imperial Hotels Group's activities to promote sustainability) [in Japanese]. Available at: https://www.imperialhotel.co.jp/j/company/csr/. Accessed 1 Dec 2021.

Insider. (2019). *41 countries around the world that charge a tourist tax*. Available at: https://www.insider.com/countries-that-require-a-tourist-tax-2019-2. Accessed 23 Nov 2021.

Investopedia. (2021). *How Airbnb works*. Available at: https://www.investopedia.com/articles/personal-finance/032814/pros-and-cons-using-airbnb.asp. Accessed 29 Dec 2021.

ISO. (n.d.). *ISO 14000 Family: Environmental management*. Available at: https://www.iso.org/iso-14001-environmental-management.html. Accessed 24 Nov 2021.

Itoen Hotels. (2021). *Oshirase (notice)* [in Japanese]. Available at: https://www.itoenhotel.com/uomisaki/news/detail/978/. Accessed 29 Nov 2021.

Japan National Tourism Organisation. (2020). *Press release on 17 January 2020* [in Japanese]. Available at: https://www.jnto.go.jp/jpn/statistics/data_info_listing/pdf/200117_monthly.pdf. Accessed 4 Dec 2021.

JGLA. (n.d.). *Glamping* [in Japanese]. Available at: http://glamping.or.jp/about-glamping.html. Accessed 16 Dec 2021.

JYHG. (n.d.). *Sekai no Youth Hostel* (Youth Hostels around the world) [in Japanese]. Available at: http://www.jyh.or.jp/international/index.html. Accessed 8 Sep 2023.

Jimura, T. (2011a). The websites of Japanese ryokan and eWOM: Their impacts on guests' expectation and experience. *International Journal of Asian Tourism Management, 2*(2), 120–133.

Jimura, T. (2011b). The impact of world heritage site designation on local communities - A case study of Ogimachi, Shirakawa-mura, Japan. *Tourism Management, 32*(2), 288–296.

Jimura, T. (2019). *World heritage sites: Tourism, local communities and conservation activities*. CABI.

Jimura, T. (2022). *Cultural and heritage tourism in Japan*. Routledge.

Jimura, T., & Lee, T. (2020). The impact of photographs on the online marketing for tourism: The case of Japanese-style inns. *Journal of Vacation Marketing, 26*(3), 354–364.

JTBF. (2019). *Kosho kara miru Nihon no shukuhaku-jigyo* (Accommodation businesses in Japan according to old books) [in Japanese]. Available at: https://www.jtb.or.jp/gallery/hotel-history-japan-201910/. Accessed 27 Nov 2021.

Kagaya Group. (n.d.). *Kaisha gaiyo* (About us) [in Japanese]. Available at: https://www.kagaya.co.jp/company/outline/. Accessed 7 Dec 2021.

Kubo, T. (2019). *Todofuken-betsu camp-jo su* (The number of campsites by prefecture) [in Japanese]. Available at: https://todo-ran.com/t/kiji/23956. Accessed 16 Dec 2021.

LeBlanc, R. M. (2017). Designing a beautifully poor public: Postgrowth community in Italy and Japan. *Journal of Political Ecology, 24*(1), 449–461.

Liang, S., Leng, H., Yuan, Q., & Yuan, C. (2021). Impact of the COVID-19 pandemic: Insights from vacation rentals in twelve mega cities. *Sustainable Cities and Society, 74*, 103121.

Mainichi Shimbun. (2021). *Corona-ka ni 'anshin no tabi': Camping car juyo kyuzo* (Safe travels under the COVID-19 circumstance: A rapid increase in the demand for RVs) [in Japanese]. Available at: https://mainichi.jp/articles/20211117/ddl/k08/020/072000c. Accessed 17 Dec 2021.

Matsubara, S. (2019). Implementation status of events and experience programs related to way of living in guest houses [in Japanese]. *Sugiyamajogakuen Daigaku Kenkyu-ronshu, 50*, 73–90.

Matsunaga, M. (2019). Activation of the resale housing market for unoccupied house solutions to the problem [in Japanese]. *Toyo University Graduate School of Bulletin, 55,* 1–15.

Ohno, M. (2019). *Hotel ryokan no business model* (Business models adopted by hotels and *ryokan*) [in Japanese]. : Gendai Tosho.

Oriental Hotel. (2021). *About us.* Available at: https://www.orientalhotel.jp/concept/. Accessed 27 Nov 2021.

Redelman, M. (2012). 3. Shukubo. *AOFS Newsletter, 4,* 3.

Super Hotel. (2021). *ISO eno torikumi* (Efforts to obtain ISO certifications) [in Japanese]. Available at: https://www.superhotel.co.jp/kaisya_r/company/iso.html. Accessed 5 Dec 2021.

Takizawa, N. (2021a). *Bakuzoshita 3man booths no capsule hotels: Boom shuen no riyu wa corona-ka dakejanakatta 5* (The number of beds *capsule hotels* have increased a lot, more than 30k beds: the COVID-19 pandemic was not only the reason why its success ended 5) [in Japanese]. Available at: https://www.itmedia.co.jp/business/articles/2107/28/news042_5.html. Accessed 13 Dec 2021.

Takizawa, N. (2021b). *Bakuzoshita 3man booths no capsule hotels: Boom shuen no riyu wa corona-ka dakejanakatta 4.* (The number of beds *capsule hotels* have increased a lot, more than 30k beds: The COVID-19 pandemic was not only the reason why its success ended 4) [in Japanese]. Available at: https://www.itmedia.co.jp/business/articles/2107/28/news042_4.html Accessed 13 Dec 2021.

TBS News. (2021). *Kocho! Candeo Hotels* (Good business performance of Candeo Hotels) [in Japanese]. Available at: https://www.youtube.com/watch?v=BQycJNb0n04. Accessed 4 Dec 2021.

Tokyo YMCA. (n.d.). *Business Hotel to City Hotel no chigai towa* (Differences between *business hotels* and *city hotels*) [in Japanese]. Available at: https://hotel.ymsch.jp/column/cat/hotel-hikaku.html. Accessed 3 Dec 2021.

UNWTO. (n.d.). *Glossary of tourism terms.* Available at: https://www.unwto.org/glossary-tourism-terms. Accessed 23 Nov 2021.

WWF Japan. (n.d.). *Shinrin-hozen to jizokukano na kami-riyo* (Forest conservation and sustainable use of papers) [in Japanese]. Available at: https://www.wwf.or.jp/activities/basicinfo/1382.html. Accessed 6 Dec 2021.

Yamada, H., Honma, Y., & Bando, M. (2018). Investigation of the indoor hygienic environment of private lodging [in Japanese]. In *The 42nd symposium on human-environment system,* pp 145–148.

Yasuda, S. (2021). Spiritual legitimacy in contemporary Japan: A case study of the power spot phenomenon and the Haruna Shrine, Gunma. *Religions*, *12*(3), 177. https://doi.org/10.3390/rel12030177

Yokohama Archives of History. (2007). *Hotels* [in Japanese]. Available at: http://www.kaikou.city.yokohama.jp/q-a/hotel_01.html#:~:text=1860%E5%B9%B4%EF%BC%88%E4%B8%87%E5%BB%B6%E5%85%83%E5%B9%B4,%EF%BC%93(1770)%E5%B9%B4%E9%96%8B%E6%A5%AD%E3%80%82. Accessed 23 Nov 2021.

Yokozeki, M. (2018). *Minpaku jorei towa* (What the New Act on Private Lodging) [in Japanese]. Available at: https://minpaku.yokozeki.net/minpaku-jourei/. Accessed 11 Jan 2022.

7

Sustainability of Food and Beverage Sector in Japan

1 Introduction

According to Maslow (1943), eating and drinking are physiological needs, the most basic needs of human beings, that are vital to satisfy their hunger and thirst. Consuming foods and beverage is also an essential activity that every single excursionist or tourist does whilst he/she is away from home for leisure, business or other purposes. Moreover, the value and importance of foods and drinks, especially those reflecting national, regional or local characteristics and/or being associated with national, regional or local identity, as tourism resources and cultural heritage have been acknowledged and examined well in academic research (Jimura, 2022). Timothy (2021) further states that food and culinary traditions are cultural heritage that could have a power to influence on the decision making of day trippers or tourists. Foods and drinks are particularly important and influential for certain types of visitors such as foodies who are likely to be allured to visit specific localities mainly to have new and authentic food experiences (Getz et al., 2014). Foods and beverage that are unique to or prominent in peculiar regions with potentials to attract travellers would include pasta and pizza (Italy), tapas and paella (Spain), falafel (Middle East), couscous (North Africa) and dim sum (Hong

Kong). As for Japan, *washoku* (also called *Nihon-ryori*) can be viewed as the food and culinary traditions whose popularity has been increasing in foreign countries and amongst inbound tourists coming to Japan (Jimura, 2022). In addition, the significance of *washoku* as cultural heritage is endorsed by the listing of 'Washoku, traditional dietary cultures of the Japanese, notably for the celebration of New Year' as Intangible Cultural Heritage by UNESCO in 2013 (UNESCO, 2013; Jimura, 2022).

In tourism settings, visitors, including day trippers and tourists, usually dine out to consume foods and/or drinks. Under the circumstances of COVID-19, furthermore, travellers often arrange the delivery of foods and/or beverage or take foods and/or drinks away to consume them in their accommodations. Thus, it is natural for visitors to include places to eat and/or drinks, typically restaurants (see Sect. 2), cafes (see Sect. 3) and bars (see Sect. 4), in their itineraries. Regarding this, it should be noted that traditional eateries offering national, regional or local dishes have been playing an important role in the conservation of intangible cultural heritage and raising people's awareness of national, regional or local cultures. In some nations, such eateries may include indigenous restaurants and their presence has been getting stronger in popular tourist destinations where cultures of indigenous peoples are utilised as cultural heritage products in tourism settings (Timothy, 2021). Examples of such foods and restaurants can be found in Taiwan (Austronesian Taiwanese) and Australia (Aboriginal Australians). In Japan, the cuisine of Uchinanchu (Okinawan) people can be understood as Japan's indigenous people's cuisine (Jimura, 2022). Many Uchinanchu people have moved to the largest mainland of Japan, Honshu, to find a job or build a new life. Particularly, Taisho Ward in Osaka City (Osaka Urban Prefecture) and Tsurumi Ward in Yokohama City (Kanagawa Prefecture) are famous for a large population of the Uchinanchu who relocated to the cities and their descendants, and have districts called 'Little Okinawa'. For this reason, there are also a lot of restaurants offering Uchinanchu cuisine in and around these districts. According to Tabelog (2022), one of the most influential restaurant search websites in Japan, in fact, there are 16 and 12 Uchinanchu restaurants in and around the Little Okinawa districts in Taisho Ward and Tsurumi Ward respectively.

The businesses offering services related to provision of foods and/or drinks have been working on the TBL of sustainability and relevant key agendas such as SDGs in many different ways. Nevertheless, it could be stated that there would be five major domains that the businesses focus on as follows:

* Procurement of ingredients and development/improvement of menus
* Restaurant operations
* Employees
* Local communities, and
* Management (Nautical Star Strategy & Analysis, 2021).

Like many other nations with established tourist destinations, Japan also has a wide variety of places to eat and/or drink. It is challenging to establish a classification of these different places that can satisfy the needs and views of all key stakeholders. However, the classification adopted by Statistics Bureau of Japan (hereafter SBJ) can be seen as one of the well-known examples of classifications of places for eating and drinking (see Table 7.1). This chapter discusses two main types of places to eat and drink, namely 'eateries' (in Sects. 2, 3 and 4) and 'food/drink takeaways and deliveries' (in Sect. 5). Regarding the eateries, Sect. 2 looks at those other than 'bars, cabarets and night clubs' and 'cafes'. Section 3 examines 'bars, cabarets and night clubs', whilst Sect. 4 explores 'cafes'.

2 Restaurants

In Table 7.1, the categories and subcategories included in the type of 'eateries' are divided mainly by cuisine or dish they offer to their customers (e.g. *sushi* and hamburger). However, these categories and subcategories cannot be seen as a comprehensive list of restaurants currently existing in Japan. For example, Jimura (2022) lists major international cuisines in Japan based on the number of restaurants recorded in Tabelog as follows:

* Chinese (42,182)
* Italian (especially pizza and pasta) (24,660)
* French (11,034)
* Korean (9038)

Table 7.1 Eateries and food/drink takeaways and deliveries in Japan

Type	Category	Subcategory
Eateries	Offices for administration and management	
	General restaurants	
	Specialised restaurant	Japanese restaurants
		Chinese restaurants
		Yakiniku barbecue restaurants
		Other specialised restaurants
	Japanese noodle (*soba* and *udon*) restaurants	
	Sushi restaurants	
	Izakaya (Japanese bar restaurants) and beer halls	
	Bars, cabarets, and night clubs	
	Cafés	
	Other eateries	Hamburger restaurants
		Okonomiyaki, yakisoba and *takoyaki* restaurants
		Other unclassified restaurants
Food/drink takeaways and deliveries	Offices for administration and management	
	Food/drink takeaways	
	Food/drink deliveries	

Source: SBJ (2019)

- Indian (4569)
- Thai (2088)
- Spanish (1621)

Of these, however, only 'Chinese restaurants' is shown as a subcategory in Table 7.1 that is created following the classification employed by SBJ. In other words, other six different cuisines popular in Japan with a large number of restaurants are all included in the subcategory, 'Other specialised restaurants', although especially Italian, French and Korean restaurants have been established as popular specific type of cuisine in the

7 Sustainability of Food and Beverage Sector in Japan

Japanese food and drink market. '*Izakaya* (Japanese bar restaurants) and beer halls' have characteristics of both restaurants and bars but are discussed as 'restaurants' in this section for subsequent reasons.

Izakaya and beer halls serve alcoholic drinks like 'bars, cabarets and night clubs'. Nonetheless, the quality and variety of foods/dishes and those of drinks are equally important when customers evaluate their services. In addition, lightweights, including the author, can use *izakaya* or beer halls without a problem or hesitation, ordering non-alcoholic drinks and enjoying a range of foods/dishes available there. On the contrary, it is usually challenging for lightweights to use bars, cabarets or night clubs as their customers are strongly expected to order alcoholic drinks. Bearing these points in mind, following paragraphs look at sustainability and sustainability management of restaurants in Japan.

Like other sectors in the tourism industry such as transport (e.g. airlines) (see Chap. 5) and accommodation (e.g. Japanese-style inns) (see Chap. 6), overall the food and beverage sector is also labour-intensive. This means that a large amount of human labour is constantly required to continue to provide their customers with excellent services. Thus, labour costs can put pressure on the economic sustainability of restaurant businesses. In addition, it is often pointed out that the restaurant market is highly competitive and Japan's market is not an exception. For these reasons, the economic sustainability of restaurant businesses across the globe and in Japan is inclined to be fragile. Moreover, jobs available in the restaurant market tend to be seasonal and low-waged and this also applies to Japan. In summary, restaurants businesses usually try to minimise wages and increase flexibility of work contracts (Shiva Foundation, 2021) to keep themselves economically sustainable. Such situations signify that the economic sustainability of employees in the restaurant market is also unlikely to be stable. In the case of Japan's restaurant market, subsequent issues are raised as key problems related mainly with the economic sustainability of restaurant businesses or their workers:

- Low wages and long working hours (Shinmura et al., 2018),
- Shrinking market size and a large number of bankruptcy cases, especially in the *izakaya* market (Morishima & Sato, 2012), and

- Short length of continuous service and low proportion of full-time permanent employees (Ikeda, 2020).

Besides, the COVID-19 pandemic has been negatively influencing these economic or financial challenges Japan's restaurant companies face. According to Morishima and Sato (2012), around 77% of restaurants in Japan are run by small and medium-sized enterprises or families. This implies that these restaurants have rather limited financial resources and are likely to be hit hard by a crisis like the pandemic. In addition, many restaurant enterprises close their businesses temporarily, reduce their business hours or stop offering alcoholic drinks, following central, regional and/or local government guidance. All of these factors have also damaged the economic sustainability of restaurant businesses and their employees. In fact, 842 food and drink businesses listed in Table 7.1 went bankrupt with liabilities of 10 million Japanese Yen (hereafter JPY) or more in 2020, and this number was the highest since 1992 (Tokyo Shoko Research (hereafter TSR) 2022). The number of bankruptcy cases decreased to 648 in 2021 mainly thanks to financial support from national, regional or local government (TSR, 2022). Of all kinds of restaurants discussed in this section, *'izakaya* (Japanese bar restaurants) and beer halls' have especially seriously damaged by the impact of the COVID-19 pandemic. This is evidenced by the fact that 174 and 152 *izakaya* or beer halls went into administration in 2020 and 2021 respectively with debts of 10 million JPY or more (TSR, 2022).

Waldfogel (2020) examines dining out and enjoying various international foods at restaurants as 'cultural trade'. His research reveals that cuisines of five countries, namely Italian, Japanese, Chinese, Indian and American, have established a solid position in foreign countries, gaining popularity amongst the general public of these nations (Waldfogel, 2020). Waldfogel (2020) also concludes that excluding fast food, the largest net exporters of their national cuisines are Italian and Japanese people, whilst the largest net importers of foreign cuisines are American citizens followed by Brazil, China and the UK. These facts and figures demonstrate socio-cultural impacts as well as economic impacts of internationalisation of foods and cuisines across a number of countries in different regions of the world. Dining out has also been recognised widely as one of the major leisure activities for people all over the world, including Japan. For instance, Kitada (2003) argues that dining out is the most popular leisure activity amongst women in Japan aged between 20 and 59 years old. In relation to the aforementioned Maslow's hierarchy of needs (see Sect. 1), dining out can satisfy not only basic needs of human beings such as physiological needs but also their psychological needs such as love and belonging. In fact, local restaurants, particularly established ones, can function as meeting places where local inhabitants get together frequently. Such strong bonds with local communities are quite important to maintain or enhance the socio-cultural sustainability of eateries. Being recognised well and utilised regularly by residents is essential for the economic and socio-cultural sustainability of restaurants, especially those are not branches of famous international or nationwide restaurant chains or are not located in well-known tourist destinations.

According to Japan Productivity Center (hereafter JPC) (2020, 2021), furthermore, dining out for special occasions is the second popular leisure activity amongst the general public of Japan, and 43.5 million people enjoyed this leisure activity in 2019. In 2020, however, the rank of dining out for special occasions dropped to the sixth with 33.3 million people who enjoyed it mainly due to the COVID-19 pandemic (JPC, 2021). Thus, it could be said that economic and socio-cultural sustainability of restaurant businesses had been established and solid by being used widely by the general public and visitors up until the pandemic. Unfortunately, however, it is also true that their economic and socio-cultural sustainability has weakened due to a massive decrease in the number of opportunities for socialising activities, including having foods and beverage at restaurants, since the spread of COVID-19 around the world began in 2020. Regarding this situation, it also needs to be remembered that a much-reduced number of occasions for dining out has led to the rise and development of takeaways and deliveries (see Sect. 5 for details).

Like the transport sector, especially airlines, (see Chap. 5) and the accommodation sector, particularly hotels and Japanese-style inns, (see Chap. 6), many businesses in the food and drink sector of Japan have been working on the environmental sustainability through their activities for SDGs. Such activities are better confirmed amongst large food and drink companies such as international or domestic restaurant chains rather than SMEs, including local/family-run businesses. Within the tourism industry of Japan, this inclination is commonly observed in both accommodation and food and beverage sectors. Table 7.2 shows Japan's top 10 fast food businesses by sales in Japanese fiscal year of 2020 (between April 2020 and March 2021), and representative brand(s) of each of the top 10 companies (Gyokai-doko Search n.d.). Of these, for instance, Mos Food Services has been well-known not only for their unique products (e.g. MOS Rice Burger) but also for their activities for CSR or SDGs (Nishihara, 2021). The company has been conducting various activities for CSR or SDGs as follows:

- Disclosing vegetable-producing areas and information on producers to enhance the level of traceability,
- Reusing tableware and recycling cooking oil, and
- Separating a smoking area from a non-smoking area in a restaurant and increasing the number of non-smoking restaurants (Nishihara, 2021).

Table 7.2 Japan's top 10 fast food businesses by sales between April 2020 and March 2021

Rank	Name	Representative brands	Sales (billion Japanese Yen)
1	McDonald's Holdings (Japan)	McDonald's (hamburger)	288.3
2	Zensho Holdings	Sukiya (beef bowl), Coco's (general restaurant)	216.2
3	Torildoll Holdings	Marugame Seimen (*udon*)	134.7
4	Yoshinoya Holdings	Yoshinoya (beef bowl)	105.6
5	Matsuya Foods Holdings	Matsuya (beef bowl)	94.4
6	KFC Holdings Japan	KFC (fried chicken)	89.6
7	MOS Food Services	MOS Burger (hamburger)	71.9
8	Ichibanya	Coco Ichibanya (Japanese curry)	44.2
9	Arcland Service Holdings	Katsuya (Japanese pork cutlet)	38.6
10	Duskin	Mister Donut (donut)	36.5

Source: Gyokai-doko Search (n.d.)

Of these, the concepts and practice of 'reuse' and 'recycle' confirmed in the second point are the elements of 3Rs. In addition, the concept and practice of the other element of 3Rs, 'reduce', is also confirmed through Mos Food Services' approaches towards CSR or SDGs. Mos Food Services' hamburger restaurants, Mos Burger, offers their meals on a 'cooked-to- order' basis since its foundation in 1972 (Mos Food Services, 2022). This style needs to ask their customers to wait for a while until they receive meals they ordered; whilst it can 'reduce' the amount of food waste and enables Mos Burger restaurants to always provide their customers with fresh meals.

Once, McDonald's Japan, the long-standing market leader, focused very much on the speed of their services and offered their popular products in a 'made-ahead' manner. Between 2004 and 2005, however, McDonald's Japan introduced the 'Made For You' system at all of their restaurants throughout Japan (McDonald's Japan, 2022). Compared with 2001, McDonald's Japan could reduce the amount (kg) of unused completed products per sale of one million Japanese Yen by 51.5% in 2005, the year when the Made For You system was introduced at all of their restaurants across Japan (McDonald's Japan, 2022). Completed products of McDonald's Japan consist of food, paper, plastic and package resources, and the Made For You system could reduce the usage of all of these resources. In 2017, moreover, the system won a *mottainai* award that is offered by the Ministry of Agriculture, Forestry and Fisheries for the system's great contribution to the reduction of food waste (McDonald's Japan, 2017). It should also be noted that the Made For You system is also related to three SDGs, namely SDG 9 Industry, Innovation and Infrastructure; SDG 12 Responsible Consumption and Production; and SDG 17 Partnerships for the Goals (McDonald's Japan, 2022). As a company as a whole, whilst, McDonald's Japan particularly focuses on six SDGs, namely SDG 2 Zero Hunger, SDG 8 Decent Work and Economic Growth, SDG 12 Responsible Consumption and Production, SDG 13 Climate Action, SDG 15 Life on Land, and SDG 17 Partnerships for the Goals. This signifies that the company is aware of the importance of the economic and socio-cultural sustainability of their businesses and wider society as well as the environmental sustainability of these.

Compared with international (e.g. McDonald's) or even domestic (e.g. Mos Burger) restaurant chains, generally what local, independent and/or family-run restaurants can do for CSR or SDGs would be rather limited. Nonetheless, examples of such schemes or actions can still be confirmed. One of representative approaches for CSR or SDGs taken by the above-mentioned small food and drink businesses is 'local production for local consumption' (*chisan-chisho*). According to Eguchi Holdings (n.d.), local production for local consumption is directly associated with and can make a great contribution to achieving SDG 14 Life below Water and SDG 15 Life on Land. Many local seafood restaurants and vegetable restaurants, and some steakhouses in Japan try to use locally produced foods as much as possible. For example, seafood restaurants and *sushi* restaurants situated in the Numazu Fishing Port area (Numazu City, Shizuoka Prefecture) fully utilise locally sourced seafood for their dishes. Figure 7.1 shows a popular seafood bowl at Nishiyo restaurant in the Numazu Fishing Port

Fig. 7.1 A popular seafood bowl at Nishiyo restaurant. (Source: Author)

area. The three kinds of toppings on the bowl, namely whitebait (*shirasu*), sakura shrimp (*sakura ebi*) and horse mackerel (*aji*) that are caught locally. All of these three, especially whitebait and sakura shrimps, have been valued as important ocean resources that are also part of local identity. Hence, it could be stated that this example is closely associated with SDG 14 Life below Water. Local production for local consumption is also practiced widely at motorway service stations, roadside stations (*michi no eki*) and seaside stations (*umi no eki*) (see Sect. 6 of Chap. 6) all over Japan. Tamba-Sasayama City (Hyogo Prefecture) is famous for several sorts of locally produced foods. Restaurants at the motorway service stations (Nishiki Service Areas) located in the city have developed and offer a range of dishes that make the most of various locally produced foods such as beef, pork, chicken, black soybean and milk. Some of them are also established brands (e.g. Tajima Beef and Tamba Black Beans) and have been valued a lot by the general public as well as local inhabitants. Thus, this case can be seen as a good example of activities for SDG 15 Life on Land.

In addition to SDGs 14 and 15, the concept and practice of local production for local consumption is also associated with SDG 7 Affordable and Clean Energy; SDG 9 Industry, Innovation and Infrastructure; and SDG 13 Climate Action (Eguchi Holdings, n.d.). SDGs 7 and 9 refer to the significance of energy's local production and local consumption. Energy, especially electricity, required to sustain business and human activities, including dining out at restaurants, should be produced locally as much as possible. To this end, the infrastructure and services (e.g. power stations and power transmission) that need to provide customers with energy must be developed and available locally. In the case of Japan, overall this has not been realised regarding electricity. That is because; the areas that consume a considerable amount of electricity (e.g. Tokyo Metropolitan Prefecture (hereafter TMP) or Osaka Urban Prefecture (hereafter OUP)) are often far from major electricity-producing areas (e.g. Fukushima Prefecture and Niigata Prefecture for TMP and Fukui Prefecture for OUP). On the other hand, SDG 13 Climate Action in the context of foods or drinks offered at restaurants can be discussed in terms of 'food miles'. Food miles means a travel distance of food between its production area to its consumption area (Weber & Matthews, 2008). As any major transport modes for the transport of foods or drinks, especially air transport, consume energy and cause environmental impacts, decreasing or minimising food miles is essential to contribute to SDG 13 Climate Action. With regard to restaurants in Japan, several international cuisines are very popular amongst Japanese people as mentioned at the beginning of this section, and restaurants offering these cuisines often need to import foods and drinks from the countries where the cuisines originate. In recent years, however, many restaurants and their owner chefs have been keen to find and use locally produced foods/drinks as much as possible, establishing and enhancing their relationships with local producers. To cite a case, French restaurants such as Veronica Persica (Iruma City, Saitama Prefecture) and Petale de Sakura (Yokohama City, Kanagawa Prefecture) are representative examples of restaurants that adopt and implement a local production for local consumption approach continuously.

3   Bars, Cabarets and Night Clubs

'Bars, cabarets and night clubs' is one of the categories of eateries specified in Table 7.1. As signified in Sect. 2, in principle, bars, cabarets and night clubs are the places to enjoy drinking alcoholic drinks rather than non-alcoholic drinks or foods. A major difference between bars, cabarets and night clubs and other categories of eateries is that the former must be licensed by the Prefectural Public Safety Commission that exercises jurisdiction over the area where the business office is located, following Article 3 (1) of the Act on Control and Improvement of Amusement Business. This implies that a need for alcoholic drinks is less essential than that for foods or non-alcoholic drinks in relation to physiological needs in Maslow's hierarchy of needs. This also signifies that although bars, cabarets or night clubs are recognised as eateries in Table 7.1, their main purpose as service providers is not to satisfy people's hunger and/or thirst but to provide them with comfort and/or amusement (Jimura, 2022). In addition to bars, cabarets and night clubs, Japan has other types of businesses whose main service is to offer alcoholic drinks. All of these businesses can be divided into two subcategories by with or without of services provided by hostesses or hosts.

The economic sustainability of the businesses whose main product is alcohol drinks is usually supported by a high profit margin generated by selling alcohol drinks to their customers. At the same time, however, the economic sustainability can be threatened by a poor rotation of customers, especially for bars, and a high wage for hostesses for cabarets or night clubs. Compared with other kinds of food and drink businesses, this sort of business has been hit more severely by the COVID-19 pandemic. That is because, some prefectural governments such as TMP asked food and drink business located in TMP to close their businesses temporarily, reduce their business hours and finish their businesses earlier, and/or stop offering alcoholic drinks, providing the business agreeing to do so with subsidies, during a state of emergency. Basically, the state of emergency is declared by the central government often responding to a request from prefectural governors. Even the subsidies are provided, the impact of the declaration of a state of emergency can still be immense for bars, cabarets or night clubs, because running their business late at night is a key feature of the business and alcoholic drinks are often the most profitable amongst their products.

Globally, the importance of night-time economy for many cities, especially large ones such as London, UK, has been growing in recent years (BBC News, 2019). This is also a subject that has been explored in several different study fields such as tourism and urban studies especially since 2010s (Ikeda, 2017). These international trends in academia as well as real world can also be applied to Japan, typically TMP. Jimura (2020) claims that together with recent inbound-tourism boom and diverse cultural heritage of TMP, the urban regeneration linked to Tokyo 2020 is expected to revitalise Tokyo and Japan as a whole. More specifically, the significance of night-time economy and potential of night-time tourism, particularly those in Tokyo, have been a centre of discussions in academia (e.g. Ikeda, 2017) and the real world (NHK World-Japan, 2019). If Tokyo 2020 were held normally as originally planned, it might have been able to economically contribute to Tokyo and possibly whole of Japan, including their night-time businesses such as bars, cabarets and night clubs. As everybody knows, however, unfortunately almost opposite happened due to the COVID-19 pandemic. Amongst various restrictions related to COVID-19, travel bans for international travellers visiting

Japan and holding the Games without international or domestic spectators hit the tourism industry of Japan, particularly Tokyo's, very hard. If held normally with international tourists and spectators, Tokyo 2020 could be a trigger or key driver to make bars, cabarets and night clubs more thriving as nightlife is one of key attraction factors for tourists, especially for those from Western countries (Ikeda et al., 2017) or English-speaking countries (Isono, 2020). In other words, the economic sustainability of bars, cabarets or night clubs could not be strengthened thanks to Tokyo 2020 and was actually weakened by the COVID-19 pandemic.

The presence of bars, cabarets or night clubs is generally accepted by the general public of Japan and these services have been utilised by a certain proportion of adults, normally men, for a long time. In this sense, it could be stated that the socio-cultural sustainability of these services is stable and their presence has been established in Japanese society. In Japan, '*sakariba*' is a traditional word that describes specific locales where people get together for amusement purposes (Jimura, 2022), including consuming alcoholic drinks. Although what '*sakariba*' means precisely can differ by person, it is safe to say that the term generally refers to certain areas that consist of shopping streets/districts (*shoten-gai* or *hanka-gai*) and/or entertainment streets/districts (*kanraku-gai*) (Jimura, 2022). In relation to this point, Jimura (2022) also argues that venues for consuming alcoholic drinks are necessary elements for areas to be understood as *kanraku-gai*. This also implies that businesses for drinking such as bars, cabarets and night clubs can create a flamboyant and licentious mood of *kanraku-gai*, especially at night, working together with businesses for socialising, dining out and sexual services (Jimura, 2022). For these reasons, some people, for example women and families with small children, may want to avoid living in/near *kanraku-gai*. Moreover, opportunities to use bars, cabarets or night clubs to entertain people, business clients or important customers have been getting smaller under the COVID-19 circumstances. In this sense, the socio-cultural sustainability of these services has been facing important challenges.

Overall, initiatives or activities to maintain or enhance the environmental sustainability of bars, cabarets or night clubs do not seem to have been developed or conducted well compared with restaurants discussed in Sect. 2. Their approaches or works for CSR or SDGs also do not seem to have been advanced well. Nevertheless, some practices associated with the spirit of *mottainai* and 3Rs, especially 'reuse', can be observed in the food and drink sector of Japan, including bars, cabarets and night clubs. The concept of 'reuse' is practiced when an existing bar, cabaret or night club is closed. For example, bar/kitchen facilities and equipment, wine cellars, lighting appliances and/or bar stools and sofas can be sold to second-hand stores to be reused by people who are going to open their businesses. By doing so, new owners of these facilities or equipment could obtain them with cheaper prices, and the facilities and equipment can be reused by new owners. This represents the spirit of *mottainai*. Alternatively, business venues for bars, cabarets or night clubs can be rented again to new tenants with all their existing furnishings. In Japan, these properties are called '*inuki bukken*'. Renting '*inuki bukken*' is advantageous for new tenants in many ways particularly if they are going to deliver a type of service that is the same or similar to previous tenants'. By renting *inuki bukken*, entrepreneurs can save initial costs and start their businesses quickly and smoothly. In addition, it should also be noted that the facilities and equipment left at *inuki bukken* could have longer live as products. All of these practices are useful to strengthen the environmental sustainability of bar/kitchen facilities and equipment and businesses of bars, cabarets and night clubs. Like restaurants, unfortunately, many bars, cabarets or night clubs have been closed temporarily or permanently because of the COVID-19 pandemic. However, it is also true that many people also decided to newly start their food and drink businesses, including bars, cabarets or night clubs, because rents of properties located in many popular urban districts have dropped.

4   Cafés

In this book and chapter, the word, 'café', is used to indicate a place to take a rest, have a chat and/or relax, enjoying non-alcoholic drinks (e.g. coffee, tea) and sweets or savouries. It could be stated that this notion of café is equivalent to the concept of '*kissaten*' in Japanese. Table 7.1 includes 'cafés' as one of the categories for eateries, but actually it is written as '*kissaten*' in Japanese in the source of Table 7.1. Nowadays, there are a wide variety of cafés in Japan, including international, domestic or regional café chains and independent cafés. Concerning international café or coffee/tea shop chains in Japan, Starbucks Coffee is a representative example. Since its arrival in Japan in August 1996, Starbucks Coffee has been very successful in their business and expanding its store network rapidly. Today, Starbucks Coffee is the largest café chains in Japan in terms of the number of stores. As of December 2020, there are 1628 Starbucks Coffee stores across Japan, covering all of Japan's 47 prefectures (Gyokai-doko Search, 2021). Several different factors are pointed out by researchers as secrets of Starbucks Coffee's huge business success in Japan. For example, a proper balance between standardisation across the world and adaptation for the Japanese market is seen as a key factor for Starbucks Coffee's success in Japan (Grinshpun, 2009). In addition, Hisashige (2007) states that Starbucks Coffee has successfully established its presence in the Japanese market as 'a third place' for its customers, offering its customers with a bit special or luxurious experience. Here, 'a third place' denotes a place neither home nor office. This concept has been highly attractive for a specific market segment, young Japanese people in 20 s or 30 s, especially women. Regarding domestic café or coffee/tea shop chains in Japan, whilst Doutor Coffee is most popular in terms of the number of stores. As a company, Doutor Coffee opened its first store in 1980 and has 1286 stores under six different brands as of March 2022 (Doutor, n.d.). Of these brands, the largest brand is Doutor Coffee and there are 1074 Doutor Coffee stores in Japan as of February 2022 (Doutor, 2022). The concept or characteristics of Doutor Coffee is somewhat different from Starbucks Coffee's. Overall, the prices of Doutor Coffee's products are less expensive than those of Starbucks Coffee's products. The interior of Doutor Coffee's stores also tends to be simpler than Starbucks Coffee's. Such features could make Doutor Coffee's stores handier and more approachable cafés than Starbucks Coffee's. These kinds of character are related to the main target segment of Doutor Coffee such as persons who want to have a business meeting or a quick rest (Iwata, 2012).

Although the number of stores has been decreasing gradually, independent cafés still share an important position in Japan's café market. According to Tanaka and Umezaki (2012), after the Second World War, café culture of Japan revived in around 1947. Until the end of 1970s, independent cafés are major players in the café market of Japan. During these three decades, independent café with various characteristics emerged and they include cafés with retro atmosphere and those play classical (*meikyoku kissa*) or jazz music (jazz *kissa*) (Tanaka & Umezaki, 2012). For instance, Sabouru (TMP) and Tsukiji (Kyoto Urban Prefecture) are representative examples of Japanese cafés with retro atmosphere, whilst Lion (TMP) and JAMJAM (Hyogo Prefecture) are good examples of *meikyoku kissa* and jazz *kissa* respectively. As confirmed above, however, key players in Japan's café market have gradually shifted to domestic (e.g. Doutor Coffee) and then international (e.g. Starbucks Coffee) café chains. In addition to two big names, Starbucks Coffee and Doutor Coffee, Komeda Coffee, founded in Aichi Prefecture in 1968, has developed into the third largest coffee shop chain in Japan since the early twenty-first century. Key features and main target markets of Komeda Coffee's stores are different from Starbucks Coffee's or Doutor Coffee's. Komeda's stores are often located along main roads in suburban areas rather than city centre. This signifies that their stores are usually spacious and have a large personal space per customer. Although the prices of their foods and drinks are rather expensive, these products are also famous for their good qualities and/or generous portions. Consequently, the popularity of Komeda Coffee is prominent amongst senior citizens (Shima, 2018). During the past decade, Japan's café market also saw the rise and development of international tea shop chains. This phenomenon is characterised by the third wave of tapioca balls boom, especially huge bubble tea boom, in Japan between 2018 and 2020. The boom was triggered by the arrival of two Taiwanese tea shop chains in the 2010s, namely Chun Shui Tang in 2013 and Gong Cha 2015. The boom was promoted further by an increased popularity of Taiwan as a tourist destination amongst Japanese people, particularly the youth.

Like other types of eateries in Japan, overall cafés have also been negatively affected by the COVID-19 pandemic regarding their economic sustainability. In fact, the market size of Japan's café sector in 2020 was around 805.5 billion that was 31.6% smaller than 2019 (Nikkei Telecom, 2022). Delivery and takeaway culture and practice have been fostered during the pandemic time and this could be somewhat helpful for the economic sustainability of cafés in Japan (see Sect. 5 for details). The rise and development of convenience stores (e.g. Seven-Eleven, Lawson) and fast-food restaurants (e.g. McDonald's, McCafé) as takeaway coffee shops have also been a threat for the economic sustainability of cafés, especially independent ones due to their cheap prices and relatively good tastes.

As for the socio-cultural sustainability of cafés in Japan, it is fair to say that the aforementioned independent cafés often mirror personality of owners and/or the culture(s) they are interested in (e.g. jazz music). The Nagoya area in Aichi Prefecture is famous for its distinct café culture that is difficult to spot in other areas in Japan. Nagoya's café culture can be characterised by key features such as its highly value-for-money morning coffee sets and unique local dishes (e.g. Ogura toast, *ankake* spaghetti). There is no single view why such exceptional café culture appeared and has been established in this peculiar locale. Nonetheless, it is safe to say that this café culture is closely associated with local identity of the area and generally local people seem to enjoy and be proud of the culture. It can also be stated that nowadays this distinct café culture is spread across Japan. That is because; the café culture has been embedded in the nature and characteristics of the above-mentioned Komeda Coffee originated in Nagoya City in Aichi Prefecture and today Komeda's coffee shop network covers all 47 prefectures of Japan. The business success of Komeda Coffee and diffusion of the café culture of the Nagoya area would be helpful for the socio-cultural sustainability of this local café culture in the future. It should also be noted that cafés, particularly independent local cafés, have been playing a vital role in maintaining or enhancing the socio-cultural sustainability of local communities, especially ties amongst elderly people (Tanaka & Umezaki, 2012; Tajima et al., 2018). That is because; these cafés can work as regular gathering points for local residents, functioning as social capitals in local communities (Tanaka & Umezaki, 2012; Tajima et al., 2018). In light of this, the existence of cafés in local communities can be one of the main factors that may influence the socio-cultural sustainability of certain local communities and networks/bonds amongst people in the same communities.

Like the environmental sustainability of restaurant sector, the environmental sustainability of café sector has also been examined well in academia. For example, Starbucks has been explored well in terms of CSR (e.g. Kang & Namkung, 2018; Li et al., 2019), SDGs (e.g. Park, 2018;

Kim & Jang, 2021) and 3Rs (e.g. Ottman, 2017). In November 2019, Starbucks Coffee Japan made an important announcement about its new policy to improve the environmental sustainability of surrounding/related natural environment. Starbucks Coffee Japan (2019) announced that the company would start replacing plastic straws with paper ones from January 2020 at all of their coffee stores in Japan. This notice evoked diverse responses from the general public of Japan. When the announcement was made, overall customers seemed to understand the meaning of the new policy, because many of them should know that plastic waste had been a major environmental concern across the world. In fact, plastic pollution in the ocean has been particularly serious due to its negative impacts on the life of sea creatures, including seabirds, sea turtles and whales (e.g. De Stephanis et al., 2013). Nonetheless, it would also be true that many customers still feel somewhat uncomfortable with enjoying a glass of iced coffee or other drinks with a paper straw, although they will get used to it more as time goes by.

Last but not least, the concept and practice of fair trade are important for main products of café businesses, coffee and tea. Fair trade is a trading partnership that intends to realise a greater level of equity between product producers and buyers in international trade (De Ferran & Grunert, 2007). Through this specific trade channel, food and textile products from developing countries are exported to developed countries (Adriani & Becchetti, 2004). Such a greater level of fairness between the two parties can be realised by guaranteeing fair prices for products of farmers in developing countries (De Pelsmacker et al., 2005) and marketing these products in developed countries at an ethical premium (Bird & Hughes, 1997). The philosophy and meaning of fair-trade products have been acknowledged and sympathised by Japanese coffee companies, including wholesalers, retailers and cafés. These coffee companies include the aforementioned Starbucks Coffee Japan, Mount Hagen and Ogawa Coffee. Amongst these, Ogawa Coffee originating in Kyoto is a wholesaler and retailer of coffee and equipment. Its subsidiary, Ogawa Coffee Creates runs cafés in three different cities, including its hometown, Kyoto City. Ogawa Coffee Group compliances to Fairtrade International Standards consisting of three key pillars of sustainability, namely economic, social and environmental criteria (Ogawa Coffee n.d.). The enterprise also sets

May as 'Fairtrade Month'. Ogawa Coffee develops new menu items for its cafés and promotes people's awareness of its fairtrade certified products, including coffee (Ogawa Coffee n.d.). Although the splendour of the philosophy and concept of fair trade would not have room for doubt, enough attention needs to be paid to the reality – how fair trade is actually implemented on site. In some cases, the 'fair' price guaranteed by the system does not go to local farmers due to factors difficult to identify for consumers such as exploitation by cooperative leaders as management fees or labour costs.

5 Takeaways and Deliveries

In Table 7.1, food/drink takeaways and deliveries are the other type of places for eating and drinking. Except pizza chains (e.g. Pizza Hut, Domino Pizza), takeaway/delivery-only food and drink shops/brands were rather limited and they comprised specific *sushi* shops (e.g. Chiyoda Sushi, Kyotaru, Kozosushi), and certain Japanese or Western confectionary stores prior to the COVID-19 pandemic. However, the pandemic has changed this situation. People are willing to and/or expected to decrease the number of opportunities and length of time they spend for dining out under the COVID-19 climate to minimise chances to spread or catch the virus. This has made a huge contribution to the rise and expansion of takeaway and delivery services since spring 2020. On the contrary, the condition has been totally different for eateries where consumers enjoy foods and drinks on site. As a result, the economic sustainability of food/drink stores that do not or cannot offer takeaway or delivery services appear to have been hit severely by the COVID-19 pandemic.

On the other hand, food and drink businesses that could successfully launch or further develop their takeaway and/or delivery services seem to have been able to maintain the economic sustainability of their businesses or even improve their business performances. To cite a case, Marugame Seimen, a domestic fast-food chain whose main product is *udon* noodle with various tastes and toppings. *Udon* restaurants of Marugame Seimen had been financially struggling with a decrease in sales and profits due to the COVID-19 pandemic since spring 2020. However, the release of four different types of *udon bento* with affordable prices in April 2021 worked as a game changer for the firm. This means that customers of Marugame Seimen could have another option, takeaway, to enjoy Marugame's tasty *udon* noodle. This also means a lot for its customers in the COVID-19 climate. Initially, selling *udon* menu items as takeaways were not possible mainly because of difficulties in keeping freshness of *udon* noodle. Nonetheless, new ideas and devices could make offering *udon* noodle as *bento* to customers possible. *Udon bento* could improve the business performance and economic sustainability of Marugame Seimen considerably. The enterprise could achieve a 4.7 billion Japanese Yen surplus between April and June of the fiscal year of 2021, selling more than nine million *udon bento* during this period (Foodist Media, 2021). Another successful example is McDonald's Japan. Surprisingly, the company achieved six-month profit of 17.2 billon Japanese Yen between January and June 2021 and it was the highest ever half-year profit for the firm (Foodist Media, 2021). All kinds of services with non or limited contacts between service providers and consumers, namely drive-through, takeaway and delivery, made a great contribution to this successful business performance of McDonald's Japan under the COVID-19 climate (Foodist Media, 2021).

Although drive-through has not been adopted widely by other food and drink businesses, takeaway and/or delivery have been employed by a number of food and drink businesses as new types of service provision. Consequently, these food and drink companies have been able to retain or even enhance the level of their economic sustainability under the COVID-19 circumstance. For example, Sushiro is a leading conveyor belt *sushi* restaurant chain, whilst Gyoza no Ohsho is a top Chinese restaurant chain in Japan. Although Sushiro and Gyoza no Ohsho offered takeaway services prior to the start of the pandemic, both have newly launched their takeaway-only brands called 'Sushiro to go' (its first store opened in February 2021 in Abiko City, Chiba Prefecture) and Gyoza no Ohsho Joy Naho (its first store opened in June 2021 in Setagaya Ward, TMP). Obviously, the launch of new brands intends to meet an increasing demand for takeaway foods by consumers and to increase their sales and profits. On the other hand, the take-off or expansion of delivery services often involves and relies on external business partners that are specialised in delivering foods (and drinks) to designated places (usually customers' houses) quickly and certainly. That is probably because; increasing the workloads of existing members of staff and/or recruiting new members of staff mainly for delivery service would not be ideal and can be a financial burden for their businesses. In Japan, there are several online food ordering and delivering companies, but it would be safe to say the market is dominated by two giants, namely Uber Eats and Demae-can. It is intriguing that the former is an international pioneer brand, whilst the latter is a very domestic one. The emergence and development of online food ordering and delivering companies and services have led to the birth of a new type of job, delivery driver (or delivery worker). Today, delivery drivers are part of typical cityscapes, especially in urban areas such as TMP. This implies that their existence has been more and more socially accepted by the general public of Japan, particularly during the COVID-19 pandemic era. This also generates employment opportunities for people who have a lot of energy and access to a bicycle or motorbike. This type of job can be conducted as a second/part-time job, spending drivers' spare time. Thus, it can also enhance the economic sustainability of drivers' household income.

Traditionally, the majority of local restaurants in Japan, usually independent ones, have been offering delivery services called *demae* for their (regular) customers' convenience. A member of restaurant staff brings dishes to customers' houses or offices and visit there later again to collect dishes after eating. This can be viewed as an admirable practice from the point of view of the environmental sustainability and the spirit of *mottainai*. This practice also includes two elements of 3Rs: It can 'reduce' the volume of business waste and 'reuse' tableware repeatedly. Representative meals available through *demae* contain Chinese dishes, *sushi* and *soba* and *udon* noodles. In the author's view, however, *demae* culture seems to have started declining around when Japanese names of era (*gengo*) changed from Showa to Heisei (1989). There were some possible reasons for the weakening of *demae* culture, including nuclearisation of families and an increase in labour costs. Since the beginning of the Heisei period (1989–1990), *demae* culture had been gradually replaced with the delivery service. At that point, however, the delivery service was available only at delivery/takeaway pizza restaurant chains (e.g. Pizza California, Pizza

Hut). Throughout the Heisei period (1989–2019), delivery and takeaway services has been spread across the food and beverage sector in Japan. Since around 2000, a domestic online food ordering and delivering company, Demae-can, has been expanding its service. The online food ordering and delivering system has established its presence and has been able to make the business economically and socio-culturally sustainable since international online food ordering and delivering companies, namely Uber Eats and Wolt, arrived in Japan in 2016 and 2020 respectively. These shifts in main trends in food delivery service available in Japan are characterised by weakened economic and socio-cultural sustainability of *demae* practice and strengthened economic and socio-cultural sustainability of online food ordering and delivering scheme.

In relation to economic and socio-cultural sustainability of food and drink businesses, particularly takeaways', there is another phenomenon to be discussed in this section. The popularity of food trucks (*kitchen cars* in Japanese English) as a way to provide and receive food and drink services has also been increasing since the COVID-19 pandemic began. Some food trucks are run by existing restaurants or cafés to grasp more opportunities and to outreach new market segments, whilst others are started as new business ventures operated by entrepreneurs. According to T-ARA (n.d.), food trucks should be located in or near any of following places to attract a certain number of customers and to be visited by them regularly:

* Business districts or apartment buildings,
* Shopping malls, visitor attractions or amusement parks,
* City halls, town halls or public parks,
* Motorway service stations or roadside stations (*michi no eki*) (see Sect. 6 in Chap. 6 for details), and
* Universities or junior colleges.

Not waiting for customers to come to restaurants or cafés but getting to new places to find customers indicates a major change in a business approach employed by food and drink businesses from a passive to active one. This may also lead to more chances of survival for food and drink businesses during this challenging pandemic period, contributing to their economic sustainability. This active approach can also be beneficial for the socio-cultural sustainability of food and drink companies, because the businesses can explore and reach new people and new places, and the existence of food trucks has been increasingly recognised by the general public during the COVID-19 pandemic time. Nowadays, food trucks as well as takeaways and deliveries can be regarded as established phenomena in Japanese society.

The growth of takeaways, deliveries and food trucks as modes to provide people with foods and drinks, however, may also induce or worsen environmental problems. Like the café businesses such as Starbucks Coffee in Japan (see Sect. 4), containers used for takeaways, deliveries or by food trucks have also been changing from plastic to paper ones. Nonetheless, a rapidly and extensively increased demands for food containers and packages under the COVID-19 situation have still been causing an upsurge in the amount of non-biodegradable waste, typically plastic one (Otsuka et al., 2021). Moreover, both supply and demand sides of takeaway and delivery services wear or are expected to wear a non-woven face mask and the former also wears gloves whilst cooking or serving not to pass coronavirus onto their customers or colleagues, or not to spread the virus widely. Unfortunately, not all of these non-biodegradable wastes have been properly dealt with (Otsuka et al., 2021). As a result, the environmental sustainability of takeaway or delivery businesses themselves and the natural environment surrounding them, especially water and soil, can be negatively influenced by the non-biodegradable wastes.

6   Conclusion

The food and beverage sector is another essential component of tourism industry all over the world, including Japan. The products offered by this sector can satisfy the most fundamental needs of human beings, namely hunger and thirst. As everyone knows, however, consuming foods and drinks is also enjoyment for people and works as socialising experience when sharing them together with others. To this end, places and services providing the general public with enjoyment/socialising opportunities as

7 Sustainability of Food and Beverage Sector in Japan

well as offering foods and drinks have been playing a key role in society regardless of nation or culture. Although some tourists may want to consume internationally standardised foods and drinks at international restaurant chains (e.g. Big Mac at McDonald's), many tourists look forward to having foods and/or drinks that are unique to, originate in or are prominent in a certain region of the world, country, domestic region or locale. As the presence of tourists with special interest in food/drink such as Getz et al.'s (2014) 'foodies' shows, enjoying specific foods/drinks at certain places can be a primary reason for them to travel. Also in academia, the emergence of and studies on 'niche tourism' (Novelli, 2005), including types of tourism whose main focuses are specific foods or drinks, can be well confirmed. For example, 'wine tourism', part of food/drink tourism, can be seen as one of the most studied types of niche tourism that covers multiple nations or regions across the world (e.g. Australia, France, Italy, Spain). In Japan, Katsunuma Town (Yamanashi Prefecture) has been recognised and studied as a representative destination of wine tourism (e.g. Kingsbury, 2013). Linking these points back to the main focus of this chapter, food and drink businesses such as both eateries (Sects. 2, 3 and 4) and takeaways/deliveries (Sect. 5) can act as mediators who bridge between producers/producing regions of peculiar foods/drinks and consumers. By doing so, the food and drink businesses can directly or indirectly help to increase or stabilise local producers' income; enhance the level of recognition of certain food/drink brands amongst people, including domestic and international tourists; and maintain fields, farms and orchards. These effects can be comprehended as the food and beverage sector's contribution to the economic, socio-cultural and environmental sustainability of producers and producing regions respectively. Retaining or improving the three pillars of sustainability for these people and places can also lead to a better level of three kinds of sustainability of food and drink businesses. In relation to these points, the movement of 'local production for local consumption' (*chisan-chisho*) should also be noted (see Sect. 2). That is because; implementing *chisan-chisho* can generate a multiplier effect within local economies (economic sustainability), foster local pride and enhance the level of recognition of the locale (socio-cultural sustainability), and reduce food miles (environmental sustainability).

Although there are some differences in the approaches and practices between different types of food and drink businesses in relation to the sustainability of their own businesses and surrounding environment and people, there are also many similarities. Like the cases of transport (see Chap. 5) and accommodation (see Chap. 6) sectors of Japan, generally the COVID-19 pandemic has been negatively affecting the business performance and economic sustainability of the food and beverage sector of Japan since spring 2020. Amongst diverse kinds of eateries, the businesses whose main products are alcoholic drinks have been especially hit hard by the pandemic as food and drink businesses were frequently requested to offer non-alcoholic drinks only and/or to finish their daily business earlier. In this chapter, such businesses are *izakaya* restaurants (Sect. 2); and bars, cabarets and night clubs (Sect. 3). Although some financial supports were available from public sector, the aids often do not seem to have been distributed fairly or timely for these businesses. That is because, the amount of monetary support was more than enough for small businesses with a low level of sales but was not enough at all for large business with a high level of sales. Although regional government or city/town council seems to have done their best to provide the businesses with financial aids, the payment was not always prompt enough from a perspective of the businesses affected by the pandemic.

Even this challenging time for the food and drink sector, some food/drink companies have been able to maintain or strengthen the economic and socio-cultural sustainability of their businesses mainly through the launch or expansion of takeaway and/or delivery services. Although takeaway and delivery services already existed in the Japanese food and drink market prior to the COVID-19 pandemic, the services have developed and expanded rapidly and extensively during the COVID-19 time. That is because; consumers wanted or were expected to dramatically decrease the frequency and opportunities to go out for dining or drinking, particularly with people other than their family members. However, it needs to be remembered that not all food and drink businesses could newly start or further develop their takeaway and/or delivery services due to various factors such as a lack of labour, cost or know-how. Overall, however, takeaway and delivery services have been much more embedded in people's daily lives and the increasing number of people seem to have used takeaway or delivery service compared with the time before the COVID-19 pandemic. This also signifies that the socio-cultural sustainability of takeaway and delivery services have been strengthened, changing the scenery of cityscapes of Japan. That is because; in case of delivery services, the presence of people/companies who bring foods and drinks from eateries to customers' houses is essential. They are typically online food ordering and delivering companies, and Uber Eats and Demae-can are two big names in this business field. This sort of business has also been accepted by Japanese society, especially in urban areas. The prosperity of takeaway and delivery services, however, should be understood as a double-edged sword, considering its impact on the surrounding natural environment due to an increase in the amount of packaging waste. It depends on country and business, but it could be stated that not all packaging waste is biodegradable. In recent years, there is an urgent need to mitigate the impact of plastic waste on water and soil and creatures there, especially sea creatures. Without improving the issue, takeaway and delivery services will not be environmentally sustainable enough.

References

Adriani, F., & Becchetti, L. (2004). Fair trade: A 'third generation' welfare mechanism to make globalisation sustainable. Available at *SSRN*: https://doi.org/10.2139/ssrn.625562. Accessed 20 Mar 2022.

BBC News. (2019). *The growing importance of the night-time economy*. Available at: https://www.bbc.com/news/business-49348792. Accessed 3 Mar 2022.

Bird, K., & Hughes, D. R. (1997). Ethical consumerism: The case of "fairly-traded" coffee. *Business Ethics: A European Review, 6*(3), 159–167.

De Ferran, F., & Grunert, K. G. (2007). French fair trade coffee buyers' purchasing motives: An exploratory study using means-end chains analysis. *Food Quality and Preference, 18*(2), 218–229.

De Pelsmacker, P., Driesen, L., & Rayp, G. (2005). Do consumers care about ethics? Willingness to pay for fair-trade coffee. *Journal of consumer affairs, 39*(2), 363–385.

De Stephanis, R., Giménez, J., Carpinelli, E., Gutierrez-Exposito, C., & Cañadas, A. (2013). As main meal for sperm whales: Plastics debris. *Marine Pollution Bulletin, 69*(1–2), 206–214.

Doutor. (2022). *Doutor Group sotenpo-su* (Total number of Doutor Group's coffee stores) [in Japanese]. Available at: https://www.doutor.co.jp/about_us/ir/report/fcinfo.html. Accessed 14 Mar 2022.

Doutor. (n.d.) *Brand no goannai* (Brands). [in Japanese]. Available at: https://www.doutor.co.jp/business/brand/. Accessed 14 Mar 2022.

Eguchi Holdings. (n.d.). *SDGs ni okeru 'chisan-chisho' no okina sonzaikan* (Local production for local consumption plays an important role in SDGs) [in Japanese]. Available at: https://eguchi-hd.co.jp/resolabo-sdgs-local-production/. Accessed 17 Feb 2022.

Foodist Media. (2021). *Gaishoku-ote no 4-6gatsu kessan, 'take out' de gyoseki ni meian* (Business performances of leading restaurant companies in the first fiscal year of 2021) [in Japanese]. Available at: https://www.inshokuten.com/foodist/article/6191/. Accessed 20 Mar 2022.

Getz, D., Robinson, R., Andersson, T., & Vujicic, S. (2014). *Foodies and food tourism*. Goodfellow Publishers.

Grinshpun, H. (2009). *My cup of coffee: Analyzing Starbucks as a social and cultural space in Japan and in Israel*. Doctoral thesis, Kyoto University.

Gyokai-doko Search. (2021). *Café gyokai* (Café industry) [in Japanese]. Available at: https://gyokai-search.com/3-cafe.html. Accessed 14 Mar 2022.

Gyokai-doko Search. (n.d.). *Fast food gyokai uriagedaka ranking (2020–2021)* (Japan's top 10 fast food businesses by sales between April 2020 and March 2021) [in Japanese]. Available at: https://gyokai-search.com/4-fast-food-uriage.htm. Accessed 14 Feb 2022.

Hisashige, T. (2007). Third place kara toshi-saisei wo kangaeru (Consider urban regeneration from the concept of a third place) [in Japanese]. *Urban Study, 46*.

Ikeda, M. (2017). A review of nightlife literature and suggestions for future research in Japan [in Japanese]. *Chiri Kukan, 10*(2), 67–84.

Ikeda, T. (2020). Service-gyo no jinzai-mondai to jinzai-ikusei (Issues with and development of human resources in the service industries) [in Japanese]. *Chiba Shodai Ronso, 57*(3), 91–106.

Ikeda, M., Uda, T., Isono, T., Sugimoto, K., Ota, K., Koike, T., & Iizuka, R. (2017). The features of night-life tourism in Tokyo through the focus on clubs and live music venues [in Japanese]. *Chiri Kukan, 10*(3), 149–164.

Isono, T. (2020). Development of guided night tours for Foreign Tourists in Shibuya City, Tokyo [in Japanese]. *The Tourism Studies, 31*(1), 5–18.

Iwata, S. (2012). Sports business to chiiki innovation (Sports business and innovation of local community) [in Japanese]. *Shodai business review, 2*(1), 21–36.

Jimura, T. (2020). Changing faces of Tokyo: Regeneration, tourism and Tokyo 2020. In N. Wise & T. Jimura (Eds.), *Tourism, cultural heritage and urban regeneration – Changing spaces in historical places* (pp. 141–155). Springer.

Jimura, T. (2022). *Cultural and heritage tourism in Japan*. Routledge.

JPC. (2020). *Leisure Hakusho 2020* (Annual Report on Leisure 2020) [in Japanese]. Available at: https://www.jpc-net.jp/research/detail/004580.html. Accessed 6 Feb 2022.

JPC. (2021). *Kanto Yoyaku: Leisure Hakusho 2021* (Summary of Annual Report on Leisure 2021) [in Japanese]. Available at: https://www.jpc-net.jp/research/detail/005478.html. Accessed 6 Feb 2022.

Kang, J. W., & Namkung, Y. (2018). The effect of corporate social responsibility on brand equity and the moderating role of ethical consumerism: The case of Starbucks. *Journal of Hospitality & Tourism Research, 42*(7), 1130–1151.

Kim, E., & Jang, Y. J. (2021). Restaurants can innovate and recover from the Covid-19 pandemic. *Boston Hospitality Review, 2021*, 1–9.

Kingsbury, A. (2013). The historical geographies of growing and fermenting the Delaware grape in the Kōfu Basin of Yamanashi Prefecture, Japan. *Journal of Wine Research, 24*(4), 278–290.

Kitada, A. (2003). Gendai Nihon no asobi jijo (Leisure activities in contemporary Japan) [in Japanese]. *Osaka Shoin Joshi Daigaku Gakugei-gakubu ronshu, 40*, 129–137.

Li, Y., Liu, B., & Huan, T. C. T. (2019). Renewal or not? Consumer response to a renewed corporate social responsibility strategy: Evidence from the coffee shop industry. *Tourism Management, 72*, 170–179.

Maslow, A. H. (1943). A theory of human motivation. *Psychological Review, 50*(4), 370–396.

McDonald's Japan. (2017). *News release* (2017.03.09) [in Japanese]. Available at: https://www.mcd-holdings.co.jp/news/2017/release-170309a.html. Accessed 16 Feb 2022.

McDonald's Japan. (2022). *Made for you* [in Japanese]. Available at: https://www.mcdonalds.co.jp/sustainability/environment/madeforyou/. Accessed 15 Feb 2022.

Morishima, T., & Sato, D. (2012). Izakaya gyokai ni okru dominant senryaku to kikaika (Dominant strategies and mechanisation in the izakaya market in Japan) [in Japanese]. *Keiai Daigaku Kenkyu Ronshu, 81*, 37–54.

Mos Food Services. (2022). *3R katsudo* (Activities for 3Rs) [in Japanese]. Available at: https://www.mos.co.jp/company/csr/environment/recycle/. Accessed 15 Feb 2022.

Nautical Star Strategy & Analysis. (2021). *Itsutsu no ryoiki: Gaishoku sangyo no SDGs eno torikumi jirei – 18 no theme* (Five domains: Examples of approaches adopted by Japan's restaurant businesses for SDGs – 18 themes) [in Japanese]. Available at: https://www.nauticalstar-sa.com/news-commentary/844/. Accessed 31 Jan 2022.

NHK World-Japan. (2019). Boosting Japan's nighttime economy. Available at: https://www3.nhk.or.jp/nhkworld/en/news/backstories/578/. Accessed. 8 Sep 2023.

Nikkei Telecom. (2022). *Kissaten and café* (Cafés) [in Japanese]. Available at: https://www.nikkei.com/telecom/industry_s/0641. Accessed 16 Mar 2022.

Nishihara, H. (2021). The Future of Internationalization and Globalization in MOS Food Service: An Interview Survey with CEO A. Sakurada [in Japanese]. *Bulletin of Institute for Research in Business and Economics Meiji Gakuin University, 38*, 1–18.

Novelli, M. (Ed.). (2005). *Niche tourism: contemporary issues, trends and cases*. Routledge.

Ogawa Coffee. (n.d.). *Ogawa coffee SDGs declaration*. Available at: https://www.oc-ogawa.co.jp/sdgs/. Accessed 20 Mar 2022.

Otsuka, Y., Takada, H., Nihei, Y., Kameda, Y., & Nishikawa, K. (2021). Current status and issues of microplastic pollution research [in Japanese]. *Journal of Japan Society on Water Environment, 44*(2), 35–42.

Ottman, J. A. (2017). *The new rules of green marketing: Strategies, tools, and inspiration for sustainable branding*. Routledge.

Park, S. K. (2018). Social bonds for sustainable development: A human rights perspective on impact investing. *Business and Human Rights Journal, 3*(2), 233–255.

SBJ. (2019). *Sangyo Bunrui Ichiran* (Industrial Classification) [in Japanese]. Available at: https://www.stat.go.jp/data/e-census/2019/bunrui.html#m. Accessed 31 Jan 2022.

Shima, K. (2018). Seikatsusha no insight no toraekata (A way to understand insights of consumers) [in Japanese]. *Seni-seihin Shohi-kagaku, 59*(1), 21–26.

Shinmura, T., Fujii, N., & Nonaka, T. (2018). *Improving labor productivity for Japanese cuisine restaurant using simulator* [in Japanese]. Available at: https://www.jstage.jst.go.jp/article/pjsai/JSAI2018/0/JSAI2018_2O3OS24b03/_article/-char/ja/. Accessed 4 Feb 2022.

Shiva Foundation. (2021). *Hospitality: A high-risk industry for labour exploitation*. Available at: https://shivafoundation.org.uk/hospitality-a-high-risk-industry-for-labour-exploitation/. Accessed 3 Feb 2022.

Starbucks Coffee Japan. (2019). *Press release* (26/11/2019) [in Japanese]. Available at: https://www.starbucks.co.jp/press_release/pr2020-3248.php. Accessed 19 Mar 2022.

Tabelog. (2022). *Home*. Available at: https://tabelog.com/. Accessed 30 Jan 2022.

Tajima, M., Ohara, K., & Fujioka, Y. (2018). Kojin-keiei no kissaten ga chiiki-fukushi ni hatasu yakuwari ni kansuru kenkyu (Study on the role independent cafés play for community welfare) [in Japanese]. *Yokohama National University Global-Local Education and Research Center, Research Report*, 58–59.

Tanaka, M., & Umezaki, O. (2012). Social capital in a local community – Case study of a coffee shop in Kagurazaka [in Japanese]. *Journal for Regional Policy Studies, 5*, 9–20.

T-ARA. (n.d.). *Kitchen car no shutten ni osusume no basho wa?* (Where are food trucks should be located to attract customers?). [in Japanese]. Available at: https://kitchencar-rental.jp/column/store/opening-a-kitchen-car/. Accessed 21 Mar 2022.

Timothy, D. J. (2021). *Cultural heritage and tourism: An introduction* (2nd ed.). Channel View.

TSR. (2022). *Izakaya no tosan kako nibanme no osa – gyoshukan de meian wakeru* (The number of bankruptcy cases differs a lot by type of food and drink business – The number of bankruptcy cases of *izakaya* was the second highest in 2021) [in Japanese]. Available at: https://www.tsr-net.co.jp/news/analysis/20220111_01.html. Accessed 5 Feb 2022.

UNESCO. (2013). *Washoku, traditional dietary cultures of the Japanese, notably for the celebration of New Year*. Available at: https://ich.unesco.org/en/RL/washoku-traditional-dietary-cultures-of-the-japanese-notably-for-the-celebration-of-new-year-00869. Accessed 30 Jan 2022.

Waldfogel, J. (2020). Dining out as cultural trade. *Journal of Cultural Economics, 44*(2), 309–338.

Weber, C. L., & Matthews, H. S. (2008). Food-miles and the relative climate impacts of food choices in the United States. *Environmental Science and Technology, 42*, 3508–3513.

8

Sustainability of Visitor Attractions and Events Sector in Japan

1 Introduction

Like transport (Chap. 5), accommodation (Chap. 6) and food and drink (Chap. 7) sectors, both visitor attractions and events are also integral components of the tourism industry. Visitor attractions can also be called 'tourist attractions' and basically what these two signify are the same. Although there are many different definitions of visitor attractions, an essential element common to most of them is their power and appeal that can be a main reason to visit a certain tourist destination or motivate people to come to a specific place, spending their time and money. Visitor attractions are cultural (built) or natural resources that have been created or converted into a permanent visitor experience (Leask & Barron, 2021). As signified in this definition of visitor attractions, they can be either cultural or natural assets and may also have the nature of both as an example of Machu Picchu (Peru) shows. In fact, the United Nations Educational, Scientific and Cultural Organization (hereafter UNESCO) designated Historic Sanctuary of Machu Picchu in 1983 as a mixed World Heritage site (hereafter WHS) that has qualities of both cultural and natural World Heritage (Jimura, 2019). In addition to the dichotomy between 'cultural' or 'natural', Leask (2003) suggests some more factors/elements to categorise diverse kinds of visitor attractions in a comprehensive manner as follows:

* For which market(s) – International, national, regional or local market,
* Private or public ownership, and
* Paid or free to enter.

For example, the British Museum (London, UK) is an international cultural visitor attraction, whose annual visitor numbers have been around six million before the COVID-19 pandemic. The museum is a public visitor attraction and is free to enter except its special exhibitions, although a donation from visitors is always welcome. On the other hand, POLA Museum of Art (Kanagawa, Japan) is a cultural visitor attraction and the majority of its visitors are Japanese people. The museum is a private visitor attraction and most of its collection were collected by the founding family of POLA Cosmetics.

In relation to the discussion above on the classification of visitor attractions, Jimura (2022a) notes that being tangible or intangible is another key element to categorise cultural heritage that is often a main feature of visitor attractions across the globe. As for this point, visitor attractions are 'tangible' tourism resources. On the contrary, the other principal theme of this chapter, 'events', are a representative example of 'intangible' tourism resource. Like visitor attractions, each event has a certain theme that is associated with specific culture or nature; and whose market can be international, national, regional or local. Organisers of events can also be public or private organisations, and in case of some events, both kinds of organisations may work collaboratively to make their events happen and successful. Events can also be free or paid to participate in and enjoy. To cite a case, traditional local events mainly for children tend to be free to take part in, whilst music or food/drink events are more likely to be paid ones to fully enjoy or even to just enter event premises. In principle, each event has a peculiar theme(s) and can be held at any place, including a visitor attraction or tourist destination, on a regular or ad-hoc basis. An important relation between events and visitor attractions is also endorsed

8 Sustainability of Visitor Attractions and Events Sector in Japan

by Leask (2003) who states that 'events' are one of the main products visitor attractions can offer to visitors along with resource, interpretation, catering and retailing. As visitor attractions do, events are also strongly associated with heritage, especially cultural heritage. In fact, for instance, 'festive events' are listed by UNESCO as one of the representative types of Intangible Cultural Heritage (hereafter ICH) together with 'social practices' and 'rituals' (Jimura, 2022a).

In academia, both visitor attractions and events have been examined well in terms of their sustainability and sustainability management. For example, critical issues for economic sustainability of visitor attractions such as revenue management, visitor spending and labour costs (e.g. Lennon, 2004) and those for economic sustainability of events, including event finance and sponsorship (e.g. Tichaawa & Bob, 2015), have been examined extensively. In addition, key agendas for socio-cultural sustainability of visitor attractions and events are also studied well. Such agendas include the access for people with disabilities, cultural democracy and inclusion of local communities (e.g. Baltà Portolés & Dragićevic Šešić, 2017; Cloquet et al., 2018; Jimura, 2022b). Regarding environmental sustainability, moreover, there are also major challenges for visitor attractions and events such as rubbish, trampling the ground, soil pollution and wear and tear (e.g. Krupar, 2018; Jimura, 2022b). Bearing the key points discussed above in mind, Sects. 2 and 3 explore sustainability and sustainable management of visitor attractions (tangible tourism resources) and events and festivals (intangible tourism resources) in Japan, respectively.

2 Visitor Attractions

This section looks at representative types of visitor attractions in Japan. It could be stated that all of them were not originally created for tourism and have their primary purpose other than tourism except amusement parks or theme parks (Jimura, 2022a) (see Sect. 2.6).

2.1 Religious Sites

Needless to say, the fundamental and main purpose of religious sites is to serve a peculiar religion or a sect of a religion. Currently, however, most religious sites are also seen by visitors and actually function as visitor attractions (Olsen, 2006; Jimura, 2022a). Japan has two dominant religions namely Shintoism and Japanese Buddhism (Jimura, 2022a). Typically, Shinto shrines are holy places for the former, whilst Japanese Buddhist temples are sacred sites for the latter. For instance, Nikko Toshogu Shrine (Tochigi Prefecture) is one of the most famous examples of Shinto shrines (see Fig. 8.1). If the above-mentioned Leask's (2003) classification of visitor attractions is applied, the shrine is a cultural (built) visitor attraction with private ownership. Since Japan's inbound tourism has become noticeable in 2014, the shrine has attracted international tourists widely except the COVID-19 period. Its admission fee for an

Fig. 8.1 Yomeimon Gate of Nikko Toshogu Shrine. (Source: Author)

8 Sustainability of Visitor Attractions and Events Sector in Japan

adult is 1300 JPY (7.76 GBP or 9.70 USD) as of June 2022. Another example referred to here is Kawasaki Daishi Temple (Kanagawa Prefecture). The temple is an established religious visitor attraction and attracts around three million visitors during the New Year period (see Fig. 8.2). The profile of the temple in terms of Leask's (2003) classification is similar to Nikko Toshogu Shrine's except the admission fee. Unlike the majority of well-known Japanese Buddhist temples, Kawasaki Daishi does not charge the entrance fee.

The economic sustainability of religious bodies owning and managing a Shinto shrine or Japanese Buddhist temple has been maintained by the income from different sources such as the admission fees, prayers, holding various ceremonies and rituals, hosting exhibitions of religious arts, and/or selling religious and secular souvenir. As they are religious organisations, their income from religious activities is tax-free and only the income from non-religious commercial activities is taxable. This special

Fig. 8.2 Main Hall (Hondo) of Kawasaki Daishi Temple. (Source: Author)

treatment has played an important role in maintaining the economic sustainability of religious bodies and sites in Japan. Simultaneously, however, this handling has been one of financial burdens for local governments that have a number of Shinto shrines and Japanese Buddhist temples. A typical example of local government having such a financial problem is Kyoto City. Kyoto City's finance has been facing a risk of bankruptcy, although it is a world-famous tourist destination. In addition to a large number of religious bodies, Kyoto City has other financial issues such as the construction of a new subway line that has been operating in the red, a large proportion of university students who are exempt from paying resident tax, and the negative impact of COVID-19 on inbound tourism.

Regarding the socio-cultural sustainability of religious sites, overall it has been maintained or even enhanced by working as visitor attractions. That is because, their presence in Japanese society and beyond has been increasingly established through being visited and appreciated by a range of same-day visitors and domestic and international tourists as well as by their religious believers/sympathisers and local people (Jimura, 2022a). For the environmental sustainability of religious structures or properties, main threats include vandalism, litter and wear and tear. These are problems commonly confirmed at many visitor attractions all over the world. More and more religious sites in Japan have introduced security cameras in recent years, and this seems to have improved the aforementioned issues, especially vandalism. On the other hand, the environmental sustainability of natural environment surrounding religious places such as forests can be damaged by careless behaviours of human beings, including forest fire and unauthorised logging. Kumano Hayatama Taisha Shrine (Wakayama Prefecture) is a component of a cultural WHS. In 2011, trees in Mount Gongen, which are managed by the shrine, were logged by a local forestry cooperative without obtaining the approval of the shrine or a relevant local government because the cooperative did not recognise that the forest is part of the WHS. As many shrines and temples in Japan are located in a rural area and surrounded by rich natural environment, enough attention needs to be paid to not only religious sites themselves but also such natural environment in order to retain the environmental sustainability of these sites.

2.2 Historic Buildings

Many of the religious structures and properties discussed as religious visitor attractions in Sect. 2.1 can also be viewed as historic buildings that are open to the general public as visitor attractions today. As shown in Chap. 2, such historic structures in Japan are protected through public schemes for their recognition and conservation as follows:

- National Treasures (*Kokuho*)
- Important Cultural Properties (*Juyo Bunkazai*)
- Registered Tangible Cultural Properties (*Toroku Yukei Bunkazai*).

Thus, to keep exploring and realising a best balance between conservation and tourism is one of key requirements for the sustainability management of historic buildings open to the general public as visitor attractions. To this end, for example, closing historic buildings during the low season is a strategy employed by National Trust to maintain their cultural properties in England, UK. Typically, their historic houses (e.g. Fenton House and Garden, London) are closed annually for four months between November and February, and essential works for their maintenance are conducted during that time. Such a regular closure of historic buildings on an annual basis can be seen disadvantageous in terms of their economic sustainability as there are no income raised through tourism during this period. Their socio-cultural, especially social, sustainability may also be weakened temporarily through this approach. That is because, all sorts of visitors, including local inhabitants, students on school trip and domestic and international tourists, should lose the access to the historic buildings for a certain period of time. It is also true that the vast majority of people working at the buildings would lose their jobs for four months, although many workers are volunteers who are often retired people in case of National Trust properties. On the contrary, closing historic buildings annually for essential maintenance works would be ideal for the environmental sustainability of the structures themselves and their surrounding nature. The neighbouring nature could secure a certain time for recovery under the visitor-free circumstance. It would be particularly important for sustainability management of historic buildings that have a large number of visitors regularly and are situated in countryside.

In Japan, whilst annual closure of historic buildings for upkeep does not seems to be a well-adopted strategy to retain an ideal balance between conservation and tourism. Rather a more popular method for sustainability management of historic buildings appears to be closing historic buildings for a much longer period than the case of National Trust (England) to complete even extensive renovation or restoration at one time. To cite a case, the National Museum of Western Art (hereafter NMWA) (Tokyo Metropolitan Prefecture (hereafter TMP)) had been closed for one and half years between 19 October 2020 and 8 April 2022 for the conservation of the museum structures, including restoration of the front yard (NMWA, 2021). In other cases, historic buildings may remain open even during the large renovation. For instance, Konpon Chudo, the original main hall, of Enryaku-ji Temple (Shiga Prefecture) remains open while the extensive repair work is conducted (see Fig. 8.3). Here, however, it should be remembered that the situations of NMWA and Konpon Chudo of Enryaku-ji are somewhat different. The key difference would be that the period required to complete renovation of the latter (ten years between 2016 and 2025) is much longer than the case of renovation of the former (one and half years). If totally closed for a decade, the economic and socio-cultural sustainability of Enryaku-ji Temple can be hugely damaged, although the environmental sustainability of the temple itself and its surrounding nature can be dramatically improved mainly thanks to a lack of visits and limited human impacts.

2.3 Gardens

In relation to the two kinds of visitor attractions in Japan discussed in Sect. 2.1 (religious sites) and 2.2 (historic buildings), Japanese gardens (*nihon teien*) are closely associated with both. Furthermore, some of them are established visitor attractions in their own right. The majority of religious sites in Japan, particularly Japanese Buddhist temples, have a Japanese garden (*jisha teien*) in their premises. Moreover, the origin of

8 Sustainability of Visitor Attractions and Events Sector in Japan

Fig. 8.3 Konpon Chudo of Enryaku-ji Temple. (Source: Author)

many Japanese gardens existing today is the gardens created by feudal lords (*daimyo*) in their territories or Edo (Today's Tokyo) during the Edo period (1603–1868) (*daimyo teien*). Throughout most of the Edo period, the Tokugawa Shogunate based in Edo required feudal lords (*daimyo*) to change their place of residence annually (Edo or their domains). This system is called *sankin-kotai*. Thus, many *daimyo teien* were built near or by their mansions in Edo as well as in their domains.

The aforementioned *jisha teien* or *daimyo teien* is the way to categorise Japanese gardens, focusing chiefly on their origins or roots. Nonetheless, a more popular way to classify Japanese gardens would be the one that is based on their appearance and elements. According to this classification, following three would be basic categories that are widely accepted today:

- Water gardens (*chisen teien*)
- Japanese rock gardens (*karesansui*)

- *Roji.*

Amongst these, water gardens encompass a pond and streams/brooks. Water gardens can be further classified into three sub-groups depending on how to appreciate their beauty namely from a boat floating on the pond, looking out the garden from a nearby building or walking around the garden. For example, Rikugien (TMP) is a representative example of *daimyo teien*. It is regarded as a water garden and visitors walk around the garden to enjoy and appreciate it (see Fig. 8.4). On the contrary to water gardens, Japanese rock gardens express the world of Buddhism, typically *zen*, with rocks and pebbles as their alternative name, Japanese dry gardens, indicates. In many cases, the sizes of Japanese rock gardens are smaller than those of water gardens. The other type of Japanese gardens, *roji*, is much smaller than other two types of Japanese gardens. *Roji* means a very small and simple Japanese garden leading to a tea-ceremony room.

Fig. 8.4 Rikugien (a Japanese garden). (Source: Author)

In other words, *roji* functions as a path to the tea-ceremony room and guests are expected to be ready for the ceremony whilst they are walking through the *roji*.

Like religious sites (Sect. 2.1) and historic buildings (Sect. 2.2), nowadays a number of Japanese gardens are open to the general public as visitor attraction, and they are usually paid attractions. Admission fees for *jisha teien* are usually included in those for the temples or shrines and the prices are typically between 500 and 1500 JPY. Entrance fees for *daimyo teien* are likely to be cheaper than those for *jisha teien*. For instance, the aforementioned Rikugien's admission fees are 300 JPY for adults and 150 JPY for elderly people as of June 2022. Considering the maintenance costs required for Japanese gardens, the income raised through entrance fees are not always large enough. Nevertheless, it is also true that the economic sustainability of Japanese gardens is surely supported by this type of income. As the case of Selected Conservation Techniques (*Sentei Hozongijutsu*) discussed in Sect. 4 of Chap. 3 shows, specific knowledge and skills that have been inherited from generation to generation are essential for socio-cultural sustainability of cultural heritage. Conservation of Japanese gardens also needs such special knowledge and techniques. To this end, for instance, organisations such as the Society for the Conservation of Culturally Important Gardening Techniques was established in 2002 (Nippon-no-waza expo, 2022). With regard to environmental sustainability, activities related to 3Rs, especially 'recycle' has been implemented well in the maintenance process of Japanese gardens. To cite a case, regular tree pruning is crucial to retain the beauty and health of trees in Japanese gardens. Nowadays, pruned branches generated through tree pruning in Japanese gardens are recycled as natural garden materials such as portable hedge walls (Hanatoyo Landscape, 2022).

2.4 Museums and Galleries

Referring to the classification of visitor attractions by Leask (2003), most visitor attractions in the world are regarded as 'built' (cultural) attractions. In terms of visitor numbers in 2016, the National Art Centre (TMP) and the National Museum of Nature and Science (TMP) are

Japan's most popular gallery and museum respectively (Kaiga no Arukikata, 2021). Both of the two are situated in TMP. In fact, however, Japan's established museums or galleries are scattered across Japan. For example, the 21st Century Museum of Contemporary Art is located in Kanazawa City (Ishikawa Prefecture) and the Kure Maritime Museum is situated in Kure City (Hiroshima Prefecture). As the case of Machu Pichu (Peru) in Sect. 1 indicates, however, there are also some visitor attractions that have dual nature of cultural and natural places. An illustrative example of such visitor attractions is open-air museums that are found in many different nations, including Japan. One of the most famous examples of open-air museums outside Japan is Skansen located in Stockholm (Sweden). Skansen describes itself as the world's oldest open-air museum whose history commenced in 1891. In Japan, the Hakone Open-Air Museum (Kanagawa Prefecture) and the Museum Meiji-mura (Aichi Prefecture) are well known examples of open-air museums (The Travel, 2019). Concerning other three elements of Leask's model, namely markets, admission and ownership, Japan's museums and galleries are highly varied.

Since around 2015 or 2016, International Council of Museums (hereafter ICOM) has been working on the revision of its existing definition of museums that was adopted in 2007. The proposed new definition was examined and approved at the Extraordinary General Assembly on 24 August 2022. ICOM's previous and current definitions of museums are shown respectively as follows:

Previous –

A museum is a non-profit, permanent institution in the service of society and its development, open to the public, which acquires, conserves, researches, communicates and exhibits the tangible and intangible heritage of humanity and its environment for the purposes of education, study and enjoyment. (ICOM, 2022)

Current –

A museum is a not-for-profit, permanent institution in the service of society that researches, collects, conserves, interprets and exhibits tangible and intangible heritage. Open to the public, accessible and inclusive, museums

8 Sustainability of Visitor Attractions and Events Sector in Japan

foster diversity and sustainability. They operate and communicate ethically, professionally and with the participation of communities, offering varied experiences for education, enjoyment, reflection and knowledge sharing. (ICOM, 2022)

The aforementioned current definition is not the one originally proposed as the new one. The definition suggested in 2019 was criticised heavily by the majority of delegates of ICOM General Conference of the year because it was 'a fuzzy collection of political correctness and trendy posturing that would have little legal value' (The Art Newspaper, 2020). Consequently, another new definition that was examined in August 2022 had been developed through a number of discussions.

In relation to one of the main themes of this book, sustainability, it is crucial that ICOM's current definition contains the word, 'sustainability'. Considering its context and content, socio-cultural sustainability would be the most relevant and important pillar of sustainability for the current definition. This can be confirmed from the inclusion of words in the current definition such as 'the participation of communities'. Nakao (2021) states that museums or galleries are regarded as educational facilities according to relevant Japanese laws. This implies that museums and galleries, especially public ones, are essentially not profit-driven. It should also be noted that the business income of museums/galleries are often less than 10% of their annual expenditure (Nakao, 2021). This is especially true for small or medium-sized public museums whose main exhibits are cultural heritage (Nakao, 2021). Thus, lots of museums and galleries attempt to maximise their business income through admission fees, retails, restaurants and cafés, and/or hosting a ceremony, aiming to enhance their economic sustainability. A number of museums and galleries in Japan have also been working on the environmental sustainability of themselves, their themes and/or their surrounding natural and cultural environment. Such works have been implemented often in the forms of their activities to take cooperate social responsibility (hereafter CSR) and their contributions to Sustainable Development Goals (hereafter SDGs). Generally, workshops are typical CSR activities for SDGs that are employed by a large number of museums or galleries. Amongst these, those for children or students are very much common. For instance, the

Kyoto Railway Museum organises four different workshops for children, namely introductory, beginner, intermediate and advanced depending on their knowledge and learning experience so far (Kyoto Railway Museum, n.d.).

2.5 Industrial Heritage Sites

In his book on cultural heritage and tourism in Japan, Jimura (2022a, 129) refers to the definition and management of industrial heritage suggested by Alfrey and Putnam (2003) as follows:

- Gathering the remains of lost industry to understand how it functioned,
- Conserving buildings, sites and machinery due to their technical, historical or aesthetic interest,
- Finding new usages for redundant but irreplaceable elements of the industrial landscape,
- Restoring disused machinery and working practices to use,
- Recording the knowledge, skills and experience of industrial populations, and,
- Using the results of the above to show how past generations lived and worked.

These points signify that industrial heritage and sites having it may need to alter their quality and/or purposes to keep up with ever-changing external circumstance surrounding them. Such attitudes should be beneficial for industrial heritage and its sites to make them sustainable in every aspect. To cite a case, many countries, especially developed countries whose main industry has changed from (primary and) secondary industry to service industry, have industrial heritage sites whose nature and purposes have been converted from places of/for production to those of/for consumption (Jimura, 2019, 2022a). The UK is a distinctive example of such nations. Ironworks in Blaenavon (Wales) was diverted to a museum, whilst a textile mill in Saltaire (Bradford) has been used as a complex including an art gallery, a restaurant, a café and a bookshop after the mill stopped serving its original purpose (Jimura, 2007, 2019, 2022a).

8 Sustainability of Visitor Attractions and Events Sector in Japan

Needless to say, these places of consumption are providers of services and can also be regarded as visitor attractions.

Like the UK, Japan is also a country whose main industry has been changing from manufacturing to services. In relation to this, a lot of industrial heritage and its heritage sites in Japan finished working on their original purposes. Such places include main players in the second industry during the Edo period and key contributors to Japan's modernisation since the beginning of the Meiji period. For instance, a former silver mine in Oda City (Shimane Prefecture) and a former textile mill in Tomioka City (Gunma Prefecture) are now open to the general public as visitor attractions. Through changing their nature from places of productions to those of consumption, these industrial places have been able to improve their economic sustainability at least to some extent, for example, by introducing or increasing admission fees, or providing visitors with a range of services such as audio guides.

Regarding the three main pillars of sustainability, the socio-cultural sustainability of industrial heritage and industrial heritage sites are retained or enhanced in many countries often through recognition and conservation schemes unique to each. Such systems are usually led and managed by governmental bodies at various levels, non-governmental organisations, or non-profit organisations. In Japan, for example, a historic district including the above-mentioned silver mine was listed as an Important Preservation District for Groups of Traditional Buildings (*Juyo Dentoteki Kenzobutsugun Hozonchiku*) in 1987, whilst three wings of the aforementioned textile mill were designated as National Treasures (*Kokuho*). The socio-cultural sustainability of these two industrial heritage sites in Japan have also been secured by an international scheme for recognition and conservation of cultural, natural and mixed heritage, namely WHSs designated by UNESCO. The aforementioned silver mine and its related heritage were inscribed as a cultural WHS named Iwami Ginzan Silver Mine and its Cultural Landscape (hereafter WHS Iwami) in 2007. On the other hand, the above-mentioned textile mill and its related heritage were designated as a cultural WHS called Tomioka Silk Mill and Related Sites (hereafter WHS Tomioka) in 2014.

In light of a considerable value of WHS listing for many Japanese people, especially destination communities and visitors (Jimura, 2011), the

WHS inscription may further enhance the socio-cultural sustainability of Japan's industrial heritage sites listed as WHSs. Thanks to keen interests of Japanese visitors in WHSs, the number of people coming to such industrial heritage sites may increase after their WHS listing. This surge can enhance the economic sustainability of these sites and their nearby communities but can also weaken their environmental sustainability. In reality, however, such an upsurge cannot be confirmed or may be temporary even confirmed depending on some factors Jimura (2011, 2019) suggests (e.g. how famous a site is without World Heritage (hereafter WH) status). In the cases of WHS Iwami and WHS Tomioka, both experienced an increase in the number of visitors just before and soon after their WHS designation, but visitor arrivals began to decline a few years after the listing (Jimura, 2019). As for the environmental sustainability of industrial heritage sites, it should be noted that some of them have dual nature of cultural and natural heritage. As its name as a WHS signifies, the components inscribed as WHS Iwami are not only its cultural properties but also its natural environment. The natural environment paramount for WHS Iwami is the forest surrounding its cultural properties. Hence, the environmental sustainability of both cultural and natural components needs to be maintained well in order to retain its WH status.

2.6 Amusement Parks and Theme Parks

According to Jimura (2022a), the essence of amusement parks or theme parks as visitor attractions differs from that of other types of visitor attractions discussed earlier in Sect. 2. That is because, amusement parks or theme parks are planned and built as visitor attractions from the beginning, and working as such, giving enjoyable experience to visitors, is always their primary mission. In contrast, other kinds of visitor attractions are developed originally to serve their prime purposes other than tourism but start playing a role as visitor attractions later, meeting emerging or new needs of people and society (Jimura, 2022a). In relation to differences between amusement parks and theme parks, Jimura (2022a, 231) suggests that "'amusement parks' is a broader concept than 'theme parks', and the former includes the latter". Basically, a peculiar theme that

8 Sustainability of Visitor Attractions and Events Sector in Japan

is consistent throughout all components of a theme park can be confirmed in the theme park, whilst such a theme usually cannot be confirmed in other types of amusement parks. Stated differently, amusement parks other than theme parks appear to focus much more on offering and delivering enjoyable experience to their customers rather than sticking to representation and delivery of a particular themes in their everyday businesses. Concerning theme parks in Japan, Jimura (2022a) argues that two major types of the theme parks are American-origin ones and the ones featuring Europe. Representative examples of the former are Tokyo Disney Resort (hereafter TDR) consisting of Tokyo Disneyland and Tokyo DisneySea (Chiba Prefecture) and Universal Studios Japan (hereafter USJ) (Osaka Urban Prefecture) (hereafter OUP) (see Fig. 8.5), whilst those of the latter include Parque España (Shima Spain Village) (Mie Prefecture) and Huis Ten Bosch (Nagasaki Prefecture) (Jimura, 2022a). Amongst these four, the socio-cultural sustainability of TDR and

Fig. 8.5 Universal Studios Japan. (Source: Author)

USJ, especially the former, has been well maintained since their opening, establishing theme park culture in Japanese society and amongst Japanese people.

The above-mentioned four theme parks, especially TDR and USJ, are rare examples of Japan's theme parks that have been achieving business success for many consecutive years. In fact, the vast majority of theme parks in Japan, particularly those located in a suburban or rural area, were short-lived mainly due to a lack of their economic sustainability (Jimura, 2022a). Generally, theme park businesses are labour-intensive services as well as capital-intensive services. Thus, it is vital for them to keep attracting a certain number of visitors continuously throughout a year and for many years. Nevertheless, the aforementioned short-lived theme parks could not attract a large enough number of visitors after one or two years since their opening. Consequently, many theme parks in Japan went into administration, and abandoned structures and attractions often became bitter legacies called 'white elephants'. This is not ideal at all in terms of the spirit of *mottainai*, and the environmental sustainability of theme park premises and their neighbouring areas. As Jimura (2022a) states, however, ruins of theme parks can be converted into places for new purposes such as public parks for local communities. This can improve the environmental sustainability of the sites once used as theme parks and their adjacent communities. This also signifies that former theme park sites are able to regain or even strengthen their links with local people and beyond, and it is beneficial for the socio-cultural sustainability of these sites.

3   Events and Festivals

This section is devoted to discussing economic, socio-cultural and environmental sustainability of events and festivals, both of which are intangible tourism resources. In tourism and events study field, events and festivals are the notions that are closely interrelated. Generally, events are understood as a broader concept than festivals, and the latter is seen as part of the former. In other words, festivals can be regarded as a specific

8 Sustainability of Visitor Attractions and Events Sector in Japan

kind of events. With regard to this, Cundy et al. (2012) list following characteristics as key features of festivals:

- Varied in terms of theme and purpose,
- Special events that are not associated with work,
- Aim to celebrate significant elements for the life of local communities,
- Often related to the culture and religion of local communities,
- Usually consist of many different social and cultural events,
- Held on a regular basis, (e.g. annually) and can be combined with competitions (e.g. music, film, art, sport).

The power of events and festivals and their impacts on tourism and urban regeneration are illustrated clearly by Jimura and Wise (2020). This section examines Japan's events and festivals separately in terms of their sustainability management, focusing on mega and hallmark events (see Sect. 3.1) and traditional festivals (see Sect. 3.2).

3.1 Mega Events and Hallmark Events

Events can be categorised in various ways with different emphasises. If classified following their nature, 'cooperate', 'private' and 'charity' are often viewed as three main groups, and 'live' events may be added as the fourth group. On the other hand, Bowdin et al. (2001) consider the size, level of appeal, and main markets of events, and suggest subsequent four as main types of events:

- Mega events,
- Hallmark events,
- Major events, and
- Local events.

Regarding this, however, it needs to be noted that this classification is just one of the many, and difference in the meaning between these fours are not always clear for other events/tourism researchers. To cite a case, Olds (1998) does not seem to distinguish mega events and hallmark events in his paper on urban mega events in Canada. On the contrary, there are scholars who state that mega events and hallmark events are different with varied reasons. Getz et al. (2012) argue that both mega events and hallmark events are large, but they are surely different as the former tends to be one-time only, whilst the latter is likely to be recurring. They also mention that hallmark events play a key role in building or enhancing destination branding or community identity (Getz et al., 2012). In addition, another character of hallmark events is an increase in the level of community or national pride resulting from the feelings of enthusiasm (Ritchie, 1984; Waitt, 2001), although the majority of mega events can also bring such a positive impact to hosting communities. Compared with mega and hallmark events, major and local events tend to have a smaller size and a lower level of recognition and appeal. This implies that the involvement of external people or agencies such as tourists is likely to be limited in major and local events, particularly in the latter. Thus, this section puts mega and hallmark events in the centre of following discussions.

Considering mega events that have been investigated in previous tourism/events studies, it can be stated that probably the Olympics and Paralympics, especially summer ones, are the type of mega events that have been looked at most. In light of the characteristics of hallmark events discussed above, moreover, basically the Olympic and Paralympic Games can also be comprehended as hallmark events. Amongst a number of hosting cities and games held there, subsequent ones have been studied in terms of sustainability and its relevant notions:

- Barcelona 1992 (e.g. Aragón-Pérez, 2019; Solanellas et al., 2019)
- Sydney 2000 (e.g. Lochhead, 2005; Davidson & McNeill, 2012)
- London 2012 (e.g. Kim, 2013; Monica et al., 2015)
- Rio 2016 (e.g. Trendafilova et al., 2017; Sartore-Baldwin & McCullough, 2018).

Probably, the second most examined kind of mega events in terms of sustainability would be the World Expos, and these studies include:

8 Sustainability of Visitor Attractions and Events Sector in Japan

- Shanghai 2010 (e.g. Krupar, 2018; Li, 2018)
- Millan 2015 (e.g. Guizzardi et al., 2017; Gallo et al., 2020)
- Dubai 2020 (e.g. Manikas et al., 2022)

Like Olympic and Paralympic Games, World Expos are also understood as hallmark events for the reasons mentioned above. In the past, mega and hallmark events such as Olympics and World Expos were hosted by capital or large cities of countries. In addition, these mega and hallmark events were held when the aforementioned countries were making key economic development in order to increase the level of civic pride and show off their ability and power to the whole world.

Concerning representative kinds of mega events, the Olympics and Paralympics and World Expos, Japan hosted six mega events to date, and is going to host its seventh mega event, Expo 2025, welcoming visitors from all over the world to its main venue in Osaka City (OUP) (see Table 8.1). With regard to these mega events, particularly the Olympic and Paralympic Games, all of the three main pillars of sustainability are deeply associated with the events. It is not limited to these mega events held in Japan, but their cost-benefit performance has always been a main concern of their key stakeholders and has also been examined well in academia. Stated differently, cost-effectiveness of hosting the Olympics and Paralympics or World Expos has been looked at in terms of their

Table 8.1 Olympics and Paralympics and World Expos held in Japan

Name	Type of mega event	Hosting city	Year
Tokyo 1964	Summer Olympics & Paralympics	Tokyo	1964
Expo '70	World Expo	Osaka	1970
Sapporo 1972	Winter Olympics & Paralympics	Sapporo (Hokkaido Prefecture)	1972
Nagano 1998	Winter Olympics & Paralympics	Nagano	1998
Expo 2005	World Expo	Aichi Prefecture	2005
Tokyo 2020	Summer Olympics & Paralympics	Tokyo	**2021**
Expo 2025	World Expo	Osaka	[Scheduled in 2025]

Source: Author

economic sustainability. Generally, such mega events are expected to bring a considerable or at least a certain amount of economic benefits to the hosting city and beyond. As for this point, for instance, even Tokyo 2020 was not an exception before the COVID-19 arose in early 2020 (Jimura, 2020). As for the Olympics, usually candidate cities and their countries bid for hosting the Games when the nations' economy is flourishing, but the economy often starts declining by the year of the Olympics as the Games are held often seven to eleven years later (Flyvbjerg et al., 2021). Flyvbjerg et al. (2021) also look at average gross domestic product (hereafter GDP) growth for host countries before, at, and after the Olympics for all Games since Rome 1960. The result shows that overall the average GDP growth after the Games is lower than before the Games. This implies that the Olympic Games do not usually have an enough power to reignite host nations' economic growth. In fact, Flyvbjerg et al. (2021) mention that hosting the Games is financially costly and risky. Thus, it could be stated that the economic sustainability of the Games is fragile and sceptical. This point is backed by Investopedia (2022) who indicates that amongst 11 summer and winter Olympic Games between 2000 and 2020 (i.e. Sydney to Tokyo), five made a profit (e.g. Salt Lake City 2002), one was breakeven (London 2012), and other fives made a loss (e.g. Tokyo 2020). In the case of Tokyo 2020, furthermore, an unforeseeable threat beyond the control of Tokyo or Japan, the COVID-19 pandemic, had a gigantic negative impact on the cost-benefit performance and economic sustainability of the Games.

As stated earlier in this section, an increase in the level of community or national pride is one of possible main outcomes of hosting hallmark events. As mega events such as the Olympics and Paralympics can also be seen as hallmark events, the Games may also cause such an effect. It should also be noted that traditionally the Games held in East Asia and South America aimed to enhance the national prestige as well as highlight the economic development as a new developed country to the world (Aramata et al., 2018). Indeed, such an effect can be confirmed in the Olympics and Paralympics and World Expo held in Japan whilst the nation had been recovering from the World War II and experiencing extensive and rapid economic development (i.e. Tokyo 1964, Expo '70 and Sapporo 1972). Nonetheless, it is doubtful whether the Games and

8 Sustainability of Visitor Attractions and Events Sector in Japan

World Expos held or scheduled in Japan in the 1990s and thereafter could still have such a positive impact. If so, the social meaning and socio-cultural sustainability of recent or scheduled the Games or World Expos would not be meaningful or solid enough. As stated in Sect. 2.6, structures and attractions of theme parks can be negative legacies named 'white elephants' if well-considered plans are not prepared before the parks were actually closed. Such outcomes are undesired from the viewpoint of the *mottainai* spirit, and the environmental sustainability of theme park sites and their nearby areas. Holding mega events and hallmark events, including the Olympics and Paralympics and World Expos, also involve such a risk. In fact, several host cities have been saddled with this negative impact (e.g. Athens 2004, Sochi 2014, Rio 2016). Unfortunately, examples of white elephants can also be found in Japan such as bobsleigh facilities of Nagano 1998. Operation of the facilities was suspended in 2018 due to the continuous money-losing operations (Jiji.com, 2021). Hosting Tokyo 2020 led to the construction of six permanent sport facilities. Of these six, however, only Ariake Arena is expected to be able to make a profit after the Games (Jiji.com, 2021). The cases of Nagano 1998 and Tokyo 2020 show a weak economic sustainability of these mega events and structures newly built for the events. This situation can also invite the emergence of white elephants that can damage the environmental sustainability of the sites and adjacent districts.

3.2 Traditional Festivals

This section focuses on the above-mentioned peculiar sort of events, festivals. Like events, festivals can be categorised into several groups depending on various elements vital for them. For instance, Jimura (2022a, 48–49) suggests 11 categories for festivals around the world based on their theme or purpose as follows:

1. Religious,
2. Harvest,
3. Seasonal,
4. Food and drink,

5. Art,
6. Books,
7. Music,
8. Culture/heritage,
9. Dance/performing arts,
10. Films/television programmes/theatre, and
11. Sports.

Jimura (2022a) also states that these 11 categories of festivals can also be applied to those in Japan. In relation to this categorisation, it should be noted that the majority of festivals have multiple themes or purposes. To cite a case from Japan, Hirosaki Neputa Matsuri (Aomori Prefecture) can be understood as a seasonal, art, or culture/heritage festival (see Fig. 8.6). Concerning the festivals of Japan, Jimura (2022a) further argues that traditional festivals with a long history and founded relationship with a particular place, custom, history and/or religion are usually called '*matsuri*', whilst those emerged or developed in modern days are likely to be called 'festivals'.

Amongst 11 major themes/purposes of festivals listed above, *matsuri* are inclined to have the themes/purposes of religion, harvest, seasonal, culture/heritage, and/or dance/performing arts. As signified from this, a range of Japan's tangible and intangible cultural heritage that is deeply rooted in Japanese society and people are well featured as key themes/purposes of *matsuri*. For instance, fireworks of Japan are called '*hanabi*' and have been entertaining Japanese people since the 17th century (Edo period) as a seasonal tradition (*fubutsushi*) of Japanese summer (Jimura, 2022b). Throughout its history, a variety of *hanabi* have been developed. They have been utilised for different occasions and enjoyed by varied types of people. Of these, *hanabi* used for fireworks displays (*hanabi-taikai*) require special knowledge and skills for their production, and these legacies have been inherited from generation to generation by individual fireworks craftsmen (*hanabishi*), groups of *hanabishi* or *hanabi* enterprises (Jimura, 2022b). Thus, *hanabi*, particularly those created for *hanabi-taikai*, are seen and valued as intangible cultural heritage of Japan. This also means that traditional *hanabi-taikai* with established history such as Sumidagawa Hanabi-taikai (TMP) can also be viewed as a

8 Sustainability of Visitor Attractions and Events Sector in Japan

Fig. 8.6 *Uchiwa* (Japanese paper fan) featuring Hirosaki Neputa Matsuri. (Source: Author)

traditional festival (*matsuri*) of Japan. It is also important that the aforementioned diverse main themes or purposes of *matsuri* are often well interrelated each other. For example, gods of Shintoism and Buddhas of Japanese Buddhism are enshrined at Shinto shrines and Japanese Buddhist temples respectively, and religious *matsuri* are held regularly to celebrate their gods or Buddhas. Buddhist *matsuri* may include a temporary open of their special cultural heritage (e.g. hidden Buddhist statues) to ordinary people and/or performances with sacred nature. Besides, harvest *matsuri* are essentially seasonal *matsuri*, because they have been conducted regularly at a specific time or times of a year since the ancient times to appreciate the harvest of the current year and pray for a good harvest of the next year.

Amongst the three key pillars of sustainability, their socio-cultural sustainability would be most crucial for traditional festivals of Japan (*matsuri*). That is because, most *matsuri* feature a certain kind of cultural heritage and have a close link with its local communities. As Jimura (2022b) indicates through the case of Japan's fireworks festivals (*hanabi-taikai*), however, local *matsuri* might develop into regional, national or even international *matsuri*, expanding their geographical markets, including a wider variety of people and organisations, and increasing the number of audiences. These changes in the nature and quality of *matsuri* would also signify that there are possibilities that local *matsuri* would become tourism resources and visitor attractions. Such alterations of *matsuri* would be a welcoming thing for persons related to tourism businesses; however, the development may alter the original purpose of the *matsuri* and/or damage its meaning for local communities (Jimura, 2022b). For example, Sanja Matsuri is a large Shinto *matsuri* of Asakusa Shrine held annually in May. In recent years, the *matsuri*'s purpose seems to have somewhat changed and its relations with local community might have weaken due to the development of the *matsuri* as a tourism resource and visitor attraction, and an increasing level of involvement of outsiders in the *matsuri* as the supply side of *matsuri* (i.e. not just as audience) (President Online 2018). At the same time, however, it must have been challenging for many local *matsuri* to have survived until today if they did not change their purposes or meanings at all, did not have the quality as a tourism resource/visitor attraction, and/or did not involve a wider range of people. Thus, it is imperative for key stakeholders of *matsuri* (e.g. local residents) to carefully consider and decide the degree and types of changes local communities should accept in order to maintain socio-cultural sustainability of their *matsuri*.

Widening participation in *matsuri* can be useful not only for their socio-cultural sustainability but also for their economic sustainability. To cite a case, not only local enterprises (e.g. local shopping centre) but also (local branches of) famous Japanese companies (e.g. Toshiba) have supported Aomori Nebuta Matsuri through sponsorship (Mitsui, 2006). In the case of Aomori Nebuta Matsuri, sponsors assist holding of the *matsuri* financially and socio-culturally mainly by asking local *nebuta* craftsmen to make their *nebuta* floats. By doing so, *nebuta* craftsmen could earn income using their knowledge and skills, and also have opportunities to pass such expertise to next generations. Nowadays, Aomori Nebuta is recognised by Japanese people (and possibly even by international tourists) as one of the most famous summer *matsuri* in Japan. Before the COVID-19 pandemic hit, more than 2.5 million visitors come to Aomori City during the *matsuri* period (2-7 August every year) to enjoy the *matsuri* and appreciate *nebuta*. This signifies that the economic sustainability of the city itself and local businesses could also be maintained or strengthened through this established *matsuri*. Regarding the environmental sustainability of festivals, the most reported issue across the world would be a large amount of rubbish left after the festivals, especially solid one (Wan & Chan, 2013). This is applied to large *matsuri* in Japan. In fact, the problem has been confirmed at the venues of Gion Matsuri (Kyoto Urban Prefecture) and Tenjin Matsuri (OUP). In recent years, both *matsuri* have been planning and conducting various measures to minimise the amount of *matsuri* waste. These measures include adoption of reusable trays and recruitment of volunteer staff who pick up rubbish on the *matsuri* premises.

4   Conclusion

Visitor attractions and events are tourism resources located in tourist destinations, the supply side of tourism. In many cases, visiting certain visitor attractions or taking part in specific events can be a main motivation for same-day visitors or tourists to come along to peculiar tourist destinations. Stated differently, visitor attractions or events can function as a key attraction factor of the tourist destinations. With regard to their nature, visitor attractions are tangible tourism resources, whilst events are intangible tourism resources. This chapter looks at six different sorts of cultural heritage that functions as visitor attractions today (see Sect. 2). Of these, however, five types of cultural heritage except amusement parks/theme parks are not originally developed as visitor attractions but built to serve their original objectives other than tourism. Thus, it is fair to say that the quality of these cultural heritage sites or properties have been changing, acquiring new meaning as tourism resources in the context of today's society and responding to the demands of the general public. Such alterations might have been affecting the socio-cultural sustainability of the cultural heritage utilised as visitor attractions in a positive or negative manner, or both. An example of positive socio-cultural changes is that the value of abandoned industrial sites might be recognised by external people such as heritage researchers, and the sites may develop into industrial museums or visitor centres (e.g. Iwami Ginzan Sliver Mine (Shimane Prefecture)). In this case, the socio-cultural sustainability of this cultural heritage is secured and will be maintained or even enhanced if the heritage can be passed onto future generations through working as a visitor attraction. This could also be beneficial to strengthen the economic sustainability of the industrial heritage and visitor attractions featuring it as they should be able to raise money through admission fees, retailing/souvenir shops, cafés and/or restaurants, and/or hosting meetings or ceremonies. If the sites can be managed in a proper way, like using them as visitor attractions, it is also advantageous for the environmental sustainability of the sites and their neighbouring communities.

On the other hand, an example of negative socio-cultural changes is that a type of local crafts exhibited or sold at a gallery or museum may become famous and popular amongst visitors, and fake versions of the crafts can be developed by unqualified persons or outsiders to meet the ever-increasing demands of visitors (e.g. Nambu ironware (Iwate Prefecture)). In this case, commoditisation of the cultural heritage occurs in an inappropriate way. This implies that neither the economic sustainability nor the socio-cultural sustainability of this cultural heritage can be enhanced and, in fact, both are rather deteriorated. That is because, financial benefits collected through selling fake versions of cultural heritage go to the outside of relevant professionals or local communities, and the link between the cultural heritage and local communities may not be recognised or respected enough by the general public. Thus, the original meanings and purposes of cultural heritage need to be retained or ideally enhanced even if the cultural heritage is featured in or utilised as tangible tourism resources, namely visitor attractions, especially for its socio-cultural sustainability.

8 Sustainability of Visitor Attractions and Events Sector in Japan

Concerning amusement parks or theme parks, whilst the environmental sustainability of them and their neighbouring environment would be the pillar of sustainability that requires enough attention from their stakeholders. Except a few successful cases such as TDR and USJ, most of Japan's amusement parks, particularly theme parks, tend to be short-lived. Consequently, their premises, especially large facilities or attractions, can be negative legacies called white elephants if there is no well-considered plan for a new way to make the most of the places and structures. If this happens, it really hurts not only the environmental sustainability but also the socio-cultural sustainability of the sites and nearby areas as these places will lose associations with their surrounding communities. This risk is also pointed out or the problem actually occurred at many post-mega events sites across the world as discussed in Sect. 3.1. The issue coming from post-mega events sites such as the Olympic and Paralympic Games or World Expos can be even more serious than the one steming from short-lived theme parks, because durations of the Games (typically around one month in total) or World Expos (generally around six months) are usually even shorter than the period the short-lived theme parks are active.

On the other hand, the other topic discussed in Sect. 3 as intangible cultural heritage and tourism resources is traditional festivals of Japan called *matsuri*. Of the main three pillars of sustainability and its management, the socio-cultural sustainability is particularly significant for *matsuri*. That is because, *matsuri* have been closely associated with a wide variety of cultural heritage of Japan for a long time, developing and maintaining strong bonds with certain localities and local inhabitants. Part of *matsuri* have been altering their nature from local events chiefly for community members to a popular regional, national or even international festivals for wider communities, including excursionists and tourists. In this process, some *matsuri* might lose or weaken their connections with local communities, although the consequence of this change can increase the level of recognition of *matsuri* that can lead to a better level of the economic sustainability thanks to spending by visitors. Different from the Olympics and Paralympics or World Expos, almost all *matsuri* are held outdoor. Furthermore, the venues for *matsuri* are likely to be larger than those for the aforementioned international mega and hallmark events. For instance, therefore, practices reflecting the *mottainai* spirit such as reducing the amount of rubbish from visitors and using reusable tableware for foods and drinks are crucial for the environmental sustainability of *matsuri* and the lives of local residents who reside near the *matsuri* premises.

References

Alfrey, J., & Putnam, T. (2003). *The industrial heritage: Managing resources and uses*. Routledge.

Aragón-Pérez, A. (2019). The influence of the 1992 Earth Summit on the 1992 Olympic Games in Barcelona: Awakening of the Olympic environmental dimension. *The International Journal of the History of Sport, 36*(2–3), 244–266.

Aramata, M., Oshiro, N., Yamaguchi, S., Koizumi, R., & Sugiyama, K. (2018). Thinking about the 2020 Tokyo Olympic games: Globalization, urban and regional development, and security [in Japanese]. *E-Journal GEO, 13*(1), 273–295.

Baltà Portolés, J., & Dragićevic Šešić, M. (2017). Cultural rights and their contribution to sustainable development: Implications for cultural policy. *International Journal of Cultural Policy, 23*(2), 159–173.

Bowdin, G., McDonnell, I., Allen, J., & O'Toole, W. (2001). *Events management*. Butterworth-Heinemann.

Cloquet, I., Palomino, M., Shaw, G., Stephen, G., & Taylor, T. (2018). Disability, social inclusion and the marketing of tourist attractions. *Journal of Sustainable Tourism, 26*(2), 221–237.

Cundy, W., Korec, P., & Rouba, R. (2012). Resident's perception of festivals – The case study of Łódź. *Slovak Sociological Review, 44*, 704–728.

Davidson, M., & McNeill, D. (2012). The redevelopment of Olympic sites: Examining the legacy of Sydney Olympic Park. *Urban Studies, 49*(8), 1625–1641.

Flyvbjerg, B., Budzier, A., & Lunn, D. (2021). Regression to the tail: Why the Olympics blow up. *Environment and Planning A: Economy and Space, 53*(2), 233–260.

Gallo, M., Arcioni, L., Leonardi, D., Moreschi, L., & Del Borghi, A. (2020). GHG Accounting for sustainable mega-events: How lessons learnt during the Milan Expo 2015 world fair could lead to less carbon-intensive future mega-events. *Sustainable Production and Consumption, 22*, 88–109.

Getz, D., Svensson, B., Peterssen, R., & Gunnervall, A. (2012). Hallmark events: Definition and planning process. *International Journal of Event Management Research, 7*(1/2), 47–67.

Guizzardi, A., Mariani, M., & Prayag, G. (2017). Environmental impacts and certification: Evidence from the Milan World Expo 2015. *International Journal of Contemporary Hospitality Management, 29*(3), 1052–1071.

Hanatoyo Landscape. (2022). *Environment-friendliness, awareness-building*. Available at: https://www.hanatoyo.co.jp/en/company/csr/. Accessed 13 June 2022.

ICOM. (2022). *The ICOM Advisory Council selects the museum definition proposal to be voted in Prague*. Available at: https://icom.museum/en/news/the-icom-advisory-council-selects-the-museum-definition-proposal-to-be-voted-in-prague/#:~:text=%E2%80%9CA%20museum%20is%20a%20non,of%20education%2C%20study%20and%20enjoyment. Accessed 20 June 2022.

Investopedia. (2022). *The best and worst Olympics financial planning*. Available at: https://www.investopedia.com/financial-edge/0912/the-best-and-worst-olympic-financial-planning.aspx. Accessed 8 July 2022.

Jiji.com. (2021). *Gorinkaijo "fu no isanka" kenen: go-shisetsu ga akaji mitoshi – Tokyo-to* (Becoming white elephants? Five facilities from Tokyo 2020 will be in red – Tokyo Metropolitan Prefecture) [in Japanese]. Available at: https://www.jiji.com/jc/article?k=2021090800834&g=pol. Accessed 8 July 2022.

Jimura, T. (2007). *The impact of World Heritage Site designation on local communities – A comparative study of Ogimachi (Japan) and Saltaire (UK)*. Doctoral Thesis, Nottingham Trent University.

Jimura, T. (2011). The impact of world heritage site designation on local communities – A case study of Ogimachi, Shirakawa-mura, Japan. *Tourism Management, 32*(2), 288–296.

Jimura, T. (2019). *World Heritage Sites: Tourism, local communities, and conservation activities*. CABI.

Jimura, T. (2020). Changing faces of Tokyo: Regeneration, tourism and Tokyo 2020. In N. Wise & T. Jimura (Eds.), *Tourism, cultural heritage and urban regeneration – Changing spaces in historical places* (pp. 141–155). Springer.

Jimura, T. (2022a). *Cultural and heritage tourism in Japan*. Routledge.

Jimura, T. (2022b). Events and intangible cultural heritage. In N. Wise & K. Maguire (Eds.), *A research agenda for event impacts* (pp. 117–128). Edward Elgar.

Jimura, T., & Wise, N. (2020). Expanding perspectives in tourism, cultural heritage and urban regeneration. In N. Wise & T. Jimura (Eds.), *Tourism, cultural heritage and urban regeneration – Changing spaces in historical places* (pp. 205–213). Springer.

Kyoto Railway Museum. (n.d.). SDGs Gakushu Programme (SDGs Learning Programmes) [in Japanese]. Available at: https://www.kyotorailwaymuseum.jp/sdgs/. Accessed 8 Sep 2023.

Kaiga no Arukikata. (2021). *Nyujosha-su ranking* (Top 10 museums and galleries by visitor numbers) [in Japanese]. Available at: https://www.venven.jp/%E6%97%A5%E6%9C%AC%E3%81%AE%E7%BE%8E%E8%A1%93%E9%A4%A8%EF%BC%86%E5%8D%9A%E7%89%A9%E9%A4%A8-%E6%9D%A5%E9%A4%A8%E8%80%85%E6%95%B0-%E5%85%A5%E5%A0%B4%E8%80%85%E6%95%B0%E3%83%A9%E3%83%B3%E3%82%AD%E3%83%B3/. Accessed 20 June 2022.

Kim, H. D. (2013). The 2012 London Olympics: Commercial partners, environmental sustainability, corporate social responsibility and outlining the implications. *The International Journal of the History of Sport, 30*(18), 2197–2208.

Krupar, S. (2018). Sustainable World Expo? The governing function of spectacle in Shanghai and beyond. *Theory, Culture and Society, 35*(2), 91–113.

Leask, A. (2003). The nature and purpose of visitor attractions. In A. Fyall, B. Garrod, & A. Leask (Eds.), *Managing visitor attractions: New directions* (pp. 5–15). Butterworth-Heinemann.

Leask, A., & Barron, P. (2021). Factors in the provision of engaging experiences for the traditionalist market at visitor attractions. *Tourism Management Perspectives, 38*, 100810.

Lennon, J. J. (2004). Revenue management and customer forecasts: A bridge too far for the UK visitor attractions sector? *Journal of Revenue and Pricing Management, 2*(4), 338–352.

Li, Y. (2018). Research of the ecological environment in Shanghai World Expo park. *Journal of Environmental Engineering and Landscape Management, 26*(3), 177–189.

Lochhead, H. (2005). A new vision for Sydney Olympic Park. *Urban Design International, 10*(3), 215–222.

Manikas, I., Sundarakani, B., Madmoune, A., & Alvares, R. (2022). Integrated supply chain sustainability for mega-events: An empirical study of Dubai Expo 2020. *Event Management.* https://doi.org/10.3727/152599522X16419948391032. Accessed 4 July 2022.

Mitsui, I. (2006). Chiiki-bunka to kigyo no kakawari ni kansuru keiei-jinruigaku-teki kosatsu: Aomori Nebuta Matsuri no jirei wo chushin to shite (A study on relations between local cultures and enterprises in the view of anthropology of administration: A case study of Aomori Nebuta Matsuri) [in Japanese]. *Shogaku-ronshu, 75*(1), 5–18.

Monica, B. M., Sabina, M., & Sofia, M. G. (2015). Sustainable development in the context of the Olympic Games. *Science, Movement and Health, 15*(2), 111–116.

Nakao, T. (2021) Hakubutsukan wa akaji nanoka (Are museums in red?) [in Japanese]. *Nihon no Hakubutsukan no Korekara IV* (Preprint).

Nippon-no-waza expo. (2022). *The conservation of culturally important landscape gardening techniques.* Available at: https://www.nippon-no-waza.jp/expo/en/teigikyo-en.php. Accessed 13 June 2022.

NMWA. (2021). *Kokuritsu Seiyo Bijutsukan no renewal open ni tsuite* (On reopening of NMWA after renovation) [in Japanese]. Available at: https://www.nmwa.go.jp/jp/information/. Accessed 12 June 2022.

Olds, K. (1998). Urban mega-events, evictions and housing rights: The Canadian case. *Current Issues in Tourism, 1*(1), 2–46.

Olsen, D. H. (2006). Management issues for religious heritage attractions. In D. J. Timothy & D. H. Olsen (Eds.), *Tourism, religion and spiritual journeys* (pp. 104–118). Routledge.

Ritchie, B. W. (1984). Assessing the impact of hallmark events: Conceptual and research issues. *Journal of Travel Research, 23*(1), 2–11.

Sartore-Baldwin, M. L., & McCullough, B. (2018). Equity-based sustainability and ecocentric management: Creating more ecologically just sport organization practices. *Sport Management Review, 21*(4), 391–402.

Solanellas, F., Ferrand, A., & Camps, A. (2019). *Barcelona 92: A legacy case study.* Springer Nature.

The Art Newspaper. (2020). *Icom in turmoil after row over new definition of museums.* Available at: https://www.theartnewspaper.com/2020/08/13/icom-in-turmoil-after-row-over-new-definition-of-museums. Accessed 20 June 2022.

The Travel. (2019). *The 10 best open-air museums in the world, ranked.* Available at: https://www.thetravel.com/best-open-air-museums-ranked/. Accessed 20 June 2022.

Tichaawa, T. M., & Bob, U. (2015). Leveraging mega-events beyond the host nation: A case study of the 2010 FIFA World Cup African Legacy Programme in Cameroon and Nigeria. *Leisure Studies, 34*(6), 742–757.

Trendafilova, S., Graham, J., & Bemiller, J. (2017). Sustainability and the olympics: the case of the 2016 Rio summer games. *Journal of Sustainability Education, 16*(3), 1–22.

Waitt, G. (2001). The Olympic spirit and civic boosterism: The Sydney 2000 Olympics. *Tourism Geographies, 3*(3), 249–278.

Wan, Y. K. P., & Chan, S. H. J. (2013). Factors that affect the levels of tourists' satisfaction and loyalty towards food festivals: A case study of Macau. *International Journal of Tourism Research, 15*(3), 226–240.

9

Sustainability of Tourism Intermediaries in Japan

1 Introduction

Tourism intermediaries are another essential component of the tourism industry, and it is the last sector looked at in this book. Tourism intermediaries can also be called travel intermediaries, and there does not seem to be clear established differences between these two terms. Probably, the most important character of tourism intermediaries that differentiates it from other key elements of the tourism industry examined in Chaps. 5, 6, 7, and 8 is that they exist between the supply and the demand sides of tourism. More specifically, tourism intermediaries function as middlemen between service providers and service consumers, bridging these two types of key players in tourism businesses. It is generally agreed across the world that tourism intermediaries primarily consist of two kinds of enterprises, namely 'tour operators' and 'travel agents' (Yen et al., 2021). Both tour operators and travel agents have been playing various key roles in tourism distribution channels. However, there are differences in their roles. Traditionally, tour operators purchase diverse tourism services (e.g. air tickets, hotel rooms) from different service providers (e.g. airlines, hoteliers) in bulk to reach discount price deals and this leads to the development of their own products such as package holidays and all-inclusive holidays that can give convenience and reassurance to tour participants. Tour operators not only create their tourism products but also sell them to travel agents or directly to consumers. On the other hand, customarily travel agents work only as retailers, selling the aforementioned products to consumers on behalf of tour operators. Figure 9.1 shows the positions tour operators and travel agents share in the tourism distribution system and their relations with other main actors in the system.

As signified in Fig. 9.1, the roles of tour operators in the tourism distribution system are similar to those of wholesalers in the distribution system of other industries that deal with goods and/or services. Conventionally, tour operators have been highly influential not only for other main players in the tourism distribution channels included in Fig. 9.1 but also for tourist destinations as a whole. That is because, tour operators have been affecting consumers' awareness of certain tourist destinations and have been influencing their demands for travelling to specific destinations. They have also been powerful as marketing channels for service providers whose level of recognition amongst consumers can be enhanced by being involved in package or all-inclusive tours created by tour operators. Traditionally, travel agents have also been influential for consumers as well as service providers as they have a lot of information about different tourist destinations and service providers and can directly tell their views towards them to consumers. This suggests that

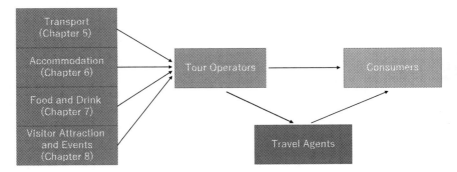

Fig. 9.1 Tour operators and travel agents in the tourism distribution system. (Source: Author based on Holloway and Taylor (2006))

their information and opinions have a power to affect consumers' decision-making process.

Generally, tourism as a whole is seen as a fragile and unstable industry, and tourism intermediaries are not exceptions. This means that tourism intermediaries can be easily affected by changes in each company (internal environment), those within the industry (external (micro/near) environment), or those in our society (external (macro/far) environment). Amongst them, changes in our society tend to be the most challenging ones for businesses as these changes are usually beyond the control of one company or even the industry as a whole, although they can also be great opportunities for an enterprise or industry it belongs to. In the past 30–40 years, probably the most influential change for tourism intermediaries would be the emergence and advancement of the Internet. The development and adoption of a range of information technology (hereafter IT) in the tourism industry, including tourism intermediaries have caused both advantageous and disadvantageous changes for tourism intermediaries. Thanks to the development of IT, for instance, tourism intermediaries could have another type of marketing channel on the Internet. This addition could increase business opportunities for these companies as consumers who are difficult to visit their physical shops could also access and look at their products on websites. Nonetheless, not all tourism intermediaries can fully benefit from IT, because the vast majority of tourism intermediaries are small and medium-sized enterprises (hereafter SMEs) that are likely to have limited financial and human resources (Lin, 2016). That is why most of them need to spend their resources primarily on their core businesses.

Although the rise and advancement of IT gave new business opportunities to existing tourism intermediaries, it also invited the emergence of competitors within the industry typically online travel agents, including Expedia, Booking.com, Hotels.com and lastminute.com especially between the late 1990s and the early 2000s. Moreover, an increasing number of service providers in tourism, once part of their sales more or less relied on tourism intermediaries, have started selling their products directly to consumers, developing user-friendly webpages for direct marketing and direct selling. This phenomenon is widely confirmed across different tourism service providers, but in the author's view, particularly noticeable in the accommodation sector. Many hoteliers across the globe, typically international hotel chains, even adopt a 'best price guarantee' policy (e.g. NH Hotel Group). The policy makes a promise to hotel guests who purchased a hotel room directly from the hotel's own webpage to offer the cheapest price. This trend can be understood a real threat for tourism intermediaries, especially for traditional non-online ones, because main selling points of traditional package holidays, convenience and discount, may not work as their competitive advantages over their rivals any longer. Nowadays, consequently, more and more consumers, including the author himself, seem to arrange their travels using direct marketing and selling. This signifies that the market size of tourism intermediaries has also be shrinking. This should be particularly challenging for tourism intermediaries that are SMEs. One of the common ways for these SMEs to survive is to focus on a niche market. The fields where these tourism intermediaries specialise are varied such as travels by rail or those to a less established tourist destinations. The number of small or medium-sized tourism intermediaries specialising in ecotourism or responsible tourism, has also been growing, mirroring changes in consumer concerns/interests and an important global agendas.

Needless to say, COVID-19 is another key external factor that has been affecting tourism intermediaries all over the world in recent years. The pandemic has been a major threat for the tourism industry as a whole, including tourism intermediaries. It is reported from all over the world that a number of tour operators and travel agents have gone into administration.

This section outlines major characteristics of tourism intermediaries. The next section (Sect. 2) looks at those of tourism intermediaries in Japan. As can be suggested from key points above, overall the sustainability management of tourism intermediaries has been increasingly demanding, especially for those categorised as SMEs. The matters related to sustainability and those associated with issues surrounding sustainability are explored in Sects. 3 and 4, respectively.

2 Tourism Intermediaries in Japan

Like other countries whose internal, inbound and outbound tourism have highly developed, the modern history of Japan's tourism cannot be fully understood without looking at Japan's tourism intermediaries. As shown in Sect. 1, in many nations, two major types of tourism intermediaries are tour operators and travel agents. Indeed, tourism intermediaries in Japan can also be categorised in this way. Regarding Japan's tourism intermediaries, however, a classification of 'tour operators' suggested by the Japan Association of Travel Agents (hereafter JATA) is accepted and used widely. Although JATA describes themselves as a group of 'travel agents', this classification is about 'tour operators'. It is intriguing and this gap stems from how JATA understands and uses the term, 'travel agents'. Specifically, JATA seems to use the term, 'travel agents', meaning 'tour operators' defined in Sect. 1. According to JATA (2022), the three categories of tour operators, the number of JATA member companies by category (as of 22 June 2022), and the business fields of companies in each of the three categories are as follows:

- First category (572):
  Companies that can sell and implement overseas and domestic tours they create and those they develop following their customers' needs, arrange overseas and domestic travels, and sell overseas and domestic tours planned by other tour operators on their behalf.
- Second category (253):
  Companies that can sell and implement domestic tours they create and overseas and domestic tours they develop following their customers' needs, arrange overseas and domestic travels, and sell overseas and domestic tours planned by other tour operators on their behalf.
- Third category (275):
  Companies that can sell and implement overseas and domestic tours they develop following their customers' needs, arrange overseas and domestic travels, and sell overseas and domestic tours planned by other tour operators on their behalf. In addition, they can sell and imple-

ment domestic tours they create that visit only certain designated areas within Japan.

For a long time, JTB has been the number one tour operator in Japan in terms of annual sales. Prior to the COVID-19 pandemic, for instance, JTB's annual sales in the fiscal year of 2019 (April 2019–March 2020) was around 1.29 trillion JPY (Travel Voice, 2020). JTB is a representative tour operator belonging to the aforementioned 'first category' and has several affiliated companies in the tourism industry and beyond. JTB has multiple brands for their domestic and overseas tours, and well-known examples from the company include 'Tabi Monogatari' (budget/domestic and overseas) and 'Look JTB' (luxurious/overseas). On the other hand, Shinki Travel based in Osaka City is a good example of tour operators in the 'second category'. The enterprise sells package holidays arranged by Nippon Travel Agency as well as those created by themselves. An example of tour operators belonging to the 'third category' is ELTAS Tohoku that sells and conducts domestic tours visiting Tohoku (northeast) region of Japan.

The rise and advancement of IT, especially the Internet, has also been affecting tourism intermediaries in Japan. Like in other major tourist-generating and tourist-destination regions of the world, once physical shops were a main marketing channel for Japan's tourism intermediaries. In the last 20–30 years, however, the intermediaries have also been launching and developing their official websites as another key marketing channel for them. In many cases nowadays consumers can not only search the information on their products (e.g. package tours) but also purchase these products. Hence, it is fair to say that the importance of the Internet and tourism intermediaries' official websites has been increasing year by year. Consequently, the number of tour operators' or travel agents' physical shops across Japan, especially those in local cities or rural areas has been generally decreasing. NHK (2022) looks at branches of tour operators in the first category that are situated in Matsuyama City. Matsuyama is a prefectural capital of Ehime Prefecture in Shikoku region. The region is located in Shikoku Island that is Japan's fourth largest island, southwest of Japan's main island Honshu, and consists of four prefectures, namely Tokushima, Kagawa, Ehime and Kochi. There are no cities with over a million population in Shikoku region. Matsuyama is the largest city in the region in terms of population, but its population is around 0.52 million followed by Takamatsu City in Kagawa Prefecture (around 0.42 million). According to NHK (2022), the branches of Nippon Travel Agency, Nokyo Tourist Corporation and Meitetsu World Travel, all of which are the first-category tour operators, were closed in 2021 or 2022.

Needless to say, the biggest reason of these closures is the impact of the COVID-19 pandemic on internal, inbound and outbound tourism. However, the aforementioned trend in Japan's tourism intermediaries already started well before the emergence of the COVID-19 pandemic due to the rise and development of the Internet as a new business place. As suggested in Sect. 1, this virtual and online trading space has enabled tour operators or travel agents in Japan to increase the number of opportunities to see potential customers. This has also been beneficial for consumers as they can easily check a lot of information on products of tour operators/travel agents and, in many cases, they can even purchase a product without visiting physical shops. On the other hand, phenomena that can work as threats for traditional tourism intermediaries have also risen. The first phenomenon is the rise and diffusion of direct marketing/selling from service providers to service consumers. For example, a 'best price guarantee' policy discussed in Sect. 1 is also employed by many of Japan's nationwide hotel chains. A good example of this is SUPER HOTEL. The hotel chain guarantees lowest price for their customers who book a hotel room via the company's official website. The second phenomenon is the emergence and development of online travel agents. Major examples of Japan's online travel agents are Rakuten Travel and Jalan (Jimura, 2011). The above-discussed two phenomena have led to a decrease in the number of business opportunities, particularly with individual tourists, for traditional tourism intermediaries of Japan, although such a shift can also be confirmed in other nations whose tourism has been highly developed.

Last but not least, it should also be remembered that most of tourism intermediaries are SMEs, and this feature also applies to those in Japan. In other words, almost all Japan's tour operators in the second and third categories and many of them in the first category are SMEs. In addition to the issues illustrated above, this can also be understood as a reason why tourism intermediaries in Japan, particularly traditional SMEs, have been suffering from challenging and fast-changing business environments for the past 20-30 years. Bearing these key points in mind, the subsequent section (Sect. 3) sheds a light on the sustainability and its management in Japan's tourism intermediaries, referring to relevant examples from the sector.

3   Sustainability Management in Japan's Tourism Intermediaries

3.1   Economic Sustainability

As pointed out in Sects. 1 and 2, the impacts of the COVID-19 have been immense for Japan's tourism intermediaries in a negative manner. As can be confirmed in other sections in Part 3 of the book, almost all changes caused or escalated by the pandemic have been disadvantageous for the tourism industry. Of various sectors in the tourism industry in Japan, tourism intermediaries seem to have been especially hit badly according to various information and data from real world. For instance, 90% of bankruptcies of Japan's tourism intermediaries were affected by the COVID-19 pandemic for the first seven months of 2021 (Travel Voice, 2021). Amongst these, SMEs specialising in overseas travels and tours were hit worst (Travel Voice, 2021). Working together with IT related changes argued earlier in this section, the COVID-19 pandemic has negatively been influencing not only tourism intermediaries that can be viewed as SMEs but also leading tour operators in the first category.

According to NHK (2022), JTB has decided to close 115 physical shops in the near future, and this means a quarter of their shops currently exit will be gone. Other leading tour operators of Japan also plan to decrease the number of their physical stores. Kinki Nippon Tourist will decrease the number of their physical shops from 130 to around 40–45, whilst Nippon Travel Agency plans to reduce the number of their physical stores from 190 to 90 by the end of the fiscal year of 2022 (NHK, 2022). These can be comprehended as their business strategy to survive in the challenging market with their weakened economic sustainability under many negative factors. Moreover, this movement also mirrors a current trend in the businesses of Japan's tourism intermediaries generally, less focus and less priority on sales on individual customers over the counter. That is mainly because, this type of sales is not cost effective enough and rather disadvantageous in terms of economic sustainability of their businesses. Generally, tourism enterprises need to rent business spaces often in prime locations for their stores. Each store also needs financial resources for their sales representatives, interior, office furniture, utility fees, and paper brochures. Furthermore, not all the people visit tour operators' or travel agents' physical stores purchase tickets or packages from them. In fact, many people came to the stores just to listen to sales staff's advice and/or talk with them. In such cases, no profits can be raised for tour operators or travel agents even if their sales representatives spend a considerable amount of their time for these people. Thus, maintaining physical stores for individual customers are unlikely to be seen as a sensible strategic selection in terms of economic sustainability of tour operators or travel agents. In fact, other major tour operators in the first category, namely Tobu Top Tours and the aforementioned Meitetsu World Travel, have started closing their stores for individual customers in Kanto region and Tokai region respectively (NHK, 2022), although these regions are the companies' main geographical markets.

3.2 Socio-cultural Sustainability

It is important to look at the history of Japan's tourism industry when the socio-cultural sustainability of Japan's package holidays and tourism intermediaries is considered. It was on 1 April 1964 when overseas travels were liberalised for ordinary Japanese citizens (Japan Times, 2014). In relation to this milestone event, it should be noted that JTB Tourism Research & Consulting (2014) points out that this major policy change did not primarily intend to ease the limitations for people's movement but to mitigate those for foreign currencies. Specifically, Japanese people were allowed to travel abroad once a year and to bring up to 500 USD. In fact, the Japanese Government needed to do so as this policy change was one of the requirements from the Organisation for Economic Co-operation and Development (hereafter OECD) to welcome Japan as a new OECD member country. It should also be remembered that 1964 is the year when Tokyo 1964 was held as the first Olympic Games held in Japan or Asia. It was not a coincidence that both the aforementioned liberalisation and Tokyo 1964 occurred in the same year but these two were actually interrelated. The year 1964 also had other memorial events for Japan's tourism industry such as the opening of Tokaido Shinkansen bullet train in October, the launch of Hakone Sightseeing Cruise in Lake Ashi (Kanagawa Prefecture) in July and the opening of Kyoto Tower (Kyoto Prefecture) in December.

Since 1964, travelling overseas has gradually and steadily established its position as one of major hobbies or leisure activities amongst ordinary Japanese people. It is fair to say that Japan's tour operators and travel agents and package holidays they created and/or sold have been playing a crucial role in this process. These points imply that socio-cultural sustainability of tourism intermediaries, package holidays and overseas trips have also been enhanced amongst Japanese people and society since 1964. It could also be stated that package holidays have been playing an essential role in the development of Japan's tourism intermediaries and popularisation of overseas trips amongst Japanese citizens in the past around 60 years. Bearing this in mind, Takenaka (2011) views that it is not an exaggeration that the history of Japan's package holidays can be seen as the history of Japan's tourism industry as a whole.

As discussed in Sect. 3.1, nonetheless, generally Japan's tourism intermediaries have been financially struggling due to a range of factors, including the advancement of direct marketing and selling from service providers to service consumers and the development of online travel agents followed by the COVID-19 pandemic. This suggests that the economic sustainability of Japan's tourism intermediaries has been facing a considerable risk. The above-mentioned latest news such as the bankruptcy of small and medium-sized tour operators or travel agents and the closure of physical stores also indicate that the position tourism intermediaries have shared in the tourism industry and Japanese society as a whole has been weakening and Japanese people's culture to utilise tourism intermediaries and package tours has also been degrading. This implies that the socio-cultural sustainability of tourism intermediaries in Japan may have also been declining. However, leading tour operators such as JTB and HIS have started using these challenges as opportunities for them. For example, both companies started selling and conducting package holidays to popular overseas destinations (e.g. Hawaii) with a pre-departure COVID-19 test at the destination for tour participants' return to Japan (HIS, 2022; JTB, 2022). As of August 2022, the Japanese Government still required all the people arriving in Japan to take an approved COVID-19 test within 72 hours before their flight departure time and obtain proof of a negative result in the format approved by the Japanese Government (GOV.UK, 2022). After a long wait, this restriction was lifted in September 2022.

3.3 Environmental Sustainability

A typical way for Japan's tourism intermediaries to contribute to the environmental sustainability of tourist destinations, their natural and cultural environments, and local communities there have been the promotion of ecotourism by planning and implementing eco tours. Nowadays, many tour operators and travel agents in Japan arrange and/or sell eco tours (e.g. ECOLO-no-MORI (Toyama Prefecture)) or tours that can be seen as eco tours (e.g. Kaze no Ryokosha (Tokyo Metropolitan Prefecture)). Representative tourist destinations of eco tours include Hokkaido Prefecture, Kyoto Prefecture, Kagoshima Prefecture and Okinawa Prefecture. Of ecotourism destinations in these prefectures, Shiretoko Peninsula in Hokkaido and Yakushima Island in Kagoshima Prefecture are also natural World Heritage sites and both have established history of eco tours. Major destinations of eco tours in Okinawa Prefecture include Ishigaki Island. The sea zone surrounding the island is famous for its coral reefs. Rinpana, a local tour operator, has implemented measures to protect the coral reefs, whilst utilising them as key visitor attractions in a sustainable manner. On the other hand, the majority of eco tours conducted in Kyoto Prefecture focus more on its cultural heritage, although its surrounding natural environment is also invaluable. In Kyoto Prefecture, eco tours visiting Miyama Town have been developed well. A key visitor attraction of Miyama is traditional Japanese houses with a thatched roof (*kayabuki*). In addition, the landscape of *satoyama* is also an irreplaceable asset of the town. *Satoyama* are places where local inhabitants and local natural environment meet. In other words, proof of interactions between human beings and nature can be found there as traces of human activities such as agriculture or forestry.

Eco tours arranged and/or run by Japan's tour operators are supported by various stakeholders, including public sector. For instance, the Japanese Government enforced the Act on Promotion of Ecotourism in 2008. Non-governmental organisations (hereafter NGOs) or non-profit organisations (hereafter NPOs) have been playing a crucial role in the development of eco tours in Japan and the awareness-raising of ecotourism and conservation of natural and cultural heritage. The Japan Ecotourism Society (hereafter JES) and its predecessor has been working on promotion and awareness-raising of ecotourism since its establishment in 1998. Moreover, ecotourism societies at local level can also be confirmed across Japan. The aforementioned major destinations of ecotourism (Shiretoko, Miyama and Yakushima) have such local societies. Unfortunately, however, an ecotourism society for a whole of Okinawa Prefecture was dissolved in 2020 after 14 years since its establishment in 2006 (ECO-Okinawa, 2020). The main reason for the dissolution of Okinawa's ecotourism society was a fragile system of the society (ECO-Okinawa, 2020). ECO-Okinawa (2020) asserts that Okinawa Prefecture should take a leading role in developing a new system that is more stable and can obtain more supports from relevant stakeholders. It is a shame as Okinawa Prefecture has a wide variety of natural and cultural heritage whose environmental sustainability is paramount for the future of Okinawa's tourism. Thus, Okinawa's tourism in a sustainable manner such as ecotourism must be supported more by all actors involved in the tourism industry and heritage conservation.

4 CSR, SDGs, Mottainai Spirits and 3Rs

4.1 Activities for CSR and SDGs

As can be confirmed from other chapters in Part 3 (Chaps. 5, 6, 7, and 8), most CSR activities conducted in various sectors belonging to the tourism industry, namely transport, accommodation, restaurant and café, and visitor attraction and event sectors, can also be interpreted as those for SDGs. The year 2003 is usually seen as the first year of CSR practice in Japan as a number of large enterprises have begun to publish their annual CSR reports and establishing their CSR divisions since that time (see Sect. 5.2 in Chap. 1). On the other hand, 17 SDGs were adopted at the UN General Assembly on 25 September 2015. This indicates that there is a 12-year time difference between the beginning of CSR history and the creation of SDGs for Japanese society and Japan-based enterprises. Moreover, there should be many overlaps between the things to take and complete a responsibility as a member of society and those to make a good contribution to the realisation of more sustainable future of humans and environment. Thus, it is natural for Japanese companies, including those in the tourism industry, that in many cases, the activities they originally planned and carried out as their CSR activities have been developed into their activities for SDGs.

The relations between activities for CSR and those for SDGs are particularly strong for the tourism industry, especially tour operators, as the products they create and sell cannot exist without tourist destinations where local residents live and work, their cultures survive, and surrounding natural environment subsists. In fact, JTB states that the most important thing for the company is tourist destinations and the starting point of JTB's CSR activities is to maintain the beauty of tourist destinations and spread their attractiveness widely amongst new and repeat customers (Vane Online, 2020). For instance, JTB Brighter Earth Project is one of the CSR activities the company has been conducting. The project aims to bring their customers, local residents and JTB Group employees together to carry out diverse activities that can lead to a brighter future for every party (JTB, n.d.). The activities held as part of the project include clean-up activities at tourist destinations, conservation activities for the natural environment of tourist destinations, and awareness-raising activities on local history and culture, making the most of local characteristics (JTB, n.d.). Ultimately, the enterprise aims to bring vitality to the earth and smiles to people through the human and environmental interchange in a sustainable manner (JTB, n.d.). In light of the activities held as JTB Brighter Earth Project and the aim of the project, it is safe to say that these CSR activities also work as JTB's activities for SDGs. Such a close link between activities for CSR and those for SDGs can also be found at other leading tour operators such as the companies belonging to the first category of JATA. In the case of Kinki Nippon Tourist, for example, their CSR section is also in charge of the company's activities for SDGs (KNT-CT Holdings, 2021). Furthermore, activities for CSR and those for SDGs and close links between these two can also be confirmed at some SME-type tour operators or travel agents such as the ones belonging to the second or third category of JATA. This also applies to some members of All Nippon Travel Agents Association (hereafter ANTA) whose members are dominantly the enterprises equivalent to the ones belonging to the second or third category of JATA as ANTA's annual membership fees are cheaper than JATA's. To cite a case, MapTravel based in Fukui Prefecture clearly states on their official website that their CSR activities are also those for SDGs (MapTravel, 2022). Such integration of activities for CSR and those for SDGs is also well confirmed on the official website of Saiyu Travel that is a tour operator belonging to JATA's first category and specialising in arranging tours to relatively unknown regions of the world.

In addition to the aforementioned diverse activities for CSR or SDGs, Japan's tour operators also try to incorporate elements of CSR or SDG, particularly the former, in the tours they arrange. In 2008, JTB and Okinawa Prefecture agreed to start selling tours called 'CSR Tourism' for cooperate clients (Web-Nile, n.d.). More specifically, employees of a company that decides to join CSR Tourism tours take part in cleaning-up activities, educational programmes to enhance their knowledge on natural environment, or other activities beneficial for natural environment (Web-Nile, n.d.). By participating in these activities, CSR Tourism intends to enable joining companies to fulfil their social responsibility and to strengthen the value of the companies in society (Web-Nile, n.d.). By doing so, joining enterprises will be able to make consumers aware of the companies, increase the size of market for their products, enhance the level of their brands' recognition amongst consumers, and motivate their employees (Web-Nile, n.d.). These expected outcomes look great at a glance. In the author's view, nonetheless, these anticipated results seem to focus too much on advantages for the companies rather than those for wider society. If so, it is not sure whether or not these activities should still be understood and accepted as enterprises' 'CSR' activities.

On the other hand, as a whole, tours containing elements of SDGs are more likely to be planned and implemented by tourist destination governments or communities, although it is often more or less led and/or supported by local tour operators or branches of leading tour operators. Nowadays, tours incorporating SDGs elements are available at many tourist destinations across Japan, especially at the destinations whose key attraction factor is the natural heritage that is unique to or prominent in the destinations. A good example of such destinations is Toyama Prefecture. The prefecture is blessed with beautiful and rich natural heritage, including 3000-meter-high Tateyama mountain range, several forests parks, deep snow in winter and Toyama Bay, and these resources also function as important visitor attractions of the prefecture. Seibu Travel, a Toyama-based small-sized tour operator, arranges SDGs tours by working together with their business clients, reflecting companies' views towards SDGs and their practice to contribute to SDGs (Seibu Travel, n.d.). Chichibu-Tama-Kai National Park extends over four prefectures in Kanto region of Japan, namely Saitama, Tokyo, Yamanashi and Nagano. The national park is famous for its mountains, primeval forests and valleys, and a main venue for SDGs tours organised by Tokyo Mountain, a Tokyo-based local tour operator (Tokyo Mountain, 2020). Activities included in their tours are therapeutic walks in forests, cleaning up Tama River, and revitalisation of local *wasabi* fields (Tokyo Mountain, 2020). In the case of Maniwa City in Okayama Prefecture, whilst local government and local communities play a more leading role in planning and implementing local SDGs tours compared to the cases of the above-discussed Toyama Prefecture or Chichibu-Tama-Kai National Park. Maniwa describes itself as 'the city of biomass industry' (Maniwa SDGs Biomass

Tour, 2021). The city fully utilises this uniqueness when they plan their SDGs tours. Specifically, two out of six SDGs tours for educational purposes feature the city's biomass industry. Tour participants, including students, can observe the process of electricity generation by burning wood biomass or the procedure of recycling kitchen rubbish into biomass compost (Maniwa SDGs Biomass Tour, 2021). Here, it should be noted that a relation between activities for SDGs and an element of 3Rs (recycle) is confirmed in a real-world setting.

Under the COVID-19 situation, moreover, SDGs tours have also been developed as online tours, although it should still be somewhat controversial whether or not online tours should be viewed and treated as real travel experiences. HIS, one of Japan's leading tour operators belonging to JATA's first category, has 22 different online SDGs tours as of 20 August 2022 (HIS, n.d.). Although destinations and purposes of these tours are diverse, some of these are directly linked to specific SDGs. For example, HIS teams up with Save the Children and organises an online tour that allows participants to study historical and social backgrounds of poverty and education for young people, relaying scenes from Uganda, Lebanon or Mongolia (HIS, n.d.). These are the countries where Save the Children engages in their mission actively. In light of the contents of the online tour, it could be stated that the tour is directly linked with SDG 1 No Poverty and SDG 4 Quality Education. As for online SDGs tours to domestic destinations, Okinawa Prefecture is the destination of four out of their 22 online SDGs tours. These tours shed a light on diverse aspects of Okinawan nature such as conservation of coral reefs, cleaning up beaches, and growing aloe vera (HIS, n.d.). Online tours have also been employed by other leading tour operators in Japan (e.g. JTB), although a clear connection between online tours and SDGs is usually not confirmed well. Online tours as a whole are regarded as one of excellent opportunities that has been created by a dramatic change (i.e. IT, especially the Internet) in the external environment surrounding the tourism industry, including tourism intermediaries (see Sect. 1). Although it is not sure how effective online tours can be to raise customers' awareness of SDGs or sustainable development overall, at least this can make some contribution to this end under the COVID-19 situation.

4.2 3Rs and *Mottainai* Spirit

The two themes of the previous section (Sect. 4.1), CSR and SDGs are also closely connected with the concept and practice of 3Rs (reduce, reuse, recycle) across diverse business fields. Like CSR or SDGs, for instance, 3Rs can be a main theme of the tours that tourism intermediaries develop and/or sell. Considering examples of such tours planned and conducted in Japan, however, regional or local government oftens plays a leading role in planning and conducting tours that aim to learn about 3Rs. It could also be stated that main targets of 3Rs tours tend to be school children, students or families. Ehime Prefecture has been keen to promote recycling of resources in every field of society. To this end, the prefecture gives a certificate of 'sugo-eco' (meaning 'super eco-friendly') to offices, shops and factories that have been practicing 3Rs continuously in their daily businesses (Ehime Prefecture, 2022). It is not sure whether or not any tour operator is involved in planning and/or conducting Ehime's 3Rs tours. However, it is clear from their relevant web page that the prefecture leads the arrangement and practice of their 3Rs tours, targeting both children and adults. Their 3Rs tours usually visit offices, shops, or factories of the businesses that received the 'sugo-eco' certificate (Ehime Prefecture, 2022). Ehime Prefecture arranges two 3Rs tours in the fiscal year of 2022 by region within the prefecture. One visits the businesses in the Eastern part of the prefecture, whilst the other visits those in the middle part. Places these tours call in include recycling factories for discarded glass bottles or food residues, a biodiesel fuel manufacturing plant, and farms adopting the sharing solar scheme (Ehime Prefecture, 2022).

On the other hand, families are the main target of 3Rs tours held in Fukuoka City during school summer break in 2018 (Fukuoka City, 2018). With regard to planning and implementation of the city's 3Rs tours, the city was supported by a NPO called Happy Ride. The families who took part in the tour engaged in 'eco-cooking' that is a cooking way aiming to minimise the amount of food waste from home cooking (Fukuoka City, 2018). The participants also attended a lecture on food waste issues, how to 'reduce' the amount of food waste, and how to 'reuse' leftovers to cook a different meal (Fukuoka City, 2018). Developing an original 3Rs tour is also used as a learning activity of university students. To cite a case, the aforementioned Nippon Travel Agency made a call for 3Rs tours suggested by university students in Japan. Suggested 3Rs tours should aim to enable families to learn about SDGs (Nippon Travel Agency, 2021). A student group supervised by a professor at Kwansei Gakuin University won the prize and their 3Rs tour to Shiga Prefecture was commoditised as an optional tour that can be added to a package holiday (Nippon Travel Agency, 2021). This case shows that tour operators are still interested in supporting 3Rs activities, even if they do not play a leading role in it. JTB's plans to set their CO2 reduction target by the end of the fiscal year of 2022 through their own activities for 3Rs, namely Responsible Business, Responsible Tourism, and Responsible Value Chains (JTB, 2022; Travel Voice, 2022). JTB's CSR seems to be integrated in their own 3Rs each of which starts with the word, 'responsible'. It is also noteworthy that 'responsible tourism' is one of JTB's 3Rs. Generally, responsible tourism shares the goals same as sustainable tourism and both of them should be understood as approaches or movements rather than (niche) types of tourism. Unlike sustainable tourism that is related to local communities, tourist destinations and tourism industry as a whole, responsible tourism focuses more on actions and responsibilities each stakeholder of tourism takes, and their implications for the future.

These 3Rs activities can be comprehended as embodiment of the *mottainai* spirit. 'Mottainai Kitchen' is a Japanese movie released in 2020. David Gross, an Austrian film director, found the notion of *mottainai* very attractive. He explored Japan with his partner by his food truck, seeing different places where the *mottainai* spirit was practiced and opening *mottainai* kitchens where unused foods were reborn as new dishes. HIS teamed up with key stakeholders of the movie and developed a one-day coach tour that calls in the places appeared in the film (United People, n.d.).

'*Mottainai*' is also employed well as part of destination marketing campaign by tour operators, travel agents, local governments or local destination marketing organisations (hereafter DMOs) in order to encourage visitors to fully explore the destinations. More specifically, tourism intermediaries or agencies want people to visit not only famous visitor attractions or tourist honeypots but also relatively unknown attractions or rather unexplored districts in/around the destinations. If visitors call in more diverse visitor attractions and explore wider areas in/around tourist destinations, they are likely to spend more time and more money there. This implies that a wider community can directly benefit from tourism and economic profits can be distributed in a fairer way. This also signifies that visitor spending per person can be boosted and this can enhance the economic sustainability of the tourist destinations without much sacrificing their socio-cultural or environmental sustainability. That is because, in such cases, negative socio-cultural impacts of tourism (e.g. overtourism in tourist honeypots) or environmental impacts of tourism (e.g. visitors' rubbish) on tourist destinations would be rather limited compared with the advantages in terms of economic sustainability of the places. In fact, following tourist destinations adopt such a destination marketing strategy. First, Nagaoka City (Niigata Prefecture) is very famous for its annual fireworks display (Jimura, 2022), and visitors tend to think that this is the only major attraction in the city and visit the city only the dates of the event (in 2022, 2 and 3 August). On the official website of the fireworks display; hence, Nagaoka City encourages visitors to also visit and enjoy local *sake* breweries and bullfighting (see https://nagaokamatsuri.com/appinfo/582/ in Japanese). Second, people coming to Iwate Prefecture are likely to visit only Morioka City, the capital city of the prefecture. Thus, Morioka City and a local tour operator work together to inspire visitors to Morioka to explore Morioka's neighbouring five towns and two cities, developing a brochure for this purpose (see http://travel-link.jp/wp-content/uploads/2020/10/23057f1fabf7cf33df9236468120a03a.pdf in Japanese). Last but not least, Japanese people are inclined to see Atami City (Shizuoka Prefecture) just as a hot-spring destination. Bearing this in mind, All Nippon Airways try to raise people's awareness of other attraction factors of the city such as a Shinto shrine, a restaurant offering Japanised Western cuisine, and an herb and rose garden (see https://www.ana.co.jp/travelandlife/article/002078/ in Japanese).

5 Conclusion

Traditionally, tourism intermediaries have been playing an important part in the tourism industry as the go-between between service providers on the supply side of tourism and service consumers on the demand side of tourism. Two representative examples of tourism intermediaries are tour operators and travel agents. In principle, the former create and sell tourism products such as package holidays to consumers, whilst the latter only sell these products to customers. Overall, the tourism industry and sectors in the industry are seen as unstable businesses mainly due to fragility against external threats that are beyond the control of the sectors or industry. It is obvious that the most serious crisis for tourism intermediaries since March 2020 has been the COVID-19 pandemic. In addition, another major threat particularly for tourism intermediaries has been direct marketing and selling that emerged and has advanced thanks to the development of the Internet, especially that of Web 2.0 since around 2000. Indeed, this advancement is helpful for tourism intermediaries as they can communicate with both service providers and consumers easily and update the information for their customers quickly. At the same time and probably more importantly, however, the informative and interactive features of Web 2.0 enable service providers and service consumers to communicate each other effortlessly. In other words, service providers could share their information with potential consumers timely, and service consumers can book or purchase products directly from service providers without the assistance of tourism intermediaries. This type of marketing and distribution channel does not require the go-between like tour operators or travel agents and has been increasingly thriving in recent years. This has been threatening for traditional tourism intermediaries and damaging the economic sustainability of these enterprises. Furthermore, the rise and development of online travel agents, especially hotel booking sites such as Rakuten Travel or Jalan in the case of Japan, have also become a major threat for conventional tour operators or travel agents. This situation has been particularly tough for small and medium-sized tourism intermediaries mainly due to their rather weak economic sustainability and limited human resources. It is not a strategy unique to

Japan, however, such SMEs attempt to survive in a challenging and tricky business environment by specialising in a niche market. For example, A&A based in Tokyo is specialised in arranging and conducting tours visiting Thailand.

The above-discussed issue, weakened economic sustainability of tourism intermediaries, is also closely connected with another issue, the decline of socio-cultural sustainability of tourism intermediaries. To put it concretely, nowadays traditional tourism intermediaries do not have much of a presence in the tourism industry of Japan and wider society. Thus, securing a right strategy is crucial for tourism intermediaries, especially small or medium-sized ones. Planning and conducting eco tours is a major way for Japan's tourism intermediaries to contribute to the environmental sustainability of tourist destinations through ecotourism. Not only natural heritage but also cultural heritage that are unique to or prominent in tourist destinations are usually utilised as main themes of such eco tours. Eco tours created and/or carried out by Japan-based tour operators are supported by diverse kinds of stakeholders such as central, regional or local government, NGOs and NPOs. Such NGOs or NPOs include ecotourism societies at different levels (e.g. national and local). As shown in Sect. 3.1, local ecotourism societies work as key players in the development of ecotourism in different tourist destinations.

Activities for CSR and those for SDGs are closely connected in the tourism industry of Japan. This phenomenon is especially distinctive amongst Japan's tourism intermediaries. As the businesses of tourism intermediaries deal with tourist destinations, these enterprises are responsible for the destinations as a whole, including local communities and cultural and natural heritage. Thus, supporting local inhabitants and conserving cultural and natural environments of the destinations can often be one of the purposes of Japanese tourism intermediaries' CSR activities since around 2003. After SDGs were established in 2015, many of tourism intermediaries' CSR activities have started having a nature as those for SDGs. Moreover, some tourism intermediaries have also begun to arrange and sell tours including CSR and/or SDGs elements, and their main customers are companies and students. CSR and SDGs are also well related to the notion and practice of 3Rs. Tours aiming to learn about 3Rs are often planned by regional or local government supported by local tour operators. The main target of 3Rs tours would be students and families, and they learn about the idea and practice of 3Rs usually through a combination of lecture, workshop and/or factory tour. Last but not least, it needs to be noted that activities for 3Rs are understood as embodiment of the *mottainai* spirit. '*Mottainai*' is also utilised well for destination marketing campaign launched by tour operators, travel agents, local governments or local DMOs. Including the term, *mottainai*, in their slogans or names of campaign intends to urge visitors to fully explore the destinations. If the visitors do so, the local DMOs believe that these people really make the most of opportunities they could have on site. Moreover, it is fair to say that such a way to appreciate a tourist destination embodies the spirit of *mottainai*.

References

ECO-Okinawa. (2020). *Top* [in Japanese]. Available at: http://www.ecotourism-okinawa.jp/. Accessed 14 Aug 2022.

Ehime Prefecture. (2022). *Reiwa 4nendo 3R taiken tour no kaisai ni tsuite* (About 3Rs tours in the fiscal year of 2022) [in Japanese]. Available at: https://www.pref.ehime.jp/h15700/4731/ecotour/04bosyu.html. Accessed 21 Aug 2022.

Fukuoka City. (2018). *Natsuyasumi oyako 3R taiken tour wo jisshi shimashita* (3Rs tours for families were held during the summer break) [in Japanese]. Available at: https://www.city.fukuoka.lg.jp/data/open/cnt/3/71112/1/natuyasumioyako3rtua.pdf?20191206155558. Accessed 21 Aug 2022.

GOV.UK. (2022). *Foreign travel advice – Japan*. Available at: https://www.gov.uk/foreign-travel-advice/japan/entry-requirements. Accessed 11 Aug 2022.

HIS. (2022). *An interview with Takamitsu Jimura*. 20 June 2022.

HIS. (n.d.). *SDGs online taiken tour kensaku kekka* (Search results of SDGs online tours) [in Japanese]. Available at: https://www.his-j.com/oe/search/T114/. Accessed 20 Aug 2022.

Holloway, J. C., & Taylor, N. (2006). *The business of tourism* (7th ed.). Harlow: Financial Times Prentice Hall.

Japan Times. (2014). *No substitute for overseas travel*. Available at: https://www.japantimes.co.jp/opinion/2014/01/06/editorials/no-substitute-for-overseas-travel/. Accessed 11 Aug 2022.

JATA. (2022). *Taking on a new era of travel*. Available at: https://www.jata-net. or.jp/wp/wp-content/uploads/press/2022-JATAPROFILE.pdf. Accessed 3 Aug 2022.

Jimura, T. (2011). The websites of Japanese ryokan and eWOM: Their impacts on guests' expectation and experience. *International Journal of Asian Tourism Management, 2*(2), 120–133.

Jimura, T. (2022). Events and intangible cultural heritage. In N. Wise & K. Maguire (Eds.), *A research agenda for event impacts* (pp. 117–128). Edward Elgar.

JTB. (2022). *Interview with Takamitsu Jimura*. 22 June 2022.

JTB. (n.d.). *What is JTB Brighter Earth Project?* Available at: https://www.jtb-corp.jp/jp/csr/clean/. Accessed 18 Aug 2022.

KNT-CT Holdings. (2021). *SDGs eno torikumi hajimemasu* (The company launches activities for SDGs) [in Japanese]. Available at: https://www.knt.co.jp/cb/common/pdf/sdgs.pdf. Accessed 18 Aug 2022.

Lin, S. W. (2016). The critical success factors for a travel application service provider evaluation and selection by travel intermediaries. *Tourism Management, 56*, 126–141.

Maniwa SDGs Biomass Tour. (2021) *Topics: 2021.08.20* [in Japanese]. Available at: http://biomass-tour-maniwa.jp/topics/1710/. Accessed 20 Aug 2022.

MapTravel. (2022). *CSR katsudo* (CSR activities) [in Japanese]. Available at: https://www.maptravel.co.jp/corporate/csr/. Accessed 18 Aug 2022.

NHK. (2022). *Sugata wo kesu ryoko-gaisha: korekara do ikinokorunoka* (The number of tour operator/travel agent branches has been decreasing: how they can survive) [in Japanese]. Available at: https://www.nhk.or.jp/matsuyama/insight/article/20220518-1.html. Accessed 8 Aug 2022.

Nippon Travel Agency. (2021). *SDGs wo kazoku de manabu '3R Trip in Shiga' wo shohinka* (Commoditising '3Rs tour to Shiga' that aims to enable families to learn about SDGs) [in Japanese]. Available at: https://www.nta.co.jp/news/2021/__icsFiles/afieldfile/2021/06/25/3r_trip_in_shiga.pdf. Accessed 21 Aug 2022.

Seibu Travel. (n.d.). *SDGs eno torikumi ni tsuite* (Activities for SDGs) [in Japanese]. Available at: https://www.seibu-travel.co.jp/company/sdgs%E3%81%B8%E3%81%AE%E5%8F%96%E3%82%8A%E7%B5%84%E3%81%BF/. Accessed 20 Aug 2022.

Takenaka, M. (2011). Nihon no kaigai package tours: sono kozai to mirai (Japan's package holidays to overseas countries: their pros, cons, and future) [in Japanese]. *Nihon Kokusai Kankogakkai ronbun-shu, 18*, 123–129.

Tokyo Mountain. (2020). *Tokyo SDGs tours* [in Japanese]. Available at: https://tokyomountain-tours.jp/sdgs/. Accessed 20 Aug 2022.

Travel Voice. (2020). *JTB renketsu-kessan 2019nendo* (JTB's consolidated settlement of accounts for the fiscal year of 2019) [in Japanese]. Available at: https://www.travelvoice.jp/20200529-146290. Accessed 7 Aug 2022.

Travel Voice. (2021). *90% of bankruptcies of travel firms in Japan were affected by COVID-19 for the first seven months of 2021*. Available at: https://www.travelvoice.jp/english/90-of-bankruptcies-of-travel-firms-in-japan-were-affected-by-covid-19-for-the-first-seven-months-of-2021. Accessed 10 Aug 2022.

Travel Voice. (2022). *JTB, 2022nendo ju ni CO2 sakugen-mokuhyo wo settei e* (JTB plans to set their CO2 reduction target by the end of the fiscal year of 2022) [in Japanese]. Available at: https://www.travelvoice.jp/20220126-150534. Accessed 21 Aug 2022.

United People. (n.d.). *Mottainai kitchen and HIS* [in Japanese]. Available at: https://unitedpeople.jp/archives/3499. Accessed 22 Aug 2022.

Vane Online. (2020). *SDGs Kigyo jichitai no torikumi – JTB* (Efforts made by companies and municipalities for SDGs – JTB [in Japanese]. Available at: https://www.vane.online/interview/page01.html. Accessed 18 Aug 2022.

Web-Nile. (n.d.). *JTB ga hojin-muke 'CSR Tourism' wo hatsubai* (JTB decided to start selling tours called 'CSR Tourism' for cooperate clients [in Japanese]. Available at: https://www.web-nile.com/article/article.php?category=CSR&article=000015&page=1. Accessed 19 Aug 2022.

Yen, H. P., Chen, P. C., & Ho, K. C. (2021). Analyzing destination accessibility from the perspective of efficiency among tourism origin countries. *SAGE Open, 11*(2), 21582440211005752.

Part IV

Conclusions

10

Conclusions – Reflections and Futures

1 Revisiting Sustainability Management in Japan's Heritage and Tourism Industries

1.1 Sustainability, Sustainability Management and *Mottainai*

Indeed, the year 1987 is a monumental year for the idea of sustainability and sustainable development, because Our Common Future (also known as the Brundtland Report), a key publication for these themes, was published in October 1987 by the United Nations (hereafter UN). Overall, however, sustainability or sustainable development does not seem to have been well integrated into the theory and practice of the management of organisations or enterprises in the heritage or tourism industry of Japan until around the end of the 1990s. One of the reasons for this was lack of clarity and concreteness in themes and objectives (See Sect. 2.2 in Chap. 1). Around ten years after, however, sustainability or sustainable development started to have become embedded in the theory and practice of the management of Japan's heritage and/or tourism businesses. It is the time when following Millennium Development Goals (hereafter MDGs) were established as a result of the UN's Millennium Summit in 2000:

1. To eradicate extreme poverty and hunger.
2. To achieve universal primary education.
3. To promote gender equality and empower women.
4. To reduce child mortality.
5. To improve maternal health.
6. To combat HIV/AIDS, malaria, and other diseases.
7. To ensure environmental sustainability.
8. To develop a global partnership for development.

Moreover, an increasing number of Japan-based organisations or companies engaging in heritage and/or tourism businesses have begun to reflect the concept of sustainability or sustainable development on the practice of their activities and businesses since around 2016. In light of relevant discussions in preceding chapters, it is fair to say that the UN's Sustainable Development Goals (hereafter SDGs), the successor of MDGs, adopted in 2015 have been working as a key catalyst for this trend/movement (see Table 1.1 in Chap. 1).

In everyday businesses of organisations or enterprises in Japan's heritage or tourism sector, sustainability of themselves and their activities can be checked and evaluated through different aspects of sustainability. Amongst these, three pillars of sustainability or sustainable development, namely economic, socio-cultural and environmental sustainability, are particularly important and can be associated with daily activities of most parties or cooperations across the globe, including Japan. Needless to say, these organisations and businesses in the heritage or tourism industry in Japan are not an exception. Since around 2016, Japan's heritage and tourism industries really started working to enhance the level of sustainability of their surrounding environments and external stakeholders as well as themselves and their activities by integrating the concept of sustainability into their vision and by practicing the notion of sustainability management in their daily activities. In relation to this, internationally well-recognised and widely adopted SDGs function as a trigger to encourage organisations or enterprises to work on sustainability management of their activities.

As can be suggested above, Japan and its heritage or tourism industry may not have been regarded as a forerunner or leading figure in sustainability management. In reality, however, an important notion and practice, sharing similar goals to sustainability, has been handed down from generation to generation in Japan. This key concept and practice is called *mottainai* in Japanese. The notion is originated in Japan and unique to the country, and its spirit has been inherited amongst Japanese people for a long time through many different ways. For instance, the author learned about this concept as an attitude towards people and surrounding environments from his grandmother and as a key principle to follow as a human being at a moral education class at his primary school. Nonetheless, the notion of *mottainai* has not been well-known amongst people outside Japan until Professor Wangari Maathai, a Kenyan environmental activist and the first African woman to win the Nobel Prize, introduced this concept to international audience in 2005. She encountered the *mottainai* concept and was deeply impressed by it during her visit to Japan in 2005. Since then she referred to the idea during her speeches at various international events. The value and magnitude of the *mottainai* spirit have also been re-appraised in the heritage or tourism sector of Japan in the past 15–20 years. Regarding this, more are discussed in the subsequent section (Sect. 1.2).

1.2 Heritage and Tourism Industries and Mottainai Spirit

This book suggests that Japan has two major groups of heritage, namely cultural heritage and natural heritage like many other countries do (see Chaps. 2, 3 and 4 in Part II of the book). Moreover, the former can be sub-divided into two sub-categories called tangible cultural heritage (see Chap. 2) and intangible cultural heritage (see Chap. 3). The above-mentioned spirit of *mottainai* has been practiced in Japan's heritage industry for a long time well before the *mottainai* spirit becomes famous all over the world and/or the value of such heritage is recognised by international organisations (e.g. the United Nations Educational, Scientific and Cultural Organization (hereafter UNESCO)). As for tangible cultural heritage, to cite a case, basically original structures and materials are adopted as much as possible when historic buildings of Japan, especially Shinto shrines and Japanese Buddhist temples, are restored. To this end, not only original structures and materials but also knowledge on how to use them for repairments is equally imperative. Such know-how is seen as conservation techniques for cultural heritage and is valued domestically and internationally chiefly through the listing systems such as Selected Conservation Techniques (*Sentei Hozongijutsu*) and Intangible Cultural Heritage (hereafter ICH) (one of UNESCO's conservation schemes for cultural heritage) respectively. Concerning the listing at international level, more specifically, the aforementioned conservation techniques were designated as ICH by UNESCO and the official name of the ICH is 'Traditional skills, techniques and knowledge for the conservation and transmission of wooden architecture in Japan'. As the official name implies, listed conservation techniques are for the maintenance or repairment of wooden architecture. Experts who are specialised in the conservation of large-sized wooden architecture are called *miyadaiku* in Japanese. Examples of the maintenance/restoration works conducted by *miyadaiku* can be confirmed in Shinto shrines and Japanese Buddhist temples in many municipalities in Japan, especially those in and around the Kansai region. For example, *miyadaiku* from the Kaneyasu Building were in charge of the repairment of wooden pillars of a signboard located in Kasuga Shrine in Sakurai City (Nara Prefecture), using the *kanawatsugi*, one of traditional joint techniques for wooden structures (Kaneyasu Building, 2021). On the other hand, *miyadaiku* of Imasa Kensetsu conducted repair work of the main hall (*hondo*) of Yamanaka Fudo Temple in Kakamigahara City (Gifu Prefecture), considering the safety of worshippers and visitors (Imasa Kensetsu, 2020).

In addition, practice of the *mottainai* spirit can also be confirmed at places with natural heritage. Like many overseas countries like the USA or the UK, Japan's most popular type of tourist destinations with natural heritage are its National Parks, Quasi-National Parks and Prefectural Natural Parks (see Sect. 1 of Chap. 4). Activities embodied the spirit of *mottainai* can be found there. For instance, Oze National Park extends over four prefectures, namely Fukushima, Tochigi, Gunma and Niigata, in the Honshu Island of Japan. Around 65 km boardwalk is placed to protect its natural environment, especially wetland, and ensure safety for hikers. The boardwalk lasts for only around ten years and around 2 km of it has been replaced with a new one every year (Sanjo Insatsu, n.d.). To make the most of discarded old boardwalk, it has been recycled as Oze Boardwalk Paper (Sanjo Insatsu, n.d.). This project represents the *mottainai* spirit of Oze National Park itself and Sanjo Insatsu, a Niigata-based printing company, which has been leading the project since 2005.

Tourism industry comprises many different sectors and they are inter-related and interdependent each other (Lubbe, 2003). Amongst these, this book looks at five sectors, namely transport, accommodation, food and beverage, visitor attractions and events, and tourism intermediaries (see Chaps. 5, 6, 7, 8 and 9 in Part III of the book). It should be noted that heritage and tourism industries are closely associated and heritage has been serving as key attraction factors in tourism settings. With regard to this, use of cultural or natural heritage in the context of visitor attractions/events or food and beverage can be understood as the most founded relations in heritage and tourism. In reality, for instance, all of historic buildings (tangible cultural heritage), local foods (intangible cultural heritage) and mountains (natural heritage) have been functioning as visitor attractions or events all over the world, including Japan. Regarding accommodation, some historic structures of Japanese-style inns or Western-style hotels in Japan are also formally recognised as its cultural heritage by the national, regional or local government. Concerning transport, basically a steam-locomotive train (hereafter SL) has finished its role as a passenger train in Japan like many other nations of the world. Nevertheless, there are still a large number of adults who are keen fans of SLs. Moreover, SLs are also very attractive for kids, especially boys, partly thanks to a British children's television series, Thomas & Friends. Thus, some passenger train companies of Japan (e.g. Tobu Railway) arrange special or seasonal train services (e.g. SL Taiju), using SLs, mainly at weekends or holiday seasons. Figure 10.1 shows Tobu Railways' SL Taiju that runs between Nikko and Kinugawa areas both of which are established tourist destinations in Tochigi Prefecture (Tobu Railway, n.d.). As confirmed from the above, there is a solid association between Japan's heritage and four out of five main sectors in the tourism industry examined in this book. Compared to these four, there is a limited relation

Fig. 10.1 SL Taiju departing from Kinugawa-Onsen station. (Source: Author)

between Japan's heritage and tourism intermediaries. Nonetheless, the rise of tour operators and travel agents specialised in inbound travels may indirectly indicate that these tourism intermediaries are expected to be familiar with and then build or strengthen the level of their engagement in a wide range of Japan's cultural and natural heritage. For instance, Tokyo Asian Service (or TAS) based in Tokyo Metropolitan Prefecture and Asia Sales Agency (or ASA) based in Fukuoka Prefecture can be seen as representative examples of such inbound-specialised tourism intermediaries in Japan.

Of the business and service fields of the aforementioned five sectors in the tourism industry, personally the author has been experiencing the concept and practice of *mottainai* most regarding 'food and beverage' through eating at home and dining out. The author's grandparents, especially grandmother, hammered the notion of *mottainai* into him when he was a child and lived with them. She also encouraged, or almost enforced, the author to practice the *mottainai* spirit in his everyday life. At that time, the author was annoyed by her approach and could not understand at all why she was so keen to enable him to absorb the *mottainai* concept, particularly the spirit associated with food and drink. The author's grandparents already passed away and more than 40 years have passed since the author learned the idea of *mottainai* from his grandparents. Now, the author could understand their passion for *mottainai*. When the grandparents were young, Japan was not a developed country. Moreover, both of them experienced World War II, more precisely the Pacific War, in their youth. In those days, their daily lives were filled with challenges and sorrow. Their families were also struggling with securing their safety and foods and drinks. Such harsh reality of wartime life they had to have when they were young should be a basis of their, especially the author's grandmother's strong belief in the *mottainai* spirit. I was strongly advised to avoid leftovers at home or a restaurant, even a grain of rice.

In relation to the scope of this book, leftovers are one of the main issues in the sustainability management of food and drink businesses, especially the management of the environmental sustainability of their businesses. The issue also affects the sustainability management of other tourism-related businesses such as accommodation. As for leftovers at a restaurant, asking a doggy bag to take it away reflects the idea of *mottainai* and would still be the most common practice to tackle the problem in the environmental sustainability of Japan's food and drink sector and its customers. Allowing customers to take their leftovers away can be advantageous for restaurants in terms of the economic sustainability of their businesses as it can cut their food waste disposal costs. According to the author's observation and experience, however, bringing leftovers to home with a doggy bag does not seem to have been adopted widely by either customers or restaurants in Japan. In the author's opinion, there are mainly three reasons. First, a restaurant may take a certain level of responsibility if their customers feel unwell after leftovers from the restaurant. Although there are no laws that prohibit restaurants from allowing their customers to take leftovers away, the socio-cultural sustainability of restaurants' businesses can be potentially endangered if the aforementioned problem happens. Indeed, the philosophy of *mottainai* is invaluable in its own right and crucial for the sustainability management of tourism-related businesses. Nevertheless, it is meaningless, especially in terms of socio-cultural (and economic) sustainability, if customers become ill and/or restaurants take a legal responsibility for compensation. Second, customers may judge the quality of foods and/or drinks based on leftovers if they do not eat or drink a lot at a restaurant. This can influence prospective customers negatively mainly through the spread of e-word-of-mouth such as reviews on various websites (*kuchikomi*) (Jimura, 2022). Third, allowing customers to bring their leftovers to home may damage brand image or reputation of restaurants or accommodation facilities. This can be a major concern for high-end restaurants, including Michelin-Starred ones, and restaurants in luxurious hotels such as five-star hotels. Even if these restaurants and hotels are happy to allow leftovers to be taken away, other customers or the general public of Japan may find such a practice shabby or unsightly and is not appropriate for lavish establishments. In such a case, these service providers would need to seek a balance between promotion of their activities realising the *mottainai* spirit and maintenance of their brand images or reputations.

Regarding accommodation facilities, room cleaning is another area deeply related with the *mottainai* spirit. Jumping on the bandwagon, Japan's accommodation sector has worked actively on environmental sustainability of their businesses and surrounding environments. As can be imagined, such efforts often mean practicing the *mottainai* spirit in the context of accommodation sector. Specifically, an increasing number of accommodation facilities, typically Western-style hotels whose guests may stay two or more nights, allow some options for room cleaning such as full cleaning, changing towels and amenities only or nothing at all (totally 'do not disturb'). If some guests choose the second or the third option, hotels can save the amount of water for washing.

In this book, the word, visitor attractions, are used to indicate tangible tourism resources, whilst the term, events, are used to show intangible tourism resources. Nonetheless, it is commonly important for both that they feature cultural heritage that is unique to or prominent in a certain locality such as a village/town/city, geographical region or even a country as a whole. Here, as discussed earlier, the integration of heritage and tourism can be confirmed clearly in visitor attractions and events. Therefore, the *mottainai* spirit must be incorporated in the conservation policy for visitor attractions or events with specific heritage. Furthermore the spirit

10 Conclusions – Reflections and Futures

needs to be reflected in the everyday management of visitor attractions or events to maintain their socio-cultural sustainability. It is also true that the economic sustainability of visitor attractions and events, featuring certain heritage, must be retained. Otherwise, these establishments will not be able to survive in the future due to lack of financial resources. This is particularly significant for those owned and/or managed by private organisations that do not rely on the assistance from the public fundings. For visitor attractions, particularly gigantic ones such as theme parks, the management of environmental sustainability as well as that of economic sustainability are crucial. Basically, theme parks in Japan are managed by enterprises, and unfortunately the vast majority of them have been short-lived (Jimura, 2022). A key reason of this problem is that these theme parks were failed to keep attracting a large enough number of visitors constantly for a long time. The most serious issue comes after the closure of theme parks is often how to deal with the extensive spaces and abandoned facilities. Unused facilities of former theme parks or mega-event spaces (e.g. Olympics) are called 'white elephants'. These facilities can negatively affect both environmental and economic sustainability of enterprises or organisations owning or managing them. Stated differently, the *mottainai* spirit is not embodied in such a condition.

Concerning the transport sector, overall the environmental sustainability of their facilities and services has been improved through the advancement in technology such as renewable energy and eco-friendly vehicles. Of these, the former well represents the essence of *mottainai* spirit. Representative examples of renewable energy are as follows:

* Solar energy,
* Wind energy,
* Geothermal energy,
* Hydropower,
* Ocean energy, and
* Bioenergy (Biomass energy) (UN, n.d.)

Amongst these, for example, solar energy and bioenergy have a potential to be alternative energy for local busses. In fact, Seibu Bus, operating local regular bus services in Tokyo Metropolitan Prefecture and Saitama

Prefecture, started their bus operations, using biodiesel, in September 2020 (Seibu Bus, n.d.). In addition, the bus company has also been operating hydrogen fuel cell busses since December 2020. Like its relations with heritage, Japan's tourism intermediaries' association with the mottainai spirit is also relatively limited. For example, however, the case that HIS, Japan's large tourism intermediary, worked together with Mottainai Kitchen, a Japanese movie by an Austrian director, to organise and conduct a one-day coach tour exploring filmed locations, may have made some contribution to the spread and penetration of the spirit in the general public of Japan (see Sect. 4.2 of Chap. 9).

This section sheds light on Japan's heritage and tourism sectors and interrelationships between these two. It also reviews how the spirit of *mottainai* is considered and practiced in the activities or businesses of main players in these sectors. The following section revisit other key notions for the book, namely business ethics, corporate social responsibility (hereafter CSR), 3Rs (reduce, reuse and recycle), considering their connections with sustainability management, SDGs (Sect. 1.1) and the idea of *mottainai* (Sect. 1.2).

1.3 Theory and Practice of Sustainability in Heritage and Tourism Industries

Sections 4 and 5 of Chap. 1 discuss theory and practice of sustainability, referring to those across the world (Sect. 4) and then those in Japan (Sect. 5). In each of these chapters, the first notion examined is ethics, especially business ethics. That is because, organisations and companies involved in the heritage or tourism industry, particularly the latter, usually conduct their activities as businesses (see Sect. 4 of Chap. 1). In light of discussions in the above-mentioned two sections, it could be stated that ethics is the notion associated with 'morally' right or wrong, or acceptable or unacceptable. Thus, this contains an element of evaluation or judgement. To this end, a certain or series of standard needs to be developed. This is especially true to the business environment where various agencies and enterprises with diverse aspirations or concerns communicate and influence each other. Business ethics is expected to play a key role in preventing the occurrence of morally wrong or unacceptable behaviours or actions caused by organisations or individuals. As shown in Sect. 5.1 of Chap. 1, business ethics is called *kigyo rinri* in Japan. Typically and traditionally, it has been seen that collectivism is a dominant principle in Japanese society. In fact, however, the rise of individualism can be confirmed throughout the society in the past 20–30 years. In the author's view, main features of Japan's collectivism is passive attitudes towards something new; tacit request, acceptance or pressure; and expectation to read between the lines. In general, it is also true that doing or saying nothing tends to be viewed more preferably than doing or saying wrong. For these reasons, people, organisations or companies in almost all industries, including heritage and tourism, are inclined to be passive when they newly begin to do something related to sustainability or sustainability management of their businesses as they can be blamed easily. Therefore, it would be natural that actions for securing business ethics have been often led by companies with innovative or progressive nature or established enterprises/organisations followed by many others. In the heritage industry, Shinto shrines or Japanese Buddhist temples led by relatively young leaders tend to have such a progressive character. In the tourism industry, family-owned companies are likely to be open to adopt a new approach with rather limited forces of resistance. As demonstrated in Sect. 5.1 of Chap. 1, examples of ethical actions/behaviours employed in the heritage or tourism industry includes the manifestation of company's personal information protection policy and presentation of nutrition facts. Although part of these are required by relevant Japanese laws, many are doing more to implement their businesses in an ethical manner. Moreover, it is fair to say that the aforementioned examples of actions can contribute to SDGs 12 Responsible Consumption and Production and 17 Partnerships for the Goals. Furthermore, the presentation of nutrition facts, including allergens, can be useful to practice the *mottainai* spirit as it enables customers to avoid buying the products they do not or cannot consume.

As for SDGs, it has become clear that nowadays CSR activities conducted in Japan's heritage or tourism industry often includes their activities for SDGs. Soon after the concept of CSR was really put into practice in 2003. Enterprises' CSR activities did not seem to have focus heavily on matters in sustainability or sustainability management, although MDGs having eight goals and 18 targets for 2015 were already established by that time because of the UN's Millennium Summit in 2000. Since 17 SDGs were set up in 2015, however, CSR activities of a much larger number of heritage/tourism businesses, particularly the latter, have become focused much more on those for sustainability, especially environmental sustainability, of human society and natural environment. To this end, sustainability management of their businesses themselves has been increasingly significant for organisations/enterprises in Japan generally, including those in heritage or tourism.

According to Kyo no Rekishi Navi (2022), good examples of approaches adopted by heritage organisation and tourism business can be found around Kiyomizu-dera Temple in Kyoto City. Kiyomizu-dera Temple is an established visitor attraction located in the east of the city and one of the 17 elements forming a cultural World Heritage sites called Historic Monuments of Ancient Kyoto (Kyoto, Uji and Otsu Cities). An example of CSR/SDGs activity implemented in the heritage industry is the work conducted by Shinpuku-ji Temple and a local private technical college called TASK. TASK is a technical college where students can learn knowledge on and skills for Japan's traditional crafts. Their students made a wooden statue of Dainichi Buddha, using a pine tree fallen by tsunami caused by Great East Japan Earthquake, and dedicated it to the temple (Kyo no Rekishi Navi, 2022). This example also includes all of 3Rs elements. This approach could 'reduce' the amount of wasted pine trees in Takata-Matsubara (Rikuzen-Takata City, Iwate Prefecture), one of the areas designated as Places of Scenic Beauty (*Meisho*) by Japanese Government. This measure also 'reused' the fallen pine tree and allowed it to be 'recycled' as cultural heritage and visitor attraction. On the other hand, an example of CSR/SDGs activity carried out in the tourism industry is the plan conducted by the Hotel Seiryu Kyoto Kiyomizu. The hotel uses the buildings of Kiyomizu Primary School that was closed in 2011. The location, interior and exterior of the primary school were highly valued; hence, it was contradictory to the spirit of *mottainai* if the school buildings were demolished. Bearing this in mind, Kyoto City was seeking the best way to make the most of the school site, inviting great plans from a wide range of private businesses. Consequently, the school buildings had been converted into the hotel that was opened in 2020. This idea could 'reduce' the volume of construction waste. As a result, the buildings of the primary school was 'reused' as a luxurious hotel. This can be seen as a successful example of conversion, although it cannot be viewed as a case of 'recycling'.

2 New Themes Emerged

2.1 SDGs and Relevant Concepts Now Everywhere in Japan

Section 2.1 explores how the concept of SDGs and the notions relevant to SDGs have become ubiquitous in Japan, shedding light on their historical aspects and development. Several important ideas related to SDGs, including key notions for this book such as sustainability and *mottainai*, have been discussed throughout the book. First, as examined in Chap. 1 and this chapter, *mottainai* is a long-standing concept in Japan, although it had not been exported to all over the world until 2005 when Professor Wangari Maathai encountered the notion during her stay in Japan. The author moved to the UK in August 2002 and enrolled on the Master's programme called MSc Tourism, Conservation and Sustainable Development offered by the University of Greenwich. At that time, the terms/concepts of 'sustainability' (*jizokukanousei* in Japanese) and 'sustainable development' (*jizokukanouna kaihatsu* in Japanese) neither spread much across Japanese society nor permeated into the general public of Japan, although MDGs for the year 2015 were already set up in 2000 by UN.

In contrast, spreading and penetration of the notion, CSR, occurred much earlier than those of sustainability and/or sustainable development in the case of Japan. As stated in Sect. 1.3, generally the year 2003 is viewed as the time when a number of enterprises in Japan, including those engaging in tourism-related businesses, started practicing CSR activities. CSR activities in Japan have begun to develop gradually since 2003 together with concepts and approaches connected with CSR. A representative example of such a notion and approach is 'environmental, social, and (corporate) governance' (hereafter ESG). These two are interrelated but are different each other. For instance, CSR is a notion that intends to contribute to wider society as a member of the society, whilst ESG is an idea that aims to maximise a company's value for investors and shareholders. The other example of the concepts that have been intimately working together with CSR is the Global Reporting Initiative (hereafter GRI). GRI is an independent organisation that sets up international benchmarks. Their benchmarks support private and public organisations to comprehend their activities' impacts on key agenda in the triple bottom line (economic, socio-cultural and environmental (hereafter TBL)) of sustainability. GRI launched the first version of GRI guidelines in 2000. The guidelines have been updated three times in 2002, 2006 and 2013, covering wider kinds of industries or businesses (ICDJ, 2022). In 2016, GRI guidelines were replaced with GRI standards, and the standards have been updated in 2021 as their second version (ICDJ, 2022). As the names imply, a main difference between GRI guidelines and GRI standards is that the former serve like recommendations without obligations, whilst the latter work as obligations rather than recommendations (ICDJ, 2022).

Another key notion associated with SDGs is 3Rs (reduce, reuse, recycle). It is not totally clear when and how this notion emerged. However, the origin of 3Rs can be traced back to the 1970s of the USA. This was during the late stage of the Vietnam War when American people thought that air pollution, waste, and water quality need to be improved (Pantheon Enterprises, 2014). The US Congress passed the Resource Conservation and Recovery Act in 1976, aiming to increase recycling and conservation efforts to tackle a waste problem that had become serious, and it can be stated that the concept of 3Rs was born at this time (Pantheon Enterprises, 2014). Since then, the concept started spreading in the USA followed by Canada. For example, the idea of 3Rs appeared in the state law of the State of Oregon in the 1980s, and in the city policy of Toronto City, Canada in 1990 (Ideas for Good, n.d.). In Japan, on the other hand, the concept of 3Rs was embedded in Basic Act on Establishing a Sound Material-Cycle Society (*Junkangata Shakaikeisei Suishin Kihon-ho*) that was promulgated in 2000 (Ideas for Good, n.d.). Four years later, Japan's Prime Minister Junichiro Koizumi proposed '3R Initiatve' at the G8

10 Conclusions – Reflections and Futures

Summit held in Sea Island, Georgia, USA in June 2004 (Ministry of the Environment (hereafter MOE), n.d.). The initiative aimed to build a circulation-type society through the practice of 3Rs and got the support of leaders of other G8 nations (MOE, n.d.).

As can be confirmed from the arguments above, all of the concepts related to sustainability, sustainable development or sustainable management that are discussed in this book are relatively new for Japanese society, organisations, companies and people. It is also applied to the heritage and tourism industries of Japan. The only exception is the spirit of *mottainai* that has been inherited from ancestors of Japanese persons to current generations. Stated differently, the level of diffusion and penetration of the notion of sustainability and sustainable development had been immature and its practice had also been ad hoc until SDGs were established and imported to Japan in 2015. In addition, it is also safe to say that sustainable management of organisations' and enterprises' activities have not been focused enough by themselves and have not been paid enough attention from the general public of Japan before the emergence of SDGs. Regarding Japan, however, this situation seems to have changed dramatically thanks to SDGs. 17 SDGs consist of simple and clearly written targets that address diverse and interrelated issues vital for sustainability of life on earth and earth itself. It is also noteworthy that these SDGs have been made available in many different languages, and each SDG has a logo unique to each. Furthermore, UN, UNESCO and many other organisations and businesses prepared a diverse kinds of learning materials for ordinary people, especially students and children. In the author's view, all of these efforts have made SDGs much more approachable and interesting for people across the world than other concepts related to sustainability or sustainable development. This would be particularly true in the Japanese context, including its heritage and tourism industries. In other words, SDGs has been working as a breakthrough for the diffusion and penetration of sustainability and sustainable development in Japanese society.

The pace of diffusion and penetration of the idea of sustainability and sustainable development in Japanese society, including heritage and tourism arenas, seems to have been accelerating in the past two or three years (i.e. since around 2020). As far as the author is aware, there have been no specific reasons supported by the vast majority of scholars or practitioners in relevant fields. In the author's opinion, nonetheless, there would be at least two factors that can be regarded as main reasons. One is Tokyo 2020 that was extended to 2021. The sustainability of the Games, particularly the sustainability of the Games' venues, has been a key concern of the general public of Japan as well as key stakeholders of the Games (Okada & Greyser, 2018; Jimura, 2020). Thus, economic, socio-cultural and environmental sustainability of the Games may have raised Japanese people's awareness of sustainability of such a mega event that can be understood as both cultural heritage of Japan and a powerful visitor attraction of the country. The other factor is the COVID-19 pandemic emerged in early 2020. The pandemic has been affecting economic, socio-cultural and environmental sustainability of heritage and tourism industries of Japan often negatively but sometimes positively. Its impacts have been extensive enough to increase the level of people's interest in the sustainability of organisations and businesses in heritage and/or tourism industries. The issues associated with COVID-19 are discussed in detail in the subsequent sub-section (Sect. 2.2). Nowadays, consequently, the concept and practice of sustainability and/or sustainable development have also been embodied by businesses closely associated with heritage or tourism, or even by municipalities as a whole, often indicating relevant SDGs. For instance, Fig. 10.2 shows three kinds of plastic or paper shopping bag sold at a shop of Kasho Sanzen, a Japanese confectionery company. The company donates part of the income raised through the sale of bags for environmental preservation activities. Figure 10.2 also signifies that Kasho Sanzen believes that their businesses and activities can contribute to four out of 17 SDGs, namely 12 Responsible Consumption and Production, 13 Climate Action, 14 Life below Water, and 15 Life on Land. In 2020, Akashi City (Hyogo Prefecture) was selected by the Cabinet Office of the Japanese Government as the city that plans to conduct excellent activities to achieve SDGs (it is called 'SDGs Future City') (Akashi City, 2020). Figure 10.3 exhibits a SDGs logo with the name of the city on the surface of the pavement near the Akashi railway station. This implies that the city is very proud of being selected as a SDGs Future City and quite eager to carry out activities for SDGs.

10 Conclusions – Reflections and Futures

Fig. 10.2 Plastic or paper shopping bag sold at a shop of Kasho Sanzen. (Source: Author)

Today, SDGs can be found everywhere in Japan. For instance, a slogan including 'SDGs' can be found even at a nursery in Tokyo Metropolitan Prefecture (hereafter TMP) (see Fig. 10.4). In fact, it is difficult to find official websites of large companies or organisations in tourism industries that do not address relations between their activities, often CSR activities, and SDGs. In fact, such relations can be confirmed at official websites of Japan Airlines, JR West (railway), Imperial Hotel, Mos Food Services (fast-food restaurant chain), OLC Group (theme park), and JTB (tour operator/travel agent). In addition, relations between cultural/natural heritage and SDGs can also be found on the heritage sites' official websites and other relevant media'. Different from tourism-related businesses, heritage organisations' activities for SDGs are usually planned and conducted by working together with their partners in the public and/or private sectors. For instance, organisations with cultural heritage (e.g.

Fig. 10.3 Akashi City's logo for being selected as a SDGs Future City. (Source: Author)

Fig. 10.4 Slogan including SDGs at a nursery in TMP. (Source: Author)

specific Japanese Buddhist temples in Kyoto City or Nara City) or those with natural heritage (e.g. Yakushima Island) often team up with a local government, local tour operator, or relevant non-profit or non-governmental organisation to plan and implement their activities for SDGs. Moreover, these activities for SDGs tend to be presented at websites of local government (e.g. Kyoto City, Hiroshima City) rather than those of owners/managers of heritage. As a whole, it could be stated that SDGs are now well-known to not only stakeholders of heritage or tourism industry but also ordinary people residing in Japan. Nevertheless, the author has a concern that sometimes 'SDGs' appears to be used just as a 'buzzword' without considering what they really mean or what they can do in the context of organisations' or companies' activities. For example, some organisations/enterprises in heritage or tourism industry just include the term, SDGs, on their websites without explaining what kinds of activities they are doing or which SDGs their activities are linked with. In such a case, the word, SDGs, seems to be used with other 'positive' term such as 'CSR' or '3Rs' to improve the image of companies or organisations.

2.2 The Impacts of COVID-19 Pandemic

The COVID-19 pandemic is the phenomenon that cannot be ignored when writing up this book as it has influenced every sector in heritage or tourism industry all over the world, including Japan. Amongst TBL of sustainability, overall the pandemic has affected the economic sustainability of Japan's heritage and tourism-related organisations and their activities and businesses in a negative manner. Especially, the latter, Japan's tourism industry, have suffered from devastating economic impacts of the COVID-19 pandemic. Travelling between different regions or even prefectures was discouraged by the central or regional government. This has negatively influenced the business performance of not only transport companies but also hoteliers, restaurants, visitor attractions/events, and tourism intermediaries. Eateries were also asked to temporarily close their business, shorten their business hours, or not to serve alcohol by local government. Some kinds of financial support have been available for affected individuals and businesses, although many have closed their businesses or went into administration. Since Japan's inbound tourism boom has flourished in 2014, an increasing number of tourism-related businesses, particularly part of accommodation or food and drink businesses, started relying too heavily on inbound tourists. Moreover, more and more people and enterprises entered Japan's inbound tourism market, launching new businesses and targeting at inbound tourists, especially those from Asia, Europe and North America. Since the outbreak of the COVID-19 in early 2020; however, Japan had closed its borders to foreign tourists for more than two years until reopening of its borders in October 2022 (BBC News, 2022). Thus, many tourism-related businesses, focusing too much on inbound tourism, could not survive the highly challenging business environment caused by the pandemic. Basically, the economic sustainability of organisations owning and/or managing cultural and/or natural heritage has also been negatively affected by the COVID-19 pandemic as the income raised through tourism activities such as admission fees often plays an important role in sustaining their financial status.

Unlike inbound tourism to Japan, outbound tourism from Japan was not completely banned by the Japanese Government. However, the number of outbound Japanese tourists has also dropped significantly due to various factors that could discourage people in Japan to go abroad. These factors include a compulsory PCR test within 72 hours before Japanese tourists' returning flights to Japan, and a negative result from the PCR test. During the peak periods of the COVID-19 pandemic, moreover, Japanese tourists needed to be in self-isolation for several days (often three to seven days) on their arrival at a foreign country and/or their return to Japan. Furthermore, what Japanese tourists could enjoy in a destination country tended to be highly limited as a number of visitor attractions, shops and restaurants were closed. This situation has changed Japanese people's travel patterns or preferences, and some of the altered patterns or preferences may continue even after the end of the pandemic. In other words, people in Japan has paid more attention to domestic tourism, especially visits to nearby destinations with day trips or trips with one or two nights, compared with the pre-COVID-19 time. By doing so, many persons in Japan seem to have discovered or rediscovered the attractiveness of close destinations that were likely to be overlooked by them prior to the pandemic. Such a movement could be advantageous to strengthen the socio-cultural sustainability of regions or local areas of Japan, because the significance of their cultural or natural heritage can be found or even valued by not only local residents but also much larger number of people coming from various places in Japan. This trend has been further encouraged by the schemes developed and adopted by the Japanese or regional government such as 'Go to Travel', 'Zenkoku Ryoko-shien' and 'Kenmin-wari'.

It should also be noted that there is a recent phenomenon associated with the socio-cultural sustainability of 'tourism', the rise and development of online tours. Hori et al. (2022) argue that an 'online tour' is a tour that uses a web conference system as a place where guests meet hosts and they can communicate each other in real time. According to them, Japan has three kinds of online tour platforms as follows:

1. Video streaming sites, such as YouTube,
2. Web conferencing applications, such as Zoom, and
3. Original websites.

In most definitions of tourism, '(physical) movement of people to places outside their usual environment' is one of the requirements to be seen as tourism. Needless to say, however, an online tour does not include this element. Hence, there should be various or even conflicting views amongst scholars regarding whether or not an online tour should be accepted as a new type of tourism, although Hori et al. (2022) regard an online tour as a close substitute for a group tour. As stated above, however, it can be stated that an online tour has been effective to maintain the socio-cultural sustainability of tourism, because at least the online tour has given people in Japan an additional choice or new option to see and experience something extraordinary for them.

Decreased or suspended business activities, including international and domestic movements of people, has made a positive contribution to the environmental sustainability of natural heritage across the world and the whole of the earth. For example, Japan's National Greenhouse Gas Emissions in the fiscal year of 2020 (April 2020 to March 2021) decreased from those in the fiscal year of 2019. This was caused by the reduced energy consumption because of decreased production in manufacturing industries and decrease in the amount of passenger and freight traffic, resulting from the spread of the COVID-19 pandemic (MOE, 2022). Ironically, it has been reported from all over the world that natural heritage (e.g. forests, rivers, lakes) of/near popular nature-based tourist destinations have been recovering naturally thanks to the absence of excursionists or tourists. In other words, the COVID-19 pandemic has contributed to the enhancement of the environmental sustainability of natural heritage. Nonetheless, it should be remembered that the amount of money that can be spent for conservation activities of natural heritage has decreased a lot due to the pandemic. Thus, the environmental sustainability of natural heritage may start weakening in the near future if the number of visitors appreciating natural heritage has not recovered. For organisations responsible for certain cultural heritage, especially tangible one, a decrease in tourism income can be a much more serious issue for their environmental sustainability because cultural heritage cannot recover from vandalism or wear and tear naturally. On the other hand, it is also true that many organisations in charge of conservation of specific cultural heritage could secure a certain amount of time, generally much longer than usual, for repairment works under the COVID-19 circumstance due to extended closure time. Therefore, relatively large renovation works could be carried out during the COVID-19 period if their budgets permit.

In summary, the COVID-19 pandemic have functioned as a catastrophe for the economic sustainability of heritage and tourism industries, particularly for the latter. As for the socio-cultural sustainability of heritage and tourism industries, the pandemic has somewhat altered the nature or characteristics of these industries rather than influencing them in a positive or negative way. On the contrary, lack or even absence of visitors has generally worked positively for the environmental sustainability of cultural or natural heritage, especially the latter. Considering these points, it should be noted that the impacts of the COVID-19 pandemic on TBL of sustainability is not always negative and can also be positive, although its negative impacts on the economic sustainability have been immense. In light of Sects. 1 and 2, the following section (Sect.

3) suggests recommendations for the future of heritage and tourism industries, focusing on inclusion of *mottainai* sprit in sustainability management of Japan's heritage and tourism industries.

3 Reflections and Recommendations for the Futures

3.1 Introducing Mandatory Entrance Fees for Mountains Popular amongst Climbers

In Japan, generally, people, especially consumers, are intolerant of price increase and demanding regarding the level of services they receive. That is why the vast majority of Japanese businesses whose main customers are the general public have been to reluctant or unable to pass on their costs to their sales prices. Part of Japanese people have been aware of risks this situation involves, but most of them seem to have enjoyed low prices of products with high level of services for a long time, probably too long. In recent years, at last, an increasing number of people in Japan have started recognising negative implications resulting from the aforementioned situation, including a stagnant or even lower level of real income since the 1990s and an increase in the number and percentage of non-regular or non-permanent workers. In 2022, moreover, the aftermaths or still-ongoing impacts of the COVID-19 pandemic and the influence of Russian invasion of Ukraine make matters worse. As a result, the prices of almost all products have dramatically increased within a year and many households state that they are struggling.

Thus, it is natural for the general public of Japan to prioritise daily necessaries when they decide what to spend, although many still want to enjoy tourism. In fact, the schemes adopted by the Japanese Government such as 'Go to Travel' have been financially beneficial for same-day visitors/tourists as well as tourism-related businesses, particularly accommodation and food and beverage sectors (see Sect. 2.2). However, the author still believes that visitors need to pay a fair amount of money for the services they receive and experiences they have in every setting, including heritage and/or tourism settings. This would be crucial for TBL of sustainability of these industries, especially their economic and environmental sustainability. Nowadays, many bodies owning and/or managing cultural heritage acting as visitor attractions charge admission fees on visitors (e.g. museums, Japanese Buddhist temples), whilst many of those having and/or running natural heritage serving as visitor attractions do not (e.g. national parks, mountains). For instance, mountain climbing has become an established hobby of Japanese people since the late 1980s (Yamagata, 2013). Since around that time, people started regarding climbing as a general hobby rather than an adventurous activity. Since around 2009 or 2010, climbing has become even more approachable for larger number of people and popular amongst a wider variety of people. This was caused by various factors spread by mass media such as the emergence of term/concept of *'yama girl'* (mountain girls) who enjoy climbing in a casual and fashionable way in 2009 and the broadcast of television programme called *'Nippon hyaku-meizan'* (100 great mountains of Japan). This latest climbing boom still continues.

The above-mentioned situation means that the number of people in Japan who enjoy climbing as their hobby has increased, and this leads to more pressure on the natural environment of mountains. It also signifies that more services and facilities are required to meet an increasing needs and demands of climbers. As the number of climbers who lack knowledge on mountains and climbing, physical strength required for climbing, and/or do not take responsibility for their decisions and/or actions has also increased, the amount of costs to rescue climbers have also increased. Nevertheless, the majority of mountains popular amongst Japanese climbers have not charged a mandatory entrance fee on their climbers. Even Japan's highest and most popular mountain, Mount Fuji (Yamanashi and Shizuoka Prefectures), has not introduced a mandatory entrance fee as of writing (November 2022), although the idea of the introduction of such a fee was approved by the committee consisting of the key stakeholders in 2021 and the donation for conservation costs (1000 JPY per climber) was introduced in 2014. Unfortunately, however, the percentages of climbers to Mount Fuji who agreed to make donation in summer 2022 were not so high in both Yamanashi and Shizuoka, 72.8% and 57.3% respectively (Yomiuri Shimbun, 2022).

Considering the fairness amongst climbers and the amount of costs required to support climbing, however, the entrance fees for the mountains popular amongst climbers, typically Mount Fuji, should be compulsory and also reviewed regularly to cover necessary costs. This policy can also lead to a decrease in the number of climbers and this should be beneficial for the environmental sustainability of super-popular mountains like Mount Fuji.

3.2 Encouraging Travelling by Public Transport

As discussed in Sects. 3 and 4 of Chap. 5, generally railway is regarded as the most eco-friendly travel mode followed by coach/bus. Needless to say, walk or bicycle is ideal in terms of the environmental sustainability of travel mode. In light of day trippers' or tourists' travel distances between home and destinations, however, it is unrealistic for many to complete their travels only with walk and/or bicycle except very short trips from their home. Of course, travellers may need to use rent-a-car or a car-sharing service when they explore countryside or rural area, and call in a visitor attraction, enjoy restaurant or join an event there. In fact, public transport facilities and services are developed well in and around urban areas of Japan. Amongst these, those in and around Special Wards of Tokyo (hereafter SWT) and Osaka City are highly developed. In the author's opinion, therefore, same-day visitors or tourists explore SWT or Osaka City do not need to come by car. Instead, they can make the most of public transport facilities and services to get to there and explore the destination. In reality, however, many people still get to SWT or Osaka City by car. One of the reasons for this situation would be that there are often no distinct disadvantage for visitors to get to and travel around tourist destinations in urban areas by car. Simultaneously, it is also true that there are usually no clear advantage for travellers visiting these areas, using public transport. Thus, there is a need to develop ways to discourage people to come by car and encourage them to visit by public transport.

An approach to stop people from coming by car is an introduction of congestion pricing (charges) scheme. Congestion charges intend to reduce the amount of inner-city motorised traffic and require drivers to pay a toll when entering a pre-defined inner-city area (Kley et al., 2012). The scheme was first introduced in Singapore in 1975, but there have not been many followers until the early 2000s. In the past 20 years or so, since London introduced its congestion charges in 2003, the system has been adopted by many urban areas, especially in the West such as Los Angeles, Millan and Stockholm. In the author's view, congestion pricing can be applied to, for instance, Asakusa, Ginza, Ikebukuro, Shibuya and Shinjuku in SWT, and Kita (Umeda) and Minami (Shinsaibashi and Namba) in Osaka City. On the other hand, a measure to promote the use of public transport would be any favourable treatment for those who come by public transport. In the UK, for example, Castle Howard, a stately home located in Yorkshire open to the general public as a visitor attraction, offered discount on entrance fees for visitors coming by local bus. In fact, when the author lived in the City of York (2008–2015), he could enjoy the castle with a discounted fee after he showed a bus ticket at the ticket office. As far as the author is aware, however, this type of discount is not well adopted by Japan's visitor attractions, including those in urban areas where public transport is highly developed. In Japan, instead, a joint ticket for two or three attractions nearby seems to be much more popular way to encourage visitors to come. This strategy is effective for the economic and socio-cultural sustainability of these attractions as it can increase the number of visitors and income from them. On the other hand, the strategy does not appear to be useful for the environmental sustainability of surrounding natural environment. In light of this, if a joint ticket for multiple visitor attractions nearby can offer further discount for people travelling by public transport, the scheme can contribute to TBL of sustainability in a more comprehensive and exhaustive manner.

3.3 Promoting Pedestrianisation of City Centres or Tourist Honeypots

Encouraging the use of public transport as a way to travel to and explore around tourist destinations (see Sect. 3.2) is a recommendation closely associate with another recommendation discussed here, promoting

10 Conclusions – Reflections and Futures

pedestrianisation of city centres or tourist honeypots. Based on the author's observation in many city centres in urban areas and tourist honeypots across Japan, the author feels that experience of visitors and quality of life of local residents who do not use/own a private car are inclined to be negatively affected by heavy and/or busy motor traffic. The author has resided in and/or has been to more than 1000 cities all over the world and thinks that Japan can be seen as the most convenient country to live in or travel around without a car. This is especially true in and around a megalopolis like SWT and metropolis like Osaka City. Nonetheless, many people, including local residents, still come to a city centre or tourist honeypot, say Ginza in SWT, by car. Generally, Ginza is regarded as the most prestigious shopping quarter in SWT and even across Japan (Jimura, 2022). The district can be easily accessed and explored by public transport. In fact, there are three subway stations (Ginza, Ginza-itchome and Higashi-ginza) and an East Japan Railway station (Yurakucho) in and around the quarter. Moreover, frequent regular bus services are available throughout the quarter. Nevertheless, many people still come to the Ginza area by car. It is almost impossible for the author to understand why they need to come to Ginza by car, making noise, polluting air and threatening pedestrians.

Things cannot be simple and there are no single correct answer applied to all urban spaces due to differences in the history and practice of urban planning amongst various city centres and uniqueness of their characters and structures. In light of the situation above, nonetheless, the author still believes that pedestrianisation of city centres in urban areas and tourist honeypots should be advanced much further in Japan. Across the world, pedestrianisation of certain roads or areas can be temporary or permanent. Compared with other countries, especially Europe, pedestrianisation in Japan are likely to be temporary rather than permanent. A key reason for it should be the presence of 'historic centres' in historic European cities and the lack of such quarters in city centres or tourist honeypots in Japan (Jimura, 2019, 2022). Soni and Soni (2016, 140) suggest that 'the most common positive impacts of pedestrianisation can be categorised into following five categories:

- Transportation-related,

- Social,
- Environmental,
- Economic, and
- Health-related'.

Soni and Soni (2016) also explain each positive impact in detail and most of them are more or less related to sustainability of humans and their surrounding environments. As can be confirmed from the aforementioned five categories, each TBL of sustainability is included in these categories. This signifies that these positive impacts will be able to contribute to the economic, socio-cultural or environmental sustainability of people's lives and built and natural environments surrounding them. Some of the benefits of pedestrianisation for economic, socio-cultural or environmental sustainability suggested by Soni and Soni can also be benefits for pedestrianised city centres or tourist honeypots in Japan. They are as follows:

- Economic: Increase in footfall, sales and rent, increase in employment, and income from public transit users (2016, 142–143).
- Social (socio-cultural): Social interaction and relations, sense of belongingness, responsibility and pride, increase in security and safety, and heritage preservation and urban renewal (2016, 141).
- Environmental: Reduction of air pollution and noise (2016, 142).

Amongst these benefits for economic, socio-cultural or environmental sustainability, 'heritage preservation and urban renewal' is closely connected with the final recommendation explained in the subsequent section (Sect. 3.4).

3.4 Enhancing a Holistic Approach for Heritage Conservation

Soni and Soni (2016) argue that pedestrianisation has been the most useful way for heritage preservation as it is basically low-cost and eco-friendly. Pedestrianisation can protect historic buildings from traffic-induced

10 Conclusions – Reflections and Futures

vibration and vehicular air pollution, and also secure heritage place and space from the threat of expansion of roads and creation of parking spaces (Soni & Soni, 2016). Referring a successful case from Singapore, they also note that pedestrianisation of a street with historic buildings has been helpful for the conservation of this tangible cultural heritage (Soni & Soni, 2016). Thanks to this, visitors as well as local inhabitants can still enjoy appreciating the heritage there and walking around this area. Consequently, the street has become one of tourists honeypots in the country (Soni & Soni, 2016). A lesson from this case is that a holistic approach would be required to ensure an excellent level of heritage conservation on a long-term basis in tourism and community contexts. The aforementioned case is about cultural heritage; however, overall such an approach would also be needed for the conservation of natural heritage.

In Japan, some examples of such a comprehensive approach can be found in the cases adopting an international or domestic conservation scheme. As for the international system, a representative example is UNESCO's World Heritage sites (hereafter WHSs). Japan has 25 WHSs, 20 cultural and five natural, as of writing (November 2022). The system has two different zones, namely properties (a core zone) and a buffer zone. In principle, a buffer zone is (much) larger than properties (a core zone) and the latter is surrounded by the former to avoid or minimise any risk that can arise outside the zones. This can be seen as a good example of a holistic approach towards heritage conservation and signifies the importance of heritage conservation as a surface rather than a point or linear. This kind of approach should involve a wide geographical area filled with different types of stakeholders, including local residents and visitors. Hence, the socio-cultural and environmental sustainability of a whole area rather than only properties (a core zone) needs to be considered in its sustainability management.

A comprehensive approach towards heritage conservation similar to the aforementioned core and buffer zones for WHSs is also suggested in Japan. The Agency for Cultural Affairs (hereafter ACA), (n.d.) develops some plans to realise a holistic approach towards cultural heritage conservation, and one of the plans focuses on the significance of surrounding areas as well as cultural heritage itself. In tourist honeypots, several different kinds of cultural heritage co-exist contiguously in a certain area. In such a case, a comprehensive approach for conservation would be particularly important to understand possible impacts of tourism that can differ significantly by property. The socio-cultural sustainability of each property in a certain area, especially rather unknown ones', can be enhanced by highlighting the cultural significance of the area as a whole and each property in tourism or educational settings, for example, through good interpretations. Moreover, the environmental sustainability of each heritage property, particularly well-visited one's, can be ensured by a good distribution of visitors amongst multiple properties.

In the author's opinion, the above-mentioned holistic approach for heritage conservation should closely work with the Japan Heritage (hereafter JH) (*Nihon Isan*) scheme also managed by ACA. Compared to the holistic approach for heritage conservation adopted by ACA, JH can be seen as a system for regional promotion and community revitalisation. ACA also emphasises the importance of comprehensive promotion or revitalisation of certain areas with different sorts of cultural heritage through the JH initiative. This implies that a unique and attractive 'story' each locality has should be packaged and developed into a new heritage/tourism product through the JH scheme. Consequently, JH aims to raise people's awareness of appeal of cultural heritage of a certain region and the region a whole and encourage them to visit the region. By doing so, the socio-cultural sustainability of the cultural heritage and its region can be strengthened by the increased level of recognition amongst the general public, including prospective visitors. Their economic sustainability can also be enhanced by attracting many visitors to the region as a whole rather than to already famous heritage properties.

References

ACA. (n.d.). *Bunkazai no sogoteki na hogo wo okonautameno shisaku nit suite* (About measures to conserve Japan's cultural properties in a holistic manner). [in Japanese]. Available at: https://www.bunka.go.jp/seisaku/bunkashingikai/bunkazai/kikaku/h18/02/shiryo_6.html. Accessed 24 Nov 2022.

Akashi City. (2020). *SDGs Mirai Toshi* (SDGs Future City) [in Japanese]. Available at: https://www.city.akashi.lg.jp/seisaku/sdgs_torikumi/sdgsmirai-toshi.html. Accessed 6 Nov 2022.

BBC News. (2022). *Japan to lift restrictions on foreign tourists*. Available at: https://www.bbc.com/news/world-asia-63003802. Accessed 7 Nov 2022.

Hori, K., Yoshida, I., Suzuki, M., Yiwen, Z., & Kurata, Y. (2022). Emergence and rapid popularization of paid web-conferencing-application-based Tours in Japan: An analysis of their business potential. In *ENTER22 e-tourism conference* (pp. 41–54). Springer.

ICDJ. (2022). *GRI standards towa nanika* (What are GRI standards?) [in Japanese]. Available at: https://note.com/idcj_sdgs/n/n2a4ad3cbb0c8. Accessed 5 Nov 2022.

Ideas for Good. (n.d.). *3R towa* (What are 3Rs?) [in Japanese]. Available at: https://ideasforgood.jp/glossary/3r/. Accessed 6 Nov 2022.

Imasa Kensetsu. (2020). *Genba fukei blog* (Blog on work scenes) [in Japanese]. Available at: https://imasakensetu.com/genbanikki/post-11277/. Accessed 9 Oct 2022.

Jimura, T. (2019). *World heritage sites: Tourism, local communities and conservation activities*. CABI.

Jimura, T. (2020). Changing faces of Tokyo: Regeneration, tourism and Tokyo 2020. In N. Wise & T. Jimura (Eds.), *Tourism, cultural heritage and urban regeneration – Changing spaces in historical places* (pp. 141–155). Springer.

Jimura, T. (2022). *Cultural and heritage tourism in Japan*. Routledge.

Kaneyasu Building. (2021) *Miyadaiku no shigoto – jinja no Kanban-hen* (A work of miyadaiku – a signboard in a Shinto shrine) [in Japanese]. Available at: https://kabu-kaneyasu.com/blog/detail/20210319160900/. Accessed 9 Oct 2022.

Kley, F., Wietschel, M., & Dallinger, D. (2012). Evaluation of European electric vehicle support schemes. In M. N. Nilsson, K. Hillman, A. Rickne, & T. Magnusson (Eds.), (pp. 75–95). Routledge.

Kyo no Rekishi Navi. (2022). *Kyoto wa SDGs no Hoko* (There are a number of cases associated with SDGs in Kyoto) [radio programme in Japanese]. Available at: https://voicy.jp/channel/1134/381951. Accessed 31 Oct 2022.

Lubbe, B. (Ed.). (2003). *Tourism management in southern Africa*. Pearson South Africa.

MOE. (2022). *Japan's national greenhouse gas emissions in fiscal year 2020* (Final Figures). Available at: https://www.env.go.jp/en/headline/2599.html. Accessed 7 Nov 2022.

MOE. (n.d.). *3R initiative*. Available at: https://www.env.go.jp/recycle/3r/initiative/en/index.html. Accessed 6 Nov 2022.

Okada, I., & Greyser, S. A. (2018). *After the carnival: Key factors to enhance Olympic legacy and prevent Olympic sites from becoming white elephants*. Harvard Business School Working Knowledge.

Pantheon Enterprises. (2014). *The story behind "reduce, reuse, recycle"*. Available at: http://pantheonchemical.com/reduce-reuse-recycle/. Accessed 6 Nov 2022.

Sanjo Insatsu. (n.d.). *Introduction: Oze boardwalk paper* [in Japanese]. Available at: https://oze-boardwalk-pj.sanjo-prn.co.jp/. Accessed 10 Oct 2022.

Seibu Bus. (n.d.). *Environment*. Available at: https://www.seibuholdings.co.jp/en/sustainability/environment/. Accessed 24 Oct 2022.

Soni, N., & Soni, N. (2016). Benefits of pedestrianization and warrants to pedestrianize an area. *Land Use Policy, 57*, 139–150.

Tobu Railway. (n.d.). *About the SL Taiju*. Available at: https://www.tobu.co.jp/en/sightseeing/nikko_kinugawa/sl/. Accessed 30 Oct 2022.

UN. (n.d.). *What is renewable energy?*. Available at: https://www.un.org/en/climatechange/what-is-renewable-energy. Accessed 24 Oct 2022.

Yamagata, T. (2013). Climbing Trend in Heisei Period [in Japanese]. *Shohoku Kiyo, 34*, 189–204.

Yomiuri Shimbun. (2022). *'Hitori sen-en' no Fujisan nyuzan-ryo. Nini no kyoryoku ga hajimete mokuhyo no nanawari uwamawaru* (More than 70% of climbers donated 1000 JPY when climbing Mount Fuji) [in Japanese]. Available at: https://www.yomiuri.co.jp/national/20221007-OYT1T50351/. Accessed 12 Nov 2022.